D0745465

Understanding

ISLAM

and Muslim Traditions

Understanding
ISLAM
and Muslim Traditions

*An Introduction to the Religious Practices, Celebrations,
Festivals, Observances, Beliefs, Folklore, Customs, and Calendar System
of the World's Muslim Communities, Including an Overview
of Islamic History and Geography*

By Tanya Gulevich

Foreword by Frederick S. Colby

615 Griswold Street • Detroit, Michigan 48226

Omnigraphics, Inc.

Cherie D. Abbey, *Managing Editor*
Amy Marcaccio Keyzer, *Editor*
Allison A. Beckett, Mary Butler, and Linda Strand, *Research Staff*

* * *

Peter E. Ruffner, *Publisher*
Frederick G. Ruffner, Jr., *Chairman*
Matthew P. Barbour, *Senior Vice President*
Kay Gill, *Vice President — Directories*

* * *

Liz Barbour, *Permissions Associate*
Dave Bianco, *Marketing Director*
Leif A. Gruenberg, *Development Manager*
Kevin Hayes, *Operations Manager*
Barry Puckett, *Librarian*
Cherry Stockdale, *Permissions Assistant*

Shirley Amore, Don Brown, Margaret M. Geist, Kevin Glover,
Martha Johns, and Kirk Kauffman, *Contributing Staff*

Library of Congress Cataloging-in-Publication Data

Gulevich, Tanya.
Understanding Islam and Muslim traditions : an introduction to the
religious practices, celebrations, festivals, observances, beliefs, folklore,
customs, and calendar system of the world's Muslim communities,
including an overview of Islamic history and geography / by Tanya Gulevich ;
foreword by Frederick S. Colby.
p. cm.
Includes bibliographical references and index.
ISBN 0-7808-0704-9 (hardcover : alk. paper)
1. Islam. 2. Muslims. 3. Islam — Essence, genius, nature. 4.
Islam — Doctrines. 5. Islam — Customs and practices. I. Title.
BP161.3.G85 2004
297—dc22
2004024462

Copyright © 2004 Omnigraphics, Inc.
ISBN 0-7808-0704-9

The information in this publication was compiled from the sources cited and from other sources considered reliable. While every possible effort has been made to ensure reliability, the publisher will not assume liability for damages caused by inaccuracies in the data, and makes no warranty, express or implied, on the accuracy of the information contained herein.

This book is printed on acid-free paper meeting the ANSI Z39.48 Standard. The infinity symbol that appears above indicates that the paper in this book meets that standard.

Printed in the United States

Table of Contents

Section One:
A Brief Introduction to Islam

THE HISTORY OF ISLAM

MUSLIMS TODAY

Section Two:
Religious Customs and Folklore

Section Three: Calendar System, Holidays, and Other Days of Observance

ᏸᏋ

Foreword

Islam is one of the most widely practiced, and most widely misunderstood, religions in the world today. Second only to Christianity in the sheer numbers of adherents, Islam is truly a world religion, with followers in every part of the world. Many people in Europe and the United States associate Islam with Arabs and the Middle East, and they are often surprised to find out that only a fraction of Muslims are Arabs or live in the Middle East. With all the problems facing our world today, more and more people have begun to realize the need to become educated global citizens. For many non-Muslims around the world, a key component of that education involves a better understanding of Islam and Muslims.

Many non-Muslims think that they know nothing about Islam, that Muslim beliefs and practices are a complete mystery to them. Yet they do in fact already possess certain ideas on the subject, for the mainstream media in many countries continually presents them with images of Muslims. Unfortunately, however, too often these media images repeatedly depict Muslim men as violent fanatics who appear to oppose all modern ways of living and Muslim women as veiled victims who appear to suffer under a sexist system. These images are selective representations that do not do justice to the diversity of Muslim beliefs and practices around the world. Furthermore, the negative stereotypes about Islam that these images invoke are woefully inadequate for a balanced and nuanced understanding of the more than one billion Muslims who are our neighbors in this ever-shrinking global village.

The attacks of September 11, 2001, brought new attention to Islam and Muslims in the United States and around the world. U.S. president George W. Bush insisted that Islam is not to blame for the horrific acts of a few individuals, and in this he is correct. Nevertheless, many Americans still treat Muslims as a generic "other," wondering why "they" hate "us" to such a degree. While the desire to ask such a question is commendable, and while investigating the roots of contem-

Opposite page: Silhouetted against the sky, this striking bronze sculpture — one of some 300 monumental works scattered through Jiddah, the western gateway to Saudi Arabia — enlarges a sampling of Arabic calligraphy that reads "In the name of God, the merciful, the compassionate."

porary conflicts is an important part of becoming informed global citizens, approaching the study of Islam in terms of a simplistic us versus them opposition may obscure more than it illuminates.

Do all Muslims hate the United States? Surely not. A number of Muslims, in fact, proudly defend the United States as members of the U.S. military. Other Muslims are proud to be American citizens, yet they see it as their patriotic duty to oppose those U.S. foreign policies with which they disagree. Some Muslims outside the United States oppose its policies or its cultural exports for a variety of reasons. Other Muslims outside the United States support America and all that it stands for. This example illustrates how crucial it is not to assume that all Muslims think and act the same way, nor to assume that all Muslims are somehow hostile to or different from non-Muslims. Like any other large group of people, Muslims have diverse attitudes, opinions, customs, and motivations. In light of the one-dimensional stereotypes that confront us on a daily basis, it seems that we need to remind ourselves that Muslims are human beings. No one individual or sect speaks or acts for all Muslims, just as no one individual or sect speaks or acts for all Christians.

Given such diversity among Muslims, it becomes crucial to investigate what Muslims have in common. What do Muslims do or believe that makes them Muslims? Are there certain traditions and customs, or certain doctrines and beliefs, that are characteristically "Islamic"? What books or teachings do many Muslims look to as sources of religious authority? What beliefs and practices unite the majority of Muslims around the world into a single religious community? And what beliefs and practices give rise to divisions or controversies among Muslims? Approaching the subject of Islam in this fashion helps to demonstrate the unity in diversity, as well as the diversity in unity, present among Muslims today.

Once one moves beyond overly simplistic assumptions about all Muslims being the same, other sorts of questions arise. If Muslims around the world are not all the same, how do distinct groups of Muslims differ? How does the practice of Islam vary from country to country? What holidays do Muslims celebrate, and how do these holidays vary from place to place? To what degree might some things that are often thought to be "Islamic," such as certain styles of women's dress, be a product of cultural or regional practices rather than a product of the religion itself? These questions point toward the need to understand the complexities of the diverse groups of people around the world who identify themselves as Muslims. In this book, Tanya Gulevich offers a fine introduction to the variety of ways that religion forms part of the lives of contemporary Muslims in different parts of the world.

With this impressive text, Gulevich makes accessible to a general audience a wealth of material on the concrete beliefs and practices of contemporary Muslims. Not only does she present the core beliefs of Muslims and some of the highlights of Islamic civilizations in a concise and readable fashion, she also conveys the intricacies of the divergent ways that Muslims practice their faith. One of the great strengths and contributions of this work is that it shows how the folklore and popular customs of Muslims represent a significant and valuable component of "lived Islam." Unlike the approach of many introductory works on Islam that seldom go beyond abstract and general characterizations of Muslims, in this book Gulevich weaves a colorful tapestry that illustrates how the unifying thread of Islam brings together diverse strands of Muslim experiences from South East Asia to South Carolina.

Gulevich treats the reader to a rich description of rituals, celebrations, and recipes that convey a sense of the unity and diversity of Muslim practices around the world. From the stages of ritual prayer to methods for warding off the evil eye, from the political activism of some Afghani women to the mystical dance of some Turkish Sufis, Gulevich surveys the length and breadth of Muslim practices in a way that few authors have ever attempted. While an exhaustive inventory of Muslim customs and traditions is beyond the scope of any one work, the amount of detail included here is truly astounding.

Drawing upon the works of both Muslim and non-Muslim specialists, this book explains the intricacies of many complex issues in a manner that readers on a variety of levels will be able to understand and appreciate. It makes available for perhaps the first time a basic introduction to Islam, intended for the general reader, that focuses attention not upon political strife or stereotypical images but upon the lived experiences of Muslims around the world. The author and the publisher are to be congratulated for producing this valuable work, contributing to a richer understanding of Islam that is so crucial in this day and age.

> — Frederick S. Colby, Ph. D.
> *Assistant Professor of Comparative Religion,*
> *Miami University*

Preface

Many Americans knew little about Islam before the September 11, 2001, terrorist attacks on the World Trade Center and the Pentagon. Upon discovering that the attacks were perpetrated by a small handful of Muslims who believed their atrocious actions were necessary to defend their religion, many Americans began to ask questions about Islam. Librarians and booksellers often found their shelves understocked and themselves unprepared to meet this need.

Over the next several years continuing world events — namely the U.S. invasion of two Muslim countries, Afghanistan and Iraq, as well as the continuing occupation of the latter nation — presented Americans with an ever-increasing flow of media images concerning Islam. For the most part, these images linked Muslims to social strife, political violence, oppressive governments, rigid and backward societies, and dislike if not outright hatred of the United States. These media images may have served to illustrate certain current events, but did not provide Americans with a well-rounded picture of Islam. *Understanding Islam and Muslim Traditions* is dedicated to the task of broadening the reader's acquaintance with Muslims and their religion. The book seeks neither to promote Islam nor to criticize it, but rather to present it in a balanced way that also suggests the diversity of interpretation, practice, and custom that exists throughout the Muslim world.

Opposite page: Muslims of every nationality flood toward the prayer hall of the Faysal Mosque in Islamabad, Pakistan, for their Friday prayers.

No single book could ever hope to cover all aspects of Islam, however. Therefore *Understanding Islam and Muslim Traditions* focuses primarily on the cultural aspects of the religion. Fully two-thirds of the book is devoted to holidays, festivals, ways of worship, devotional practices, social customs, manners, celebrations and ceremonies associated with the life cycle, folklore, foods, artistic traditions, and Islamic calendar system. Since this information would be considerably less useful, and even less intelligible, to those without a general knowledge of Muslim history, geography, and religious beliefs, these subjects, too, are summarized. Thus *Understanding Islam and Muslim Traditions* devotes more attention to describing how ordinary people around the world express their Muslim identity in everyday life than it does to providing detailed accounts of Islamic theology derived from the writings of Muslim religious authorities and other experts in the field.

Scholars point out that Islam, along with Christianity and Judaism, is one of the three major religions of the Western world. Moreover, it is the second most popular religion in the world today. Only Christianity can claim more believers than Islam. Population statistics reveal that some four to six million Muslims live in the United States and that their numbers are growing. In fact, some experts believe that if these population trends continue, Islam will replace Judaism as the second most popular religion in the United States some time in the first half of the 21st century. These facts underscore the need for Americans to become familiar with the beliefs and customs of their Muslim neighbors, here and abroad.

Plan of the Work

Understanding Islam and Muslim Traditions is divided into three sections. The first section provides a brief introduction to Islam's most important religious beliefs and practices, a short history of the founding and growth of the religion, and a review of the great achievements of Islamic civilization. It also furnishes a discussion of commonly held stereotypes, as well as an overview of the world's Muslim population and the religion's major holy sites.

The second section of the book describes and explains religious and folk customs. Here, for example, the reader will find a detailed explanation of the words, postures, and rituals associated with prayer, descriptions of various Muslim devotional customs, and a review of beliefs and practices associated with the Quran and the Prophet Muhammad. In addition, section two discusses beliefs about the body, customs concerning the separation of the sexes, celebrations associated with stages in the life cycle, and practices related to food and clothing. Greetings and sayings, commonly held superstitions, folklore, symbols, and traditional forms of entertainment are also covered in section two.

The third and final section of the book begins with an explanation of the Islamic calendar. It continues with descriptions and explanations of the religious activities and festivities associated with Muslim holidays, festivals, and regularly occurring religious observances. Ramadan (the month of fasting that occurs annually) and Eid al-Fitr (the holiday celebrating the end of the fast) receive the most in-depth coverage, including descriptions of religious observances and festivities that take place in 20 different countries. Other holidays covered include Ashura, Eid al-Adha, the First of Muharram, Hidrellez, Laylat al-Bara'ah (the Night of Forgiveness), Laylat al-Miraj (the Night of the Ascension), Laylat al-Qadr (the Night of Power), and Mulid al-Nabi (the Prophet's Birthday).

The special days known as the Lamp Nights and the White Nights also receive attention, as well as an assortment of festivals commemorating saints' days. Friday, the Muslim holy day, and the annual Hajj pilgrimage are also treated here.

Understanding Islam and Muslim Traditions was written with the assumption that most readers would be using the book to look up specific pieces of information. In order to make it more convenient for these readers, a number of definitions and key points of information are repeated in various places throughout the book. The intention in so doing was to save these readers from having to hunt for this information elsewhere.

Audience

Understanding Islam and Muslim Traditions was designed for non-Muslim readers. It was written with middle and high school students in mind, but will also be of interest to the general reader who would like to know more about Islam. Detailed coverage of customs and holidays is provided with the hope that this information will make the book especially useful to students researching the customs and holidays of foreign countries and world religions. In addition to students, the general reader, too, will find this book of interest, especially if he or she is looking for a text that shines light on the human face of Islam.

Scope

Understanding Islam and Muslim Traditions takes an international approach to studying Islam. Many Americans may associate Islam with the geographical region we call the Middle East, but in fact the Muslims of Asia far outnumber those of the Middle East. Numerous adherents of Islam can also be found in Africa. In addition, Europe and the Americas host minority Muslim populations. *Understanding Islam and Muslim Traditions* addresses this diversity by providing information on how Muslim holidays are celebrated in various parts of the globe. Cultural variations in the ways in which certain ceremonies are performed—for example burial and male circumcision—are also addressed.

Understanding Islam and Muslim Traditions also includes photographs and other illustrations selected to help readers familiarize themselves with people, places, objects, and activities described in the text. Holiday-related poems and recipes have been included as well in order to broaden readers' understanding and appreciation of Muslim celebrations.

Glossary

The text of *Understanding Islam and Muslim Traditions* contains a significant number of foreign words, most of them Arabic. The first time a foreign word

This symbol appears on the first page of each chapter. This square Kufi calligraphy represents the words "Allahu Akbar" (God is Greater) and is based on a 14th-century tile design in the ceiling of an iwan in Friday Mosque in Isfahan, Iran.

appears in each section of the book, it is italicized and defined in context. After this initial usage, the word may appear again without definition. For the reader's convenience, all foreign words used in the text appear in the glossary. A reminder notice about this section is appended to the beginning of each chapter, ensuring that readers will locate this helpful feature. A few English words (such as "mosque," "Sufi," and "arabesque") are also listed in the glossary.

Most of the foreign words that appear in this book have several English language spellings. The spellings chosen for *Understanding Islam and Muslim Traditions* are among the simplest in use. Diacritical marks have been omitted. Readers who know Arabic may find that these spellings oversimplify the Arabic words they are intended to represent. Nevertheless, these simple spellings were chosen to help the vast majority of readers—who we assumed would not know Arabic—digest a text that of necessity includes many foreign words. (*For an expanded discussion of this matter, see the glossary on page 423.*)

Additional Resources and Bibliography

A list of additional resources appears at the end of each section of the book. The list is broken down by topic, in order to help readers find books that address their particular interests. A number of children's books have been included in these lists, as an aid to librarians and other readers who are searching for materials appropriate for that audience. These texts have been grouped together under their own subheading, "resources for children." Web sites and videos also appear in the list of additional resources. The web sites were checked for accessibility during late July 2004.

A general bibliography of sources has been included at the back of the book. The bibliography is also broken down by topic. Its division into three sections and various subsections mirrors that of the book itself.

Understanding Islam and Muslim Traditions contains quite a number of quotes from the Quran, the holy book of Islam. Unless otherwise noted, they were taken from *Al-Qur'an: A Contemporary Translation*, Ahmed Ali translator, revised definitive edition, Princeton, NJ, Princeton University Press, 1988.

Index

Understanding Islam and Muslim Traditions contains an easy-to-use, comprehensive index to the personal names, place names, and subject terms that appear in the book. It covers such topics as important people, holy places, fundamental principles and practices of Islam, prayer and other devotional customs, religious sects, holiday symbols and ceremonies, and other subjects crucial to an understanding of Islam.

Photo captions have also been included in the index, with these page references marked in italic type. To facilitate use of the glossary, the index also features references for its definitions of terms. For these entries, the page reference for each glossary term is marked after the heading "defined."

Acknowledgements

First and foremost I would like to thank Frederick S. Colby, assistant professor of comparative religion at Miami University, for giving so generously of his time and expertise. His detailed feedback on the manuscript was invaluable. Thanks also to editor Helene Henderson, with whom I had ongoing discussions during the conceptualization and writing of this manuscript. I appreciate both her listening ear and her wise advice. The support given me by Kitty Lehman during the writing of this book is also much appreciated. Many thanks go to graphic designer and illustrator Mary Ann Stavros-Lanning, for her enthusiasm for this project and her hard work, and to Dick Doughty and the photographers of *Saudi Aramco World,* for access to their photo archives and the generous permission to include more than 275 images in this book. Appreciation goes as well to Breen Mullins, for hunting down the answers to a number of questions, and to Michael Graebner, for the loan of some books. Finally I would like to thank my parents for their continuing support of all my endeavors.

Dedication

For Achmed Effendi and the three Muslim women
who saved my grandmother's life long ago in Semendre, Turkey,
and for the merciful and compassionate people of every
faith and every nation.

ೞ

. . . whosoever saves a life
Saves the entire human race
(The Quran, 5:32)

ೞ

Blessed are the merciful
For they shall obtain mercy
(The Gospel According to Matthew, 5:7)

ೞ

He has told you, O Mortal, what is good;
And what does the Lord require of you
But to do justice, and to love kindness,
And to walk humbly with your God?
(The Book of Micah, 6:8)

Section One

A Brief Introduction to Islam

Section One:
A Brief Introduction to Islam

Overview

*U*nderstanding Islam and Muslim Traditions* introduces readers to Islam through an examination of its religious observances, customs, holidays, calendar system, and folk beliefs. About two-thirds of the book is dedicated to these subjects. Thus, rather than approach Islam simply as a set of abstract religious beliefs, this book takes as its primary task the description of what Muslims do and the meaning they attribute to these practices. Nevertheless, in order to make some sense of these customs and observances, the reader needs to have a basic understanding of Islamic religious beliefs. It may also be helpful to know something of the history of Islam, as well as the ethnic identity and geographic distribution of today's Muslim peoples. Therefore, these subjects are all covered in the first section of the book.

Section one is broken down into three parts. The first of these parts — The Teachings of Islam (Chapters 1-2) — offers those readers with little knowledge of Islam an introduction to the religion's basic beliefs and practices. The second part — The History of Islam (Chapters 3-6) — gives a brief history of Islam, concentrating on the founding of the religion and the major achievements of Islamic civilization. The third part looks at Muslims today (Chapters 7-9). It begins by examining commonly held stereotypes about Muslims and balancing them against profiles of accomplished and admirable Muslim men and women from around the world. It then includes a review of the geography of Islam, which explains the distribution of the world's Muslim population and concludes with a list of Islam's major holy sites.

*Opposite page:
Light filters
through the stained
glass windows to
reveal the elegant
Moroccan-style
interior of Masjid
Raya, the largest
mosque in
Sumantra,
Indonesia.
More than 220
million Muslims
live in Indonesia.*

The Teachings of Islam

Chapter 1
Essential Beliefs and Practices

Islam

"Islam" is an Arabic word meaning surrender, submission, or obedience. Thus the very name of this religion sums up its central message: that human beings must surrender themselves to God. Followers of Islam are called Muslims, meaning "those who submit." The holy book of Islam, called the *Quran*, tells Muslims how to obey the will of God. Arabic speakers know that the word Islam contains another important message about the religion. They point out that it comes from the Arabic word *salam*, which means peace. Muslims believe that humanity can achieve peace—both inner peace and social harmony—by following the teachings of Islam. In addition, those who adopt the religion must do so in peace, without being subjected to pressure or force of any kind.

Since it was founded in the seventh century, many people consider Islam to be the youngest of the world's major religions. Muslims don't think Islam is a new religion, however. Rather they view it as a return to what they believe to be an ancient religion: belief in and submission to the one, all-powerful God spoken of in the earliest Hebrew scriptures (for example, the Bible's Book of Genesis). What's more, whereas Christians and Jews tend to view Islam as a separate religion that has no bearing on their own faith, Muslims see their religion as closely related to Judaism and Christianity. In fact, they tend to view Islam as the fulfill-

Opposite page: A Saudi student of computer science and his wife, a biology student, read from the Quran in their Texas apartment, during one of their five prayer periods of the day, which all devout Muslims observe.

Foreign words used in the text are defined in the Glossary, pages 423-40.

33

ment of those earlier religions, which got off track due to human error and the human tendency to invent false gods and to place faith in things other than God. Muslims deem that God sent Islam to humanity through the prophet Muhammad in order to correct these errors. They believe that Muhammad's prophecies will be God's last revelation to the people of the earth.

The Five Pillars of Islam

The core of Muslim religious life revolves around one central belief and four religious practices. Together these are called the five pillars of Islam. Muslims may differ with one another on other matters, but the vast majority unite to proclaim the importance of these principles. Muslim thinkers assert that Islam is a total way of life for individuals and communities, rather than just a private belief system. The five pillars reflect this understanding of Islam, in that they affect both communal life and the private life of individual believers. What's more, they demonstrate the great importance that Islam places on reverence for God and charity to one's neighbor.

The First Pillar

One all-important religious teaching stands at the very heart of Islam and must be adopted by all Muslims. This is the belief that there is only one God. Religious scholars call this belief monotheism and contrast it to polytheism, the belief in many gods and/or goddesses. Muslims refer to God as *Allah*, an Arabic word meaning God. Some writers note that the exact, literal translation of Allah is "the God." In this case, the word "the" serves to reinforce the idea that there is only one God. Muslims also assert that God has no associates,

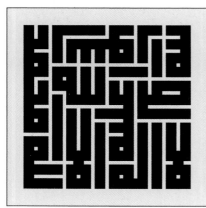

SHAHADAH SQUARE

There is no divinity but God,
Muhammad is the Messenger of God,
may God pray upon him.

Stone carved panel from Khan al-Saboun, Aleppo, Syria,
early 16th century. Square Kufi calligraphy.

partners, or offspring, and that he does not share his power with anyone or anything. Those who adopt these wrong ways of thinking about God are committing a sin known in Arabic as *shirk* (association). Along with failure to believe in God, shirk is the worst sin one can commit in Islam. According to the Quran, the holy book of Islam, these are the only sins God finds it impossible to forgive. Some Muslim scholars suggest that this may be because those who commit them cut themselves off from God's absolute power, and thus separate themselves from God's power to forgive.

Muslims link their faith in one God of limitless power and majesty with the belief that Muhammad, a man who lived in Arabia during the seventh century, was chosen to serve as God's prophet. The centrality of these beliefs is reflected in the fact that the first pillar of Islam requires all Muslims to affirm them daily in prayer. Muslims testify to these beliefs by reciting the *shahada* in their daily prayers. Shahada means "affirmation" or "witness" in Arabic. In English this declaration of faith may be rendered thus: "I witness that there is no god but God, and Muhammad is the messenger of God." The shahada is so central to Islam that to recite it with belief is all that is necessary for new members to convert to the religion.

The Second Pillar

Formal prayer, or *salat*, is the second pillar of Islam. Muslims make a distinction between this kind of ritualized prayer—where believers speak required words and perform required actions—and informal prayer, called *dua*, where believers may pour out their individual feelings and concerns to God. Devout Muslims perform salat five times each day: at sunrise, at midday, in the middle of the afternoon, at sunset, and in the evening. These prayers are offered in Arabic, regardless of the native language of the worshiper. Muslims prepare to worship by washing their feet, hands, face, and mouth. Salat begins with the proclamation "God is most great." It also includes a recitation of the *Fatiha*, the very first chapter in the Quran:

> In the name of God, the Merciful and Compassionate. Praise be to God, the Lord of the Universe, the Merciful and Compassionate. Ruler on the Day of Judgment. You do we worship and call upon for help. Guide us along the Straight Path, the road of those who You have favored, those with whom You are not angry, who are not lost. (Quran 1:1-7, Cleary trans.).

A young Muslim girl, holding a pair of prayer beads, performs dua.

Muslims from Dhakar, Bangladesh, performing some of the different body positions required of worshipers during salat.

The prayer session continues with other passages from the Quran as well as affirmations of faith. Each cycle of prayer closes with a repetition of the phrase "God is most great," after which the entire cycle is repeated two, three, or four times. Although it is preferable to offer these prayers in a group, those who find themselves alone also pray. At the end of the entire session worshipers offer a peace greeting — "Peace be upon all of you and the mercy and blessings of God" — to those on either side of them.

Certain body positions, as well as certain words, are required of worshipers during salat. First, worshipers stand facing the direction of Mecca, a city in Saudi Arabia. The worshipers then raise their hands as they begin to recite the prayers. As the prayers continue they stand with arms folded across their stomach, bow, kneel and prostrate themselves (bowing until the forehead touches the ground), and return to a sitting position. This cycle of movement is repeated with each cycle of prayer.

Salat may be performed at home, in a mosque, or anywhere the worshiper happens to find him or herself at the correct time. On Friday, the Muslim holy day, many people go to the local mosque for their noonday prayers. At this time the prayers are followed by a sermon. In predominantly Muslim countries, considerably more men than women perform salat in mosques. Women have customarily prayed at home, but in recent years more have been attending mosque prayer services.

The Third Pillar

Zakat, or almsgiving, is the third pillar of Islam. Each year all adult Muslims must give two and one-half percent of all their wealth (goods as well as income) to the poor. The truly poor are exempted from this duty, because Muslim law specifies that a person must possess a minimum amount of wealth before he or she is eligible to give. In some predominantly Muslim countries the government collects zakat. In others people make these payments to charitable institutions, mosques, or needy individuals. Muslims distinguish zakat, which is viewed as a kind of tax, from charity, which is seen as a voluntary contribution. In addition to paying zakat, Islam encourages Muslims to make frequent charitable donations.

The Fourth Pillar

Fasting, or *sawm*, is the fourth pillar of Islam. Muslims fast during the entire month of Ramadan by not eating or drinking during the daylight hours. In this way Muslims learn first-hand about the suffering of the poor and hungry. Husbands and wives must also refrain from marital relations, and everyone must avoid evil thoughts and bad deeds. Children, pregnant and menstruating women, the sick, and the very elderly do not have to observe the fast. Fasting reminds Muslims of their dependence on God and helps them to focus on spiritual matters. In Muslim countries people experience the Ramadan fast as a special, joyful time.

Muslims understand salat, zakat, and sawm to be closely related activities. As one famous Muslim religious teacher put it, "Prayer carries us half-way to God; fasting brings us to the door of his praises; almsgiving procures for us admission" (Zepp 2000: 89).

Muslims understand salat, zakat, and sawm to be closely related activities. Each advances the common goal of bringing the individual believer and the community closer to God. As one famous Muslim religious teacher put it, "Prayer carries us half-way to God; fasting brings us to the door of his praises; almsgiving procures for us admission" (Zepp 2000: 89).

More than two million Muslims from all parts of the globe have traveled to Mecca, in modern-day Saudi Arabia, to complete the fifth pillar of Islam.

The Fifth Pillar

The fifth pillar of Islam is pilgrimage to Mecca, in modern-day Saudi Arabia. Believers who can afford it are expected to make this journey, called *Hajj*, at least once in their lifetimes. Tradition specifies that only those who can make the pilgrimage without going into debt can make a valid Hajj. Because of the expense involved, most of the world's Muslims do not complete this act of devotion. They are not considered less devout if they fail to meet this religious obligation for financial reasons.

The Hajj takes place at the same time every year according to the Muslim calendar, during the first ten days of the month that Muslims call *Dhu al-Hijjah*. According to the calendar used in the United States and most of the world, however, the dates of the Hajj change from year to year. Since the Muslim calendar has 11 fewer days than our own (called the Gregorian calendar), the dates of the Hajj according to our calendar shift backward by 11 days each year. In recent years, more than two million Muslims from all parts of the globe have traveled to Saudi Arabia during these ten days to complete this religious duty. Making the Hajj is a powerful experience in the life of a Muslim, a chance not only to visit the religion's holiest of sites, but also to worship with a great cross-section of the worldwide Muslim community. Male pilgrims wear identical white robes, and many women wear white too, although their dress code is less strict. No perfume or jewelry is allowed, and certain behaviors are also forbidden. Islam teaches the equality of all believers before God.

Many pilgrims report that the experience of making the Hajj alongside thousands of other pilgrims — rich, poor, and of all colors and ethnicities — makes that teaching a reality for them.

Jihad

The Arabic word *jihad* means "struggle" or "striving." This concept is so important to Islam that some Muslims call jihad the sixth pillar of Islam. Although Muslims have sometimes used it to refer to warfare against non-Muslims, the term is most often used to describe the struggle within the self to overcome selfishness, greed, and other weaknesses. The Quran urges Muslims to improve themselves and their communities through jihad. For the vast majority of Muslims this means working to overcome their own personal failings, striving to live a charitable and ethical life, building a just society, and spreading the teachings of Islam.

Although Muslims have sometimes used it to refer to warfare against non-Muslims, the term "jihad" is most often used to describe the struggle within the self to overcome selfishness, greed, and other weaknesses.

The Quran's teachings on jihad also approve of the defense of the Islamic community against aggressors. Certain passages, too, seem to suggest that it is permissible to use warfare to spread Islamic rule (9:5, 9:29). When used in these senses the word jihad has sometimes been mistranslated as "holy war." While religious scholars contend that the concept of jihad does not justify military aggression, certain groups in past and present times have used the concept and the passages from the Quran to justify violent attacks against people deemed to be their enemies. For example, the terrorist group al-Qaeda (an Arabic phrase meaning "the base") has declared a jihad against the United States and other nations that its leaders believe to be the enemies of Islam. In addition, there are a number of Islamist terrorist groups operating in the Middle East who conceive of their political and military activities as jihad. Examples include the

Palestinian Islamic Jihad Organization and Hamas (Movement of Islamic Resistance), both of which are fighting to establish some form of Palestinian rule in what is now the state of Israel. While these groups often receive a good deal of media attention, especially after staging an act of violence, not all Muslims agree with their methods.

In the Muslim world the number of organizations that define their mission in terms of jihad has increased throughout the twentieth century, especially after 1970. Nevertheless, as one expert in the field has written, this increase "does not say as much about Islam, as is often assumed in the West, as it says about desperate attempts to exploit Islam politically" (AbuKhalil 1995: 373). Muslims as well as non-Muslims have fallen victim to violent jihad movements. Often these militant jihadists will label Muslims who do not agree with them as "unbelievers," a label which in their minds legitimizes the use of violence against them. For example, the Egyptian president Anwar Sadat (1918-1981), himself a Muslim, was assassinated by religious extremists from an Egyptian group called al-Jihad. They killed Sadat because they opposed his efforts to make peace with Israel. In another Muslim country, Afghanistan, a group of religiously trained soldiers called the Taliban took over the country in 1996. Taliban is an Arabic word meaning "seekers," and usually refers to students of religion. Although Islam was already the prevailing religion (about 99 percent of the population is Muslim), the Taliban claimed that the takeover was necessary in order to restore order and to establish its own version of strict Islamic law. Once in power, the Taliban government imposed harsh punishments, including beatings, amputations, and death, on those who disobeyed their laws.

The Egyptian president Anwar Sadat (1918-1981), himself a Muslim, was assassinated by religious extremists from an Egyptian group called al-Jihad. They killed Sadat because they opposed his efforts to make peace with Israel.

Other Important Beliefs

In addition to the beliefs and values addressed in the five pillars, there are other concepts that are important to Islam. These include the absolute unity of God (which is implicit in the first pillar, the shahada), the existence of angels, and the understanding that one's personal destiny, whether for better or for worse, is determined by God. Muslims also accept both the Jewish and Christian scriptures as divinely inspired (although they think that Jews and Christians have distorted to some degree these messages and their meaning). Therefore, Muslims accept Jesus and the Hebrew prophets as authentic prophets of God. They do not accept the divinity of Jesus, however. Muslims also believe in a Day of Judgment and life after death. They believe that the dead will appear before God to be judged according to how they lived their lives. Evildoers and the irreverent will go to a place of torment. The righteous and devout will live forever in paradise.

The Quran

Muslims believe the Quran literally to be the words of God. Some even say that an exact copy of the book, in its original Arabic, exists in heaven. Although they believe that the prophet Muhammad transmitted the words to humanity, they are considered to be God's words, not Muhammad's. Muhammad's followers wrote down what he said, and these statements were collected and bound together as a single book some time after Muhammad's death (in the year 632).

The Quran is the single most authoritative guide for those trying to live a Muslim life. No person, body of writings, or institution has more authority than does the Quran. Nevertheless, over the centuries religious scholars have played an important role in interpreting the Quran for ordinary believers. The opinions of scholars are still sought today, although many contemporary believers would also argue that all Muslims should study the Quran for themselves and strive to come to their own understanding of the book.

The Quran is composed of 114 chapters containing some 6,000 verses. It is just about four-fifths as long as the Christian New Testament. The Quran often con-

The Quran is the single most authoritative guide for those trying to live a Muslim life. It is composed of 114 chapters containing some 6,000 verses.

Illuminated page from Quran: Sura 96 (complete).

fuses Christian and Jewish readers because it appears to skip from one topic to the next. Unlike the Bible, the Quran was not composed as a series of stories arranged roughly in chronological order. Instead, it is a collection of recitations that are not arranged according to any kind of master narrative (that is, a guiding story line). When the early Muslims compiled the Quran, they arranged its chapters by length, with the longest chapters first and the shorter ones at the end (the exception being chapter one, which is very short). Muslims are not bothered by the way in which the book is arranged and find that it permits them to dip into the text, even if they have only enough time to read a paragraph or two, and extract valuable insights.

Readers familiar with the Quran have identified a number of its most important themes. These themes, rather than a master narrative, help to unify the book. The Quran repeatedly urges believers to pay attention to and follow God's teachings as presented in the Quran, to let good motives and conscientious intentions guide their actions, to strive to improve themselves and their community, to be generous with their wealth and possessions, and to be grateful for what God has done for them.

The Importance of Arabic

The Arabic language has a very important place in Islam. Muslims believe that God composed the Quran in Arabic. Since translation would change the meaning of the original words even slightly, it is viewed by many as dubious tinkering with the word of God. Translations of the Quran are available, but believers are expected to study the holy text in Arabic. Even those Muslims for whom Arabic is not a native language learn enough of the language to perform their daily prayers in Arabic.

The Prophet Muhammad

The Islamic religion was transmitted to humanity by Muhammad, a man who lived in Arabia from 570 to 632 C.E. Muslims do not consider him the founder of their religion, because they believe that God founded their religion. Instead they understand Muhammad to be a prophet, that is, someone who delivers a message from God to humankind. Muhammad is taken to be the "seal" of the prophets, meaning that Muslims understand him to be the last prophet that God will send to humanity.

Muslims do not view Muhammad in the same way that most Christians view Jesus. They emphasize that Muhammad was just a human being and was in no way divine (a belief which would be considered shirk, or a great sin, in Islam). Nevertheless, they assert that Muhammad was the most perfect of human beings, a man who was known by his companions to be profoundly spiritual, deep-thinking, generous, kind, and just. Even before he became a prophet at the age of 40, he had earned the nickname *al-Amin* "the trustworthy one." Though he was human, Muslims believe Muhammad's virtues far outshone those of an ordinary person. A well-loved Arabic poem, in comparing Muhammad to other people, describes him as "a jewel among the stones."

Many Muslims also assign a great deal of authority to the way in which Muhammad conducted his personal life and the practices that he is known to have approved of. His example, referred to as *sunna* in Arabic, provides guidance on many issues not addressed in the Quran. For example, although the Quran does not require male circumcision, Muhammad approved of the procedure. Thus, though not required, it is widely practiced among Muslims.

Hadith and Legends

A book of hadiths written in 1027 C.E. (418 A.H.).

Muslims understand Muhammad to have been the ideal believer and strive to model their belief and conduct after his. Not long after his death, Muslims began to collect reports of Muhammad's sayings and deeds. Religious experts attempted to weed out the unreliable reports and wrote down the ones deemed to be of some value, rating them as more or less likely to be true and accurate statements. These statements are called *hadith*, an Arabic word meaning "account," "report," or "speech," but also sometimes translated as "tradition." In addition to the Quran the hadith form an important body of knowledge for Muslim believers attempting to pattern their own lives after Muhammad.

Many pious legends concerning Muhammad also circulate throughout the Muslim world. Though not considered authoritative by religious scholars, they reflect the great love and esteem that Muslims have for their prophet and the importance of these thoughts and feelings in the religious lives of many believers.

Relationship to Christianity and Judaism

Islam shares certain basic beliefs with Christianity and Judaism. Followers of all three religions profess belief in one God, life after death, and accountability before God for one's actions on earth. Each faith claims to have been granted a special covenant, or relationship, with God: the Jews through Moses, the Christians through Jesus, and the Muslims through Muhammad. While Jews and Christians often fail to recognize a connection between their faith and Islam, Muslims acknowledge a relationship between Islam and the biblical faiths. In fact, the Quran refers to Christians and Jews as "the people of the Book" and grants the validity of their scriptures. In this case, the phrase "people of the Book" refers to the Bible, but Muslims have also taken the phrase to refer to followers of other scripturally-based religions, such as Hinduism. Jesus and the major Hebrew prophets are accounted prophets in Islam. Muslims often refer to them by the Arab versions of their names, for example, Nuh (Noah), Ibrahim (Abraham), Ismail (Ishmael), Ishaq (Isaac), Loot (Lot), Yaqub (Jacob), Yusuf (Joseph), Musa (Moses), Daoud (David), Sulaymen (Solomon), Ayyub (Job), and Issa (Jesus). Like Christians and Jews, Muslims see themselves as descendants of Abra-

ham. Whereas the Jewish people claim descent though Abraham's son Isaac, Arabs believe themselves to have descended through Abraham's son Ishmael. The story of Abraham's sacrifice found in the Bible's Book of Genesis differs from that accepted by most Muslims, however. The Bible declares that Abraham intended to sacrifice his son Issac, while most Muslims claim that Ishmael was the intended victim.

Opposite page: Miniature of Noah's ark in the shape of nef with lateen sail. Note the animals in the port holes in detail shown above.

Islamic Law

Many observers have commented that Islam places more emphasis on how people should behave than on what they think about God. Over the years, Muslim scholars have developed a great number of rules used to govern people in Muslim societies. English speakers call this body of knowledge Islamic law. Muslims often refer to these rules as *sharia*, an Arabic term that may be translated as "path to the spring" or "the watering hole." Devout Muslims view sharia, or correct behavior, as important because it is seen as the path to God. Because Islam does not accept the separation of religion and politics, many predominantly Muslim countries have made sharia the law of the land either in part or in whole. Nevertheless, not all Muslims agree with this policy. The past several decades have witnessed a prolonged debate among Muslims about whether or not government should become involved in enforcing sharia.

> *Sharia comes from four major sources: the Quran, the example set by the prophet Muhammad and those traditions recorded as hadith, analogical reasoning, and the consensus of religious scholars.*

Sharia comes from four major sources: the Quran, the example set by the prophet Muhammad and those traditions recorded as hadith, analogical reasoning, and the consensus of religious scholars. The prohibition against alcoholic beverages and narcotics provides an example of a law developed through analogical reasoning. The Quran asks believers to abstain from date wine (5:90-91). After examining the passage in question most religious scholars reached the conclusion that its intent is to forbid all intoxicants. Laws arrived at via the consensus of religious scholars derive their validity from Muhammad's teaching that his followers would never all agree upon an error.

Islamic law covers a wide range of topics, from serious crimes to the arrangement of domestic affairs, such as inheritance, marriage, and divorce. It also concerns itself with the regulation of daily activities, such as hygiene, eating, and drinking. For example, in addition to abstaining from alcoholic beverages, Islamic law insists that Muslims refrain from eating pork. The punishments required under Islamic law may seem severe to Americans. Under Islamic law as it is carried out in Saudi Arabia, for example, the punishment for theft is to cut off the thief's hand. And yet Islamic law may also appear unusually flexible in that it divides its rules for human conduct into five categories: required, recommended, permitted, reprehensible (permitted yet best to avoid), and forbidden. The five pillars of Islam, described above, are required according to Islamic law. Charity, beyond the zakat tax, is classified as a recommended action. The consumption of all vegetables falls under the heading of permitted behaviors. Divorce is permitted yet best to avoid. Forbidden behaviors include the serious crimes of murder, adultery, and theft, as well as the consumption of forbidden foods, such as pork and wine.

Chapter 2
Divisions Within Islam

Sunni, Shia, Ibadi

Although Muslims are united on the important points of their religion, some divisions do exist. The main split occurs between Sunni and Shia (or Shi'ite) Muslims and concerns who should lead the Muslim community. About 85 percent of all Muslims worldwide are Sunnis. The word Sunni comes from the Arabic term *sunna*, which means "example" and refers to exemplary life lived by the Prophet. The Sunnis believe that the Muslim community must be led primarily by the Quran and the example set by Muhammad. In past times they accepted the authority of the caliph, a man chosen to lead the worldwide Muslim community as a political leader and defender of the faith (though not a cleric or religious expert). Theoretically, the caliph was selected from among the upright and capable men belonging to Muhammad's extended family and their descendants, but over the years caliphs became more like ordinary kings or emperors.

The Shias constitute just under 15 percent of Muslims worldwide. They outnumber Sunnis in Iran and southern Iraq. Significant Shia communities also exist in Bahrain and Lebanon. Shias, too, believe in the authority of the Quran and the example set by Muhammad. But they also accord much importance to the teachings of their current and historical religious leaders. Shia Muslims contend that religious and political authority should be wielded by a direct descendant of the Prophet (through his daughter Fatima and his son-in-law Ali). In the period after Muhammad's death the Shias believed that Ali should

Foreign words used in the text are defined in the Glossary, pages 423-40.

47

lead them, whereas most Muslims supported Abu Bakr, the man who became the first caliph. Over the centuries Shias have accorded a great deal of authority to their own *imams*, high-ranking religious and political leaders all of whom claimed descent from Ali. (Muslims also used the word imam to refer to the men who lead the prayers at local mosques.) The respect that pious Shias give their highest-ranking imams may be compared to that offered by devout Catholics to the pope.

Since the institution of the caliphate disappeared some time ago, the main differences between the two groups today have to do with ritual practice. Shias are distinguished from Sunnis by their more open acceptance of veneration of saints and pilgrimages to the shrines of holy men, as well as by their distinctive prayer rituals. Many Sunnis look with suspicion on Shia customs, fearing that these devotions may cross the border into behavior classified as shirk. Also, Shias tend to seek out and obey the opinions and decrees set forth by their highest-ranking religious leaders, whereas Sunni Muslims see religious authority residing in a wider range of sources. Finally Shias include the opinions of the imams of old among the sources for Islamic law.

> *Shias are distinguished from Sunnis by their more open acceptance of veneration of saints and pilgrimages to the shrines of holy men, as well as by their distinctive prayer rituals.*

Another group, the Kharijites, disagreed with both Sunni and Shia Muslims on the question of who was to rule the Muslim community after Muhammad's death. The original Kharijites believed that leadership should be open to any male of exemplary belief and conduct, no matter what his ancestry. Although the Kharijites never achieved large numbers, their perspective has nonetheless wielded influence. Most of the remaining Kharijites, now called the Ibadis, live in Oman. They constitute the largest branch of Islam in that country and make up about one percent of Muslims worldwide.

Schools of Law

Among both the Sunnis and Shias there exist various schools of Islamic law. Among the Sunnis the major legal traditions are the Maliki, Hanbali, Hanafi, and Shafii. The major tradition among the Shia is called Jafari. These schools vary somewhat in their teachings concerning correct behaviors and beliefs. In addition, some of these schools of law are more conservative than others, in that they allow for very little independent opinion on the part of the judge, and tend to encourage the enforcement of the strict codes of personal behavior and strict punishments of past eras. Many consider the Hanbalis to be the most conservative of the four major Sunni schools. The Maliki school tends to

emphasize tradition and is also somewhat conservative. The Hanafi school, by contrast, allows more room for individual judgment.

Above: The Tomb of Ali is a Muslim pilgrimage site located in Najaf, Iraq.

Wahhabism

Although non-Muslim Americans are probably unfamiliar with all the schools of Muslim law discussed above, recent news-making events may have brought Wahhabi Islam to their attention. This school of thought, named after its founder Muhammad Ibn Abd al-Wahhab (1703-1791), represents what many consider to be the most conservative branch of Islam. An offshoot of the Hanbali school of law, Wahhabism advocates a return to a strict, literalistic interpretation of the Quran and the sunna of Muhammad as the only guides for Islamic law and practice. It dismisses all scholarship and jurisprudence that came afterward as "innovation," and advocates an aggressive campaign against all other schools of thought within Islam, often labeling Muslims who hold different perspectives "unbelievers." The sect has supported the destruction of shrines and other sites, fearing that the veneration that may occur there will distract people from the worship of God. Wahhabism has dominated Saudi Arabia since the early part of the twentieth century. As the official religious viewpoint of Saudi Arabia — the site of the Muslim holy land — Wahhabism has some degree of influence in the Muslim world. For example, its philosophies helped to structure Afghanistan's former Taliban government. Nevertheless, only a small minority of the world's Muslims have adopted Wahhabism.

> *Sufism itself is neither a sect nor a unified school of thought, but rather a body of teachings and practices concerned with the mystical dimensions of Islam.*

Sufism

The Sufis offer a radically different perspective on Islam. Sufism itself is neither a sect nor a unified school of thought, but rather a body of teachings and practices concerned with the mystical dimensions of Islam. Mysticism — which can be found in Christianity, Judaism, and other world religions as well — focuses on the direct experience of God. Thus Sufi religious teachers instruct their followers in various spiritual exercises that help them to sense the presence of the divine within them and around them. Sufis tend to be less interested in dwelling on the correct behaviors for Muslims outlined in Islamic law than they are with transforming their own minds, hearts, and spirits. They do not oppose more conventional versions of Islam (which most also practice), but rather seek to go beyond them. They take as their model the prophet Muhammad, whose own spiritual journey included long stints of prayer and meditation, the gift of sublime spiritual insights, and a face-to-face meeting with God. Muslims celebrate this meeting in a holiday known as Laylat al-Miraj (Night of the Ascension).

Sufism can be found among both Sunnis and Shias and has adherents throughout the Muslim world. Although scholars still debate the origins of the word "sufi," many believe it comes from the Arabic term *suf*, which means "wool" and refers to the woolen robes worn by the early Sufis. Over the centuries various Sufi masters have set up religious orders that train students to travel along the path to God established by the master. These orders may be compared to an informal network of schools, where disciples study, pray, and meditate under the guidance of a spiritual teacher. Well-known Sufi orders include the Shadhiliyyah, the Naqshbandiyyah, Chishtiyyah and the Mevlevi Order (known in the West as the "Whirling Dervishes").

Popular and Orthodox Islam

Popular religious practices add another important dimension to Islam. All the world's major religions contain certain beliefs and practices that may be considered "popular" and others that may be called "orthodox." Often popular religious practices are referred to as "folk religion." As the name implies, folk religion takes as its subject matter the religion as it is actually practiced by ordinary believers. Orthodox religion, on the other hand, may be defined as those beliefs and practices approved of by religious authorities. Orthodox religious practices and beliefs are usually defined and promoted by clergy members and those engaged in theological study. Nevertheless, rank and file believers can, and usually do, accept many if not all of them. Popular religion, on the other hand, emerges from the hearts and minds of ordinary people. Oftentimes religious officials criticize these folk ideas and customs as improper or contrary to orthodox religious teachings.

Because Muslim clerics come from different schools of thought, they don't all agree on which folk religious practices are valid according to Islamic law and which are not. Certain Shia practices, such as visiting the shrines of past imams, are accepted by Shia religious authorities. They might be criticized by Sunni clerics, however, with those representing Wahhabism likely to be the most critical.

Popular Islam includes such devotions as celebrating the birth (*mawlid*) and death (*urs*) anniversaries of holy men, making religious vows, the wearing of amulets, taking part in highly spirited sessions of religious music (*sama*), and going on pilgrimage to saints' shrines.

Above: Mausoleum and shrine of the seventh iman Musa ibn Ja'far and ninth iman Muhammad ibn Ali al-Jawad (Ali al-Taqi), Al Kadhimain (Al Kazimayn), Iraq.

The History of Islam

Chapter 3
Arabia Before Islam

Lifestyle and Values

Islam got its start in Arabia around the year 610 C.E. At that time "Arabia" was considered the lands that make up modern-day Saudi Arabia, plus Yemen, Oman, and the Persian Gulf states. In those days most of the people who lived in the deserts and steppes of Arabia made their living by herding animals. They did not build settled villages but rather moved from place to place following a nomadic lifestyle. Some towns did exist, however. Mecca and Yathrib (later Medina), located in the region of western Arabia known as the Hejaz, served as centers of trade and were among the most important settlements in Arabia.

Kinship ties were very important to the nomadic Arabs (also called Bedouins) as well as to city dwellers. The Bedouins lived together in groups of related families called clans and groups of related clans called tribes. Each tribe claimed certain grazing lands and watering holes as their own. Loyalty to one's family and devotion to protecting the family's honor, reputation, and possessions were among the

Bedouins live together in groups of related families and each tribe claims grazing lands and watering holes as their own (opposite page and above).

Camels wait patiently as their Saudi Arab Bedouin masters face meditatively toward the east and pray during one of the five prayer periods of the day.

most important virtues in Arab society. Other important values included generosity, hospitality, and courage. After their immediate family, people extended their loyalty and protection to kinfolk. Tribal members worked together to ensure the survival of the tribe. In practical terms this meant that when times were tough, groups of Bedouin kinfolk raided other tribes and trading caravans, taking camels, horses, sheep, luxury goods, slaves, and women. They also banded together to defend their own resources when attacked.

Arab culture placed tremendous emphasis on verbal skills and artistry. Poetry was a highly developed art form and poets commanded admiration and respect. Their eloquence was believed to come from contact with the divine or the supernatural. Each year, during the months when the tribes declared a truce on raiding, people gathered in the town of Ukaz for a poetry fair. Poets from each tribe recited their latest works, competing with one another for public acclaim.

Religion

At the time of Muhammad's birth Arabia was already brimming with religious ideas. Many Arabians were polytheists; that is, they believed in a variety of gods and goddesses. People often prayed and made offerings to local deities worshipped only by their own tribe. Other gods and goddesses gained a following that transcended tribal boundaries. Al-Lat, al-Uzza, and Manat were Arabia's most prominent goddesses. Al-Lat represented the sun, al-Uzza, the planet Venus, and Manat, fortune. The five most popular gods were called Suah, Wadd, Yaqhuth, Nasr, and Yauq. Some people also worshipped a god they called Allah, not as the only God but rather as a high god among many. Nevertheless, their devotion to Allah may have contained the seeds of mono-theism — the belief in one, all-powerful God. In Arabic, the word "Allah" is not a personal name, but rather means "God" (literally "the God").

Besides these gods and goddesses, many Arabians believed in spirits called *jinn*. Their personalities varied from kindly to malicious. These seldom-seen spirits lived in lush, fertile places and in harsh, forbidding ones. Arabians sought their favor through kind words and gestures, as the jinn could cause mishaps or blessings to rain down upon human beings. The English word genie comes from the Arabic word jinn.

> *Many Arabians believed in spirits called* **jinn.** *Arabians sought their favor through kind words and gestures, as the jinn could cause mishaps or blessings to rain down upon human beings.*

Many Arabians also believed that the natural world was alive and that rocks, trees, wells, oases, and other water sources contained living spirits. Some worshipped the spirits asso-ciated with these objects, and others turned these places into sites for worship of the earth's spiritual forces. In addtion, the tribes of Arabia also worshipped at locations that had been important in their history.

World religions familiar to us today, too, had gained a foothold in Arabia. By the 7th century Christians were liv-ing in Mecca and in other settlements in western and southern Arabia. Jewish communities could also be found in many Arabian towns, and Jewish mer-chants were quite active in the Hejaz. About half of the population of Yathrib (later Medina) was Jewish. Zoroastrianism was also known in the region. This ancient faith, which began in Persia perhaps as early as 1000 B.C.E., held in common with Judaism and Christianity the belief in one all-powerful God.

Amidst the practitioners of these widely varying belief systems there existed the hanifs or "pure ones." Though neither Jews, nor Christians, nor Zoroastri-ans, the hanifs attempted to merge the multiple gods, goddesses, and super-natural entities of the Arabian spiritual landscape into one marvelous and unique God. Muslims view these early hanifs as the spiritual descendants of the biblical Abraham, also an important religious figure in Islam.

Chapter 4
The Prophet Muhammad
and the Birth of Islam

The Early Life of the Prophet Muhammad

Muhammad ibn Abdullah (Muhammad son of Abdullah), the prophet who transmitted the teachings of Islam to humanity, was born in Arabia around the year 570 C.E. The name Muhammad means "highly praised one." Muhammad was born into the Hashim clan of the Quraysh tribe, which was powerful in Mecca and its environs. They were the custodians of a special shrine called the Kaba (meaning "cube") located at the center of town. This cube-shaped temple contained a mysterious black stone venerated by many Arabs. It also held the idols sacred to numerous different tribes. Pilgrims frequently visited the shrine and the Quraysh profited from the trade that travelers brought to the city.

Muhammad's father died before Muhammad was born and his mother passed away when he was six years old. Muhammad grew up under his grandfather's care, and, upon the old man's death, he passed into the custody of an uncle, Abu Talib. He joined his uncle's trading caravans on journeys to other parts of Arabia and to Syria. These expeditions not only taught him business skills, but also diplomatic ones. Many of those he encountered found him honest and reliable. During these years he acquired the nickname al-Amin, which means "trustworthy one."

Opposite page: Pilgrims perform the circling around the Kaba in Mecca, 1974.

Foreign words used in the text are defined in the Glossary, pages 423-40.

57

A pilgrim visits one of Mecca's most most famous sites—the cave on Mount Hira. It is here that the Prophet Muhammad frequently came to devote himself to religious exercises and meditation. It is also where the first verse of the Quran was revealed to him.

At the age of 25 Muhammad married a wealthy, 40-year-old widow named Khadija who had previously been his employer. They had a number of children, the most famous of whom was their daughter Fatima. Muhammad continued to manage Khadija's caravans but as he matured he devoted increasing amounts of time to prayer and meditation. He would often retreat from Mecca for days at a time, seeking solitude in a cave on nearby Mt. Hira.

The Founding of Islam

Around the year 610, when he was 40 years old, Muhammad began to experience spiritual trances, dreams, and visions. In one of them, Jibril—whom Christians and Jews call the angel Gabriel—appeared to him, commanding him to recite what was about to be revealed to him. (Jibril's command, "Iqra," means "recite," "read," or "proclaim" in Arabic.) Muhammad at first declined, explaining to the angel that he was unqualified, as he could neither read nor write. Jibril insisted. This experience is recorded in several famous lines from the Quran (Quran 96:1-5).

Muhammad never expected such a thing to happen to him and wondered if he was losing his mind. He revealed his encounter with the angel to his wife, Khadija, who in turn told it to an uncle of hers who was a Christian. The uncle recognized the message given to Muhammad as in keeping with the long biblical tradition of divine revelation. Khadija then assured Muhammad that what he had experienced was real and that he was not going crazy. So Muhammad returned regularly to the cave, where Gabriel (Jibril) continued to relay to him the teachings of Allah, who was revealed to Muhammad as the one, true God. Muhammad memorized these words, and recited them to others. He continued to receive Allah's revelations for the next 23 years. His companions recorded Muhammad's recitations of these teachings on scraps of paper, hide, or bone. These writings were later consolidated into the Quran, the holy book of Islam.

Recite, in the name of your Lord, who created: who created humankind from a clot of blood. Recite, for your lord is most generous, who taught by the Pen, Taught humankind what it did not know (Quran 96:1-5, Cleary trans.).

As Muhammad revealed the wisdom transmitted to him by the angel, his followers marveled at the splendor of the words as well as the message. Even in a culture known for its exquisite poetry, Muhammad's recitations dazzled his audiences with their lyrical beauty. This beauty helped win converts to the new religion, as many believed it a sign from God that an illiterate caravan driver should find himself transformed into an authoritative and yet sweet-tongued religious prophet.

The central message received by Muhammad was that there is only one, all-powerful God. Thus Muhammad found himself on common ground with Jews, Christians, Zoroastrians, and hanifs. In fact, the religious truths spread by Muhammad taught respect for the Hebrew and Christian scriptures, insisting that Jesus and the Hebrew prophets were valid messengers of God. Jesus was not to be taken as a divine figure, however, but rather as the most admirable of the prophets that had appeared before Muhammad. The following passage from the Quran, in which Muhammad is referred to as "His Messenger," and "His Apostle," illustrates the Muslim belief in the close connection between the three faiths. The phrase "the Books" refers to the Jewish Torah, the Psalms, the Christian Gospels, and other divinely revealed books. "The prophets" refers to Moses, Jesus, and the other prophets recognized by Islam:

O believers, believe in God and His Messenger
and the Book He has revealed to His Apostle,
and the Books revealed before. But he who believes not
in God and His angels
and the Books and the prophets and the Last Day, has wandered far
away (Quran 4:136, Ali trans.).

Muhammad remained in Mecca for the first ten years after he received the first proclamation from Jibril. He began to preach the message he received from Allah, and developed a small band of followers. He insisted that the rich had a duty to help the poor; condemned the exploitation of widows, orphans, and the destitute; and denounced usury (charging interest on loans), false contracts, theft, immodesty, and fornication. According to Muhammad, everyone faced a final judgment after death. God would send the souls of good and devout people to heaven and the wicked and irreverent to hell. Muhammad also taught the importance of five daily prayers preceded by a washing ritual. Furthermore, he explained that all true believers belonged to a single community, the umma. Muhammad argued that the values of this new, spiritual community and the needs of its members should take precedence over tribal loyalties and values.

> *According to Muhammad, everyone faced a final judgment after death. God would send the souls of good and devout people to heaven and the wicked and irreverent to hell.*

The first convert to the new religion was Muhammad's wife, Khadija. Other early converts included Zayd, a slave whom he adopted for a son, his cousin Ali (son of Abu Talib), and his friend Abu Bakr.

Muhammad's insistence on monotheism annoyed many of Mecca's prominent citizens, especially those who made a good living from the pilgrims who came to worship the many gods whose idols stood in the Kaba. Muhammad's message that there was only one God not only threatened their livelihoods, but also flew in the face of their own beliefs. Moreover, Muhammad's teachings about the umma undermined the very foundations of Arab tribal society, in which the clans and tribes continually strove to gain material, social, military, or political advantages over one another. The Meccans began to persecute Muhammad and his followers. In 615, some of these early Muslims fled to Abyssinia (modern-day Ethiopia), where the Christian king Negus granted them refuge. Muhammad's uncle Abu Talib, the head of the Hashim clan, did not covert to the new religion. He did, however, let it be known that Muhammad was under his protection. Abu Talib's support gave Muhammad some degree of safety from his persecutors.

In 619 Muhammad's wife, Khadija, and his uncle, Abu Talib, died. Another of Muhammad's uncles, Abu-Lahab, took over as head of the Hashim clan. Abu-Lahab refused to protect Muhammad. When Muhammad's enemies heard that Muhammad's clan would no longer shield him, they began to plot his death.

The First Islamic Community

In 620 a delegation from Yathrib came to Mecca to offer Muhammad a unique opportunity. Yathrib's tribal disputes threatened the stability of the city and, having heard of Muhammad's wisdom and diplomacy, the warring factions decided to ask Muhammad to come to Yathrib and judge between them. Plans and negotiations took place over the next two years, during which time groups of important citizens met with Muhammad and agreed to become Muslims and to accept his judgments if he came to their city.

In the year 622 Muhammad and his followers left Mecca and journeyed to Yathrib. This event, called the *Hijrah* (migration), marks the start of the Islamic calendar. The significance of this journey comes from the fact that it launched the establishment of the first Islamic polity, that is, a political unit run according to the teachings and rules of Islam. Traditionally, Islam has not

Over the last decade, the Prophet's Mosque in Medina has greatly expanded. Today the mosque and its plazas are roughly as large as the pre-Islamic city of Yathrib, which was renamed Medina following the Prophet Muhammad's flight from persecutors in Mecca in 622. The Hijrah (migration) marks the beginning of both the Islamic calendar and the Islamic state.

61

recognized the separation of religion and government as a valid and positive goal. In fact, Muslim leaders have often described Islam as "an entire way of life," one that includes rules for daily living as well as laws for governing peoples and nations. Muhammad's transformation of Yathrib from a town of warring tribes into a community unified under Islamic rule was the realization of a spiritual ideal. The establishment of Islamic states would later become the goal of many Muslim leaders. Some contemporary scholars believe, however, that the true goal of Islamic teaching concerning public life is to build up the *umma*, or community of believers, rather than to establish Muslim states.

In Yathrib, under Muhammad's rule, Muslims were free to follow their faith without fear of persecution for the first time. They built the first mosque there, and the first *muezzin* publicly called people to prayer in that city. Yathrib became known as *medinat al-nabi*, "the Prophet's City," or more simply as Medina. Muhammad permitted Medina's Jews to continue to practice their religion. At first the two groups got on well together, but when some Jews rejected Muhammad's claims to prophecy and others questioned his leadership, Muhammad began to view them with suspicion. Although the Muslims had originally joined the Jews in facing towards Jerusalem while praying, Muhammad one day received an instruction from God that they face Mecca instead. Other conflicts arose concerning political loyalties and, over the next several years, the Muslims drove two Jewish tribes out of the city and confiscated their wealth. When members of the last remaining Jewish tribe were found guilty of treason in a battle with the people of Mecca, its men were executed and its women and children enslaved. Though this may seem very harsh to us today, it was the fate that customarily befell conquered enemies in seventh-century Arabia.

The muezzin can still be heard five times a day from the minaret of Quba, the first mosque of Islam.

Islam and Slavery

Slavery was an accepted practice in 7th-century Arabia. Like the Hebrew and Christian scriptures, the Quran does not forbid slavery. It seeks to regulate the treatment of slaves, however, and describes the freeing of slaves as a noble act. In some parts of the Muslim world, legal forms of slavery persisted until the latter half of the 20th century. The resurgence of ethnically and religiously based slavery in Sudan in the 1990s caused an international outcry. Moreover, some experts believe that slavery is still fairly common in Mauritania, and that pockets of slavery exist in many countries of the world—non-Muslim as well as Muslim—where it is formally illegal.

The Growth of Islam in Arabia

Muhammad remained in Medina for ten years, building the Muslim community and strengthening its political position. He also married again. After Khadija's death, while still in Mecca, he had married a young widow. In Medina he married a girl named Aisha who became his favorite wife, and later a number of other women, many of them widows. This custom, polygyny (a system whereby men can marry more than one wife but women can only marry one husband), was widely practiced at the time.

During his years in Medina, Muhammad sought alliances with the wandering tribes and with nearby settlements, swaying them with religious teachings, enticing them with the promise of material benefit, and, in some cases, threatening them with the use of force. Muhammad angered the citizens of Mecca by raiding their caravans, thereby drawing the two cities into a series of battles in which, over the course of several years, no one side achieved complete victory over the other. He emerged as both a powerful religious and military leader.

Military skill, bravery in battle, and the willingness to fight were considered good and honorable traits in Arab society. Nevertheless, Muhammad preferred to settle differences by negotiation rather than warfare.

North and South Americans, Europeans, and other people raised with the ideals of Western civilization are often startled to discover Muhammad's participation and leadership in warfare. The nonviolent stance adopted by Jesus of Nazareth, the founder of Christianity, has deeply influenced Western concepts of admirable spiritual leadership, even for those who are not Christian. In defense of Muhammad, Muslims often point out that military conflict was common and accepted as normal in 7th-century Arabia. Military skill, bravery in battle, and the willingness to fight were considered good and honorable traits in Arab society. Muhammad's participation in warfare, they argue, proves no more than the fact that he was a 7th-century Arabian. Furthermore, they call attention to Muhammad's preference for settling differences by negotiation rather than warfare, which they claim demonstrates that he was considerably more peace-loving than his contemporaries. Finally they contend that Muhammad did not fight for personal gain but rather to honor God by bringing more people to what he firmly believed was the right way to live and worship — Islam. They point out that spiritual leaders from the Hebrew scriptures (the part of the Bible that Christians call the Old Testament) also were encouraged by God to wage war against people from other ethnic groups and religions. Examples include Moses, whose battles are described in the Book of Numbers, Joshua, whose life is summarized in the Book of Joshua, and Saul and David, whose conquests are told in the First and Second Books of Samuel.

In 628 Muhammad arranged a truce with the Quraysh of Mecca, in which he and his followers were granted permission to make a pilgrimage to Mecca during the following year in order to worship at the Kaba. All went well the first year, but the following year, in 630, violence marred the event and the Meccans and Medinans prepared for battle. In the end the Meccans surrendered, realizing that Muhammad commanded the much stronger army. Muhammad and his followers galloped into Mecca and rode seven times around the Kaba. Muhammad entered the shrine and acknowledged the black stone with reverence, but destroyed all the idols of pagan gods and goddesses. Muhammad taught that the Kaba had been built by Abraham, and as such it was the first shrine in the world dedicated to the worship of the one true God. After Muhammad destroyed the pagan idols, he restored the Kaba to its original purpose. He left the black stone in the shrine, however, as it was believed to have fallen from heaven.

A 16th-century painting from a Turkish manuscript depicts a scene from the time of Muhammad. Members of the powerful Quraysh tribe in Mecca debate the impact of the growth of Islam in Medina, the nearby city where Muhammad led his converts.

The Meccans fully expected that Muhammad would command his army to slay the men of Mecca and to take the women and children for slaves. Instead Muhammad spared the Meccans, requiring them to accept him as their leader, insisting that they give up their polytheism and embrace Islam, and rewarding those who did. This act of mercy increased Muhammad's reputation throughout Arabia.

The conquest of Mecca established Muhammad as the most able political and military leader in western Arabia, as well as the most inspired religious teacher. He used all these skills, especially his talent for religious persuasion, to win new converts to Islam. Many tribes sent messengers to Mecca to seek alliances with him. By the time he died in 632, Muhammad had united most of Arabia under his rule and incorporated its people into the growing community of Islam.

Chapter 5
The Spread of Islam and
the Age of Islamic Empires

For more than a thousand years after Muhammad's death Islamic empires spread to encompass vast sections of the world. Islamic laws and values served to unify and govern the diverse peoples that lived in these realms. Arab language and culture spread far beyond Arabia in the first several hundred years of this expansion. Historians divide this period up into two segments, the Caliphate period (632-1258) and the Sultanate period (1259-1922).

The Rightly Guided Caliphs

Muhammad left no clear instructions as to who was to lead the *umma* after his death. Some Arabian tribes wanted to remain together in a single large group under one leader, while others wanted to break apart into smaller groups. Most of the believers in and around the towns of Mecca, Medina, and Taif wanted to stay together, arguing that the unity of the umma was essential to Islam. They supported Abu Bakr—Muhammad's friend and the father of his third wife, Aisha—as Muhammad's successor and their leader. In this way Abu Bakr became the first caliph (from *khalifa*, the Arabic word for successor or representative) to lead the growing umma.

The caliph was not a prophet, like Muhammad, and so did not alter or elaborate on Islam's religious teachings. Instead he served as a political and military leader who ruled the people according to Islamic principles. Muslims call the

Foreign words used in the text are defined in the Glossary, pages 423-40.

65

first four caliphs the "rightly guided caliphs," because they were companions of Muhammad and had received his personal guidance during the Prophet's lifetime. At the time of the rightly guided caliphs, most Muslims agreed that the ideal candidate should be someone from the Quraysh tribe who was selected by a council of respected Muslim men. By the time of the Umayyad Caliphate, however, caliphs were passing the office down to other family members, much like a hereditary kingship.

As the first caliph, Abu Bakr's task was to bring the breakaway groups back into a unified Muslim community. He raised an army and began the campaign that later became known as the Apostasy Wars. Abu Bakr vanquished the splinter groups, and in two years united all of Arabia under the banner of Islam.

The Mosque of Umar, one of the world's oldest, has been in use since its construction was authorized by Umar ibn al-Khattab, the second caliph, or successor, of the Prophet Muhammad, in 638.

Abu Bakr, who reigned between the years 632 and 634, was the first of the four rightly guided caliphs. The others, in order of succession, were Umar ibn al-Khattab (634-644), Uthman ibn Affan (644-656) and Ali ibn Abi Talib (656-661). Many Muslims consider the time of the rightly guided caliphs a kind of golden era due to the spiritual purity of its leaders. Inspired by the belief that Allah had conferred upon them true religious teachings and divine favor, and hungry for the rich economic resources that lay outside the boundaries of Arabia, the rightly guided caliphs launched military campaigns into the surrounding countries. By the time of Ali's death in 661, the Arab Muslim empire had conquered Egypt to the west, and had expanded northward and eastward into Palestine, Syria, Iran, and Iraq. The caliph Uthman led a different but also very important campaign, successfully collecting and consolidating the Prophet's recitations into a single written volume called the Quran.

Ali ibn Abi Talib—who was both Muhammad's cousin and his son-in-law, having married Muhammad's daughter Fatima—served as the last of the rightly guided caliphs. His reign, however, was marked by a good deal of internal dissent. Ali was murdered in 661, and after his death debate over who should become caliph marked the start of the first major division in Islam. Ali's followers believed that spiritual and political leadership should be held jointly and should always come from a member of the Prophet's family, or one of his descendants. They called their chosen leader an *imam* and they themselves were known as Shias or Shi'ites. Those who believed that political lead-

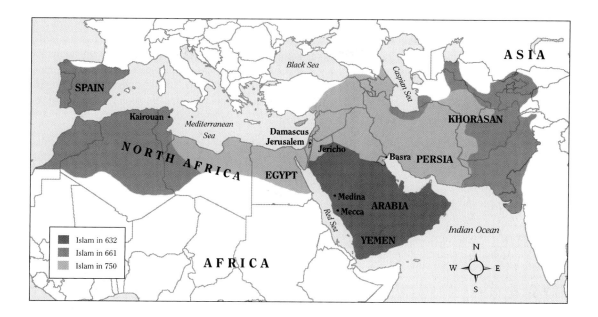

ership should come from the caliphate but religious leadership could come from religious scholars and other spiritually elevated men became known as Sunni Muslims.

Arab conquests and Muslim expansion, 7th-8th centuries.

The Umayyad Caliphate

The Umayyad Caliphate (661-750) succeeded the reign of the rightly guided caliphs and continued the expansion of the Islamic empire begun earlier. Ruling from their capital in Damascus, Syria, the Umayyads presided over military campaigns that expanded Islamic rule westward across the whole of North Africa and, crossing the Mediterranean Sea at the Straights of Gibraltar, into what is now Spain and Portugal. Eastward the Umayyads expanded the empire to the borders of India. The Arab governors and soldiers that administered Umayyad rule tended to keep top-level jobs for themselves, and did not mingle much with the peoples they conquered, even those who converted to Islam.

The Abbasid Caliphate

Whereas the Umayyad Caliphate extended Arab rule over subject peoples, the Abbasid Caliphate (750-1258) attempted to create a system of Islamic rule. They did so by embracing the technological and cultural advances of the various ethnic groups within the empire and incorporating them into an Islamic worldview. At the same time, the values and teachings of Islam filtered down to these subject peoples. They converted to the new religion in large numbers, combining the new religion with their own cultural heritage. Top positions in government and society were filled not only by Arabs but also by people of other ethnic backgrounds. The resulting blend of information, abilities, and ideas produced one of the most remarkable cultural flowerings the world has ever known.

Early brick dome of an Abbasid caliph's mausoleum.

The Abbasids moved the capital of the caliphate to Baghdad, a town whose nickname, *medinat al-Salam*, means "city of peace." Under the Abbasids, who ruled from 750 to 1258, agriculture, trade, scholarship, and industry flourished. These activities, rather than conquest, provided the empire with much of its newfound wealth and stability. The Abbasids sponsored the creation of consistent systems of Islamic law that in turn helped to unify the empire. They also became patrons of the arts, education, and architecture, providing the construction funds for many mosques. Baghdad blossomed into a city famous for its scholars and their intellectual achievements. This period produced a collection of tales known to many Westerners as *The Arabian Nights* (or *The Thousand and One Nights*). Some of the stories recount legends concerning the virtuous caliph Harun al-Rashid, an historical figure who reigned between 786 and 809.

By the 10th century rebellious regional rulers had carved chunks out of the lands under Abbasid rule. Invading Mongols and Turks — nomadic peoples from central Asia — played an important role in the final destruction of the Abbasid Caliphate. Mongol armies sacked the city of Baghdad in 1258, a date historians use to mark the official end of Abbasid rule. The victorious Mongols who had defeated the Abassids soon converted to Islam.

Other Caliphates

From the 7th to 13th centuries the Umayyad and Abbasid Caliphates spearheaded the spread of Islamic rule and nurtured the cultural and intellectual achievements of Islam. Other Islamic kingdoms and caliphates arose during the same period, however, mostly in outlying areas. The most important of these may well have been the Fatimid Caliphate (909-1171) whose rulers embraced a sect of Shia Islam. They founded the city of Cairo, Egypt, making it their capital. The Fatimids ruled much of North Africa, and expanded into parts of Arabia, Palestine, and Syria at the height of their power. The Spanish

Umayyad Caliphate, headquartered in Cordoba, Spain, provided one of the important links between what we would now call the European and Islamic worlds.

Located in Cairo, Egypt, the great mosque of al-Azhar ("The Resplendent") and university — first built in the royal compound called al-Qahira between 970 and 972 — have served for 1,000 years as Islam's most famous and most influential center of faith and scholarship.

Muslim Spain

In the year 711 Muslim armies from the north of Africa crossed over into Spain. In about three decades, these soldiers, known to the native Spanish as "Moors" (Arab and Berber Muslims from North Africa), had conquered almost all of the Iberian Peninsula and had reached southern France. A decisive battle between the French and the Moors took place between the southern French towns of Tours and Poitiers in 732. The victorious French drove the Moors out of France and sent them back across the Pyrenees Mountains to Spain.

For over 700 years, Muslims ruled some part of Spain, a land that they called "Andalus." The southernmost region of Spain, Andalucia, gets its name from this old, Arabic word. The Muslim Moors introduced new crops and industries,

The Great Mosque of Cordoba.

irrigation systems, rich trade goods from Asia, and new ideas in the sciences, medicine, philosophy, and the arts. All of these advances enriched the territory under their rule, and, with the aid of translators and travelers, some of them began to trickle back into the rest of Europe.

Around the year 756, a surviving member of the family of the last Umayyad caliph arrived in Spain and established himself in the southern Spanish city of Cordoba, which he turned into the capital of a new caliphate that ruled southern and central Spain for about 300 years. During the 10th century, at the height of its splendor, Cordoba was the most advanced city in Europe. It boasted paved streets, street lighting, public baths, a number of free schools for the poor, public libraries, numerous mosques and palaces, and a vibrant literary and intellectual life. One large library housed a collection of approximately 500,000 manuscripts, an astonishingly large number for that era. Indeed, all these facilities far outstripped what was available in other European cities at the time. What's more, the city of Cordoba claimed about 500,000 inhabitants; Paris, at that time, had a population of about 38,000. The Cordoba Caliphate, too, was known for its tolerant treatment of the Christians and Jews under its rule.

The Cordoba Caliphate broke up into a number of separate kingdoms in the middle of the 11th century. This division presented the soldiers of Christian-dominated northern Spain with an opportunity to make great strides in the Reconquest of Spain. In southern Spain tolerance for Christians diminished from the 11th century on as the Muslim kingdoms increasingly came under attack from the armies of the Christian north. In the north, Christian tolerance for Muslims also declined. From the early 13th until the late 15th century, the kingdom of Granada stood as the last remaining Muslim stronghold in Spain. The Alhambra — the graceful palace, fountains, and gardens of its Moorish kings — still stands as a lasting example of the engineering skills and artistry of this civilization. The kingdom of Granada fell to the triumphant armies of the Spanish monarchs King Ferdinand and Queen Isabella in 1492. After reuniting Spain under their rule, Ferdinand and Isabella declared that Muslims and Jews living there must convert to Christianity or leave the country.

During the 10th century, at the height of its splendor, Cordoba was the most advanced city in Europe. It boasted paved streets, street lighting, public libraries, numerous mosques and palaces, and a vibrant literary and intellectual life.

The Crusades

In the Middle Ages, both Christians and Muslims waged wars of expansion and conquest. In 1095, Pope Urban II summoned Europeans to fight in the first Crusade. The Crusades were a series of wars launched by Christian Europeans between the late 11th and late 13th centuries. The stated goals were gaining control over the city of Jerusalem, a sacred site for Christians as well as Muslims and Jews, and securing safe passage for Christian pilgrims to the Holy Land (the land where the stories in the Bible took place, located in modern-day Israel). At that time, Muslims had ruled these territories for several hundred years. At the pope's urging, a great many European Christians converged on the Holy Land as the 11th century drew to a close. In the year 1099, the armies of the first Crusade conquered the city of Jerusalem. The victorious crusaders slaughtered Muslim and Jewish civilians throughout the city.

By the early 12th century the crusaders had established a number of small Christian-ruled territories along the eastern shores of the Mediterranean Sea — the Kingdom of Jerusalem, the county of Edessa, the county of Tripoli, and the principality of Antioch — but these proved difficult to maintain once

In 1187, Saladin's victory at the battle of Hattin forced Guy De Lusignan, Crusaders King of Jerusalem, and Reynaud De Chatillon, Lord of Kerak, to negotiate surrender in Saladin's tent, an event that marked the end of Crusader hopes of enduring rule over the Holy Land.

Muslim forces regrouped themselves for battle. In 1187, the famous king and warrior Salah ad-Din al-Ayyubi (known as Saladin by the Europeans) led his troops in a decisive victory over the crusader armies, a victory that returned all but the city of Tyre to Muslim control. The Europeans not only recognized Saladin as a brilliant warrior, but also marveled at the mercy he displayed to conquered peoples, especially the weak and defenseless. By 1291, Muslims had retaken all the lands once conquered by the crusaders.

For the most part, the crusaders knew and cared little about the cultures and religions of the peoples they encountered outside of Western Europe. They did realize, however, that many riches could be found in the lands to the east. Many were tempted too, by the idea that God and the Church would forgive them their sins as a reward for their participation in the Crusades. Some historians have concluded that the average European crusader was as much motivated by a desire for adventure, loot, and the forgiveness of his or her sins, as by a desire to protect Christian access to the holy lands. Their lack of understanding and respect also

---

Political Implications of the Word "Crusade"

Scholars trace the roots of the English word "crusade" back to crux, the Latin word for "cross." In spite of the word's medieval association with Christianity, today English speakers use it to describe enthusiastic campaigns of action on behalf of any kind of cause. U.S. politicians will usually avoid describing American activities in the Middle East as "a crusade," however, even though that expression is still in common usage. This is because some Muslims still resent the Crusades of the Middle Ages, and fear the predominantly Christian countries of Europe and the Americas may still harbor a desire to attack and conquer Muslims in the Middle East.

---

extended to the Orthodox Christians they encountered in eastern Europe and the Middle East. In fact, in 1204, the soldiers of the fourth Crusade successfully attacked and looted Constantinople (today called Istanbul), the capital of the Orthodox Christian Byzantine Empire. This unprovoked attack not only further deteriorated relations between western (Catholic) and eastern (Orthodox) Christians, but also hastened the decline of the Byzantine Empire, a kingdom which had long buffered Christian Europe from the expanding empires of the Middle East.

The Spread of Islam and the Treatment of Religious Minorities

The primary goal of the Islamic conquests was not to spread Islam. In fact, the leaders who presided over these campaigns were more interested in establishing political rule over non-Muslims for the purposes of monetary gain than they were in converting them to Islam. Conquered Christians and Jews were permitted to practice their religions. Zoroastrians and Hindus sometimes fared less well than Jews and Christians, though for the most part they, too, were allowed to continue in their ways of worship. The Quranic command that "there is no compulsion in matters of faith" (2:256) was usually observed.

Under Muslim rule non-Muslims paid extra taxes and were not allowed to serve in the army. For the most part the new Muslim rulers guaranteed their safety, possessions, and religious sites. The Arabs called them *dhimmi*, or "protected ones." In this way the new Arab rulers both disarmed potential enemies and enriched the empire.

In North Africa and the Middle East, most of the conquered peoples converted to the new religion over the course of several hundred years. Many were drawn to its religious teachings. Others may have viewed conversion in a more practical way, since Muslims sometimes found it easier than non-Muslims to advance their careers and to share in the wealth of the empire. Local peoples also adopted the Arabic language and elements of Arab culture over time. In fact, in those areas first absorbed by the Islamic expansion — North Africa and the Middle East — Arabic eventually became a local language. Today it is the official language of Morocco, Algeria, Libya, Tunisia, Egypt, Sudan, Syria, Jordan, Lebanon, Saudi Arabia, Iraq, Kuwait, Bahrain, Oman, Qatar, United Arab Emirates, and Yemen. In addition, Arabic serves as one of the official languages of Mauritania, Chad, Somalia, Djibouti, and Comoros.

In those areas first absorbed by the Islamic expansion — North Africa and the Middle East — Arabic eventually became a local language.

While certain religious minorities were tolerated under Islamic rule, Islamic law favored Muslims over people from other religions in certain regards. Christians and Jews could not promote their religions, seek converts among Muslims, or build new places of worship, though they could receive permission to repair old ones. Christians, Jews, and others could convert to Islam, but Muslims were prohibited from changing their religion. In the courts of law, the word of a Muslim outweighed the word of a Christian or Jew. Nevertheless, in matters of religious or family law (for example marriage), Jews and Christians were permitted to hold their own courts governed by their own laws and customs. In some places Christians and Jews found themselves subject to additional restrictions, such as being made to wear identifying clothing and to adopt a humble and self-effacing manner in the presence of Muslims, but in other places they did not. These conditions may seem very unfair to us today. Nevertheless, many historians have concluded that Jews and Christians were treated with greater tolerance under Islamic rule than religious minorities usually received in Europe during the same era. In medieval Europe, where Christians held power, Jews were segregated in ghettos, made to wear special identifying marks on their clothing, restricted in their economic activities, and sometimes harassed or attacked. When Christian heretics — those Christians who believed differently than did the majority — grew too outspoken and influential, they were often imprisoned, exiled, or executed.

Islam spread throughout most of North Africa, the Middle East (including Iran), and part of central Asia in the wake of the Arab conquests. Outside of these areas, however, Islam spread largely through the activities of merchants, missionaries, and Sufi mystics.

This mosque, located in Isfahan, Iran, was built by Shah Abbas. The tile mosaic and glazed-tile decoration is here brought to a peak of perfection both in the iwans (semi-circular vaults) and in the great dome.

The Sultanates

After the fall of the Abbasid Caliphate its former territories were divided up into petty kingdoms. Muslim generals and tribal leaders, many of whom were not Arab, governed most of these kingdoms. For the next several hundred years these kingdoms jostled with one another for power, though no one emerged as strong enough to conquer the others. The next strong, centralized empires to arise in the Middle East were the Ottoman and Safavid Empires. Further to the east, the Mughal (also spelled "Mogul") Empire ruled large sections of the Indian subcontinent for several hundred years. These three were the most influential Muslim empires of the Sultanate period.

The Persian (Iranian) Safavid Empire (1501-1732) established Shiism as the dominant branch of Islam in Iran. Under the Safavids, Persia experienced the first independent rule it had known since the 7th century. The Safavid shahs presided over an Iranian cultural revival in the arts and in literature. The dynasty's most illustrious ruler, Shah Abbas I (r. 1588-1629), was a great supporter of scholarly study and artistic endeavors. During his reign the Safavid capital was moved from Tabriz to Isfahan and Persian replaced Turkish as the language spoken in court. He also established important trade links with Europe.

The main gateway of the Friday Mosque in Fatehpur Sikri, India, testifies to Akbar's power and complexity.

The Mughal dynasty ruled in northern India from 1526 to 1858. The great Mughal emperor Akbar (r. 1556-1605) is remembered for his religious tolerance, for the wealth he brought to the region during his reign, and for his patronage of scholars and artists. An Indian style of Islamic architecture flourished under the Mughals and is perhaps best exemplified by the world famous Taj Mahal. Sufi religious orders blossomed under Mughal rule, as did Sufi poetry and music. The Urdu language developed during the reign of the Mughals, and became a major language in the Islamic world.

The Ottoman Turks fought their way across Asia Minor (modern-day Turkey) in the 14th century, seizing Constantinople in 1453 and thus overthrowing the 1,000-year-old Byzantine Empire. They renamed this ancient city, now their new capital, Istanbul. Istanbul means "city of Islam." From there they expanded their empire into Eastern Europe, the Arab Middle East, and parts of North Africa. Sufi orders flourished in the lands under Ottoman rule, but the Ottomans became most famous in Europe for their fierce fighting forces. The greatest Ottoman ruler was Sulayman the Magnificent (r. 1520-66), whose armies reached as far into Europe as the Austrian capital of Vienna. The Muslim populations found today in the southeastern European countries of Albania, Bosnia-Herzegovina, Bulgaria, and Montenegro were largely established during the period when these lands were ruled by the Ottoman Empire.

By the 17th and 18th centuries the power and influence of the Ottoman Empire and other Islamic kingdoms had begun to wane. During this era European peoples and cultures assumed a dominant role in world affairs. Slow, steady decline dogged the Ottoman Empire throughout the 18th and 19th centuries. The Ottoman sultanate lasted until 1922, when the last sultan was removed from power. Turkey became a republic in 1923. The fall of the Ottoman Empire also marked the end of the caliphate, an office claimed by the Ottoman sultans during the declining years of their empire.

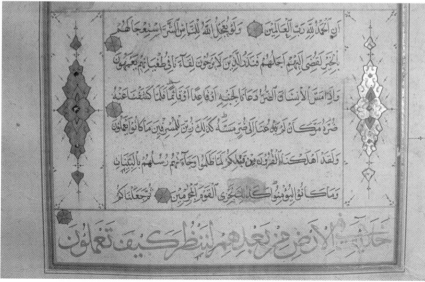

The Ottoman Empire and its art both reached their zenith during the 16th-century reign of Sultan Sulayman the Magnificent. Above: Ottoman artifacts and Quran stand produced by Ehl-i Hiref celebrating "the perplexity of spring." Left: Illuminated Ottoman Quran, 17th century.

The 20th Century and Beyond

With the fall of the Ottoman Empire in the early 20th century, the age of Islamic empires came to an end. In most places, however, Islamic rule had disappeared during the 19th century or earlier, displaced for the most part by European colonial governments or protectorates. Only Iran, Saudi Arabia, and Yemen avoided this fate. Europe's colonial holdings reached their greatest height during the 19th century. During the 20th century these colonial empires were dismantled and their former territories sorted out into nation states.

In Europe, nation states and the concepts of government that supported them developed over several centuries. By contrast, the Islamic countries had this form of political organization—with its emphasis on ethnicity and nationalism as unifying forces—suddenly thrust upon them. Many found the new system to be at odds with tradition, since in ages past Islam had served to unify people from different tribes, regions, and ethnic groups. Moreover, Islam had often functioned both as a religion and as a legal system. The imported European notion of a secular state clashed with older, established ideas enshrining the value of religiously-based government. In modern times predominantly Muslim countries have wrestled with the question of how to organize modern, effective nation states and yet still retain their Islamic heritage.

Chapter 6
The Achievements of Islamic Civilization

Located at the crossroads between Europe and Asia, the Islamic empires that ruled the Middle East during the Middle Ages stood poised to transmit knowledge from West to East and from East to West. Under the Umayyad and Abbasid Caliphates (661-1258), Muslim rulers and scholars gathered knowledge from surrounding civilizations, both contemporary and ancient. They also made their own discoveries and generated their own groundbreaking scholarship and research. In this way, they not only enriched their own people, but also preserved and generated learning that, when discovered by European scholars, helped to inspire the European Renaissance. The great power, wealth, and learning that characterized the Islamic world in that era has led some observers to call it the "golden age of Islam."

The House of Wisdom

Having heard of the wisdom of the ancient Greeks, al-Mansur (r. 754-75), the second Abbasid caliph, sent messengers to the emperor of the neighboring Byzantine Empire asking for copies of important mathematical texts. The emperor sent back a copy of Euclid's *Elements*, an important book written by an ancient Greek mathematician. This gift sparked further interest in ancient and modern scholarship. Some 50 years later, the seventh Abbasid caliph, al-Ma'mun, founded a research institute called the House of Wisdom in 830.

Foreign words used in the text are defined in the Glossary, pages 423-40.

79

Gold ink was used exclusively on one of the rarest pages in the Beit Al Qur'an collection, penned in Kairouan, Tunisia, on colored vellum. It is from a copy of the Quran said to have been commissioned by the Abbasid caliph al-Ma'mun to honor his father, Harun al-Rashid. Only three or four Quran manuscripts are known to have been written in this manner.

Located in the capital city of Baghdad, the House of Wisdom supported nearly 60 scholars and translators. Some of these scholars were Muslims, but many others were Christians and other non-Muslims. Some of these non-Muslim scholars were absorbed into the empire through Islamic military conquests; others came to Baghdad because it was a major center of learning. Together they staffed the first research institute in Muslim history, an establishment whose accomplishments made 9th- and 10th-century Baghdad one of the most cosmopolitan and advanced cities in the world. The House of Wisdom attracted students from all over the empire. It was among the most remarkable institutions of its day and predated the founding of the great European universities by several centuries.

Philosophy

When Muslim armies conquered Egypt and Syria, they found themselves in control of a land that had long been ruled by the Greek Byzantine Empire. The Byzantine Greeks had preserved much of the ancient learning of their ancestors, which had been lost to the Christians of Western Europe. Muslim translators set about decoding these ancient texts, including the works of the great philosophers Plato, Aristotle, and Socrates. These translated texts, which spread as far as Muslim Spain, eventually made their way into the hands of European scholars. In fact, some historians conclude that this influx of knowledge from the ancient world, made possible by Muslim scholars, fueled the intellectual revolution that led Europe from the Middle Ages into the Renaissance.

What's more, Muslim philosophers developed subtle philosophical insights of their own. Two of the most famous of these philosophers were Ibn Sina (d.1037) — called Avicenna in Europe — and Ibn Rushd (d.1198) — called Averroes in Europe. Their writings and translations of ancient Greek philosophers inspired the great Catholic thinker St. Thomas Aquinas (1225-1274) to compose his famous work *Summa Theologica*, which in turn influenced centuries of Christian thought. Another famous thinker, the Tunisian writer Ibn Khaldun (1332-1406), roamed the Islamic world describing and analyzing the customs of the people he encountered and inquiring into their history. His accurate observations and keen insights into the development of societies have earned him the nickname "the father of historiography" (the writing of history) and "the father of sociology."

Mathematics and Physics

Sometime around the 7th or 8th century the Arabs borrowed a basic numbering system from India. The important things about this numbering system were that it included zero as a number and that it was based on positional notion. In positional notion, the value of a particular numerical figure is understood from its position within the number. Thus, the same two numerals that are used to represent 19 can also be used to write 91. Muslim mathematicians added a decimal system to represent fractions, and used this advance to delve deeper into the world of complex mathematics. For example, the Persian scholar Muhammad ibn Musa al-Khwarizmi (ca. 780-ca. 850) went on to develop the branch of mathematics known as algebra. Other scholars made important advances in the field of trigonometry.

Ibn Rushd, or Averroes, one of the great intellects of the 12th century, is honored by a statue in his hometown of Cordoba, Spain.

Ibn al-Haytham (965-1030), a famous Muslim mathematician and scientist from Basra, Iraq, made extraordinary advances in physics and the study of optics. He offered a scientific explanation for the rainbow, argued that the movement of the stars and the earth were caused by cosmic phenomena, and stated that vision results from the eye receiving light rays, rather than sending them.

Other Muslim thinkers used their scientific understanding of the natural world to invent new machines and tools. For example, Muslim scientists developed a mechanical device for raising water that proved useful in irrigation projects, devised water clocks and fountains, and improved on the ancient Greek astrolabe, an important instrument used in navigation at sea.

Medicine

In the Middle Ages Muslim doctors moved far beyond their European counterparts in their ability to treat diseases. Again, the advances began with the translation of the works of ancient Greek physicians, such as Hippocrates and Galen. Their efforts didn't stop there, however. Medical breakthroughs attributed to medieval Muslim doctors include the use of anesthesia for surgery, the study of pharmacology as a separate branch of medicine, the preparation of prescriptions, the cauterizing of wounds, and the identification of contamination by touch or by air as the cause of epidemics.

Probably the greatest and most original of all the Muslim physicians of the classic era, al-Razi, is commemorated in a stained-glass window at Princeton University in New Jersey.

The physician Abu Bakr Muhammad al-Razi (860-940) — known as Rhazes in Europe — wrote 200 books on various aspects of medicine. Some writers have called him the greatest doctor of the Middle Ages. When printing was invented in Europe hundreds of years later, a translation of his grand 25-volume work *al-Hawi* was one of the first manuscripts to be made into a book. Ibn Sina, discussed above as a philosopher, also practiced medicine. Europeans called him the "prince of physicians." His most famous medical work, known in English as the *Canon of Medicine*, was used to teach medicine in Europe well into the 17th century.

Visual Arts

A saying of Muhammad's cautions Muslims against depicting realistic human forms lest they inspire idolatry (the worship of things other than God). Therefore, artists whose work was destined for religious settings or for use during individual prayer or group worship developed a somewhat abstract visual vocabulary. It was based largely on the combination and repetition of geometric shapes and ornate calligraphy. Many other designs appear to be based on stylized renditions of curling vines, leaves, and flowers. These motifs are sometimes called vegetal, but are more often referred to as Arabesque. The way in which one motif twirls into another, creating a pattern that seems to go on forever, gives the viewer a sense of growth and change that is somehow embedded in eternity. Thus, while avoiding realistic representational art, Islamic artists

managed to depict spiritual truths. Both of these kinds of design work can be found on tiles, rugs, fabrics, and the walls of mosques and other important buildings.

Many Muslim artists have also produced works that depict human and animal figures. Some of this artwork illustrates sacred stories or scenes from the life of the Prophet and other important Muslims. This artwork is not used in prayer or worship, however.

Calligraphy

The art of the written word — especially calligraphy and religious poetry — flourished under Islam. Their continuing popularity reflects the importance that this religion places on the word of God. Calligraphy is perhaps the most important and most prized visual art in the Islamic world. It adorns copies of the Quran, the walls of palaces and mosques, and is also produced as framed artwork. Indeed, Muslim artists have created some of the world's most beautiful calligraphy. Because the Quran is understood to be the exact words of God,

The compositions of modern artists who use a phrase or verses from the Quran testify to the tradition of Quranic calligraphy. In this 1984 stained-glass composition, Egyptian calligrapher Ahmad Mustafa rendered verses that refer to the bounty of the sea, made available by God for humankind.

Basmallah

bismallah ir-Rahman ir-Rahim

In the name of God, the merciful, the compassionate

Basmallah (Eastern Kufi)
Based on a Quran from Iraq or Persia, 11th century.

Basmallah (Kufi)

Basmallah (Modern design based on Eastern Kufi)

Basmallah (Modern design 2 based on Kufi)

Basmallah (Modern small design based on Eastern Kufi)

Basmallah (Old Kufi)
Based on a Quran from Kairouan, 9th century.

Basmallah (Naskhi)
After Hashem Muhammad al-Khattat, Iraq, 1961

Basmallah (Nastaliq)
After Najm al-Din Okyay (1883-1976)

Basmallah (Muhaqqaq)
Based on a Quran written by Baysunghur,
grandson of Tamerlane, early 15th century, Persia.

Basmallah (Thuluth Round)

to embellish these words is seen as a way of glorifying God. One hadith recalls that Muhammad said that anyone who could write the *basmallah* beautifully would be sure to go to heaven when they died. The basmallah is a religious phrase that reads "in the name of God, the merciful, the compassionate." It is found throughout the Quran. So tied is the art of calligraphy to Muslim spirituality that an Arab proverb summarizes the relationship by noting that "calligraphy is the geometry of the spirit."

Over the centuries different schools of calligraphy developed in the Muslim world. Some, like the kufic style, are more angular, and others, such as thuluth, are more rounded and curvy. Contemporary Muslim calligraphers are stretching the boundaries of the art form as they incorporate influences and materials from both Western European and East Asian art into their creations. In the Muslim world interest in calligraphy, both modern and traditional, is still strong. The International Research Center for Islamic Culture and Art (IRCICA), located in Istanbul, Turkey, holds regular contests in which artists compete to see who can produce the most beautiful examples of traditional Islamic calligraphy.

A 16th-century Indian calligrapher created this horse from a single Quran verse taken from Sura al-Baqara (Chapter 2, The Cow).

Poetry

As has been previously noted, the Arabs cherished poets and their work even before the advent of Islam. In the 9th century, about 200 years after the founding of Islam, the Arab writer Ibn Qutayba described poetry as a shrine that houses the remembrance of the great truths, great deeds, and great men and women of Arab society:

> Poetry is the mine of knowledge of the Arabs, the book of their wisdom, the muster roll of their history, the repository of their great days, the rampart protecting their heritage, the trench defending their glories, the truthful witness on the day of dispute, the final proof at the time of argument. Whoever among them can bring no verse to confirm his own nobility and the generous qualities and honored deeds which he claims for his forebears, his endeavors are lost though they be famous, effaced by the passage of time though they be mighty. But he who binds them with rhymed verse, knots them with scansion, and makes them famous through a rare line, a phrase grown proverbial, a well-turned thought, has made them eternal against time, preserved them from negation, averted the plot of the enemy, and lowered the eye of the envious (Lewis 2001: 32-33).

The Quran itself raised the lyricism of the Arabic language to new levels, and in turn inspired new efforts in religious poetry.

The Quran itself raised the lyricism of the Arabic language to new levels, and in turn inspired new efforts in religious poetry. Indeed, Islamic civilization aroused a love and respect for poetry, both sacred and secular, wherever it spread. According to the Islamic scholar Seyyed Hossein Nasr, "wherever Islam has gone, poetry has flourished, and to this day poetry is very much alive as a major cultural force in nearly every Islamic society" (Nasr, *The Heart of Islam*, 2002: 231).

In the centuries that followed the founding of Islam, inspired devotees — many of them Sufis — translated their religious insights into poetry. Important Arabic language Sufi poets include Rabi'a (713-801), Al-Hallaj (857-922), and Ibn Arabi (1165-1240). But perhaps the most famous and beloved of these Sufi poets today is Jelaluddin al-Rumi (1207-1273), who lived in what is now Turkey and wrote in Persian. New English translations of his works have contributed to making Rumi a best-selling poet in America in recent years. The well-known poet Hafiz (ca. 1325-ca. 1390) also wrote in Persian, as did Omar Khayyam (1048-ca. 1125), whose work became famous in Europe when the 19th-century English poet Edward Fitzgerald first translated it into English. Other important Sufi poets, such as Galib (1757-1799) and Nesimi (d.1417), wrote in Turkish. Contemporary writers continue to add to the treasure house of exquisite Islamic poetry.

Architecture

Islamic architects also achieved great splendor. One of the most famous buildings in the world, India's Taj Mahal, was commissioned by the Mughal emperor Shah Jahan (1592-1666) as a shrine to honor his deceased wife Mumtaz Mahal. The graceful Alhambra palace, located in Granada, Spain, was built by the region's Muslim rulers in the 13th and 14th centuries. Istanbul's fabulous, bejeweled Topkapi Palace, once the home to the Ottoman sultans, has also garnered world-wide fame. Islamic architecture has an important sacred dimension as well.

The Taj Mahal, with its mosque and reception hall, is approached through a magnificent complex of formal gardens and reflecting pool.

87

Examples of Islamic Architecture

Alhambra, Granada, Spain. The Court of the Lions, with its gallery of 128 white marble columns and its 12 oddly shaped lions clustered around a fountain, is probably the most famous part of the Alhambra.

Above: Sultan Ahmet (Blue) Mosque, Istanbul, Turkey. Built by architect Sedefkar Mehmet Agha in the 17th century, its alternative name is derived from the extensive blue-stenciled interior decoration.

Left: The Dome of the Rock in Jerusalem is a symbol of more than 1,300 years of Muslim historical and religious ties with the Holy City.

Above: Detail from the Great Mosque of Cordoba's decorative western portal illustrates the masterful usage of vegetal and arabesque design.

Muslim architects designed magnificent mosques evoking the peace and transcendence of God and inspiring worshipers to humility and reverence. Famous examples include the Blue Mosque in Istanbul, Turkey; the Dome of the Rock in Jerusalem, Israel; the Masjid i-Shah, in Isfahan, Iran; and the Great Mosque in Cordoba, Spain.

The Influence of Arabic on the English Language

Many words of Arabic origin have made their way into English and other European languages. The imported words provide a record of the inventions and innovations that Muslim society brought to Europe and the rest of the world. The sprawling but unified Islamic caliphates promoted commerce over long distances, which helped to bring new ideas, foods, and other goods not only to Muslim lands, but also to Europe. Many of the Arabic words for these products found their way into European languages. Finally, a considerable number of novelties from various Muslim societies impressed Europeans, who adopted the words into their languages. Many of these words begin with the letters "al," which corresponds to the word "the" in Arabic. The list below offers a small sampling of modern English words that came from Arabic:

English Word	Arabic Word	Meaning in Arabic
admiral	amir al-bahr	commander of the sea
adobe	al-tuba	the brick
alchemy	al-kimiya	the art of transmutation
alfalfa	al-fasfasa	the forage plant
algebra	al-jabr	to mend broken parts; knit together
algorithm	al-khwarizmi	algorithm, named after mathematician Khwarizmi
almanac	al-manakh	the climate
apricot	al-barquq	the plum
artichoke	al-khurshur	the artichoke
average	awwar	harm to ship or cargo (shared equally by investors)
azure	as-sumut	lapis lazuli, blue
camel	jamal	camel
candy	qand	crystalline evaporated sugar
cane	qanaa	hollowed out stick
caraway	karawya	caraway
carmine	qirmiz	red dye
cinnabar	zinjafr	mercuric sulfide
coffee	qahwa	coffee
cotton	qutn	cotton
crimson	qirmizi	red dye from kermes beetle
cumin	kammun	cumin
elixir	al-iksir	the drug
genie	jinni	demon, spirit
lute	al-'ud	a stringed instrument
mocha	Mukha	a port city famous for coffee
muslin	mawsili	cloth from the city of Mosul
orange	naranj	orange tree
safari	safar	journey
saffron	zafaran	saffron
satin	zaytuni	cloth from Tsinkiang (Zaytoon), a city in China
sherbet	sharba(t)	drink
sofa	suffa	bench, ledge
syrup	sharab	syrup
tambourine	tanbur	bass drum
tangerine	tanja	tangerine, from Tangiers, a city in Morocco
tariff	ta'rifa	notification, information
vizier	wazir	minister to a king
zero	sifr	zero

Al-'ud (lute) is a stringed musical instrument.

91

Muslims Today

Chapter 7
Moving Beyond Stereotypes

Until recently most Americans have paid little attention to the peoples and cultures of the Muslim world. Moreover, many Muslims feel that when the American media does cover aspects of Islam, it tends to focus on the exotic or the radical. They wish that more balanced material was more widely available. Many Muslim Americans complain that this relative lack of information has led to the creation of stereotypes. A stereotype is a one-dimensional image of a group of people that reduces the full and complex identity of each individual member down to one or two characteristics. Muslims have been stereotyped as "violent," "fanatical," "backwards," "sexist," and so on. The following discussion of stereotypes will include profiles of prominent Muslims whose ideas and achievements contradict commonly held notions about Muslims in order to help create a broader and more balanced view of Islam and its followers.

Violence and Peace

Some of the most common stereotypes about Muslims have to do with their inclination towards terrorism and other forms of violence. The publicity showered on Osama bin Laden, a Muslim terrorist who masterminded the September 11,

Opposite page: Living their faith in their daily lives, sharing it with neighbors, and building a community — those very American, very Islamic goals brought a group of Muslims to Dar Al-Islam in Abiquiu, New Mexico.

Foreign words used in the text are defined in the Glossary, pages 423-40.

93

2001, attacks on the World Trade Center and the Pentagon that killed about 3,000 people, gave this stereotype a big boost. In the following years, as Americans watched their military fight against Muslim armies and terrorists in Afghanistan and Iraq, the stereotype was developed further. In fact, the number of Americans who believe that Islam encourages its followers to perform acts of violence increased significantly between the years 2002 and 2003, from 25 to 44 percent of the population.

Unfortunately, when Muslims make the news it's often due to their association with violence and terror. For example, most Americans know the name of Osama bin Laden. They are also familiar with former Iraqi leader Saddam Hussein, a savage ruler who brutalized both the country's Kurdish and its Arab populations. But sensational stories about violent Muslims neglect the millions of ordinary believers who prefer to live in peace with their neighbors and work for justice though political, social, and spiritual means. Even famous Muslims who have devoted themselves to resolving conflicts through nonviolence are still relatively unknown in the United States.

Abdul Ghaffar Khan and Indian prime minister Indira Gandhi in 1969, upon Khan's visit to India for the centennial of Mahatma Gandhi's birth.

Such is the case with Abdul Ghaffar Khan (1890-1988), an ethnic Pathan (or Pashtun) from Pakistan who worked side by side with Mahatma Gandhi (1869-1948) to end British colonial rule in India and Pakistan. For decades the two men labored to inspire the people of India, Pakistan, and Afghanistan to join together in nonviolent resistance to the British. From among the Muslim Pashtuns, a people noted for their willingness to take up arms against the British and against each other, Khan raised an "army" of 100,000 people dedicated to community service and to nonviolent resistance to British rule. Though initially inspired by Ghandi, Khan also modeled his nonviolence on the behavior of Muhammad during his first ten years as a prophet in Mecca. He described his religion in this way: "It is my inmost conviction that Islam is *amal, yakeen, muhabat* [work, faith, love]" (Easwaran: 63). Khan's devoted followers dubbed him "Badshah Khan," which means "king of khans." Though repeatedly imprisoned by the British, Khan never wavered from his nonviolent principles.

The movement led by Ghandi and Khan was eventually successful in driving the British from India. Sadly, Khan was soon imprisoned by the very Pakistani government that he helped to bring into existence. The government did this because Khan, like Ghandi, spoke out in opposition to the division of India and Pakistan that occurred after independence. At the age of 80, Khan made a brief visit to India to join in the festivities marking the centennial of Mahatma Gandhi's birth.

Israeli prime minister Menachem Begin, United States president Jimmy Carter, and Egyptian president Anwar Sadat, September 1978.

When religious violence between Hindus and Muslims marred the celebrations, Khan began to fast as a plea for peace. So beloved was he by both Muslims and Hindus that as word of the fast spread, the riots ceased. All told, he spent about one-third of his life in jail, but he died at the age of 98, still convinced that non-violence was the way to move his people, his country, and the world forward towards justice and peace.

Anwar al-Sadat (1918-1981) presents a more worldly example of a Muslim peacemaker. Sadat became president of Egypt in 1970, and in 1973 started the Arab-Israeli War, hoping to gain back the territory lost to Israel during the 1967 Six-Day War. When the Arab-Israeli war ended in Egypt's defeat, Sadat turned to the peace-making process. He agreed to recognize the existence of the state of Israel. The Israeli prime minister, Menachem Begin, in turn agreed to return the Egyptian territory taken in the Six-Day War. For their ability to turn away from the cycle of violence and bring their two countries to a nego-tiated agreement, the two men were awarded the Nobel Peace Prize in 1978. Unfortunately, Sadat was assassinated in 1981, by members of a group of Muslim extremists opposed to peace between Israel and Egypt.

In 2003 the Nobel Peace Prize was again awarded to a Muslim, this time to Iranian judge and college professor Shirin Ebadi. At considerable risk to her own safety and well-being, Ebadi has tirelessly campaigned for human rights in Iran, and has also championed the rights of women and children. Ebadi

Shirin Ebadi is shown speaking below portraits of Iran's leaders (left to right): Mohammad Khatami, president of Iran; Ayatollah Ruhollah Khomeini, the late founder of the Islamic Republic of Iran; and his successor, Ayatollah Ali Khamenei, supreme leader of Iran.

served as the first woman judge in Iran, but was forced to step down from that job after the Iranian revolution in 1979. Iran's new rulers made sharia (Muslim law) the law of the land, declaring that women were too unstable emotionally to serve as judges. Ebadi eventually found a new forum for her talents at Tehran University, but that post did not save the outspoken rights leader from the wrath of government leaders and religious extremists, or from a stint in jail in the year 2000. Ebadi, a committed Muslim who believes that human rights are an integral part of Islam, hopes the award will help further the cause of human rights in Iran.

The third Muslim to win the Nobel Peace Prize is Palestinian leader Yasir Arafat, who shared the prestigious award along with the Israeli leaders Yitzhak Rabin and Shimon Peres in 1994. Although Arafat had been involved with terrorist activities in the past, the committee awarded him the prize for his part in trying to negotiate a just and peaceful settlement of the Israeli-Palestinian conflict with Rabin and Peres.

Americans may never forget the fact that the 19 hijackers who succeeded in killing almost 3,000 people on September 11, 2001, were Muslims. But it is also important to remember the expressions of shock and sympathy extended to the American people from millions of Muslims around the world. In the days after the attack, America received official condolences from political and religious leaders across the Muslim world, along with statements condemning the bombings. In Jerusalem and the Palestinian Territory, Palestinian Muslims gave blood destined for victims of the bombings and Palestinian schoolchildren observed five minutes of silence for the victims and their families. In Iran and Bangladesh, Muslims grieving over the attacks held candlelight vigils for the victims. In this country, the Islamic Society of North America, along with many other important American Muslim organizations, utterly denounced the bombings, calling them "vicious and cowardly acts of terrorism against innocent civilians." Across the nation American Muslims attended prayer vigils for the victims of the attack. A month later, in October of 2001, a rally in Pakistan supporting peace and moderation in Islam drew 500,000 attendees.

Fanaticism and Fairness

Another common stereotype of Muslims suggests that they are all given to extremism—especially in their treatment of non-Muslims and women—and that they are intolerant of debate and dissent within the Muslim community. The stereotype seems to suggest that there is something about Islam that necessarily leads to fanaticism. The leaders of Afghanistan's former Taliban government and the society they created constitute a well-known example of this kind of extremism. And yet those Muslims who work to establish standards of justice and fairness for all peoples seldom make the news.

One of them who deserves to be more widely recognized in this country is M. Cherif Bassiouni, a professor of law at Chicago's DePaul University. His studies cover American, European, and Islamic legal systems. In addition to his American law degrees he holds several honorary law degrees from overseas institutions. An expert on international criminal law and human rights, he has written 60 books and 200 articles and has served the United Nations many times over as an expert committee member. Professor Bassiouni is president of DePaul's International Human Rights Law Institute, as well as president of several prestigious international organizations, including the International Institute of Higher Studies in Criminal Sciences and the *Association Internacionale de Droit Pénal*. Along with this last organization, he was nominated for a Nobel Peace Prize in 1999 for spearheading the drive to create the International Criminal Court, a body established to try offenders for war crimes, genocide, and other crimes against humanity.

M. Cherif Bassiouni, a professor of law at Chicago's DePaul University, 1975.

The Muslims who spoke out in defense of Salman Rushdie offer another little-known example of fair-mindedness. In 1989, the Ayatollah Khomeini, the religious and political leader of Iran, issued a *fatwa* (opinion) condemning the British writer Salman Rushdie to death. Khomeini's ruling came in response to Rushdie's novel, *The Satanic Verses* (1988), which Khomeini took to be an attack on Islam and the Quran. American media coverage of the event showed crowds of angry demonstrators calling for Rushdie's death. Reporters also noted that reward money was being offered for Rushie's assassination. A few countries where the demonstrations had been the largest and fiercest, notably India, Pakistan, Saudi Arabia, Egypt, and South Africa, banned the book. The very real threat made to Rushdie's life forced him to live in hiding for a number of years. Yet many Muslims disagreed with the fatwa, and some spoke out in defense of Rushdie. Some of those who defended him did so in spite of the fact that they personally found the book offensive to their religious beliefs. In fact, in 1994, a group of about 90 Muslim and Arab writers from all over the world published a collection of essays entitled, *For Rushdie: Essays by Arab and Muslim Writers in Defense of Free Speech*. Unfortunately, Rushdie's defenders received less attention than those calling for his death.

Zainab Salbi provides an example of someone whose compassion for the suffering of others has become her life's work.

Finally, non-Muslim Americans may know of few prominent Muslims whose concern for others extends beyond the borders of their own religious community. Zainab Salbi provides an example of someone whose compassion for the suffering of others has become her life's work. Salbi grew up in Iraq during the Iran-Iraq War and learned firsthand of the psychological devastation that war brings, especially to women. She immigrated to the United States when she was 19. While studying to obtain her bachelor's degree at George Mason University and working as a translator for the Arab League in Washington, D.C., Salbi listened to reports of the atrocities taking place in Bosnia during the Bosnian Civil War (1991-95). Horrified that the Serbian Army had made rape a weapon of war and had subjected thousands of displaced Bosnian women to rape, Salbi resolved to do something to help the women recover and rebuild their lives. In 1993, after obtaining a small grant from All Souls Unitarian Church in Washington, D.C., she founded a nonprofit organization called Women for Women. The organization matches women war refugees with American and Canadian sponsors, who send them a monthly check and letter of support. Small loans and business training are also provided. When Salbi and her fledgling organization heard next of the massacres, mutilations, and mass rapes taking place in the southern African country of Rwanda during the Hutu campaign against the Tutsis, Women for Women quickly expanded operations to include that country. Today the organization is active in Bosnia, Kosovo, Afghanistan, Pakistan, Rwanda, Nigeria, Iraq, and Colombia, and may soon expand to serve Congo. It has distributed about six million dollars and aided over 11,000 women in both Muslim and non-Muslim countries. In 1995 Salbi was honored at the White House for her work, and her organization has been

been profiled in many media sources, including the *Oprah Winfrey Show* and many television news programs.

Strict Observance and Moderate Observance

When Muslims — especially foreign Muslims — make the news in the United States, it is often the ones who are strictest in their interpretation and observance of Islam. They are often portrayed as uninterested in, ignorant of, or highly critical of Western and American culture. News commentators often describe them as Islamic "fundamentalists." Many Muslims feel that the label "fundamentalist," which is a term borrowed from Christianity, does not fit Islam, and prefer the term "Islamist."

Islamic Fundamentalism

Yet "Islamic fundamentalism" is a term that many readers in the United States see nearly every day in the media. In general, fundamentalism is found in all of the major world religions, including Christianity, Judaism, Islam, Hinduism, and Buddhism. It refers to the response of believers who feel that modern culture challenges their religion's traditional beliefs. The term "Islamic fundamentalist" is used to describe some Muslim leaders and groups who are opposed to the secularization of their societies.

In general, fundamentalism is found in all of the major world religions, including Christianity, Judaism, Islam, Hinduism, and Buddhism. It refers to the response of believers who feel that modern culture challenges their religion's traditional beliefs.

As outlined in the section on "The History of Islam," various Arab nation states that emerged after World War I had a form of government imposed on them, with a structure chosen by Western powers. These states were "secular," i.e., they were structured so that there was a separation of government and religious leadership. This was an abrupt change from the previous system of leadership in many Muslim societies, for whom Islam was both a religious and legal system. During the 1960s, thinkers and leaders across the Muslim world began to advocate a return to Islamic ways of doing things, fueled in part by the recognition that their societies had not been making much progress on issues of economic development and social justice during the post-colonial era. Scholars call this movement "Islamism," because it seeks to apply Islamic solutions to social problems and advocates a return to an Islamic way of life.

Many different groups with different kinds of agendas operate under the banner of Islamism. In general they oppose secularization and seek to return to traditional Islamic beliefs and practices. Many believe that Western culture promotes a nonreligious approach to life, one that is specifically opposed to the teachings of Islam. Some of them devote their efforts to building schools, hospitals, and social welfare agencies, and in so doing they uphold the traditional Islamic emphasis on helping the less fortunate and building up the Muslim community. Others involve themselves in politics. Still others exhort less observant Muslims to return to regular practice of the devotional customs of Islam as well as what they believe to be its traditional codes of conduct. Many of these people are opposed to violence and operate within the mainstream of their societies.

> *According to Islamic scholar Hamza Yusef, "There is nothing Islamic about terrorism. To use violence against civilians to create terror is one of the greatest crimes in Islam."*

Some Islamists, or Muslim fundamentalists, are more extreme in their views, however. They may seek to impose their vision of Islam on others, and harass, threaten, or punish those who disagree with them. The most violent of these people have become terrorists. It is important to note that terrorists constitute only a small minority of those Muslims who consider themselves "fundamentalists," or "Islamists."

Many fundamentalist Islamic groups fervently contest the existence of the state of Israel, which was formed after World War II out of an area that had long been home to the Palestinian people. This created a volatile, and still unresolved, political situation in the modern Middle East. The Israeli-Palestinian conflict has often been seen, and reported, in terms of the religions of the participants: Islamic Arabs versus Israeli Jews, who have been supported by Western allies, including the United States.

This ongoing conflict has affected not only the Israelis and the Palestinians, but also the Arab nations of the Mideast and ultimately the rest of the world. Indeed, militant Muslims, including Osama bin Laden, cite the U.S. support of Israel as a major impetus for their terrorist acts. Likewise, some extremist Muslim leaders have seen it as their religious purpose to foment armed attacks and acts of terror against perceived enemies of the faithful. This interpretation of Islam is counter to the precepts of the faith. The taking of innocent life is strictly forbidden in Islam, even in war. According to Islamic scholar Hamza Yusef, "There is nothing Islamic about terrorism. To use violence against civilians to create terror is one of the greatest crimes in Islam." Instead, Islam is concerned with finding peace and reconciliation with a just and compassionate God.

Diversity of Interpretation and Practice

In reality Islam is a diverse religion that encompasses a wide range of believers, some of whom are narrow in their interpretation and strict in their observance, and others of whom are more flexible. It is very difficult to generalize about American Muslims in particular, as experts estimate that two-thirds of them have not affiliated themselves with any mosque or Islamic organization. Some of these people describe themselves as "cultural," "secular," or "moderate" Muslims." This means that they consider themselves Muslims, but do not observe all the basic religious practices, such as five-times-a-day prayer, weekly prayer at the mosque for men, and daily fasting during Ramadan.

The famous African-American basketball player Kareem Abdul Jabar, who converted to Sunni Islam as an adult, provides an example of someone who upholds the core beliefs of Islam while remaining flexible on other matters. He holds these core beliefs to be the understanding that there is one God; that Muhammad was his prophet; and that God's final message to humanity is contained in the Quran. While working as a professional athlete he did not adhere to the scheduled five-times-a-day prayer (*salat*), because it interfered with his practice and performance commitments. Moreover, in spite of the religion's teaching that Muslim parents must raise their children Muslim, Abdul Jabar let his children choose their own path. Although he does conform to Islam's prohibition against alcohol, he appeared in a beer commercial in 1998. He later apologized to his fellow Muslims about the appearance, when he realized how deeply it upset them. Abdul Jabar's legendary sporting accomplishments and long-unbroken records led to his election to the Basketball Hall of Fame in 1995.

The famous African-American basketball player Kareem Abdul Jabar, who converted to Sunni Islam as an adult, provides an example of someone who upholds the core beliefs of Islam while remaining flexible on other matters.

Seyyed Hossein Nasr provides an example of another kind of Muslim piety, one that demonstrates that a person may be a devout and observant Muslim and yet disagree with the narrow interpretation of Islam that has been dubbed fundamentalist. Born in Iran, Nasr was educated in both Iran and the United States, and currently holds the University Professorship in Islamic Studies at George Washington University. His busy academic career has led to the publication of about 25 books and 500 articles, which have been translated into a variety of languages. In addition to his Islamic studies, Professor Nasr has read deeply in Western philosophy, science, and comparative religion. A devout and learned Shia Muslim, Nasr describes himself as a religious traditionalist. He is critical of what has been called "Islamic fundamentalism" and at the same time he is critical of the materialism, secularism, and rationalism that he sees at the core of contemporary American and Western European culture. In addition to daily prayer and meditation, Nasr has sought spiritual instruction from Sufi masters. Although an active and well-respected scholar, Nasr still finds time to give spiritual guidance to those who seek him out. He encourages people of all faiths to nourish themselves on the deepest spiritual wisdom of their religion.

Male and Female Roles and Status

One of the most persistent Western images of Islam is that of the passive, secluded, and veiled Muslim woman, who is a second-class citizen in her own society as well as in her own home. On the one hand it is true that in many Muslim societies women have fewer freedoms and opportunities, less power, and lower status than men. On the other hand, some Muslims argue that these limitations come from sexist beliefs within the culture and cannot be attributed solely to Islam. Others believe that though the religion is not itself sexist, it has been interpreted in ways that repress women. Still others frankly acknowledge that in

A Muslim couple from Cairo, Egypt.

certain circumstances, Islam gives men precedence over women. Some disagree with these teachings, while others argue that they serve to protect women. This diversity of opinion makes it difficult to generalize about Islam's impact on women. Nevertheless, it is clear that the stereotype of the Muslim woman sketched above does not do justice to the variety of opinions, experiences, and activities embraced by Muslim women around the world.

Scholars note that when Islam was first introduced it served to raise the status of women in Arab society. For example, it outlawed female infanticide (the killing of female babies), a custom that the Arabs practiced frequently in Muhammad's time. Furthermore, the Quran grants women the right to inherit property, a right that Arab women did not enjoy before Islam and European women did not gain until hundreds of years later. Though it gives women the right to only half of what a man would inherit, Muslims point out that this reflects the understanding that men need more money because their culture assigns them the responsibility of supporting their families. In a society where women were often treated like possessions, the Quran gave women a say in their own marriage contracts and required men to treat their wives with kindness (Quran 4:5, Ali trans.). Finally, the Quran insists on the spiritual equality of men and women:

> But he who performs good deeds,
> Whether man or a woman,
> And is a believer,
> Will surely enter Paradise,
> And none shall be deprived
> Even of an iota of his reward (Quran 4:124).

An often-quoted hadith of the prophet Muhammad underlines this idea:

> All human beings (male and female) are equal, equal as the teeth of a
> comb. There is no superiority of a white over a black, nor of any male

over the female. Only the God-consciousness (regardless of gender) merits favor and the ultimate rewards from God (Zepp: 125).

While the Quran did much to improve the status of women in 7th-century Arabia, some passages do seem to imply that men are superior to women. Some Muslims argue, however, that these verses do not necessarily make Islam more sexist than Judaism or Christianity, since passages that suggest that wives should respect and obey their husbands can be found in the Jewish scriptures (e.g. Genesis 3:16) and the Christian New Testament (e.g. Ephesians 5:22-24, Colossians 3:18). Christian scripture also suggests that women should let men take the lead in church affairs (1 Corinthians 14:34).

Several passages from the Quran seem to grant men superiority to or authority over women. Chapter 2, verse 282, implies that a woman's legal testimony is worth half that of a man. Some modern interpreters argue that the verse was not motivated by sexism, but rather by the recognition that in 7th-century Arabia, few women were familiar with legal, business, and other worldly activities. The verse therefore reflects not the belief in female inferiority but rather the conclusion that their lack of worldliness would make their testimony less reliable. This line of reasoning would seem to suggest that because women's role in modern society has changed, the passage needs to be reinterpreted. Another passage, one that concerns the proper way to handle a divorce, assigns men more rights than women:

> Women also have recognized rights as men have
> Though men have an edge over them (Quran 2:228, Ali trans.).

Yet another (4:34) notes that husbands have authority over their wives because it is the male's job to support his family financially, but it advises that husbands use only their power of persuasion to enforce their decisions. Some interpreters translate this last passage from the original Arabic a bit more harshly, concluding that it gives Muslim husbands the right to discipline wives who disobey them by remonstrating them, refraining from sexual activity with them, and also, as a last resort, by striking them (as a means of stopping them from persisting in objectionable behavior). Again, contemporary commentators suggest that changing family arrangements, in which both men and women contribute to family finances, shed new light on the possible meanings of this last passage.

A number of experts on the Quran conclude, however, that its main thrust is not to establish marriage as a partnership of two people with *equal* rights and responsibilities, but rather to establish marriage as a partnership of *complementary* rights and responsibilities. Many who support this view would argue that a married woman's primary responsibility is to see to the day-to-day running of the household and raise the children, and a married man's primary responsibility is to support his family financially. Finally, according to both Muhammad's sayings and the Quran, a person's value does not come from their sex, race, occupation, or role within a marriage, but rather from living a good and devout life.

Polygyny, the practice whereby a man may have more than one wife, is permitted in the Quran. This is not the same as polygamy, the practice whereby a man or woman may have more than one spouse. These practices are illegal in the United States, so Muslim men living here may marry only one woman. By contrast, under Muslim law men may marry up to four wives. A Muslim woman may have only one husband, however. Misunderstandings concerning the place of polygyny in Islam have led to the stereotype of the over-sexed Muslim man. First, it must be pointed out that polygyny is rare in practice. Islam insists that a man must provide equally for his wives. Since very few men can afford to do this, most have only one wife. Some have interpreted Islam's dictate that a man may have up to four wives as a form of religious approval given to male lust. Muslims disagree. They point out that in Muhammad's day women needed both the financial support and physical protection provided by their husbands. Many men had been killed in raids and battles, leaving their wives vulnerable widows. The practice of polygyny permitted the men of the Muslim community to draw these women back into a protective family circle.

> *Although cultural traditions have kept many women from participating in public life, Islam in no way requires women to stay at home and in fact insists on the education of girls.*

Gender Segregation and Women's Involvement in Public Life

Does Islam demand that women stay at home and take no part in paid employment, civic affairs, and politics? Some conservative Muslims would say that women should leave these activities to men. Others say that although cultural traditions have kept many women from participating in public life, Islam in no way requires women to stay at home and in fact insists on the education of girls.

In certain Muslim countries, what may look to outsiders like traditional Islamic sex roles are actually of recent origin. In these cases the rise of an extremely conservative version of Islam has contributed to curtailing women's freedoms and lowering their status. The extreme limitations placed on women by Afghanistan's former Taliban government provide a case in point. These limitations included the prohibition on female education and employment, and the near

nonexistence of health care for women and girls. Laws forbidding women to leave their homes without the escort of a male family member and requiring them to cover themselves from head to toe in public in a tent-like garment called a *burqa* also severely curtailed their activities. Yet several decades earlier, none of these conditions existed in Afghanistan. They were imposed by the Taliban government, whose members were influenced by an extreme form of Wahhabi Islam. Wahhabi Islam itself only dates back to the 18th century.

Most Muslim societies practice some forms of gender segregation that are unknown to Americans and Western Europeans. Unrelated people of the opposite sex may not mingle socially, and separate areas are established for men and women in mosques, schools, and other public areas. The distinctive clothing worn by some Muslim women when in public—flowing robes, headscarves, and perhaps face veils—is another way of creating a barrier between unrelated men and women. This clothing also reflects the high value that Islam places on female modesty. While the Quran requires modest female dress, it doesn't specify the exact nature of that clothing, other than asking women to "draw their veil over their bosom" and to refrain from showing off "their ornaments" (Quran 24:30-31, 33:59). A number of commentators have interpreted this last line as a request that women keep their hair covered. Even in countries where the above forms of gender segregation are quite common, some Muslims will be more concerned with maintaining strict gender segrega-

While praying in the mosque, women are separated from the men by curtained-off sections. In the top image you can see the shadows of the women behind the curtain.

The education of women for employment is a priority in Cairo, Egypt. A girls' technical school in the city provides classes in metal work.

tion than others. Sometimes the degree of gender segregation practiced will depend on the context of a particular situation, for example, how well the people concerned know each other. In general, gender segregation tends to be less practiced in cities and more predominant in rural areas.

In a few predominantly Muslim countries, such as Iran and Saudi Arabia, women have in recent years been required by law to keep their heads and bodies covered in public. In other countries social pressure keeps local norms of modest female dress in place. In still others, some women cover themselves with robes and scarves while others choose to wear Western dress.

Is traditional Muslim clothing for women sexist? Some Muslim women believe that it lessens their freedom and symbolizes their restricted access to public life and public space. Furthermore, certain Muslim thinkers argue that veiling is not required by the Quran and was not practiced in early Muslim times. They conclude that it represents a historical and cultural innovation that has been wrongfully raised to the rank of a religious teaching.

Other Muslims think that traditional Muslim dress actually frees women from being treated like sexual objects when they appear in public. Many people presume that the clothing represents the low status of Muslim women, but some Muslim women argue that it symbolizes the high regard that Islam has for women. They point out that in Christian countries nuns often dress in a similar way and note that the nuns' religious garb usually elicits a respectful response from others. Moreover, they argue that Western dress is itself sexist, in that it steers women towards focusing excessively on their appearance and encourages men to compare and judge women according to their physical attractiveness. In recent years some predominantly Muslim countries have witnessed an increase in the number of women who voluntarily cover their heads while in public. Experts interpret this increase as a reflection of the recent revival of interest in Islam and the importance of the headscarf as a symbol of Muslim identity.

Some people measure the strength of discrimination against women or minorities in any culture by the number of educational and employment opportunities open to them and the number of women and minorities who have been successful in those fields. In that case, Americans may want to note that although the United States has not yet elected a female president or vice president, several predominantly Muslim countries, namely Turkey, Pakistan, Indonesia, and Bangladesh, have had women presidents or prime ministers. Nevertheless, it must be pointed out that the experience of these female presidents and prime ministers does not reflect the life of the average woman in these countries.

Some Muslim women believe that traditional Muslim clothing lessens their freedom and symbolizes their restricted access to public life and public space. Others think that it symbolizes the high regard that Islam has for women.

What of Muslim women in the United States? In fact, the vast majority of Muslim women in America do not embody the stereotype that many people hold about them. Many participate in joint decision-making with their husbands concerning the affairs of the household, though some choose to give the final say to their husbands. Some wear traditional Muslim clothing while others do not. Some work outside the home and some do not. Those that do work outside the home have entered every sort of profession, and many have been quite successful.

Dr. Azizah Y. al-Hibri provides an example of an influential American Muslim woman who does not conform to the stereotypes commonly held about Muslim women. Dr. al-Hibri, a lawyer and former professor of philosophy, teaches corporate law and Islamic jurisprudence at the University of Richmond in Richmond, Virginia. Professor al-Hibri founded the academic journal *Hypatia: A Journal of*

Feminist Philosophy, and an organization called KARAMAH, or Muslim Women Lawyers for Human Rights. She also serves on the editorial board of *The Journal of Law and Religion* as well as the advisory boards of the Public Religion Project (University of Chicago), the Pluralism Project (Harvard University), and the television program *Religion and Ethics Newsweekly* (P.B.S.). Dr. al-Hibri takes an active part in civic life. She is a member of the Virginia State Advisory Committee to the United States Commission on Civil Rights, and the Religious Leaders Task Force for the Prevention of Family Violence for the state of Virginia. In addition, she sits on the board of directors of the Interfaith Alliance Foundation. Dr. al-Hibri has written numerous books and articles, some of which concern women and Islam. She herself believes that Islam is not sexist, but that it has been interpreted in sexist ways.

> *The roles and status of women are continuing to evolve in the Muslim world. Like people everywhere, Muslims are debating what should and should not be changed in their societies as they move into the 21st century.*

Even in countries that offer their citizens fewer freedoms and opportunities than does the United States, Muslim women have sought to lead full lives. And in Muslim countries where women face discrimination and poor treatment due to their sex, some women are working to change these conditions. In fact, under one of the most repressive regimes the modern world has known, that of Taliban-run Afghanistan, a woman-led organization spearheaded resistance to the regime. This organization, the Revolutionary Association of the Women of Afghanistan (RAWA), set up secret schools to educate girls and provided income for widows, many of whom the Taliban had reduced to begging on the streets. After the fall of the Taliban, two accomplished Afghani women became leaders in the new government. Dr. Suheila Siddiqi, an army surgeon, headed the new department of public health. Dr. Sima Samar, an activist who had organized clinics and schools for Afghani women and girls, became Minister of Women's Affairs.

Dr. Samar's commitment to women dates back to her childhood observations about the unfairness of life for girls and women in her country. She began to put her ideas into effect at the beginning of her medical career in rural Afghanistan in 1980. Frustrated by the limits placed on her ability to work by cultural and religious beliefs about women, Samar traveled to Pakistan in the mid-1980s and spent a few years working for an international organization called Inter Church Aid. In 1989 she set up her own nongovernmental organization dedicated to providing education and medical care for women and girls, both in Afghanistan and in refugee camps inside Pakistan. Samar not only worked full days as a doctor, but also administrated projects, raised funds from the international humanitarian community to fuel these endeavors, and labored to publicize the plight of women in Afghanistan to the world community. Routine death threats from members of the Taliban did not deter her from her work. In 2001 Dr. Samar received the John Humphrey Freedom Award from the International Centre for Human Rights and Democratic Development (headquartered in Canada). After the American military campaign toppled the Taliban regime in 2001, Samar was offered a top post in the new Afghani government. However, her tenure was brief. In June of 2002, the government pressured her to resign her post as Minister of Women's Affairs after she received death threats from Islamic extremists. She was reassigned to a less powerful position as a member of Afghanistan's Human Rights Commission.

The roles and status of women are continuing to evolve in the Muslim world. Like people everywhere, Muslims are debating what should and should not be changed in their societies and their interpretation of their religion as they move into the 21st century. The roles and status of women are important subjects in that debate.

Ethnicity and Media Images

Many Americans assume that most Muslims are Arabs. In fact less than 20 percent of the world's Muslims are Arab. The largest concentration of the world's Muslim population occurs not in the Middle East, but rather in the South and Southeast Asian nations of Indonesia, India, Pakistan, and Bangladesh. The country with the greatest number of Muslim citizens is Indonesia.

Hollywood movies and television often present a distorted view of Muslims. They often portray Muslims as terrorists and other violence-prone individuals, multi-millionaire oil barons, camel-riding desert nomads, or Middle Eastern belly dancers. In reality the percentage of Muslims worldwide who are multimillionaires is very tiny. Most Muslims around the world, just like most Americans, have to work for a living. Very few of them live nomadic lifestyles. Even in the Middle East, less than 2 percent of Arabs dwell in the deserts with their camels (these people are called Bedouins). Finally, belly dancing is a Middle Eastern, not Islamic, folk tradition. Some writers say that its correct name is "oriental dancing." It began as a shimmying kind of folk dancing that women did for one another, and both men and women performed at weddings. Concerns about modesty often prevented women from dancing outside of family gatherings. With the rise of Middle Eastern nightclubs in the 20th century, belly dancing became a performance art and professional dancers began to perform it in more alluring ways than the traditional folk dancers did. The revealing "bare tummy" sequined outfit that many people associate with belly dancing got its start with these professional dancers.

Chapter 8
The Geography of Islam

Experts believe that there are 1.2 billion Muslims worldwide. That means that about one in every five people on the face of the earth is a Muslim. Though Muslims can be found in every corner of the globe, the vast majority of them live in Asia, Africa, and the Middle East. The worldwide Muslim community is thus extremely diverse.

Islam in Asia

About 45 percent of the world's Muslims live in Asia. In fact, more Muslims live in Asia than in any other region of the world. Twenty-three percent of the world's Muslims live in the South Asian nations of Pakistan, India, and Bangladesh. Fourteen percent come from Indonesia, Malaysia, and Singapore, in Southeast Asia. The Central Asian nations of Kazakhstan, Kyrgystan, Tajikistan, Turkmenistan, Afghanistan, and Uzbekistan account for over 5 percent of the world's Muslims. Though accurate statistics about religious affiliations in China are hard to come by, experts believe that that nation harbors 4 percent of the world's Muslims.

The Asian countries with the greatest percentage of Muslim citizens are Afghanistan (99 percent), Pakistan (97 percent), Bangladesh (88 percent), and Indonesia (87 percent). Of course, there are many more Muslims living in Indonesia than Afghanistan, because Indonesia has such a large population — about 220 million people compared to Afghanistan's 27 million. Indeed, more

Opposite page:
In the 14th century Islam came to Kashmir, India. Worshipers pray at Hazratbal, a shrine on the Dal Lake in Srinagar.

Foreign words used in the text are defined in the Glossary, pages 423-40.

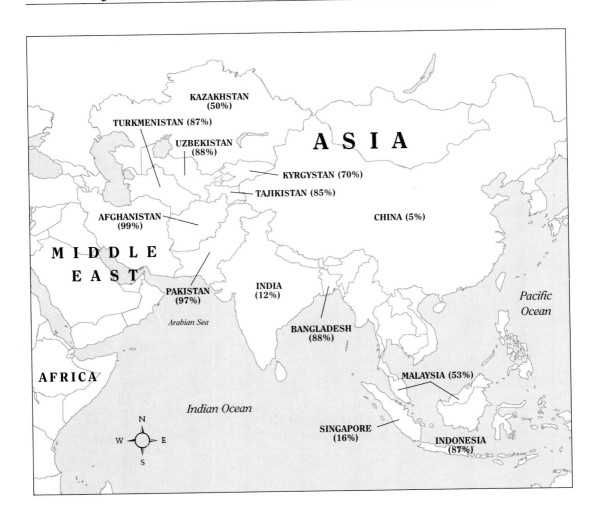

ASIA

KAZAKHSTAN (50%)

TURKMENISTAN (87%)

UZBEKISTAN (88%)

KYRGYSTAN (70%)

TAJIKISTAN (85%)

AFGHANISTAN (99%)

CHINA (5%)

MIDDLE EAST

PAKISTAN (97%)

INDIA (12%)

Arabian Sea

BANGLADESH (88%)

AFRICA

MALAYSIA (53%)

Indian Ocean

Pacific Ocean

N
W ⊕ E
S

SINGAPORE (16%)

INDONESIA (87%)

Countries in Asia with significant Muslim populations.

Muslims live in Indonesia than in any other country in the world. The rest of the central Asian nations report that 50 percent or more of their citizens are Muslims: Kazakhstan (50 percent), Kyrgyztan (70 percent) Tajikistan (85 percent), Turkmenistan (87 percent), and Uzbekistan (88 percent).

Muslims comprise only 12 percent of India's population. Yet, because 1.1 billion people live in India, that 12 percent translates to over 120 million people. Similarly, though less than 5 percent of Chinese are Muslims, the total number of Chinese Muslims has been estimated to be close to 50 million, making the total number of Chinese Muslims about equal to the total number of Muslims living in Central Asia.

Islam in the Arab Countries and the Middle East

About 15 percent of the world's Muslim population lives in the Arab countries. These countries span the northern rim of Africa, from Morocco to Egypt, and continue on into the Middle East. The Arab countries are so named because Arabic is the national language and because they all share elements of Arab culture and tradition.

The Arab nations of the Middle East include Saudi Arabia (100 percent Muslim), Bahrain (100 percent), Yemen (97 percent), United Arab Emirates (96 percent), Iraq (96 percent), Qatar (95 percent), Jordan (92 percent), Syria (90 percent), Kuwait (85 percent), Oman (80 percent or more), and Lebanon (70 percent).

Not all Middle Eastern countries are Arab. Iran, Israel, and Turkey are the exceptions. Iran's national language is Farsi and its culture is Persian, not Arab. Though not an Arab nation, it is, however, predominantly Muslim, with 95 percent of its population practicing Shia Islam and 4 percent adhering to Sunni Islam. Iran's 50 million Muslims account for a little over 4 percent of Muslims worldwide. Israel is today neither predominantly Muslim nor Arab. Nevertheless, its native Palestinian population, many of whom have escaped as refugees to the surrounding countries, is Arab and mostly Muslim, though Christians compose a significant minority. Turkey is another nation that is often considered part of the Middle East, but its population is not Arab. Its people trace their ethnic roots, and the Turkish language, back to Central Asia. Some 99 percent of Turkish citizens are Muslim. The 50 million Muslims who live in Turkey account for a little over 4 percent of Muslims worldwide.

Countries in the Middle East with significant Muslim populations.

Many Arab nations are located in Africa, north of the Sahara desert. These Arabic-speaking countries include Algeria (99 percent Muslim), Morocco (98 percent), Tunisia (98 percent), Libya (97 percent), Egypt (94 percent), and Sudan (70 percent). The sub-Saharan African countries, though not Arab, also serve as home to a considerable segment of the world's Muslim population.

113

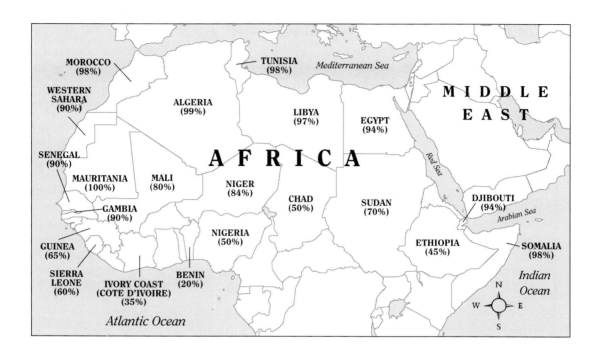

Islam in Sub-Saharan Africa

Nearly 17 percent of the world's Muslims live in sub-Saharan Africa. Among the sub-Saharan nations and territories with large Muslim populations are Mauritania (100 percent Muslim), Somalia (98 percent), Djibouti (94 percent), Western Sahara (90 percent or more), Gambia (90 percent), Senegal (90 percent), Niger (84 percent), Mali (80 percent), Guinea (65 percent), and Sierra Leone (60 percent). About 50 percent of the citizens of Nigeria and Chad adhere to Islam. Muslims make up about 45 percent of all Ethiopians, 35 percent of the population of Ivory Coast (Cote D'Ivoire), and 20 percent of the population of Benin. Other African countries also host small Muslim populations.

Islam in Europe

European Muslims account for just under 2 percent of Muslims worldwide. Albania is the only predominantly Muslim country in Europe, with 70 percent of its population adhering to Islam. A few other Balkan nations, namely Bosnia-Herzegovina (over 40 percent Muslim), Montenegro (over 15 percent Muslim), and Bulgaria (13 percent Muslim) have significant Muslim minorities. These established Muslim communities date back to the time when the region was ruled by the Ottoman Empire. Finally, migration from the traditionally Muslim countries has planted new Muslim minorities in a number of western European countries. France counts a Muslim population of close to 10 percent, or approximately five million people, many of whom trace their roots back to North African countries formerly colonized by the French. Germany calculates a Muslim population of just under 4 percent, or three million. A very large percentage of these Muslims hail from Turkey. Great Britain harbors a Muslim population of between one and two million, or 3 percent of the total population, many of whom trace their ancestry back to India and Pakistan, regions once colonized by the British.

Countries in Europe with significant Muslim populations.

Islam in North and South America

Many experts estimate that approximately six million Muslims live in North America. Population statistics from the early 1990s suggested that only about 600,000 of them lived in Canada. The rest resided in the United States. This large number of people adds up to less than 1 percent of the world's Muslim population, however. South America is home to three million Muslims.

Most North American Muslims are immigrants or the descendants of immigrants. Nevertheless, about one-third of the North American Muslim community is made up of converts. Of these converts, the vast majority are African American. Indeed, among North American Muslims, African Americans constitute the largest single ethnic group, making up 42 percent of the total. Islam continues to attract new African-American converts, many of whom see it as a return to the religious path of their ancestors. Some experts estimate that 42 percent of North American Muslims are African American.

After African Americans, the next largest group of North American Muslims are people of South Asian descent, who constitute 24 percent of the total. Arab immigrants and their descendants comprise about 12 percent of North American Muslims. People who trace their ancestry to Iran (Persia) represent

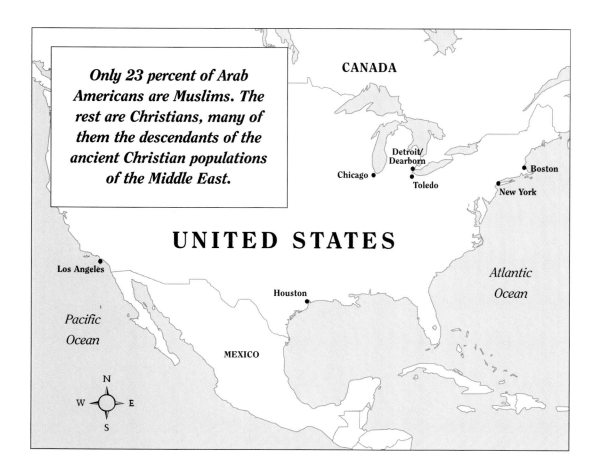

Only 23 percent of Arab Americans are Muslims. The rest are Christians, many of them the descendants of the ancient Christian populations of the Middle East.

CANADA

Detroit/Dearborn

Chicago

Toledo

Boston

New York

UNITED STATES

Los Angeles

Houston

Atlantic Ocean

Pacific Ocean

MEXICO

N W E S

Communities in the United States with significant Muslim populations.

almost 4 percent of the total. The rest is made up primarily of Southeast Asians, Turks, Europeans, and their descendants.

Somewhere between four and six million Muslims live in the United States. Many observers believe that in the first half of the 21st century, the growing American Muslim population will surpass the nation's Jewish population. This would make Islam the second largest religion in the United States after Christianity.

The United States not only has a resident Muslim population, but also is home to an offshoot of Islam called the "Nation of Islam" or the "Black Muslims." As the latter name suggests, this group is composed entirely of African Americans. An African American named Elijah Muhammad (1897-1975) founded the Nation of Islam in the 1930s, basing his creed loosely around Islamic teachings. The organization also dedicated itself to helping black Americans cope with racial prejudice by creating separate, strong, and self-sufficient African-American families and communities. In addition, the Nation of Islam preached the superiority of blacks over whites, taught that Elijah Muhammad was a prophet of God, and even claimed that the movement's founder, Wallace D. Fard Muhammad, was God. These teachings are contrary to those accepted by all branches of Islam and to the Quran itself, so Muslims do not recognize members of the Nation of Islam as true Muslims. By the late 20th century Elijah Muhammad's sons succeeded in steering most of the Nation of Islam back into the mainstream of Islamic belief and practice, and changed the group's name to the American Muslim Mission. Remnants of the Nation of Islam still remain, however. The Nation of Islam minister Louis Farrakhan and his followers represent a hold-out against these recent reforms.

Although Muslims can be found throughout the United States, certain urban areas have especially large Muslim communities. These cities include Boston, Chicago, New York, Detroit, Dearborn, Toledo, Houston, and Los Angeles.

Elijah Muhammad (seated) and his son, Warith.

Chapter 9
Holy Places of Islam

Mecca

The three most sacred cities in Islam figure significantly in the life of the prophet Muhammad. The holiest of these sites is the city of Mecca (also spelled Makkah) in Saudi Arabia. Muslims have bestowed upon it many honorary titles, including "The Ancient Place," "The Forbidden City," "The Sure Country," "The Sacred House," and "The Holiest of Cities."

At the center of the city lies the Kaba, a shrine built over the site where, according to Islamic tradition, the biblical Adam erected the first temple to God. Abraham rebuilt the temple after it was ruined in the great flood. Islam teaches that by Muhammad's time the temple had been destroyed and rebuilt several times. For Muhammad the Kaba represented the original, monotheistic religion he strove to teach the Arab people. Thus he made pilgrimage to the city one of the Five Pillars of Islam. Moreover, he taught that Muslims everywhere should face Mecca when they pray. People who live in Mecca face the Kaba when they pray. Inside the Kaba, which represents the very heart of the human relationship with God, it doesn't matter which direction one faces to pray.

The Kaba is a single-room structure, made out of stone, and shaped approximately like a cube. It's about 50 feet high, 40 feet wide, and 33 feet deep. It is covered with a black silk ceremonial cloth (called a *kiswa*) onto which verses from the Quran have been embroidered in gold thread. A new kiswa is placed

Opposite page: Entrance to the Grand Mosque in Mecca.

Foreign words used in the text are defined in the Glossary, pages 423-40.

119

The Kaba is covered by the kiswa, a black cloth with Quranic verses in gold. The photo below was taken at the Kaba Cloth Factory where kiswa are made.

on the building every year. Some 200 specially trained workers labor throughout the year making the kiswa that will protect the sacred structure in the year to come. Some time after Muhammad's death a large mosque was constructed around the Kaba, called the Great Mosque, or the Grand Mosque, of Mecca. The mosque has been enlarged many times over the centuries. Recent renovations permit the enormous mosque and its courtyard to accommodate one million people at a time. This capacity is put to the test during the annual Hajj pilgrimage, which in recent years has brought two million pilgrims to the mosque over the course of several days.

Mecca is also revered as the birthplace of Muhammad and the site of the first ten years of his ministry. In Muhammad's day the Arabs used the Kaba as a shrine for their many tribal gods. Muhammad left Mecca after trying without success to convert its population to Islam. When he returned to the city in triumph as a successful military and religious leader, one of his first acts was to destroy the stone idols of the pagan gods. Then he returned the Kaba to its original purpose, that is, a temple dedicated to the worship of the one God. Mecca is considered so holy to Muslims that non-Muslims are not allowed into the city.

This sitara, which hangs now in the United Nations delegates' lounge, was originally part of the kiswa that covered the Kaba—the sacred stone cube in Mecca that is considered to be the physical center of Islam.

Above and right: Interior and exterior of the Prophet's Mosque in Medina. Opposite page shows the prayer niche, which indicates the direction of Mecca.

Medina

The city of Medina (also spelled "Madinah"), also located in Saudi Arabia, is the second holiest city in Islam. Medina, too, played an important role in the life of the Prophet Muhammad. The city's full name, Medinat al-Nabi, means "the city of the prophet." It was here that Muhammad created the first community run according to Muslim teachings and built the mosque in which he and his followers prayed. Today the Mosque of the Prophet sprawls over the original site. The latest expansion project, completed in 1992, brought the total number of square feet covered by the mosque to 1.78 million. It can hold more than half a million people. Many pilgrims make the trip to Medina before or after completing the Hajj. The tombs of the prophet Muhammad, his daughter Fatima, and the second caliph, Umar, are located within the mosque. Only Muslims may enter the sacred city of Medina.

The tile-sheathed shrine of the Dome of the Rock in Jerusalem is built over the rock from which Muhammad is believed to have ascended on his nocturnal journey to heaven. It is the earliest great Muslim building in existence.

Jerusalem

Muslims also consider Jerusalem, in modern-day Israel, to be a sacred city. In Arabic it's called *al-Quds*, "the holy." Jerusalem's importance to Muslims stems from multiple sources: the fact that many biblical prophets lived there, its role as the city towards which Muslims first oriented their prayers, and as the earthly destination of Muhammad's Night Journey and the site of his Ascension. Muslims believe that one night, the angel Gabriel brought Muhammad from Mecca to the Temple Mount in Jerusalem. Centuries ago, the Mount had been the site of the Jewish Temple, the holiest place in the world for Jews. From this site Muhammad and the angel ascended into heaven. During his ascent Muhammad was brought past Jesus, Moses, and the other prophets until he met with God face to face. In this meeting Muhammad received God's instruction that Muslims pray five times a day.

In Muhammad's time, the ruins of the Jewish Temple stood upon the Temple Mount. Muslim rulers later built a holy shrine, called the Dome of the Rock, on the site where Muhammad was said to have risen into heaven. The building

Above: Entrance of al-Aqsa Mosque in Jerusalem.

Left: Detail of the interior dome inside the al-Aqsa Mosque in Jerusalem. It was built in 715 in memory of the Prophet Muhammad's Night Journey from Mecca to Jerusalem.

derives its name from the golden dome that crowns it, and also from a large stone (42 by 56 feet) that stands at the heart of the monument. According to Islamic teachings, Muhammad was standing on this stone when he began his ascent into heaven. On the other end of the Temple Mount stands the silver-roofed al-Aqsa Mosque, which was constructed at the end of the 7th century.

Other Holy Sites

All Muslims acknowledge Mecca, Medina, and Jerusalem to be holy cities. But there are many other holy sites that have importance for certain groups of Muslims. For example, Shia Muslims regard the Iraqi cities of Najaf—burial site of the fourth caliph, Ali—and Karbala—the site where Muhammad's grandson Husayn was martyred—to be holy places. In Afghanistan Muslims revere the Afghani town of Mazar-i-Sharif as the site of Ali's burial. Many Shias also hold in great esteem the Iranian cities of Mashad—burial site of the eighth Shia imam, Ali ibn Musa ar-Rida—and Qom—the town where the eighth imam's sister, Fatima the sinless, is buried. What's more, devotees of certain Muslim saints consider the burial places and shrines of these holy men and women to be important places of pilgrimage. These are scattered throughout the Muslim world and include monuments to local as well as internationally known saints. Among the more famous pilgrimage destinations are the tomb of Ahmad Bamba in Touba, Senegal; the "Head of Husayn" mosque in Cairo, Egypt; the burial site of Sayyid Ahmad Badawi in Tanta, Egypt; the shrine of Zaynab (granddaughter of the Prophet) in Damascus, Syria; the tomb of Data Ganj Baksh in Lahore, Pakistan; and the tomb of Mu'in al-din Chisti in Ajmer, India.

Opposite page and above: Tomb of Ali, Najaf, Iraq, and detail of dome.

Below: Shrine of Fatima, sister of the eighth Shia imam, Qom, Iran.

Additional Resources
(Including Web Sites and Videos)

The Teachings of Islam

Al-Shiekh, Abdallah. "Zakat." In *The Oxford Encyclopedia of the Modern Islamic World*, edited by John L. Esposito. Vol. 4. Oxford, England: Oxford University Press, 1995.

Bowker, John. *What Muslims Believe*. Oxford, England: Oneworld, 1995.

Braswell, Jr., George W. *Islam: Its Prophet, Peoples, Politics, and Power*. Nashville, TN: Broadman and Holman, 1996.

Chittick, William C. "Sufism: Sufi Thought and Practice." In *The Oxford Encyclopedia of the Modern Islamic World*, edited by John L. Esposito. Vol. 4. Oxford, England: Oxford University Press, 1995.

Denny, Frederick Mathewson. *An Introduction to Islam*. 2nd ed. New York: Macmillan, 1994.

Esposito, John L. *Islam: The Straight Path*. 3rd ed. New York: Oxford University Press, 1998.

Esposito, John L. *What Everyone Needs to Know About Islam*. Oxford, England: Oxford University Press, 2002.

Glassé, Cyril. *The Concise Encyclopedia of Islam*. San Francisco, CA: HarperSanFrancisco, 1991.

Gordon, Matthew S. *Islam: Origins, Practices, Holy Texts, Sacred Persons, Sacred Places*. Oxford, England: Oxford University Press, 2002.

Kepel, Gilles. *Jihad: The Trail of Political Islam*. Cambridge, MA: Harvard University Press, 2002.

Opposite page and above: Dubai Mosque and Islamic School in Phuket, Thailand.

Nasr, Seyyed Hossein. *The Heart of Islam: Enduring Values for Humanity*. San Francisco, CA: HarperSanFrancisco, 2002.

Nasr, Seyyed Hossein. *Islam: Religion, History, and Civilization*. San Francisco, CA: HarperSanFrancisco, 2003.

Newby, Gordon D. *A Concise Encyclopedia of Islam*. Oxford, England: Oneworld, 2002.

Peters, F. E. *Islam: A Guide for Jews and Christians*. Princeton, NJ: Princeton University Press, 2003.

Peters, Rudolph. "Jihad." In *The Oxford Encyclopedia of the Modern Islamic World*, edited by John L. Esposito. Vol. 2. Oxford, England: Oxford University Press, 1995.

Renard, John. *Seven Doors to Islam: Spirituality and the Religious Life of Muslims*. Berkeley: University of California Press, 1996.

Woodward, Mark R. "Popular Religion: An Overview." In *The Oxford Encyclopedia of the Modern Islamic World*, edited by John L. Esposito. Vol. 3. Oxford, England: Oxford University Press, 1995.

Zepp, Jr., Ira G. *A Muslim Primer: A Beginner's Guide to Islam*. 2nd ed. Fayetteville: University of Arkansas Press, 2000.

Resources for Children

Gordon, Matthew S. *Islam (World Religions)*. New York: Facts on File, 1991.

Knight, Khadijah. *Islam*. New York: Thompson Learning, 1996.

Web Sites

The Middle East Institute, located in Washington, D.C., offers the entire text of M. Cherif Bassiouini's *Introduction to Islam* on its web site at: **http://www.mideasti.org/indepth/islam/index.html**

Professor Alan Godlas, of the University of Georgia's Department of Religion, has compiled a comprehensive and well-regarded web site on all aspects of Islam: **http://www.uga.edu/islam/**

Scholars from three universities, members of the Carolina-Duke-Emory Institute for the Study of Islam, have put together Islamweb, an Islamic Studies Internet Guide: **http://www.unc.edu/depts/islamweb/index.html**

The Quran

Ali, Ahmed, trans. *Al-Qur'an: A Contemporary Translation*. Rev. definitive ed. Princeton, NJ: Princeton University Press, 1988.

Cleary, Thomas F., trans. *The Essential Koran: The Heart of Islam: An Introductory Selection of Readings from the Qur'an*. 2nd ed. San Francisco, CA: HarperSanFrancisco, 1993.

One of the holiest sites for Islam is Medina—the place from which the Prophet Muhammad fled—illustrated in this 1718 manuscript of Muhammad ibn Sulayman al-Jazuli's (Morocco, d. 1465) Dalail al-khayrat (Signs of Blessing).

Sells, Michael. *Approaching the Quran*. Ashland, OR: White Cloud Press, 1999. (Includes a CD)

The History of Islam

Al-Faruqi, Ismail R. *A Cultural Atlas of Islam*. New York: Macmillan, 1986.

Armstrong, Karen. *Muhammad: A Biography of the Prophet*. San Francisco, CA: HarperSanFrancisco, 1992.

Bogle, Emory C. *Islam: Origin and Belief*. Austin: University of Texas Press, 1998.

Denny, Frederick Mathewson. *An Introduction to Islam*. 2nd ed. New York: Macmillan, 1994.

Esposito, John L. *Islam: The Straight Path*. 3rd ed. New York: Oxford University Press, 1998.

Esposito, John L., ed. *The Oxford History of Islam*. Oxford, England: Oxford University Press, 1999.

Jordan, Michael. *Islam: An Illustrated History*. London: Carlton Books, 2002.

Lunde, Paul. *Islam: Faith, Culture, History*. London, England: D. K. Publishing, 2002.

Nanji, Azim A., ed. *The Muslim Almanac: A Reference Work on the History, Faith, Culture, and Peoples of Islam*. Detroit, MI: Gale, 1996.

Nasr, Seyyed Hossein. *Islam: Religion, History, and Civilization*. San Francisco, CA: HarperSanFrancisco, 2003.

Nettler, Ronald L. "Dhimmi." In *The Oxford Encyclopedia of the Modern Islamic World*, edited by John L. Esposito. Vol. 1. Oxford, England: Oxford University Press, 1995.

Newby, Gordon D. "Muslims, Jews, and Christians: Relations and Interactions." In *The Muslim Almanac: A Reference Work on the History, Faith, Culture, and Peoples of Islam*, edited by Azim A. Nanji. Detroit, MI: Gale, 1996.

Robinson, Francis. *Cambridge Illustrated History of the Islamic World*. Cambridge, England: Cambridge University Press, 1996.

Schimmel, Annemarie. "Calligraphy and Epigraphy." In *The Oxford Encyclopedia of the Modern Islamic World*, edited by John L. Esposito. Vol. 1. Oxford, England: Oxford University Press, 1995.

Sweitochowski, Maire Lukens. "Iconography." In *The Oxford Encyclopedia of the Modern Islamic World*, edited by John L. Esposito. Vol. 2. Oxford, England: Oxford University Press, 1995.

Swisher, Clarice, ed. *The Spread of Islam*. San Diego, CA: Greenhaven, 1999.

Another one of the holiest sites for Islam is the Kaba in Mecca — the sanctuary to which Muslims turn in prayer and to which they go on pilgrimage. It is illustrated in this 1718 manuscript of Muhammad ibn Sulayman al-Jazuli's (Morocco, d. 1465) Dalail al-khayrat (Signs of Blessing).

Resources for Children

Child, John. *The Rise of Islam*. New York: Peter Bedrick Books, 1995.

Husain, Shahrukh. *Mecca*. New York: Dillon Press, 1993.

MacDonald, Fiona, and Mark Bergin. *A Sixteenth-Century Mosque*. New York: Peter Bedrick Books, 1994.

Morris, Neil. *The Atlas of Islam: People, Daily Life, and Traditions*. Hauppauge, NY: Barron's Education, 2003.

Wilkinson, Philip. *Islam (The Eyewitness Guides)*. London, England: D. K. Publishing, 2002.

Web Sites

A detail from one of the Qurans housed in the Khalidi Library in Jerusalem.

Professor Barbara R. von Schlegell, a professor in the department of religious studies at the University of Pennsylvania, has posted a web site that gives maps of the Arab conquests and the expansion of the Muslim world. The maps come from W. C. Brice's *An Historical Atlas of Islam* (1981) and R. Roolvink et al *Historical Atlas of the Muslim Peoples* (1957):
http://ccat.sas.upenn.edu/~bvon/pages/maps.html

The Middle East Institute, located in Washington, D.C., offers the entire text of M. Cherif Bassiouini's *Introduction to Islam* on its web site at:
http://www.mideasti.org/indepth/islam/index.html

For an explanation of the different styles of Arabic calligraphy see "The Art of Arabic Calligraphy," by Mamoun Sakkal, professional architect, designer, and graphic artist: **http://www.sakkal.com/ArtArabicCalligraphy.html**

Videos

Islam: Empire of Faith. Baltimore, MD: Gardner Films. Distributed by PBS home video. 180 minutes.

Muslims Today

Afkhami, Mahnaz, ed. *Faith and Freedom: Women's Human Rights in the Muslim World*. New York: Syracuse University Press, 1995.

Ahmed, Akbar S. *Islam Today: A Short Introduction to the Muslim World*. London, England: I. B. Tauris, 1999.

Ahmed, Akbar S. *Living Islam: From Samarkand to Stornoway*. New York: Facts on File, 1994.

Altorki, Soraya. "Women and Islam: Role and Status of Women." In *The Oxford Encyclopedia of the Modern Islamic World*, edited by John L. Esposito. Vol. 4. Oxford, England: Oxford University Press, 1995.

Armstrong, Sally. *Veiled Threat: The Hidden Power of the Women of Afghanistan*. New York: Four Walls Eight Windows, 2002.

Benard, Cheryl. *Veiled Courage: Inside the Afghan Women's Resistance*. New York: Broadway Books, 2002.

Braswell, George W. *Islam: Its Prophet, Peoples, Politics, and Power*. Nashville, TN: Broadman and Holman, 1996.

Burke, Alison. "Women for Women." *The World and I* 18, no. 6 (June 2003): 122.

Council on Islamic Education. *Teaching About Islam and Muslims in the Public School Classroom*. 3rd ed. Fountain Valley, CA: Council on Islamic Education, 1995.

Easwaran, Eknath. *Nonviolent Soldier of Islam: Badshah Khan, A Man to Match His Mountains*. Tomales, CA: Nilgiri Press, 1999.

El Fadl, Khaled Abou, ed. *The Place of Tolerance in Islam*. Boston, MA: Beacon Press, 2002.

Esin, Emel. *Mecca the Blessed, Madinah the Radiant*. New York: Crown Publishers, 1963.

Esposito, John L. *What Everyone Needs to Know About Islam*. Oxford, England: Oxford University Press, 2002.

Fernea, Elizabeth W. "The Veiled Revolution." In *Everyday Life in the Muslim Middle East*, edited by Donna Lee Bowen and Evelyn A. Early. 2nd ed. Bloomington: Indiana University Press, 2002.

Findley, Paul. *Silent No More: Confronting America's False Image of Islam*. Beltsville, MD: Amana Publications, 2001.

Hasan, Asma Gull. *American Muslims: The New Generation*. New York: Continuum, 2000.

Lawrence, Bruce B. *Shattering the Myth: Islam Beyond Violence*. Princeton, NJ: Princeton University Press, 1998.

Lewis, Bernard. *The Crisis of Islam: Holy War and Unholy Terror*. New York: Modern Library, 2003.

Lunde, Paul. *Islam: Faith, Culture, History*. London, England: D. K. Publishing, 2002.

Mernissi, Fatima. *The Veil and the Male Elite*. Reading, MA: Addison-Wesley, 1991.

Miller, John, and Aaron Kenedi, eds. *Inside Islam: The Faith, the People, and the Conflicts of the World's Fastest Growing Religion*. New York: Marlow and Company, 2002.

Mozzafari, Mehdi. "Rushdie Affair." In *The Oxford Encyclopedia of the Modern Islamic World*, edited by John L. Esposito. Vol. 3. Oxford, England: Oxford University Press, 1995.

A young Muslim girl looks over Iqra' International's Short Surahs, which introduces her, in English, to important short chapters of the Quran. These include Fatiha, "The Opening," which some call the essence of the book.

Nanji, Azim A., ed. *The Muslim Almanac: A Reference Work on the History, Faith, Culture, and Peoples of Islam*. Detroit, MI: Gale, 1996.

Nasr, Seyyed Hossein. *Islam: Religion, History, and Civilization*. San Francisco, CA: HarperSanFrancisco, 2003.

Nimer, Mohamed. *The North American Muslim Resource Guide*. New York: Routledge, 2002.

Reese, Lyn. *Women in the Muslim World: Personalities and Perspectives from the Past*. Berkeley, CA: Women World History Curriculum, 1998.

Safi, Omid, ed. *Progressive Muslims: On Justice, Gender, and Pluralism*. Oxford, England: Oneworld, 2003.

Shaheen, Jack G. "Reel Bad Arabs: How Hollywood Villifies a People." Special issue, *Islam: Enduring Myths and Changing Realities*, edited by Aslam Syed. *The Annals of the American Academy of Political and Social Science* 588 (July 2003): 171-93.

Smith, Jane I. *Islam in America*. New York: Columbia University Press, 1999.

Wolfe, Michael. *Taking Back Islam: American Muslims Reclaim Their Faith*. New York: Rodale and Beliefnet, 2002.

Men praying in the Mohammed Younis' Mosque in Lanzhou, China.

Resources for Children

Majaj, Lisa Suhair. "Who Are the Arab Americans?" *Cobblestone* 23, no. 5 (May 2002): 3-7.

Morris, Neil. *Islam (World of Beliefs)*. Columbus, OH: Peter Bedrick Books, 2002.

Web Sites

The web site of the Arab American Institute offers a wealth of information on Arab Americans, and also some material on Islam in America: **http://www.aaiusa.org**

Professor Alan Godlas, a professor of religion at the University of Georgia, offers his insights on women, Islam, and feminism (includes many links to other important sites for those interested in the position of women in Islam): **http://www.arches.uga.edu/~godlas/Islamwomen.html**

The Muslim Women's League web site furnishes information on women's roles and rights in Islam: **http://www.mwlusa.org/**

For more on the history of women's dress in Islam see Lyn Reese's article, "Historical Perspectives on Islamic Dress," posted at: **http://www.womeninworldhistory.com/essay-01.html**

The *Detroit Free Press* maintains a page dedicated to debunking common Arab stereotypes: **http://www.freep.com/jobspage/arabs/arab10.html**

"Hollywood Widens Slur Targets to Arab and Muslim Americans Since September 11," an article by Jack Shaheen, professor of mass communications at Southern Illinois University, is available at the Pacific News Service site:
http://news.pacificnews.org/news/view_article.html?article_id=819

This PBS Global Connections site gives a page on common American stereotypes about Islam and the Middle East, and contrasts them to common stereotypes about Americans:
http://www.pbs.org/wgbh/globalconnections/mideast/questions/types/

"The Muslim Mainstream," a *U.S. News & World Report* article by Jonah Blank, describes mainstream American Muslims that defy the commonly held stereotypes about Islam: **http://www.islamicity.com/recognitions/usnews/20isla.htm**

"Islam: Stereotypes Still Prevail," an article by Rick Blasing, is available through the National Council for the Social Studies web site listed below. Also available in print form: *Social Education,* volume 60, number 2, 1996:
http://www.ncss.org/resources/moments/600208.shtml

The Saudi Embassy posts articles from the magazine *Saudi Arabia* on its web site. For more on Mecca and Medina see the articles entitled "Makkah the Blessed" (spring 1997, volume 14, number 1) and "Al-Madinah Al-Munawwarah, the City of the Prophet" (spring 1998, volume 15, number 2) at: **http://saudiembassy.net/**

The CIA's *World Factbook* provides up-to-date information on the geography, government, economies, and populations of foreign countries:
http://www.odci.gov/cia/publications/factbook/index.html

For a discussion of female dress codes in Islam, and an argument against compulsory veiling, see "Women in Islam: Veiling," an article by Dr. Ibrahim B. Syed, at:
http://www.islamfortoday.com/syed01.htm

For a 2003 study by the Pew Forum on Religion and Public Life documenting an increase in the percentage of Americans who believe that Islam encourages its followers to violence see: **http://pewforum.org/docs/index.php?DocID=26**

For more information on the organization Women for Women see its web site at:
http://www.womenforwomen.org

A Muslim from Abiquiu, New Mexico, performing dua.

Videos

Muhammad: Legacy of a Prophet. Alexandria, VA: Unity Productions Foundation, Kikim Media, 2002. Distributed by PBS home video. 116 minutes.

Muslims. New York: Mystic Fire Video, 2002. Distributed by PBS home video. 117 minutes.

Section Two

Religious Customs and Folklore

Section Two:
Religious Customs
and Folklore

Overview

This section of the book covers religious customs known to all Muslims as well as customs practiced by certain groups of Muslims. Muslims worldwide follow the same general procedure for performing their formal prayers, for example. By contrast, courting and mourning customs vary considerably by culture and by the degree of religious conservatism espoused by an individual's family and community. Some of the customs discussed in this section of the book are required or recommended by Muslim law. Examples of these kinds of customs include dietary rules and procedures for washing before prayer. Practices inspired by religious sentiment or folk belief also appear in section two. For example, the tradition of reading and reciting poems about the Prophet grew out of the depth of many Muslims' devotion to Muhammad and is not required by the Quran. Folk beliefs covered in this section of the book include beliefs about *jinn* (spirits) that are not substantiated in the Quran, legends concerning animals, and various superstitions.

The practices discussed in this section may be performed on holidays, but most are not associated with any particular holiday. Some of them, like prayer, occur year-round, on holidays as well as on ordinary days. Traditions concerning greetings and proper dress also fit into this category. Other customs are associated with the religious celebrations that take place around important events in the life cycle, such as birth and marriage. Still others form part of

*Opposite page:
Jamia Masjid,
Thatta, Pakistan.
It is not uncommon
for people perform-
ing solitary prayer
to position them-
selves directly in
front of a pillar.*

the devotional lives of many Muslims and may be practiced either occasionally or frequently. These include the use of prayer beads, chanting as a means of remembering God (*dhikr*), and charitable contributions beyond the required 2.5 percent yearly donation.

Like the world's other major religions, Islam encompasses a fair amount of diversity. Not every Muslim practices all the customs mentioned here. For instance, some Muslim women wear headscarves and some do not. Some Muslim men wear head coverings and others do not. Not all Muslims would feel comfortable participating in the singing sessions practiced by members of some Sufi orders and some Muslims openly disapprove of them.

The distinction between orthodox and popular (or folk) religion discussed in section one is important to remember here. Some customs described in this section, such as those associated with formal and informal prayer, are accepted by all or nearly all Muslim religious authorities. They may be considered orthodox religious practices. Other customs described in section two, such as the wearing of amulets and the use of henna to decorate a bride's hands, may be thought of as folk religious practices. Many Muslim clerics do not approve of the wearing of amulets, but the practice is nevertheless widespread. The use of henna decorations on women's hands has no connection with Islam, but is included because many Muslim women practice it.

Chapter 10
Formal Prayer

The Difference Between Formal and Informal Prayer

Islam teaches believers to offer formal prayers five times per day. Muslim religious teachings make a distinction between formal prayer (*salat*) and informal prayer (*dua*). Formal prayer, sometimes referred to as ritual or liturgical prayer, is a very structured activity. Tradition dictates most of the words spoken, the actions taken, and even the preparations made for prayer. This tightly scripted kind of prayer is less about expressing oneself to God than it is about putting oneself at God's service. Recalling one's service to God—all-powerful, merciful, and magnificent—refreshes worshipers' sense of closeness to the divine and brings peace. Non-Muslims may find this kind of prayer more similar to traditional Christian congregational worship than their own private prayer practices.

Informal prayers, or supplications, may be said at any time of day. These unstructured prayers provide an outlet for personal expression and special requests to God.

Call to Prayer

In Muslim societies, the call to prayer (*adhan* in Arabic) echoes through the streets five times a day. In the old days the *muezzin* (or *mu'adhdhin*), a man charged with the responsibility of announcing the arrival of prayer time,

Foreign words used in the text are defined in the Glossary, pages 423-40.

141

would climb to the top of the local mosque's minaret and chant one form of the words that appear below.

Sunni Muslims use the following call to prayer:

God is most great (repeated four times)
I witness that there is no God other than Allah
I witness that Muhammad is the messenger of God
Come to prayer (repeated twice)
Come to acts of goodness (repeated twice)
Prayer is better than sleep (only before dawn prayers)
God is most great (repeated twice)
There is no God other than Allah.

The Shia call to prayer varies a little bit from that used by Sunni Muslims:

God is most great (repeated four times)
I witness that there is no God other than Allah
I witness that Muhammad is the messenger of God
Come to prayer (repeated twice)
Come to acts of goodness (repeated twice)
Come to the best of deeds (repeated twice)
God is most great (repeated twice)
There is no God other than Allah (repeated twice)
Ali is the saint of God.
(Note: certain Shias only recite this last line.)

From the minarets of Istanbul, Turkey (above), to Cairo, Egypt (opposite page), the local muezzin's voice intones the call to prayer.

Washing

Muslims prepare for their five daily sessions of formal prayer by washing themselves. This required cleansing is known as *wudu*. Performed correctly the practice furnishes a spiritual as well as a physical washing. Moreover, the ritual reminds Muslims of the holiness, power, and awe-inspiring nature of the God that they are about to approach in prayer. The general procedure for performing wudu is outlined in the Quran:

O believers, when you stand up for the service of prayer
wash your faces and hands up to the elbows,
and also wipe your heads,
and wash your feet up to the ankles (Quran 5:6, Ali trans.).

Though there are some minor variations in the manner in which various groups of Muslims perform wudu, what follows provides an outline of generally accepted practice. First, Muslims release all worldly and impure thoughts from their mind as they focus their concentration only on God. (This focusing

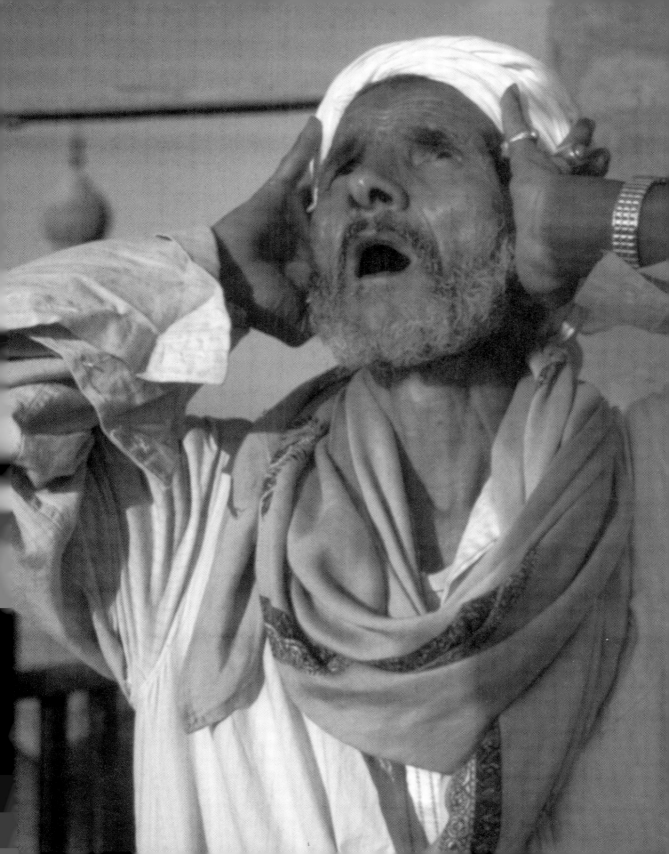

Tile and marble enrich the ablution fountains in the Faysal Mosque in Islamabad, Pakistan.

of one's intent, called *niyyah*, is important in all Muslim religious rites.) Then they must wash their hands, mouth, nostrils, face, arms up to the elbow, head, ears, and feet. Mosques usually have fountains, sinks, or basins set up for this very purpose. At home Muslims wash in their bathrooms. If one finds oneself somewhere where no water is available at prayer time, then clean sand or stones may be used. Some believers recite a blessing known as the *basmallah* before beginning to wash and say short personal prayers while they wash, for example, asking God to keep their feet on the path of Islam while rinsing their feet.

Some Muslims bathe the entire body before attending the mosque for Friday services. It helps the devout prepare physically, mentally, and spiritually for this prayerful gathering. This more complete washing, called *ghusl*, is required after sexual relations, ejaculation, menstruation, and giving birth. Prayers offered without first making the required ablution, wudu or ghusl, are considered invalid.

Muhammad's companions reported that the Prophet cleaned his teeth often with a special twig called *siwak*. He advised his followers to do the same, especially before prayer. According to a hadith, Muhammad once said, "the prayer before which the toothstick is used is seventy times more excellent than that before which it is not used" (Denny: 117).

Clothing for Formal Prayer (Salat)

Muslims clothe themselves in certain ways before their five daily prayers. Clothing worn for prayer should be clean and without stains. Women generally cover their hair and heads and wear loose-fitting clothing. Their faces and hands, however, should be visible. Men must be covered in loose-fitting clothing from at least the navel to the knees when in public. For prayer times, however, men should also cover their upper bodies. Muslim men often cover their heads with various kinds of hats or caps while praying. This gesture symbolizes humility and respect for God. Muslims remove their shoes when praying in a mosque or other indoor locations, but may leave them on when praying outside.

Prayer Rugs and Places to Pray

Prayers may be said in any place that's clean. While mosques serve as a preferred site for formal prayer, Muslims may pray in nearly any place they find themselves at prayer time, including, in the case of agricultural workers, a field, or for laborers, a factory. In many Muslim countries cultural traditions encourage women to pray at home rather than attend the mosque.

Muslims use prayer rugs to insure that the surface they pray on is clean. They should be rolled up and stored when not in use and should be used for no other purpose than prayer.

During the time of prayer, nothing should pass directly in front of the worshiper. At home, some choose to pray in front of a wall. Those performing solitary prayers inside a mosque may position themselves directly in front of a pillar. Otherwise the worshiper can place some small object, called a *sutra*, in front of him or herself, marking out the space of prayer which should not be broken. For those praying in a group, the imam — or prayer leader — serves as their sutra. The imam himself must have his own sutra.

Muslims use prayer rugs to insure that the surface they pray on is clean. These rugs vary in size, but average about three feet by five feet. They should be rolled up and stored when not in use and should be used for no other purpose than prayer. Observant Muslims often take prayer rugs with them when they travel. If no rug is available, however, a clean sheet or any clean surface will suffice. Many different kinds of designs embellish prayer rugs, depending on where the rug was woven. Some include an arch, which may be pointed in the direction of Mecca. A small defect is often woven into each rug. These imperfections remind worshipers that only God is completely without flaw. This realization inspires them to greater humility.

Exemptions

Young children are not required to perform salat. Children begin learning the rituals of formal prayer around the age of seven. Children over the age of ten are expected to pray regularly. Islam expects that both male and female believers pray, although women are not expected to pray during their menstrual periods. Though women may attend the mosque for Friday prayers, only men are expected to attend. People who are traveling may shorten and combine their prayers. People who, for good reasons, miss saying their prayers at the proper time may make them up later.

> *The morning prayer is said at dawn, the midday prayer at noon, the afternoon prayer in the mid-afternoon, the evening prayer at sunset, and the night prayer after it gets dark.*

Prayer Times

Observant Muslims offer formal prayers five times a day, at specified hours. Muslim prayer times follow the course of the sun. The morning prayer is said at dawn (before the actual sunrise), the midday prayer at noon, the afternoon prayer in the mid-afternoon, the evening prayer at sunset (between the sunset and darkness), and the night prayer after it gets dark. The exact times will vary throughout the year as the days lengthen and shorten. Mosques and Islamic centers often publicly post or furnish worshipers a list of correct seasonal prayer times, and some Islamic web sites can calculate local prayer times. Although prayers may not be said before the specified hour, there is a grace period after each scheduled prayer time in which the worshiper may still offer the prayer.

Words and Movements of Formal Prayer

Muslims face Mecca when they pray. This means that Muslims living in different parts of the world face different directions. For example, Muslims living in Turkey pray facing south, while Ethiopian Muslims pray with their faces towards the north.

Formal prayer begins in a standing position. Muslims must recite these formal prayers in Arabic, although recent converts are permitted to use their native tongue until they master the Arabic phrases. There are some slight variations in the way in which different groups of Muslims perform salat. The following description furnishes an outline of the prayer's most important elements.

The worshiper begins by raising his or her hands and placing them alongside his or her ears, palms facing forward. In this position he or she declares *Allahu Akbar*, "God is greater than all!" Then the worshiper lowers his or her hands to waist (or heart) level, and clasps the opposite forearm (or hand). In this position he or she recites the *Fatiha*, or opening chapter of the Quran:

> All praise be to Allah
> Lord of all the worlds,
> Most beneficent, ever-merciful,
> King of the Day of Judgment.
> You alone we worship, and to You alone turn for help.
> Guide us (O Lord) to the path that is straight,
> Not of those who have earned your anger, nor of
> those who have gone astray (Quran 1:1-7, Ali trans.).

When finished the worshiper adds *"ameen"* and recites a selection from the Quran of his or her own choosing. Surah (chapter) 112 is a popular choice:

> Say: "He is God
> the one most unique,
> God the immanently indispensable.
> He has begotten no one,
> And is begotten of none.
> There is no one comparable to Him"
> (Quran 112:1-4, Ali trans.).

A worshiper at the Qing Hai Mosque in Urumqi, China, raises his hands and places them alongside his ears and declares Allahu Akbar, *"God is greater than all!"*

A verse from chapter 2, known as the Throne Verse, is another common selection:

> God: There is no God but He,
> the living, eternal, self-subsisting, ever sustaining.
> Neither does somnolence affect Him nor sleep.
> To Him belongs all
> that is in the heavens and the earth;
> and who can intercede with Him except by His leave?
> Known to Him is all that is present before men
> and what is hidden
> (in time past and time future),
> and not even a little of His knowledge can they grasp
> except what He will.

His seat extends over heavens and the earth,
and He tires not of protecting them:
He alone is all high and supreme (Quran 2:255, Ali trans.).

Next the supplicant again declares, "God is greater than all." Bending from the waist, he or she places his or her hands on the knees and says "Glory to my great Lord" three times. Rising to a standing position the worshiper then affirms, "God hears those who praise Him." After that the worshiper again proclaims, "God is greater than all" and then kneels and prostrates himself or herself on the floor. In this position the forehead, hands (but not forearms), knees, lower legs, and toes press against the ground. He or she says "Glory to my Lord, Most High" three times, followed by "God is greater than all," in this position. Next the worshiper sits up, resting his or her weight on his or her lower legs and feet and again declares, "God is greater than all." He or she repeats the prostration, the three pronouncements of "Glory to my Lord, Most High" and the declaration, "God is greater than all."

After completing the required number of rakat, *or prayer cycles, the worshiper ends the prayer session by reciting the* tashahhud, *a summation of the core message of Islam, along with blessings on the Prophet Muhammad.*

The ritual described above is called a *rakah*, or prayer cycle. A complete prayer consists of two, three, or four *rakat* (pl.). In every prayer session, each rakah is basically the same except that in each cycle the believer must recite different, optional verses from the Quran. The sunrise prayer (*fajr* or *subh*) consists of two complete rakat and the evening prayer (*maghrib*) contains three complete rakat. The noon (*dhuhr*), mid-afternoon (*asr*), and night (*isha*) prayer are composed of four rakat.

Recitations from different verses in the Quran can be heard from these Chinese worshipers (opposite page).

After completing the required number of rakat, the worshiper ends the prayer session by reciting the *tashahhud* ("testimony"), a summation of the core message of Islam, along with blessings on the Prophet Muhammad:

Saluations, prayers, and good works are all for God.
Peace on thee, O Prophet, and God's mercy and His Blessings
Peace be on us and on all God's righteous servants.
I testify that there is no god but God,
And I testify that Muhammad is His servant and His Messenger
(Glasse 1991: 347).

The tashahhud is said while kneeling. While reciting it, many worshipers place their hands on their knees and lift the index finger of the right hand into the air. For many Muslims the gesture represents faith in the oneness of God. A hadith of the Prophet also teaches that it symbolizes the strength to reject the Devil and his snares.

After completing their prayer session, Muslims turn to the right and wish peace upon whoever is standing there. Then they turn to the left and do the same. They do this even if no one is standing there, as tradition teaches that angels gather around any human being at prayer. Thus an angel will receive the greeting, even if no human being does.

Students perform their noon prayers at the As-Siddiq Elementary School in Khobar, Saudi Arabia.

Rules for Congregational Prayer

Tradition advises that congregational prayer is to be preferred over solitary prayer, as worshipers will gather strength from the faith of others. So Muslims who find themselves together at prayer times — for example, family members, coworkers, and schoolmates — will often say their prayers together. In this case, someone will serve as imam, or prayer leader. He or she stands in front of the group and faces Mecca. The other worshipers form rows behind the imam, standing shoulder to shoulder. Even if only two Muslims are present, one will serve as leader and set the pattern for the others to follow.

If both men and women are present, the women will usually stand behind the men. This arrangement is viewed as less distracting to the men, since they won't have to avoid looking at a woman who is bent over in front of them. Women, too, will know that they are not being looked over by the men. In a mixed group a male serves as imam. In an all-female group, a woman may serve as imam.

Chapter 11
Informal Prayer

How and When to Offer Informal Prayers

Muslims call their informal prayer *dua*, meaning "plea" or "call." In English, this kind of prayer may be called a supplication, because the worshiper entreats or appeals to God. Unlike salat, this kind of prayer permits Muslims to communicate their personal concerns to God. It may be performed in a variety of ways at any time of night or day. Muslims may simply offer a list of their own concerns, or they may recite a traditional, composed prayer.

Though it is not obligatory, many Muslims offer dua after concluding their formal prayers. After finishing the required prayers, they may repeat an expression of thanks or praise to God 33 or more times. This act prepares them to begin the optional, informal prayers.

Examples of Composed Prayers

A composed prayer known as the *Ya Latif*, for example, is often recited in times of trouble. This prayer begins by stating the *ta'awwudh*, which translates as "I take refuge in God from Satan the stoned one." Next the worshiper says, "In the name of God, the merciful, the compassionate," a traditional formula known as the *basmallah*. This is followed by the three recitations of chapter 112 of the Quran, titled "Sincerity," or "Pure Faith":

Foreign words used in the text are defined in the Glossary, pages 423-40.

151

With forearms extended in front of him, and palms facing up, this Russian Muslim offers dua after concluding his formal prayer.

Say: "He is God
the one most unique,
God the immanently indispensable.
He has begotten no one,
And is begotten of none.
There is no one comparable to Him" (Quran 112, Ali trans.).

Next the worshiper recites this verse from the Quran: "God is gracious to his creatures, and bestows favor on whosoever He will. He is all-powerful and mighty" (Quran 42:19, Ali trans.). After this statement, one shares one's concerns with God and adds personal requests. The prayer concludes with a blessing on the Prophet Muhammad.

Another composed prayer, called the seven *salams*, may be offered in times of distress or on occasions of rejoicing. It consists of the seven verses from the Quran in which the word peace (salam) is used as a blessing on the virtuous:

> "Peace" shall be the greeting from the merciful Lord (36:58).
> Peace on Noah among all men (37:79).
> Peace be on Abraham (37:109).
> Peace be on Moses and Aaron (37:120).
> Peace be on Elias (37:130).
> So peace be on the messengers (37:181).
> It is peace till the dawning of the day (97:5) (Quran, Ali trans.).

Those who find themselves wakeful late at night might offer this traditional prayer:

> My God and my Lord, eyes are at rest, stars are setting, hushed are the movements of birds in their nests, of monsters in the deep. And Thou art the Just who knowest no change, the Equity that swerveth not, the Everlasting that passeth not away. The doors of kings are locked, watched by their bodyguards; but Thy door is open to him who calls on Thee. My Lord, each lover is now alone with his beloved, and Thou art for me the beloved (Padwick 1997: 219).

Finally, the following petition for God's forgiveness can be found in many Muslim prayer manuals:

> Forgive and show mercy for Thou art the Best of them that show mercy (Padwick: 203).

After dua it is customary to smooth one's palms over one's face and shoulders, an act which may be interpreted as covering oneself in God's blessing.

Posture and Gestures

When offering a dua prayer, the worshiper stands with forearms extended in front of him or her, palms facing up. The petitions themselves should be said silently. Afterwards it is customary to smooth one's palms over one's face and shoulders, an act which may be interpreted as covering oneself in God's blessing. The dua prayer concludes with the phrase *al-hamdu Lillah*, "Thanks be to God" or "Praise be to God."

Chapter 12
Other Devotional Customs

Prayer Beads

In certain parts of the Muslim world, it is common to meet people who carry prayer beads with them at all times. Muslims use prayer beads to help them keep track of repetitive prayers and meditations. Called *subha* or *misbaha* in Arabic or *tespih* in Turkish, they are sometimes referred to as a rosary in English, after the Roman Catholic prayer beads. Historically, however, the Muslim beads came before the Christian rosary. The Muslim beads were inspired by an even earlier tradition. Around the 9th century Muslims adopted the use of prayer beads from India, where both Hindus and Buddhists had been using them for centuries. A number of scholars believe that when the European Catholics developed the rosary in the 13th century they were inspired by their acquaintance with Muslim prayer beads. Turkish Muslims developed the custom of carrying the beads at all times, in order to remind themselves of God constantly. Eventually non-Muslim peoples living in contact with Turkish Muslims—for example Greeks and Armenians—began to carry beads, too. They busied their hands with fingering these beads as a means of soothing themselves or just keeping their hands occupied. In these cultures, the beads became known as "worry beads."

A string of Muslim prayer beads usually consists of 99 or 33 beads, with a tassel or single, long bead where the two ends of the string come together. Strings of 99 beads are usually divided into three sections of 33. This number of beads assists Muslims in reciting the 99 names of Allah, a popular devotional activity.

Opposite page and below: An elderly pilgrim who has just completed the Hajj chooses prayer beads to carry home.

Foreign words used in the text are defined in the Glossary, pages 423-40.

The worshiper passes one bead through his or her fingers for every name recited. If the string of beads is meant to be used for other kinds of meditations, the beads may vary in number or be configured differently. Members of Sufi orders often pray or chant using different lengths of prayer beads. Certain Sufi groups have used strings of 500 or even 1,000 beads. Some Sufis wear the beads around their neck, as an outward sign of their religious commitment.

The 99 Names of God

According to a hadith, Muhammad once said, "There are ninety-nine names of Allah; he who memorizes them and repeats them will get into paradise" (Braswell: 47). The Quran affirms the practice of reciting God's names: "All the names of God are beautiful, so call him by them" (Quran 7:180, Ali trans.).

Some Sufis claim that there is a secret, hundredth name. God reveals this name to those who have reached an advanced state of spiritual development.

Reciting the 99 names of God has become an important Muslim devotion. These names describe the qualities or powers attributed to God. Islam insists that God has no form and no associates. Therefore it forbids its followers to make visual images of God, fearing that these representations could lead people astray. Instead Islam encourages people to know God directly, and learn about God's qualities rather than to guess at God's appearance. For Muslims, reciting the 99 names deepens knowledge of God and strengthens faith.

Muhammad did not reveal the 99 names. Nor does the Quran provide a list of these names. Instead, scholars have poured over the holy book of Islam, culling out the names, or titles, attributed to Allah throughout the entire text. For example, the following excerpt from the Quran establishes many of these titles:

He is God; there is no God but He,
the knower of the unknown and known.
He is benevolent, ever-merciful.
He is God; there is no God but He,
the King, the Holy, the Preserver,
Protector, Guardian, Strong, the Powerful, Omnipotent.
Far too exalted is God
for what they associate with Him.
He is God, the Creator, the Maker, the Fashioner.
His are all the names beautiful.
Whatever is in the heavens and the earth
sings His praises.
He is all-mighty and all-wise (Quran 59:22-24, Ali trans.).

Other titles are inferred from Quranic descriptions of God. A few derive from Muslim tradition. More than one list of these names exists, and not all the names on these lists are exactly the same. If all the names were added up, they would total more than 99. Nevertheless, tradition has fixed the devotional practice at the repetition of 99 names.

Ninety-Nine Names of Allah

The following list of the 99 names of Allah reflects Islam's view of the tremendous power, majesty, wisdom, holiness, mercy, and justice of God:

1. The First
2. The Last
3. The One
4. The Originator
5. The Producer
6. The Beneficent
7. The Seeing
8. The Expander
9. The Inner
10. The Raiser
11. The Enduring
12. The Relenting
13. The Irresistible
14. The Majestic
15. The Gatherer
16. The Accounter
17. The Guardian
18. The Truth
19. The Wise
20. The Judge
21. The Kindly
22. The Praiseworthy
23. The Living
24. The Well-Informed
25. The Humbler
26. The Creator
27. Full of Majesty and Generosity
28. The Gentle
29. The Merciful
30. The Compassionate
31. The Provider
32. The Guide
33. The Exalter
34. The Vigilant
35. The Peace
36. The Hearer
37. The Grateful
38. The Witness
39. The Forbearing
40. The Eternal
41. The Afflicter
42. The Outer
43. The Just
44. The Mighty and also the Precious
45. The Great
46. The Pardoner
47. The Knowing
48. The High One
49. The Forgiver
50. The Forgiving
51. The Rich
52. The Opener
53. The Seizer
54. The Capable
55. The Holy
56. The Victorious
57. The Strong
58. The Self-Subsistent
59. The Great
60. The Magnanimous, the Generous, the Noble
61. The Gracious
62. The Deferrer
63. The Believer
64. The Self Exalted
65. The Superb
66. The Firm
67. The Founder
68. The Responsive
69. The Glorious
70. The Counter
71. The Giver of Life
72. The Abaser
73. The Separator
74. The Shaper
75. The Restorer
76. The Honorer
77. The Giver
78. The Enricher
79. The Maintainer, the Determiner, He who brings to pass
80. The Prevailer
81. The Bringer Forward
82. The Equitable
83. The King
84. Possessor of the Kingdom
85. The Slayer
86. The Avenger
87. The Vigilant, the Guardian
88. The Propitious
89. The Helper
90. The Light
91. The Guide
92. The Unique
93. The Loving
94. The Inheritor
95. The Vast
96. The Steward
97. The Patron
98. The Protector
99. The Bestower

(Glassé 1991: 99-100, Al Hariri-Wendel 2002: 83-85)

Allah

The most important name for God is Allah. Allah is the Arabic word for God (literally "the God"), and when Muslims use it they are referring to the same God worshipped by Jews, Christians, and all monotheistic believers. There are certain mystical teachings concerning the spiritual significance of this word and its component letters in Arabic. The word is also a favorite subject for Muslim calligraphers.

Allah (Square Kufi)

Although English-speaking Muslims sometimes retain the Arabic word Allah to refer to God, there is nothing about the word that limits its use to Islam. Arabic-speaking Christians also refer to God as Allah.

When devout Muslims speak or write the name "Allah," they follow it with one of a number of set phrases. These expressions honor God and affirm his power. The first, *subhanahu wa ta'ala*, means, "He is glorified and exalted." In English this phrase may be abbreviated with the letters SWT. Other honorific expressions include *azza wa jall,* "great and majestic," and *jalla jalaluhu,* "great is His majesty."

The 99 names teach Muslims about the many qualities of God. Ultimately, however, Allah is beyond human understanding. The following well-known passage from the Quran emphasizes the mysterious nature of God's existence and his power:

> God is the light of the heavens and the earth.
> The semblance of His light is that of a niche
> in which is a lamp, the flame within a glass,
> the glass a glittering star as it were, lit with the oil
> of a blessed tree, the olive, neither of the East
> nor of the West, whose oil appears to light up
> even though fire touches it not,—light upon light.
> God guides to His light whom He will.
> So does God advance precepts of wisdom for men,
> for God has knowledge of every thing (Quran 24:35, Ali trans.).

This passage, called the "Light Verse," is a favorite for many Muslims and has been inscribed onto many lamps.

Dhikr

Dhikr means "remembrance" or "reminder" in Arabic. The Quran urges Muslims to maintain a constant awareness of God's power and presence. One verse states, "Surely there is peace of heart in the contemplation of God!" (Quran

13:28, Ali trans.) while another commands, "O you who believe, remember God a great deal, and sing His praises morning and evening" (Quran 33:41, Ali trans.). In yet another verse God advises, ". . . remember Me, and I shall remember you" (Quran 2:152, Ali trans.). All of these verses recommend the remembrance or contemplation of God, and some Muslims see in them support for the performance of ritual acts of remembrance, also referred to as dhikr.

One of the most common forms of dhikr involves the repetition of certain phrases again and again, as a form of meditation. Some of the most frequently used phrases are, *La ilaha ill-Allah* ("There is no God but God"), *Allahu Akbar* ("God is greater than all"), *Subhana-Allah* ("Glory to you O God our Lord"), and *Al-hamdu Lillah* ("Thanks be to God" or "Praise be to God"). Reciting the 99 names of Allah may also be considered a form of dhikr. Dhikr may be practiced silently—by focusing one's mind on a single idea—or aloud—by chanting.

This Kufi octagon is based on a faience panel from the Masjid-i-Jami mosque in Isfahan, Iran. Its calligraphic design reads "La ilaha ill-Allah" ("There is no God but God").

Dhikr is one of the primary tools for expanding spiritual awareness in some Sufi orders. Members of these orders will receive specific instructions on how to perform dhikr from their teachers or spiritual masters.

In addition to being a specific set of practices, "remembrance" may be thought of as a concept or teaching that runs throughout the whole of Islam. The Quran contains numerous warnings concerning the human tendency to forget: to forget God, to forget those who suffer, and to forget the reality of our own deaths. The Quran teaches its readers that the solution to the problem of forgetfulness is remembrance. Indeed, the Quran refers to itself and other, earlier scriptures as "reminders." Prayer five times a day, memorization and recitation of the names of God, and repetitive rituals like chanting, all serve as tools with which to overcome the human inclination towards forgetfulness and replace it with a steady remembrance of God.

Mealtime Prayers

Before eating a meal some Muslims recite the *basmallah* ("In the name of God, the merciful, the compassionate"). At the end of the meal, it is appropriate to say the *hamdallah* ("Praise be to God").

Fasting

Muslims are required to fast during the month of Ramadan. From sunup to sundown they refrain from eating, drinking, smoking tobacco, and sexual relations. In Islam fasting also serves to instill compassion for and generosity towards the poor. According to a hadith, Muhammad once said, "He is not a good Muslim who eats his fills and leaves his neighbor hungry."

Muslims may also fast on other religious occasions, as a penance for misdeeds or the failure to observe a religious obligation, or simply as a means of strengthening will power and developing the soul. Muhammad recommended fasting to his followers as a spiritual discipline. Optional fast days are scheduled throughout the Muslim year. For example, the ninth, tenth, and eleventh of the month of Muharram are recommended for fasting, as are six days, of the fasting person's own choosing, in the month of Shawwal. Many Muslims consider Thursday an especially appropriate day to fast and consider the holy months of Dhu al-Hijjah, Muharram, Rajab, and Shaban as appropriate seasons for fasting. The White Nights, that is, the thirteenth, fourteenth, and fifteenth days of each month, also present a good opportunity for observing optional fast days.

> *In Islam fasting also serves to instill compassion for and generosity towards the poor. According to a hadith, Muhammad once said, "He is not a good Muslim who eats his fills and leaves his neighbor hungry."*

Charity

Islam teaches its followers to make a yearly charitable contribution of 2.5 percent of their wealth. This donation, called *zakat*, is one of the Five Pillars of Islam, the five practices and beliefs that are central to the faith. In addition to this required donation, Islam strongly recommends that Muslims make further charitable contributions, if they are able to do so without adversely affecting their families. Religious teachings stipulate that these additional donations must be made quietly, without attracting attention to the act. In Islam charity has the same value as prayer, and is viewed as just as praiseworthy by God.

Intention

The clear formation of the intention — *niyyah* in Arabic — to perform a devotional act is an important part of all Muslim religious practices. The intention may be formed silently or stated out loud. So important is intention to Islam that Muslim law stipulates that any devotional act made without niyyah is not valid.

Chapter 13
Mosque

Place of Prostration

The English word "mosque" comes from the French word *mosquée*, which in turn comes from the Arabic word *masjid*, which means place of prostration. Muslims prostrate themselves in their five daily prayer sessions. These can take place nearly anywhere, however, so long as it is clean. Muhammad is reported to have said, "The whole world has been made a masjid (mosque) for me" (Zepp: 81). Nevertheless, some Muslims prefer to congregate at their local mosque to say these prayers. Muslim men are charged with the duty of coming to the Friday noon prayer service at the mosque, but all other attendance is voluntary.

The Makkah Mosque, in Hyderabad, India, took more than 75 years to build (1617-93). It not only serves as a place of worship, but also a gathering place and hospitality center.

Gathering Place and Hospitality Center

In Muslim societies a large mosque is located at the center of most towns. Large mosques, as opposed to small neighborhood mosques, are often referred to as Friday mosques because they are roomy enough to host the large congregations that gather there for Friday noon prayers. Often a large market place is located near the Friday mosque, as are food vendors and government offices. In many towns public baths, religious schools, shrines of holy men, and decorative water fountains also spring up near the Friday mosque. Given its convenient central location, the Friday mosque serves as a gathering place that men visit during the day to take a break from their work. Here they may rest, meditate, con-

Foreign words used in the text are defined in the Glossary, pages 423-40.

161

verse with others, listen to lectures given by religious experts, and, of course, perform their daily prayers. In addition, during times of national distress or disaster people naturally congregate at the town's largest mosque. Finally, in Muslim societies mosques have traditionally permitted travelers without accommodations to sleep on their premises. This tradition reflects the emphasis that Islam places on hospitality.

Opposite page and above: Turkish tiles and a Quranic inscription adorn the mihrab of this European mosque in Munich with its distinctive parabolic arches.

Architectural Features

Nearly all mosques share the following design elements. There is a large, empty hall set aside for prayer, called a *musallah* in Arabic. This room contains neither chairs nor benches. It is usually divided into a separate men's and women's area. An alcove in one wall indicates the direction of Mecca. Called a

163

mihrab in Arabic, the alcove also serves to reflect and amplify the voice of the imam. An elevated pulpit, called a *minbar*, provides a place from which to deliver the Friday sermon. The mosque also furnishes separate areas for men and women to perform wudu, the ritual cleansing required before engaging in formal prayer.

The elevated pulpit, called a minbar, provides a place from which to deliver a sermon or speech.

In addition, most mosques include several other features. They usually have a small narrow tower called a minaret. From here the muezzin chants the call to prayer that precedes the start of the five-times-a-day formal prayers. Dome-shaped roofs are another common architectural feature. Many mosques have classrooms associated with them, which are used for religious instruction. In the United States mosques often host various kinds of large group activities, such as community dinners, so their facilities may also include kitchens and social halls, as well as rooms used as a Saturday or Sunday school for Muslim children.

Imam and Muezzin

An imam is a man who serves as a prayer leader in a mosque. Women may serve as imams for all-female congregations, but not at mixed-sex gatherings. Sunni imams are not ordained as are Christian priests or ministers and are not believed to have special authority to confer God's blessing or God's forgiveness of sin on believers. Sunni Islam rejects the idea of maintaining a special clerical class of ordained religious administrators who stand between believers and God. Instead it advocates the equality of all believers. Imams are selected for their knowledge of the Quran and their virtue. During congregational prayers the imam stands in front of the group and sets the pattern that others follow. A mosque may have several men who are capable of serving as imam. If none of them are present, a respected man from the congregation will lead the prayers.

In the United States the function of the imam has expanded somewhat to more closely resemble the kind of community leadership provided by the Christian clergy. For example, American imams may be expected to raise money for the mosque, counsel distressed community members, visit ill and shut-in members of the congregation, offer legal advice, train lay religious teachers, and preside at weddings and funerals.

The Albanian Islamic Center in Harper Woods, Michigan, was built in 1962. This mosque combines both Middle Eastern and American ideas into the architecture and design of the mihrab (prayer niche), minbar (elevated pulpit), minaret (narrow tower), and dome. The musallah (prayer hall) is also used to teach Quran classes for the children.

Shia Muslims use the word imam to refer to a select number of important religious leaders of the past as well as their current religious leaders. Unlike Sunni Muslims, Shias view their own imams as spiritually elevated people with a special role to play in transmitting God's blessings to ordinary believers.

The muezzin (or *mu'adhdhin* in Arabic) performs a different set of functions than does the imam. Traditionally the muezzin announced the approach of prayer times from the entry to the mosque or from a tower, called a minaret, attached to the mosque. Some also recited the Quran from atop the minaret, while waiting for the approach of the dawn prayer time. Pious men with good characters and strong voices are sought for this job. Nowadays many mosques use loudspeakers to call the faithful to prayer.

In addition to the regular noon prayers on Friday, the imam offers a sermon, or khutba. This sermon may touch on themes of the Quran, the political affairs of the day, or other matters.

Friday Services

Friday is the day on which Muslims gather together for communal worship. Unlike the Jewish and Christian Sabbath, however, Fridays were not traditionally observed as days of rest in Islam. In recent times this has changed. A number of Muslim countries have designated Friday as a partial or full day off from work, thereby replacing the weekly Sunday holiday that many viewed as a holdover from the time of European (and therefore Christian) colonial rule.

The Friday congregational service takes place at noon. In addition to the regular noon prayers, the imam offers a sermon, or *khutba*. This sermon may touch on themes of the Quran, problems being experienced by members of the congregation, the political affairs of the day, or other matters.

Only men are required to attend Friday noon prayers, although women may attend if they wish. In some Islamic countries, few women come to these services because cultural traditions encourage women to pray at home rather than attend the Friday service. In countries where these traditions aren't so entrenched, however — such as the United States — increasing numbers of women have been coming to these services. Although they may pray at their neighborhood mosque on other days, many people choose to attend the Friday mosque for this weekly observance.

In the United States, many Muslims find it difficult to attend Friday prayer services due to their work schedules. Some employers permit them to take long lunches on Friday, and to make up the hours at other times. Others find that they must attend the mosque on other days, perhaps even on Sundays.

Separation of Men and Women

Although men must do so, Islam does not require women to attend communal worship services. Nothing forbids women from participating in communal worship should they choose to do so, however. In some Muslim countries, custom encourages women to stay home, and few venture forth to the Friday prayer services. Nevertheless, there are signs that this convention is slowly changing. In the United States, Muslim women have participated to a greater degree in communal worship. Perhaps this is because the mosque plays such an important role in Muslim social life in countries where Muslims are a minority.

Men and women generally do not mix during communal worship. Traditionally the men occupy the front of the mosque while the women and children take their places behind them. Sometimes women and children occupy a

Despite the demands of a busy schedule, a group of Muslim students at the University of Arizona gathers for Friday noon prayers.

167

The Islamic Center of Greater Toledo in Ohio (built in 1983) uses a low sectional divider in the musallah to separate the women (left) from the men (right) during communal worship.

second-floor balcony area, which permits them to look down on the imam and male worshipers below. In the most conservative of mosques women pray in a separate room, connected to the main worship area only by television screens or speakers. In some progressive American mosques women worship on one side of the mosque and men on the other, the two sides being separated by a low divider of some sort. Before praying, men and women may use the separate wash areas provided for them at the mosque, or they may wash at home.

The various postures required in Muslim prayer are often cited as the reason for the separation of men and women. During prostration worshipers must place their foreheads on the ground and raise their seat into the air. Since men might be distracted by the sight of women in this pose, women pray in an area where men can't see them.

Muslim men and women attending prayer services at the mosque are required to follow the same clothing requirements they must adhere to when performing formal prayers at home. In addition to covering their hair, many Muslim women are also careful to cover their arms and legs completely when they go to the mosque, even if they don't always cover themselves this way when in public.

When Visiting a Mosque

When visiting a mosque in the United States non-Muslims need to be aware of the traditions of Muslim worship. Women visitors should dress modestly and bring a large scarf in case it is necessary to cover their head and hair. A long-sleeved blouse and a skirt that reaches below the knee would be appropriate. Men should wear slacks and a shirt. Both sexes should avoid obvious displays of jewelry with Christian or Jewish religious symbols on it. Calling ahead to check on dress codes and the degree of participation expected or permitted non-Muslim visitors would not be amiss, as congregations vary to some degree in these matters.

The various postures required in Muslim prayer are often cited as the reason for the separation of men and women.

Before entering the prayer hall, guests, as well as members, should take off their shoes. There will usually be shelves or a rack to place them on. Non-Muslims who visit during prayer times may enter the prayer hall to observe, but they are not expected to join in the prayers. Some more progressive mosques may invite guests who are interested to follow along with the prayers. Ask your host or the imam what is customary in their mosque. If a donation is taken, non-Muslims will not be expected to contribute.

Dress codes for non-Muslim visitors to mosques may be stricter in Muslim countries. For example, in some places women may be expected to wear floor-length skirts. In certain countries, non-Muslim visitors should not visit mosques during prayer time. In a few Muslim countries, such as Morocco, non-Muslims are not allowed to enter mosques at any time. Non-Muslims are not permitted to enter the Saudi Arabian cities of Mecca and Medina, and so may not visit the historic mosques located there.

Chapter 14
Quran

Pious Customs

The veneration that Muslims feel for the Quran comes from the belief that it records the literal words of God and that through this book God is speaking directly to them. Devout Muslims strive to receive God's word in humility and awe — through reading, chanting, or listening to the recitation of the Quran — and to let it transform them. Christians can perhaps best understand this reverence for the Quran by comparing it to their own respect for the bread and wine consumed during the ritual of Communion (also known as the Eucharist or the Lord's Supper). Some branches of Christianity teach that Christ is actually present in the bread and wine, and that consuming them invites the power of God to enter and transform them. Similarly, for many Muslims, God's voice is actually present in the Quran.

Muslims show respect for the Quran through a variety of pious customs. For example, tradition dictates that Muslims should not touch the book until they have performed the ritual cleaning required before offering formal prayers. They also should not recite the Quran in any place that is not clean or is associated with any sort of doubtful activities. Before reciting anything from the Quran, many Muslims prepare themselves by repeating the *ta'awwudh* ("I take refuge with God from the Satan the stoned one"), followed by the *basmallah* ("In the name of God, the merciful, the compassionate"). At the end of the recitation, the speaker closes with the phrase, "God Almighty has spoken truly."

Opposite page: These fine old copies of the Quran are among the Arabic manuscripts gathered by Dr. Aziz Atiya in 1979 for the University of Utah's collection.

Foreign words used in the text are defined in the Glossary, pages 423-40.

In accordance with traditional Muslim reverence for their holy scripture, nothing should ever be placed on top of a Quran, nor should anyone ever sit so that the soles of their feet point at it. (There is a greater possibility of this happening in societies where people usually sit on the floor rather than on chairs.) This Middle Eastern custom probably evolved from a notion common in that part of the world: that to point the soles of the feet towards someone or something is an insult. Many Muslims keep their copy of the book on a Quran stand (*kursi*) so that it will never be placed in an inappropriate place or position. Students who carry the book with them to school, and others who carry the Quran with them throughout the day, will sometimes place the book in a protective cover so that it will not become dirty. Some people will kiss the Quran and walk beneath it before they embark on any sort of long trip. They may bring a miniature copy of the book with them in the belief that it will confer protection upon them. Verses from the Quran may also be incorporated into amulets or written in beautiful calligraphy and displayed as an inspiring piece of religious art.

Other Names

In Arabic *al-Quran* means "the recitation." The book goes by a number of different Arabic names throughout the Muslim world, however. Some prefer to call it *al-Quran al-majid*, which means "the noble Quran." It is also called *al-Furqan*, "the Discernment." This name reflects the Muslim teaching that the book contains the principles necessary for arriving at correct ethical decisions and intellectual judgments. *Al-Huda*, meaning "the Guide," is another popular name for the Quran. For Muslims the Quran indeed serves as life's ultimate guidebook. Finally, many people speak of the Quran as *Umm al-Kitab*, "the Mother of All Books." This name comes from the belief that the original Quran exists in heaven, that all learning can be traced back to the Quran, and that the Quran serves as the model for all books.

During school hours in Dhaka, Bangladesh, children practice memorizing and reciting passages from the Quran.

Memorization and Recitation

For Muslims memorization and recitation of the Quran is a basic devotional activity as well as an art form. One well-known hadith puts it this way: "he is not one of us who does not chant the Quran" (Denny 1995: 398). Sincerity of belief is the most important quality that a Muslim can bring to his or her devotional recitations. Another hadith reports that when Muhammad was asked to judge whose recitation was the most beautiful, he replied, "The one of whom you think when you hear him recite that he fears God" (Denny 1995: 398). This is not to say that Muslims discount those who recite with precise pronunciation, pleasing rhythms, and a beautiful, sonorous voice. These people may be called on to recite the Quran for others or may become professional reciters. Their talents and skill permit them to pay a special kind of homage to the text by rendering it in such a beautiful way. Indeed, the Prophet also advised his followers to "adorn the Quran with your voices" (Denny 1995: 398). The gifted and trained, too, are expected to recite with feeling.

Muslim parents commonly train their children from an early age to memorize and recite portions of the Quran. A number of adults succeed in memorizing the entire Quran. Other people signal their respect for this accomplishment by addressing them as *shaykh* (Arabic for "old man") or *hafiz* (Arabic for "memorize" or "preserve"). They may also be referred to as *hafiz al-Quran*, or "Guardian of the Quran." In India and other parts of Asia, some people have accomplished this feat without even knowing Arabic. The sheer sound of the words, properly recited, is believed by many to impart the grace of God.

Some of those who memorize the Quran go on to master the Muslim art of Quran chanting. Masters of this art can recite the text of the Quran in particularly beautiful and expressive ways. These people may become professional Quran chanters, called *qari* or *muqri* in Arabic. Families and other groups hire them to recite at weddings, funerals, openings, inaugurations, evening gatherings during the month of Ramadan, and other observances and social occasions. Part or — on especially important occasions — all of the Quran may be recited.

A Quran from India.

Various styles of Quran recitation have developed over time. The variation between these styles results in the words flowing more or less quickly and in the reciter chanting in a more monotone or more melodic manner. Muslims also consider the call to prayer (or *adhan*), discussed above, as a form of Quran recitation.

Throughout the Muslim world, famous Quran chanters draw stadium-size crowds to their public recitations. They are often treated like celebrities and their admirers snap up their recordings. In some Muslim countries people also enjoy attending Quran chanting tournaments that feature the efforts of talented amateurs or professionals. In recent years, women reciters from Southeast Asia have won many international competitions.

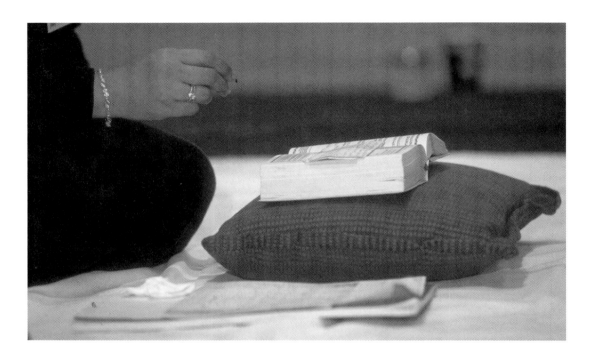

The Quran was revealed and first passed on by voice. Today, its recitation is both a popular sacred art and a pillar of worldwide Islamic education. One of Indonesia's foremost reciters, historian and college director Hajjah Maria 'Ulfah, gave her first U.S. recitations in 2000.

In Malaysia and Indonesia, Quran recitation contests developed in the second half of the 20th century. The national Indonesian tournament takes place every two years and lasts for ten days. It attracts reciters from all over the country, all of whom have emerged as champions in regional contests. Men, women, adults, children, disabled (especially blind), and able-bodied participants compete in separate divisions. A Quran knowledge contest, similar in format to an American college bowl quiz show, also takes place. In addition to a flag ceremony, music and dance performances round out the festivities. So important is the festival to Indonesians that the daily results are reported on the national television news.

Quran recitation is not limited to public performances and special events, however. In the Middle East these recitations are woven into the fabric of everyday life. Taxi cab drivers may listen to cassette recordings of Quran recitations; recitations are broadcast on the radio, and radio stations may even open and close their daily programming with recitations; finally, beggars may recite verses from the Quran hoping to inspire the generous to drop a coin into their hands.

Chapter 15
Muhammad

Although some religious scholars may reject the notion, many Muslims around the world believe that Muhammad's spiritual presence can still be felt among the community of believers. This is not to say that they think of him as still alive, however. This belief in Muhammad's spiritual presence underlies many of the folk practices of popular Islam, such as the recitation of *darud* (blessings). Practices such as these not only honor the Prophet but also help the devotee to access Muhammad's aid. Conservative Muslims may not be comfortable with all the blessing customs listed below. Even conservative Muslims, however, do not disapprove of the custom of adding the phrase, "peace be upon him," after the mention of Muhammad's name.

"Peace Be Upon Him"

When Muslims mention the prophet Muhammad, whether in speech or in writing, they follow his name with a blessing. In Arabic this blessing reads, *sala-Allahu 'alayhi wa-sallam*. It means, "God's blessings and peace be upon him." This phrase is often shortened to "peace be upon him," and may be abbreviated in English with the letters SAL. This little prayer reminds Muslims of the great blessings bestowed on humanity by Muhammad. This custom developed in response to a verse from the Quran, which asks all Muslims to salute and bless the Prophet:

> God and his angels shower their blessings upon the Prophet.
> O believers, you should also send your blessings on him,
> And salute him with a worthy greeting (Quran 33:56, Ali trans.).

Foreign words used in the text are defined in the Glossary, pages 423-40.

Faithful Muslims also interject the blessing, "peace be upon him," after speaking or writing the names of Jesus, Moses, and the other men whom Islam recognizes as important prophets. Shia Muslims will also add this blessing after the names of the first 12 Shia imams.

Publications printed in Muslim countries or by Islamic publishing companies abroad will often insert the blessing after each mention of the Prophet's name. In English-language publications, the blessing may be printed in Arabic or in English. In English it may be abbreviated by running together the first letter of each word in the phrase, "peace be upon him," and rendered thus: "PBUH."

When Muslims mention the prophet Muhammad, they follow his name with a blessing — sala-Allahu 'alayhi wa-sallam, meaning "God's blessings and peace be upon him."

Some very pious Muslims will add hand gestures to the spoken blessing. They kiss their fingers and touch them to their eyes and lips while blessing the Prophet. These gestures signify respect.

Images of the Prophet

Muslims do not use visual representations of the Prophet in their devotions. To do so would carry the danger of committing *shirk* — associating and perhaps worshiping something or someone besides God. Artwork not intended for religious use may sometimes include images of the Prophet, however. In these images, Muhammad usually appears with a white veil completely covering his face. Sometimes a flame-shaped light glows behind his head, suggesting spiritual illumination. These devices hide the Prophet's distinctive human features, thereby allowing Muslims to enjoy depictions of their religious history without being tempted into shirk.

Verbal descriptions of Muhammad are not subject to the same restrictions as are visual representations. Muslim lore has preserved various descriptions of Muhammad attributed to those who knew the Prophet personally. According to Ali, Muhammad's son-in-law, the Prophet was:

> Neither very tall nor excessively short, but was a man of medium size, he had neither very curly nor flowing hair but a mixture of the two, he was not obese, he did not have a very round face, but it was so to some extent, he was reddish-white, he had black eyes and long eyelashes, he had protruding joints and shoulder-blades, he was not hairy but had some hair on his chest, the palms of his hands and feet were calloused, when he walked he raised his feet as though he were walking on a slope, when he turned [for example, to someone] he turned completely, be-

tween his shoulders was the seal of prophecy and he was the seal of the prophets, he had a finer chest than anyone else, was truer in utterance than anyone else, had the gentlest nature and noblest tribe. Those who saw him suddenly stood in awe of him and those who shared his acquaintanceship loved him. Those who described him said they had never seen anyone like him before or since (Denny: 80).

Muhammad's Descendants

Islamic tradition suggests that Muslims treat Muhammad's descendants with special signs of respect. People who claim to be a descendant of Muhammad are called *sayyid* (other English spellings, such as *seyyed*, also exist). In Arabic the word literally means "lord" or "master," but it is also used in the same way English speakers use the words "sir" and "mister." Other titles used by Muhammad's descendants include *sharif* (Arabic for "highborn" or "honored"), and *shah* (Persian for "ruler"). In Morocco and other western Arab countries, they may be called *moulay* or *mawlay*. Certain families have incorporated these titles into their proper names. Some people who believe Muhammad to have been their ancestor cannot prove their claim, whereas others possess complex genealogical charts detailing the relationship. Etiquette requires that those who believe themselves to be related to Muhammad, no matter how distantly, set a good example to others in their admirable behavior and dignified bearing. The late King Hussein of Jordan (1935-1999), who became an internationally respected figure for working to bring about a peaceful resolution of differences between the state of Israel and the Palestine Liberation Organization, was a descendant of Muhammad through Muhammad's daughter Fatima. King Hussein's son Abdullah (b. 1962) succeeded him to the throne, so a descendant of Muhammad still rules in Jordan.

> *Etiquette requires that those who believe themselves to be related to Muhammad set a good example to others in their admirable behavior and dignified bearing.*

Muhammad's Example

Devout Muslims turn to Muhammad's example (*sunna*) not only in religious matters, but also in what non-Muslims might consider the mundane details of everyday life. Muhammad's beliefs, teachings, preferences, and daily habits have been transmitted down through the ages in collections of *hadith*. The word hadith may be translated as "speech," "report" or "tradition." One hundred to three hundred years after Muhammad's death, a small number of devoted Muslim scholars began collecting the remembrances of the many people who knew the Prophet. These people passed their recollections down to their descendants.

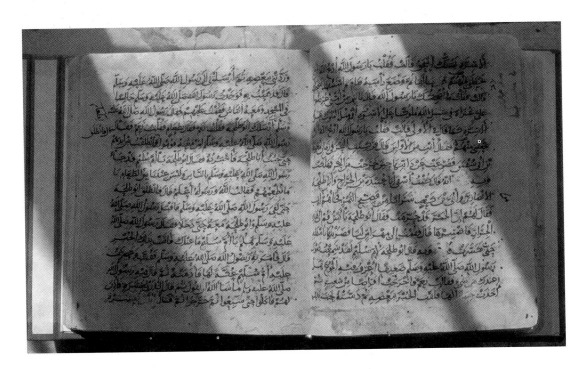

A book of hadiths written in 1027 C.E. (418 A.H.).

The scholars questioned the descendants, wrote down any saying or story they thought might possibly be genuine, rated their likelihood of being accurate as "strong" or "weak," and published them as collections of hadith. These memories of Muhammad offered a record of the everyday deeds, thoughts, and customs of the Prophet. Today Muslims still study the hadith to find answers to the problems of everyday life and to discover the best way to comport oneself in every situation.

This devotion to Muhammad reflects the belief that he was in all ways the most exemplary of human beings. Even the way in which he cleaned his nails, for instance, sets an example for others to follow. For centuries pious Muslims have cleaned their mouth with a *siwak* twig, because Muhammad did the same. In Muhammad's day siwak was used as a toothbrush. Nowadays people can purchase siwak toothpaste.

Poems and Songs

A *madh* is a poem praising a holy person, such as Muhammad, one of the Shia imams, or a saint. Muslim tradition teaches that Hassan Ibn Thabit, Muhammad's first scribe, composed the first madh. Later, Sufi poets began to compose madh. These poems may be chanted like songs. A solo singer usually performs them, but drums and a chorus may sometimes accompany the soloist. Madh performances often take place during *mulid* celebrations, such as Mulid al-Nabi, the holiday celebrating Muhammad's birthday.

A *naat* is a poem honoring and expressing devotion to Muhammad or one of his family members. These devotional verses became a common form of Muslim poetry by the 12th century. They are still very popular today. In Pakistan, newspapers publish them around the time of Mulid al-Nabi. Naat may be read or may be chanted like songs. They are usually performed without instrumental accompaniment (except perhaps drums). Many Muslims enjoy listening to accomplished naat singers. They often appear at religious events and their recordings find a ready market in the Muslim world.

Blessings

The recitation of *durud*, formulaic blessings of the Prophet, offers Muslims another way to honor Muhammad, invoke his presence, and request his guidance. For some Sufis, the repetition of durud constitutes a major channel of their religious expression. Other Muslims recite the blessings when they feel a special need for Muhammad's assistance. Devotees affirm that the practice often brings spiritual aid, such as the appearance of the Prophet in their dreams. Many Muslims recite durud while making the pilgrimage to Muhammad's tomb in Medina, Saudi Arabia. Folk belief teaches that Muhammad hears all the durud recited there.

> *The recitation of durud, formulaic blessings of the Prophet, offers Muslims another way to honor Muhammad, invoke his presence, and request his guidance.*

Muslims often preface their informal prayers with a blessing on the Prophet. One very popular blessing reads simply:

> May God call down blessing on our Lord Muhammad and on the family of our Lord Muhammad and greet them in peace (Padwick: 152).

Another blessing, popular in North Africa, is more elaborate:

> Blessing and peace be upon you, O Prophet of God;
> Blessing and peace be upon you, O Intimate of God;
> Blessing and peace be upon you, O Messenger of God.
> Thousandfold blessing and thousandfold peace upon you and
>   upon your people,
> and God's felicity upon your Companions,
> O best of the chosen of God (Glassé: 317).

> *Muhammad earned one of his names even before he became a religious prophet. Those who knew him as an honest, young caravan trader called him* al-Amin, *the Trustworthy One.*

Other Names

The name Muhammad means "highly praised one." In the Muslim world, however, people often refer to Muhammad simply as "the Prophet." Or they may use a variety of honorific names. Muslim tradition has assigned Muhammad close to two hundred other names. These names, or titles, highlight his earthly mission or his character. Muslims often refer to their Prophet by these names rather than by his given name, Muhammad. They include *Habib Allah* (Beloved of God), *an-Nabi* (the Prophet), *ar-Rasul* (the Messenger), *Sayyed al-Kawnayn* (the Lord of the Two Worlds), *Miftah ar-Rahmah* (the Key of Mercy), *Miftah al-Jannah* (the Key of Paradise), *Sayf Allah* (the Sword of God), *Sa'd Allah* (the Joy of God), *Dhikr Allah* (Remembrance of God), *Ruh al-Haqq* (Spirit of Truth), *Sahib al-Miraj* (He of the Night Ascent), and *Khatim al-Anbiya* (the Seal of the Prophets). This last name underlines the Muslim teaching that Muhammad is the last prophet that God sent to humanity. According to the teachings of Islam, no genuine prophets will follow afterwards. For that reason many Muslims do not accept any religion founded after Islam as divinely inspired.

Chapter 16
The Other Prophets,
Angels, and Jinn

Prophets Recognized by Islam

Although Muslims recognize Muhammad as their supreme prophet whose revelation surpasses those given by others, they also honor many other biblical figures as prophets. These include Jesus (Isa) and John the Baptist (Yahya) from the
Christian New Testament, as well as numerous figures from the Jewish scriptures, which Christians call the Old Testament. The Hebrew (or Old Testament)
leaders numbered as prophets by Islam include Abraham (Ibrahim), Adam, David
(Da'ud), Elijah (Ilyas), Elisha (Alyasa), Enoch (Idris), Ezekiel (Dhu-l-Kifl), Ezra
(Uzair), Isaac (Ishaq), Ishmael (Isma'il), Jacob (Ya'qub), Job (Ayyub), Jonah (Yunus), Joseph (Yusuf), Lot (Lut), Moses (Musa), Noah (Nuh), and Solomon (Sulayman). Islam also honors three Arab prophets sent before Muhammad: Salih,
Hud, and Shu'ayb (Jethro). After speaking or writing the names of one of these
prophets, it is customary to add the phrase, "peace be upon him."

Certain passages in the Quran promote religious tolerance. In one passage, for
example, God insists that He has sent a prophet to every people (Quran 4:47).
Moreover, Muslims are told to heed the prophets and to make no distinction
between them (Quran 2:285). Since even Muhammad was not told the names
of all the prophets, each religion must be treated with respect. In the Quran,
God declares:

Foreign words used in the text are defined in the Glossary, pages 423-40.

181

These miniature paintings — a nearly extinct art — were done in Pyrenees, France, by Edmond Tiffou.

Left: Noah (Nuh), the Preacher of God.

Right: Jonah (Yunus) is swallowed up by a large fish (not a whale).

Opposite page: Abraham (Ibrahim), the Friend of God, is shown about to sacrifice his son. The angel Gabriel, at the right holding a ram, descends from heaven.

We have sent revelations to you as We sent
Revelations to Noah and the prophets (who came) after him;
and We sent revelations to Abraham
and Ishmael and Isaac and Jacob, and their offspring,
and to Jesus and Job,
and to Jonah and Aaron and Solomon,
and to David We gave the Book of Psalms,
And to many an apostle We have mentioned before,
and to many other apostles We have not mentioned to you;
and to Moses God spoke directly.
All these apostles of good news and admonition
Were sent so that after the apostles
Men may have no argument against God.
God is all-powerful and all-wise (Quran 4:163-65, Ali trans.).

The Most Important Prophets

Six of the biblical prophets stand out as having special importance to Islam. Accordingly, they have been assigned special names. These names reflect the Muslim view of their prophetic mission. They are Adam, the Chosen of God; Noah, the Preacher of God; Abraham, the Friend of God; Moses, the Speaker of God; Jesus, the Word of God; and Muhammad, the Apostle of God. Muhammad, of course, is the most honored and revered of these six. As discussed above, Muslims have given Muhammad hundreds of other honorary names as well.

ذبيحة إبراهيم عليه السلام

Jesus is the second most honored prophet after Muhammad. Muslims also refer to Jesus as Spirit of God, Messiah, and Speech of Truth. Nevertheless, Muslims do not recognize Jesus as the Son of God (as Christians do), nor do they consider him in any way divine.

A Muslim artist's depiction of the angel Gabriel.

Angels

Belief in angels is central to Islam. The Quran itself is believed to have been delivered to Muhammad by the angel Gabriel. According to traditional Islamic belief, the angels do not have free will and are thus totally obedient to God in service and in worship. Some Muslims accept the notion that two angels accompany each person throughout his or her life. One angel records the good deeds and words, the other the bad deeds and words. These angels accompany the human soul on Judgment Day, when they will read their scrolls out loud before the throne of God.

Jinn

The jinn are spirits. We get our English word "genie" from the Arabic word jinn. Belief in the jinn existed before Muhammad and was incorporated into Islam. In a number of passages from the Quran, God addresses himself to both humans and jinn. Chapter 72, entitled "The Jinn," describes how some of the jinn adopted Muhammad's teaching after hearing him recite passages from the Quran. Islamic tradition teaches that God sent Muhammad to both humankind and to the jinn, to show them both the path to salvation.

In Muslim folklore the jinn prefer to reside in nature, at places connecting the earth's surface and its depths, thereby linking our world and the underworld. These kinds of places include caves, groves of trees, wells, springs, mountain passages, valleys, and desserts. Jinn prefer dark places and may also live near graves. In addition they may haunt fireplaces, or any place associated with water, such as a latrine or a bathhouse. Most of the time they are formless and invisible to humans, but may take the form of beautiful women, shifty looking men, giants, animals, or insects.

Though the jinn eat, drink and reproduce just as humans do, the jinn have magical powers that human beings lack. Human beings do well to approach them with caution, as the jinn vary widely in their attitude towards human beings. Some jinn are inclined to help humans, but others tend to hurt them; for example, by bringing on an illness. In the past, mental illnesses in particular were said to be caused by the jinn. Ill-tempered jinn also delight in causing mishaps, or by working some form of trickery upon the humans that have disturbed them. The attitude of each jinn depends on its personality, mood, and the way in which it was brought into contact with humans. Like human beings, jinn have religious preferences and will face judgment after death. Some jinn are Muslims, but others are Christians, Jews, or pagans. They are said to sit on the wall of heaven, trying to catch the words that God speaks to the angels. According to folk belief, when angels throw heavenly objects at the jinn to chase them away, the humans on the earth below see shooting stars.

Muslim folklore teaches that a devout life and manner are the best way to protect oneself against the ill-tempered jinn. In the past, people wore amulets as a means of protection against the jinn. A few people still consider a bloody handprint near the door of the house to be a good way to hold back the jinn that might seek to harm a newborn. Animal sacrifices may also help to appease an irritable jinn. Some still follow an old Middle Eastern custom of asking permission from the jinn when building a new home, pitching a tent, or establishing any new dwelling place. They call out, *dastur ya sahib al-mahall*, an Arabic phrase which means "with your permission, O owner of this place!"

Chapter 17
Greetings and Sayings

Shake Hands, Kiss, or Nod

Greeting customs vary by country, culture, and by the degree of closeness and trust in the relationship between two people. In the Arab world people may greet same sex friends with a handshake, or an embrace and a kiss on the cheek. Unrelated men and women will usually not kiss one another in greeting, although some will shake hands. Conservative Muslims may not want to shake hands with someone of the opposite sex. This is not an indication of unfriendliness, but rather reflects their adherence to a strict code of modesty when dealing with the opposite sex. A man introduced to another man's wife should take his cue from her. If she does not extend her hand, then a nod or a few words to acknowledge her presence is all that is required. When greeting someone of the opposite sex some very conservative Muslims will avoid looking directly at him or her, or will take only a quick glance.

Opposite page: Two worshipers from Khasab, Oman, greet each other with a hand shake after Friday noon prayers.

In Iran a bow or nod made while shaking hands indicates respect. In Pakistan, men may place their right hands over their hearts while greeting one another, a gesture which symbolizes friendship. In Indonesia, people often shake hands, and then touch their heart with their right hand. Although Indonesian men and women do shake hands, little other contact between men and women takes place in public. In Uzbekistan, one places one's left hand over one's heart and extends the right to shake hands.

Foreign words used in the text are defined in the Glossary, pages 423-40.

As-Salam Alaykum

Muslims typically greet each other with the Arabic phrase *as-salam alaykum*, which means "peace be upon you." The proper response is *wa-alaykum as-salam*, "peace be upon you too." The Quran instructs believers to address each other with a peace greeting. Such a greeting is meant to reflect the serenity that comes to Muslims through their submission to God. It also heralds the peaceful relations that should exist between all Muslims. According to one tradition, Muslims only offer this greeting to other Muslims. What's more, some strict authorities believe that a Muslim should not offer any greeting to a non-Muslim unless that person has saluted him or her first. Nevertheless, it is difficult to generalize about the way in which Muslims greet each other and non-Muslims. Muslims around the world tend to follow the norms of the societies in which they live.

In this large indoor/outdoor panel, the dark lettering is a naskhi variant of the basmallah. The lighter thin swirly lines are decorative only.

Basmallah

The Arabic phrase *Bismillah al-Rahman al-Rahim* means, "In the name of God, the merciful, the compassionate." Called the basmallah for short, this phrase opens every chapter of the Quran except chapter nine. Muslims utter the basmallah to bless many of their daily undertakings. Businessmen and women may say it before embarking upon sales, agreements, and various commercial enterprises. Pronounced before eating a meal, it functions in the same way as saying grace does for Christians. Taxicab and rickshaw operators may have the basmallah, or the number 786, which symbolizes it, posted in their vehicles. Students sometimes write 786 on their essays and tests. A hadith of the Prophet illuminates the centrality of the basmallah to Islam:

> All that is in the Revealed Books [other divinely revealed scriptures, such as the Bible] is contained in the Quran, all that is in the Quran is contained in the opening surah (*fatiha*) [opening chapter of the Quran], all that is in the fatiha is contained in the basmala (Chebel 2000: 19).

Inshallah

The Arabic phrase *in sha Allah* (or *inshallah*) means, "if God wills." Muslims often use this phrase when making plans for the future. Such plans might entail promising to meet with or do something for someone else, forming a resolution about one's own behavior, making a pledge, or deciding to start a new project. The *inshallah* reminds Muslims that every plan requires God's approval for its success and that they depend on God for all things.

Ma Sha Allah

Ma sha Allah essentially means "whatever God wants to be, he gives." Muslims use this Arabic phrase to express surprise and wonder, to convey congratulations, and to express humble gratitude for their success. It, too, acknowledges that all blessings and all achievements come from God. Some Muslims place a plaque with the phrase "ma sha Allah" inscribed upon it near the door of their home, office, or place of business. The sign conveys their thanks for the blessings that have been given them.

Allahu Akbar

The Arabic phrase *Allahu akbar* means, "God is most great" or "God is greater than all." It is sometimes referred to as the *takbir*. The literal translation of "Allahu akbar" is, "God is greater than. . . ." The implication is that whatever one should compare with God, God will be the greater of the two. When the muezzin calls faithful Muslims to their five-times-a-day prayers, his cry begins with "Allahu akbar!" Muslims repeat the phrase in their prayers, acknowledging the unsurpassed power and majesty of God. These words are not reserved for prayers, however. Muslims use them throughout the day to express joy, and to offer praise or to signal approval. According to Muslim law, the phrase should also be said before beginning to slaughter an animal destined for human consumption.

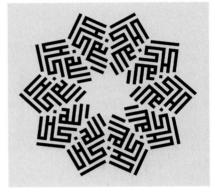

Allahu akbar, "God is most great" (Square Kufi), based on the 14th-century tile design in the ceiling of Iwan in the Friday Mosque, Isfahan.

Al-Hamdu Lillah

Many Muslims say *al-hamdu Lillah*, "Thanks be to God" or "Praise be to God," upon completing important tasks. People may also use the phrase when reporting to another that they are in good health. The full phrase, *al-hamdu Lillahi Rabb il-Alameen*, means "Praise be to Allah, the Lord of the Worlds." After the basmallah, it constitutes the first sentence in the first chapter of the Quran.

Barakallah

Barakallah, literally "the blessing of God," is used to mean "God bless you." It is often used as a means of expressing appreciation and thanks to others.

Chapter 18
Clothing and Adornment

Men's Clothing

Muslim religious teachings advise men to dress and behave modestly. A man's cultural background as well as his own vision of what constitutes modest dress will help him determine what is appropriate. Among Muslims it is widely believed that men should cover themselves from their navels to their knees at all times while in public. In addition, some Muslims think that men should not wear pure silk, gold, and certain gems. They believe that these adornments should be reserved for women. Some Muslim men wear a beard to honor Muhammad, who also wore a beard. Not all Muslims view this as a religious requirement, however.

Opposite page: The students at Muslim Seminary in Lanzhou, China, are seen wearing a headdress combination of a skullcap, scarf, and turban. Above is a skullcap.

Many Muslim men cover their heads when at prayer. This practice is meant to show modesty. Some, though not all, Muslim men, cover their heads at all times. The coverings vary from cloth skullcaps to turbans, scarves, and various kinds of caps. The kind of head coverings worn by Muslim men varies by country and cultural tradition. Members of Afghanistan's Taliban movement were expected to wear turbans. Muslim clerics from Iran also wear turbans. A black or green turban often signifies that the wearer is a descendant of Muhammad. Other Muslim men wear white turbans. Not everyone who wears a turban is a Muslim. Male members of the Sikh religion, a separate and distinct faith that developed in northwestern India, also wear turbans and beards. Prayer caps and skullcaps are particularly popular with African-American Muslims, and also with many Asian Muslims. Men who have returned from the Hajj pilgrim-

Foreign words used in the text are defined in the Glossary, pages 423-40.

191

Turban

Skullcap

Cloth prayer cap

Chupan

Hajj cap

White keffiyah

age may wear a special cap called a Hajj cap. This cap signifies their completion of the pilgrimage, their commitment to an Islamic way of life, and their status as a respected community member. Men from Jordan and Palestine often favor *keffiyahs*, large red and white scarves. Other people have begun to wear them to indicate their support for the people of Palestine. Traditional male dress in Saudi Arabia and its neighboring countries includes a white keffiyah worn over the head and secured with a dark-colored headband.

Women's Clothing

The Quran gives only a rough outline of how women should dress. Both men and women are asked to "lower their gaze," that is, to modestly avoid staring at one another. Women are also asked to "draw their veil over their bosom" and to refrain from showing off "their ornaments" (Quran 24:30-31, 35:59, Ali trans.). Many commentators have noted that before the rise of Islam, Arab women wore clothing that revealed their breasts. They argue that the Quran rejects this practice. The reference to a woman's "ornaments" is interpreted by some — but not all — Muslims to refer to her hair. The requirement of modest female dress applies only in public, the idea being that women should not seek to make themselves sexually attractive to the men they might encounter there. At home with family members, women may dress as they please.

There is disagreement among Muslims worldwide as to the exact nature of the requirements for female modesty. Some believe that Western dress or local ethnic clothing styles, as long as they are not too revealing, are acceptable. Others believe that only a woman's hands and face should show while she is in public. Women who accept this belief often cover their head, neck, and hair with a large scarf which has come to be known as a *hijab*. This Arabic word can mean several different things to Muslims. Translated literally it means "screen," "separation," "cover," or "partition." It may also refer to traditional Islamic dress codes for women, or compliance with those codes.

Muslim women who believe that they must completely cover themselves as well as hide the lines of their body sometimes wear a full length, long-sleeve robe known as a *jilbab* or an *abaya* over their street clothes. In Iran many women wear a *chador*, a full-length black cape that also covers the head and hair. Still other Muslims take the modesty requirement even further and believe that women should cover their face as well as their head and hair. Women who accept this belief add a face veil, called a *niqab*, to their clothing, which leaves only the eyes and forehead visible. Or they may wear a *burqa*, a garment that covers a woman from head to toe, with a meshwork grill area over the eyes to permit some vision.

The two young ladies have their head, neck, and hair covered with a large scarf called a hijab.

In some Muslim countries women do not have the choice to interpret the requirements of modest female dress for themselves. For example, in Iran, the law specifies that only a woman's hands and face may show while she is in public. During the 1980s Iranian women were required to wear a chador, though now

193

they may cover themselves with other loose-fitting clothing if they wish. In Saudi Arabia the law empowers religious police to enforce a dress code stipulating that women cover their head and hair as well as their bodies from the neck down while in public. In Afghanistan, the recently toppled Taliban government required women to wear the burqa. In many places in the Muslim world social pressure keeps Islamic dress codes in place, even if they are not legally mandated.

This woman is wearing a chador, *a full-length black cape that covers her head and hair, as well as a face veil, called a* niqab, *which leaves only her eyes and forehead visible.*

Some Muslim women choose to cover their hair for religious reasons, even when it is not legally or socially required of them. Social norms in non-Muslim countries may make this somewhat difficult for them. In France, newly proposed laws may in the future affect Muslim women's ability to wear the hijab. In addition, in December of 2003, a French government panel recommended banning Muslim head scarves and all other prominent forms of religious dress—such as large crosses and yarmulkes—in public schools. The French government views the proposed new law as a means of protecting the separation of religion and government. Some French Muslims have protested the plan. Others are not bothered by it, and some support it.

In at least one predominantly Muslim country, the Republic of Turkey, there are laws against veiling. These laws restrict women from wearing headscarves while performing certain activities. They forbid women to wear head coverings while taking university exams or working in government jobs. The government of the Republic of Turkey, a secular state since its founding in the 1920s, has long lobbied against the wearing of head scarves.

Some commentators have noticed that in a number of Muslim countries the number of women voluntarily wearing the hijab has increased over the past several decades. They attribute this phenomenon to the rise in interest in Islamic solutions to social ills that have occurred during this period. The subject of appropriate dress for women, and the question of whether or not traditional Islamic dress is liberating or sexist, are issues that many Muslims are currently debating.

Henna

Henna is an herb that is used for cosmetic purposes in much of the Muslim world, even though it has no formal connection with Islam. In many predominantly Muslim countries, Christians and members of other faiths also use

The night before her wedding, this Egyptian bride-to-be has her palms and fingertips hennaed, and her feet banded with the dyestuff mixture.

henna. Historians believe that the use of the herb in the Middle East predates the rise of Islam. Believers in the new religion continued to use it. Fatima, Muhammad's daughter, is said to have decorated her hands with henna. Some say that the Prophet Muhammad dyed his hair and beard red with henna.

In some Muslim countries henna designs are an everyday form of female beautification. In others they are reserved for special occasions like weddings, births, and festivals, such as Eid al-Fitr. In certain locales men returning from the Hajj color their beards with henna.

In Arab cultures, brides customarily adorn their hands and feet with elaborate henna designs on the night before their wedding. So common is this custom that the bridal eve is often called *laylat al-hinna*, the "night of the henna." The designs are made by crushing henna leaves and mixing them with lemon juice or some other liquid. Then the fluid henna paste is dabbed onto the fingernails and the skin in elaborate arabesque designs. When the paste is later removed the nails and skin retain a reddish brown stain that lasts for a couple of weeks. Bridal decorations are so intricate that they may take hours to apply. Muslim as well as non-Muslim brides in India and Pakistan may also decorate themselves with henna.

Many Arab families enjoy scenting their home with incense.

Perfume

Tradition recounts that drinking in the smell of perfume was one of the Prophet's great pleasures in life. In modern Arab culture, both men and women enjoy and use scent. Sometimes men will carry little bottles of perfume with them and offer their friends a sniff. When guests enter a home in some Arab countries they will sometimes be welcomed with rose water, which they pat on their necks and faces to refresh themselves. Many Arab families enjoy scenting their home with incense. Perfume is a popular gift. Muslim tradition recommends that after washing oneself in preparation to attend Friday services at the mosque, one dab on a bit of cologne or perfume.

Chapter 19
Separation of the Sexes

In Public

In many Muslim nations — especially in the Arab world — some gender segregation takes place in public places. Mosques furnish separate areas for men and women to perform their prayers, and some restaurants, theaters, and public beaches are divided up into male-only and family sections. Older children and teens often attend single sex classes or schools. In addition, a number of public places, for example cafes, are generally frequented by men only. These practices accord with the emphasis that Islam places on male and female modesty by eliminating situations in which unmarried men and women could encounter and perhaps become sexually attracted to one another.

The degree to which gender segregation is observed in a particular country or region not only varies according to culture, but also often varies according to social class and religious beliefs. Generally speaking, urbanites and those who espouse a more progressive interpretation of Islam are less likely than rural people and conservative Muslims to practice strict gender segregation.

In Muslim societies people often spend quite a lot of time socializing with family and extended family members. Among related people, men and women may socialize in mixed groups. Unrelated men and women, however, will tend to socialize with same sex friends rather than in mixed groups. Married men and women will generally not hold hands, kiss, or otherwise touch or show affection for one another in public. For the most part, such behavior would be viewed as immodest and as an indication of the couple's questionable moral standards. For

A woman prays in a curtained-off section of the Niu Jie Mosque, the largest of the 40 mosques that served Beijing's 180,000-strong Islamic community in 1985.

Foreign words used in the text are defined in the Glossary, pages 423-40.

unmarried couples, the judgment would be harsher. In some places in the Muslim world men sometimes walk ahead of their wives instead of by their side. While this is often interpreted as a sign of superior male status, it should be noted that cultural insiders view it as an expression of the man's responsibility to protect his wife. By contrast, it is perfectly acceptable to walk down the street holding hands with a friend of the same sex in many Arab countries. While in the United States such behavior might be deemed an expression of homosexual feelings, in these countries it is an indication of close friendship and nothing more.

In some Muslim countries there may be public places where unaccompanied women generally do not go, or times of day when they are not expected to be seen in public. In some Arab countries, for example, many men assume that any woman out in public alone after dark is a prostitute. Furthermore, there may be cafes, restaurants, and other public places in which men spend leisure time that women generally do not enter. Women who violate these unspoken rules may find their motives questioned and may be treated poorly. Nevertheless, it must be pointed out that there are other Muslim nations outside the Arab world in which the cultural rules concerning women's appearance in public places are less restrictive.

At Home

In past times, wealthy and urban Muslim homes often had a sitting room and perhaps other rooms reserved just for female family members and their guests. Male guests could not enter this area, which was referred to as *harim*; this word comes from *haram*, Arabic for "restricted," "sacred," or "forbidden." The English word "harem" developed from these terms. Male family members entertained their guests in another part of the house. This custom helped to preserve the segregation of the sexes at home, while ensuring that guests received hospitable treatment. Home layouts of this sort can still be found in some parts of the Muslim world.

In some Muslim families, women will absent themselves when male visitors come to the house. If a meal is offered, the women and children may eat separately, after the men of the household and their visitors have been served. Some observers interpret this custom as a sign of female inferiority, but some people from the cultures in question say that the real reason the practice exists is to preserve female modesty and to uphold the tradition of segregating unrelated men and women. In some parts of the Muslim world, very traditionally oriented families still practice an old custom whereby even if guests are not present, the men of the family eat first, and the women and children eat after they are finished. This is by no means the case everywhere, however. In many Muslim homes worldwide, family life is completely integrated.

Chapter 20
Beliefs and Practices
Concerning the Body

Cleanliness and Purity

Islam places a good deal of emphasis on personal cleanliness. For example, prayers are not considered valid if the proper cleansing ritual is not performed beforehand. Muhammad is reported to have advised Muslims that "the key to Paradise is prayer and the key to prayer is cleanliness."

Cleanliness is about more than the literal removal of dirt, however. Contact with that which is considered impure will make a Muslim temporarily unclean. In this state he or she cannot pray, which effectively cuts off his or her access to God. For example, contact with a corpse, a pig, or dog saliva places a Muslim into a state of impurity. So does giving in to disbelief. In order to return to a state of purity, Muslims perform one of the ritual washings used before formal prayer. Because according to Muslim law menstruating women are in a state of impurity, women are excused from prayer during their periods. Traditionally oriented Sunni religious experts often insist that they should also refrain from entering mosques at this time, though more progressive thinkers may disagree. Certain conservative Muslims consider all non-Muslims to be in a perpetual state of impurity because they have not adopted the beliefs and practices of Islam. As a result of these beliefs, some of them will refrain from shaking hands with non-Muslims. Some

In the shade of the grape arbor in Havana, Cuba, a worshiper performs his ablutions before entering the city's only functioning mosque, 1995.

Foreign words used in the text are defined in the Glossary, pages 423-40.

conservative Shia Muslims believe that they must perform the ritualized washing required for prayer (*wudu*) after touching non-Muslims, because this contact renders them temporarily impure.

Beyond preparation for prayer, Islam advocates cleanliness as a way of life. According to custom Muslims should wash their private parts with water after urinating and defecating. Custom also encourages the shaving or removal of the hair that grows in the pubic area, again out of concern for cleanliness. Frequent cleansing of the mouth or brushing the teeth is also advocated. Clean, trimmed nails are also recommended, as is a trimmed beard for men. According to a hadith of the Prophet, "cleanliness is half of faith."

A traditional bathhouse or hammam (opposite page) in Beit el-Dine, Lebanon.

The need for proper facilities in which to wash encouraged the early Arab Muslims to adopt from the ancient Romans the custom of building at least one public bathhouse in each settlement. Towns and cities commonly hosted many bathhouses which were used by all, rich and poor alike. In the days before homes were fitted with indoor plumbing, the public bathhouse, with its ample supplies of water and hot baths, elevated the level of personal hygiene in Muslim societies above that enjoyed in many European societies. The public bathhouse, or *hammam*, still serves an important function in some places in the Muslim world.

> *Islam advocates cleanliness as a way of life. According to a hadith of the Prophet, "cleanliness is half of faith."*

Left and Right

In many traditionally Muslim societies, the left hand is considered unclean. This association came about because people customarily used their left hand to clean themselves after going to the bathroom. In spite of the fact that people washed their hands afterwards, the left hand retained its association with dirtiness. Therefore, in Muslim societies one should avoid bringing food to the mouth or serving oneself from the common plate with the left hand. It is also considered impolite to give someone something with the left hand, touch someone, or use the left hand to convey a greeting. One old folk tradition advises that when using the bathroom, one should enter with the left foot, and exit with the right foot.

Custom deems the right side of the body to be better and cleaner than the left. A practice that sprang from this belief is that of stepping across the threshold of a mosque using one's right foot and exiting with one's left foot. Similarly, the devout make sure to enter a saint's shrine by stepping over the threshold with their right foot. Many people perform their ablutions for prayer by cleansing the right hand before the left, and so on.

Feet

In the Arab world and many other Muslim countries as well, one should take care that the soles of one's feet never point towards anyone. This gesture is considered insulting. For the same reason, the soles of one's feet should never be pointed towards a copy of the Quran.

Hair

In traditional Muslim societies, a woman's hair was thought to be one of her most sexually stimulating features. For that reason, some Mulims interpret the Islamic requirement of female modesty as a command that women keep their hair covered while in public. Only a woman's husband and her family were allowed to see and enjoy this component of her beauty.

Alterations

Some Muslims frown on tattooing, plucking the eyebrows, or undergoing plastic surgery intended to improve one's looks. They believe that Muhammad argued against these procedures on the basis that they were all intended to permanently alter God's creation. Some thinkers use similar arguments against the practice of female circumcision.

Chapter 21
The Evil Eye, Amulets, and Charms

The Evil Eye

Folk beliefs concerning the evil eye are common throughout the countries surrounding the Mediterranean Sea and extend from the Middle East to South Asia. (They are found in other parts of the world as well.) These beliefs suggest that when an envious or ill-intentioned person looks upon something or someone, their glance is capable of inflicting harm or passing on bad luck. Though anyone can do this to a certain degree, some people are said to possess the "evil eye," that is, to have especially strong powers in this regard. In many cultures, people with certain physical characteristics, such as blue eyes or eyebrows that run together, are believed to have the evil eye. Older women are often suspected of having this power. The usual targets for the evil eye include babies, children, pregnant women, brides, bridegrooms, and all others whose attractiveness, wealth, or distinctions might inspire envy. According to one hadith, Muhammad accepted the existence of the evil eye as a fact.

Protection from the Evil Eye

In order to avoid being suspected of envy and the evil eye, good manners dictate that one avoid staring at people and refrain from offering repeated compliments. (This is especially true regarding one's behavior towards those most vulnerable to the evil eye—babies, brides, etc.) One may safely offer a compliment or recognize an achievement by following it up with the Arabic phrase *ma*

Foreign words used in the text are defined in the Glossary, pages 423-40.

sha Allah. If one person repeatedly compliments another without saying *ma sha Allah*, or expresses envy in any other way, the complimented person may be able to ward off the evil eye by saying *Allah umma salli ala an-Nabi*, "God's blessing and grace upon the Prophet." Hand gestures; the burning of incense; amulets; the use of fire, salt, metal, or jewels; the color blue; tattoo marks; and the number five may also be invoked to deflect the evil eye.

Good Manners When Looking

Folk notions concerning the evil eye may be related to more general cultural beliefs about seeing. Some anthropologists have suggested that in Mediterranean cultures, under certain circumstances, looking—and especially staring—is viewed as an aggressive act. If an unrelated man stares at a woman (or vice versa), this prolonged glance may be considered a form of sexual advance. This view finds some support in the Quran (24:30-31) and is endorsed by pious Muslims. Therefore, unrelated men and women will usually avoid gazing at one another. Devout single people, even if formally introduced, may take no more than a single glance at one another.

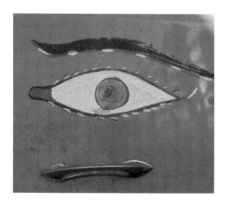

Although this stylized blue eye is not a piece of jewelry that can be worn, it, along with other symbols, can be seen painted on the doors of trucks in Saudi Arabia.

Amulet Controversies

An amulet is a small, symbolic object—often a piece of jewelry or a charm—believed to ward off harmful forces or attract good forces and good fortune. The use of amulets can be found in many different cultural and religious groups around the world. They are usually worn close to the body, and sometimes may be hidden from view. Many strict Muslims disapprove of the wearing of amulets. They feel that the use of such devices implies trust in something other than God. One hadith implies that Muhammad himself rejected the faith of those who wore amulets. Nevertheless, amulets are fairly common throughout the Muslim world.

Popular Types of Amulets

One popular amulet takes the shape of a stylized, blue eye. Its primary purpose is to guard wearers against the "evil eye," that is, the envious glance of another person which folk belief insists has the power to inflict harm. The color blue is said to confer protection. The eye shape symbolically reflects the envy back on to the envier. Another evil eye amulet is shaped like a slipper (often with a blue stone set in it). The slipper shape symbolically "kicks" the envier. Asian and African folklore teaches that the semiprecious blue-green stone called turquoise provides protection against the evil eye and attracts luck. Turquoise is also a popular amulet stone in the Middle East.

The "hand of Fatima" amulet is shaped like a stylized hand. Named after Muhammad's daughter Fatima, this charm is said to offer its wearer protection against various ills, including the evil eye. The thumb stands for Muhammad. The four fingers originally represented the four most respected women in the Muslim faith: Fatima, Khadijah (Fatima's mother), the Virgin Mary (Jesus' mother), and Asiya (the wife of Pharaoh, who saved the infant Moses from the Nile River). Among some Muslims, Asiya and the Virgin Mary have been replaced by Hasan and Hussein, the sons of Fatima. Another interpretation of the hand amulet suggests that its five fingers stand for the Five Pillars of Islam. Sometimes an eye is added to the hand of a Fatima amulet. The hand of Fatima is particularly popular with Shia Muslims.

A small sheet of metal cut into a disk, square, hand, rectangle, or an abstract shape may also serve as an amulet. These charms are often inscribed with secret names, symbols, or numbers believed to possess special powers. Some of these amulets offer protection against sickness, mishaps, envy, various kinds of losses, or demons. Others help to attract success, love, or health. People usually obtain these amulets from shayks, dervishes, and members of religious orders, who prepare them specially for the wearer. In rural areas many Muslim parents protect their children with amulets.

Another kind of amulet popular among Muslims consists of a tiny leather or metal container used to carry scraps of paper or parchment onto which verses of the Quran have been written. The names of God, prayers to God, or the names of angels frequently appear on these pieces of paper, too. Strict Muslims usually don't object to these amulets, as they invoke the power of God for protection. Out of respect for the divine, some Muslims assert that these kinds of amulets should be removed before entering a bathroom, as bathrooms are thought to be unclean places.

Another kind of amulet popular among Muslims consists of a tiny leather or metal container used to carry scraps of paper or parchment onto which verses of the Quran have been written.

Some people leave little tokens behind after visiting the shrine of a martyr, Sufi saint, prophet, or shaykh. These often take the form of a ribbon or padlock attached to the fence or building surrounding the grave. People fasten them while praying for the fulfillment of a certain request. The ribbons and locks transfer the prayer request to the person buried in the grave, urging him or her to pray to God that the request be granted. Sometimes people write their prayer requests on pieces of paper and leave these in the shrine.

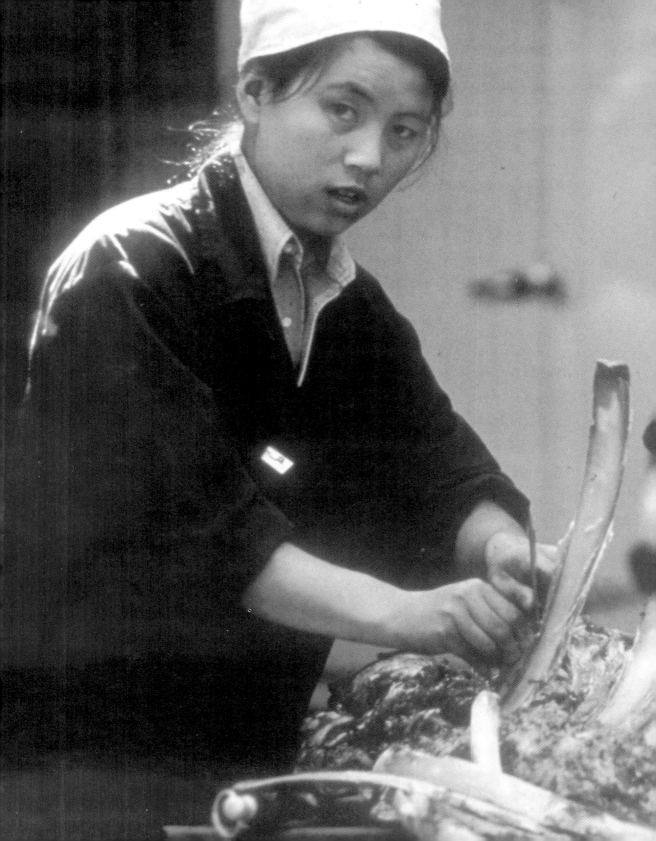

Chapter 22
Food

Forbidden and Permitted Foods

Islam forbids its followers to consume certain foods. These forbidden substances are referred to in Arabic as *haram*, which means restricted or forbidden. Permitted foods are called *halal*. Anything that is not expressly forbidden is considered halal. Forbidden foods include pork, predatory animals and birds, dead animals (that is, animals that died in ways other than having been slaughtered by a human being), alcoholic beverages of any kind, and blood. Muslims should also refrain from using intoxicating drugs. Meat slaughtered according to Muslim ritual is always preferred over other kinds of meat.

The Islamic manner of slaughtering an animal is to cut its throat with a sharp knife in one quick motion, while invoking the name of Allah. The invocation usually combines the basmallah and the takbir. Afterwards the blood should be drained from the animal. While meat butchered according to Islamic ritual — called halal meat — is preferred, Jewish kosher meats are an acceptable substitute if halal meat is not available. If kosher meat is not available, Muslims may eat regularly butchered meat, so long as it was not dedicated to any person or to any god other than Allah. Game procured while hunting is also acceptable, as long as the hunter invoked the name of God before making the kill.

Opposite page: A young Hui woman from Xian, China, works in a halal meat stall where the meat has been butchered according to Islamic ritual.

Foreign words used in the text are defined in the Glossary, pages 423-40.

Avoidance of Forbidden Foods

Some Muslims are uncomfortable eating in the home of non-Muslims for fear of being served unacceptable foods. They may also scrutinize labels on prepared foods very carefully, in order to determine whether pork fat or gelatin (which may contain pork by-products) was used in their preparation. Very observant Muslims may refrain from eating in restaurants where alcohol is served or working in places where it is sold or served.

Chapter 23
The Life Cycle and Conversion

Birth

When a child is born, Muslim parents traditionally whisper the *shahada* (the Muslim declaration of faith) into its ears. These are the first words the newborn infant hears. Some families will instead whisper the Muslim call to prayer. Both acts confirm the importance of religion in the life of the child. Some families whisper the call to prayer in the baby's right ear, and the *iqamah*, which is the formula recited just before formal prayer begins, in the baby's left ear. (The iqamah is the same as the call to prayer, except that the line "prayer has started" is added to the end.) In doing so they are following the example of Muhammad, who is reported to have done this upon the birth of his grandson Hasan. The Prophet also took a bit of chewed date and placed it in the infant's mouth. Some families follow this custom as well. Then prayers for the baby's health and protection are offered. Many families recite the first chapter of the Quran. Informal prayers are also usually offered for the baby's well-being.

A week after the birth of a baby, many Muslim families hold a naming ceremony (*aqiqah* in Arabic). Family members and friends are invited to attend. Guests often bring gifts for the newborn. The call to prayer is recited again along with the iqamah. A little bit of honey, or a bit of mashed date, may be fed to the infant. Many families practice a custom whereby the baby's hair is shaved and weighed during the ceremony. Then the family donates to charity an amount

Foreign words used in the text are defined in the Glossary, pages 423-40.

of silver equal to the weight of the baby's hair. The Prophet was said to have practiced this last custom, hence its importance for devout Muslims who have the means to follow his example. Families may sacrifice a sheep or a goat, and use some of the meat to host a festive dinner for their guests. A portion of this meat is also given to charity. Traditionally one animal was sacrificed for the birth of a girl; two for a boy. In Egypt mothers distribute packets of dried nuts to their guests, as a symbol of fertility. In Uzbekistan families celebrate with a large meal and party on the ninth day after the baby's birth. The mother appears again for the first time since the birth with the baby strapped to a brightly colored wooden cradle.

The aqiqah ceremony dates back to pre-Islamic Arabia. Muhammad incorporated the custom into Islam by linking it with Abraham's sacrifice and declaring it an expression of gratitude to God for the birth of a new baby.

Forty days after giving birth, new mothers undergo a thorough cleansing (ghusl). Childbirth is thought to render a woman unclean, so until she performs this ritual the new mother is excused from the obligation to offer formal prayers.

In Turkey, women are expected to stay in the house for 40 days after childbirth, until this ritual washing takes place.

Names and Naming

Muslims often give their boys names that have religious meanings. Boys' names sometimes make reference to one of the many names, or attributes, of God. A number of boys' names combine the Arabic word for servant, *abd*, with one of these names. For example, the name Abdullah means "servant of Allah." Another popular boy's name, Abdul Karim, means "servant of the bountiful." The names of other prophets mentioned in the Quran and the names of important figures from Muslim history are also used. Boys are frequently named Muhammad, after the Prophet. Some people believe that Muslims' strong preference for this name has made it the most popular boy's name in the world. Other common boys' names include Ibrahim (Abraham), Ali (son-in-law of Muhammad), Musa (Moses), Da'ud (David), Yusuf (Joseph), Ishaq (Isaac), Hasan (grandson of Muhammad), and Husayn (grandson of Muhammad).

> *Muhammad incorporated the naming ceremony into Islam, declaring it an expression of gratitude to God for the birth of a new baby.*

Girls are sometimes named after Muhammad's female relatives. For instance, they may be called Fatima after Muhammad's daughter, or Khadijah after his first wife, or Aisha after his youngest wife. Maryam, the Arabic form of the name of Jesus' mother, is another popular religious name. Some parents give girls names that refer to virtues becoming to women, such as Haleema, which means "gentle." Other religious names include feminine versions of the attributes (99 names) of God. For example, *al-Kareem* ("the Generous") can be turned into the feminine name Kareema; *al-Raheem* ("the Compassionate") gives rise to the feminine name Raheema; and *al-Azeez* ("the Powerful and Precious") has inspired the name Azeeza. Other popular girls' names are less tied to religion. These include Jameelah, "beautiful," and Yasmeen, "Jasmine."

When adults convert to Islam, they often choose, or are given, a Muslim name. This tradition is patterned after a custom of the Prophet. In his day, many Arabs had distinctly pagan names that made references to tribal gods and goddesses. If this was the case, Muhammad gave the convert a new name. If not, Muhammad sometimes, though not always, added a distinctly Muslim name to the one they already bore.

In the Arab world, first names are often followed by *nasab*, or lineage names. For example, the Prophet's name was Muhammad ibn Abdullah, which means

"Muhammad son of Abdullah." The words *bin, ibn,* or *ben* are used to signify "son of." *Bint* means "daughter of."

A *kunya* identifies someone by the name of one of his or her children. These names are constructed out of the words *abu,* which means "father of," and *umm,* which means "mother of." In some countries, women are often identified with the names of their offspring. For example, Umm Faysal means "Mother of Faysal." Sometimes parents combine umm with a noun in order to give their daughter a conceptual name. For example, Umm al-Sa'adah means "mother of happiness."

Some people's full names include a *nisbah,* that is, an association with a place or an occupation. For example, the name "al-Hasib" indicates that the person is a mathematician or accountant. The name of the famous Sufi poet Jela-luddin al-Rumi (1207-1273) indicates the region in which he lived; "al-Rumi" literally means "the Roman," and refers to Rumi's hometown in the heart of the old Roman — or Byzantine — Empire, now central Turkey. If "al-Ansari" is part of someone's name, that often means that they are descended from the very first Muslim converts at Medina, referred to in Arabic as *ansar,* or "helpers." People of note are sometimes called more often by their *laqab* — an adopted title describing their virtues or accomplishments — than their real name. The Abbasid caliphs, all of whom adopted laqabs, exemplify this case. For example, the name of the famous Abbasid caliph Harun al-Rashid translates as "Aaron the Righteous."

As discussed above, those people who are descended from the Prophet often have the titles *sayyid, sharif, shah, moulay,* or *mawlay* added to their names. When men return from the Hajj pilgrimage, they may add the title "Hajji" to their name to signify their accomplishment. Women add the title "Hajjah."

Male Circumcision

Circumcision — the removal of the foreskin of the penis — is a common practice among Muslims. It is not required by the Quran, but is considered *sunna,* that is, a practice approved by Muhammad. Many Muslims believe that the operation increases cleanliness. Some link the custom to the biblical story of Abraham receiving the command to circumcise his sons and their descendants (Genesis 17: 9-14) and the Quran's command to Muslims that they follow the ways of Abraham (Quran 16:23).

In some places circumcision takes place several days after birth, but it may also be performed during childhood or at the onset of puberty. In Morocco, parents often wait till the boy is three to five years old. In Uzbekistan boys are circumcised between the ages of seven and ten. In Malaysia boys undergo circumcision between the ages of ten to twelve. In Turkey, the operation is often performed on boys about the age of ten, but may be performed any time between the ages of two and fourteen.

In traditional times the local barber usually performed the circumcision. In many Muslim countries today, however, trained medical personnel are taking over an increasing percentage of these operations.

Circumcision is frequently accompanied by celebration. Traditional celebrations in the Middle East and North Africa usually entailed slaughtering a sheep and hosting a feast. In Egypt families often chose a saint's festival day as an appropriate day on which to have their boys circumcised. In this way, the saint may bless the boy and the operation. In a similar vein, some Muslims schedule their sons' circumcision for the month of Muhammad's birthday, Rabi al-Awwal. In some places parents often wait until their son has performed his first public recitation of the Quran.

> *In recent decades, educated, middle- and upper-class Muslims have increasingly tended to have their sons circumcised by doctors in hospitals around the time of birth.*

An old Arab saying states that "the Arab is king on his wedding day and his circumcision day." Indeed, in some Arab countries the boy to be circumcised is dressed as if for a wedding. In the Sudan, the boys wear jewelry and perfume, and their hands are painted with henna. Moroccan parents bathe their sons, shave off their hair, dress them in white, and also paint their hands with henna. In Egypt, Turkey, Morocco, and India the boys are dressed in feminine clothing resembling bridal wear before the ceremony. Afterwards the boys don traditional male dress. In addition to their splendid clothing, Turkish boys who are about to be circumcised also have their hands decorated with henna. Their hats bear the phrase *mashallah* (a variant spelling of *ma sha Allah*), which in this instance may be translated as "God preserve him." On the day of the circumcision, the boy is paraded about the streets dressed in his finery, accompanied by musicians. The boy's parents prepare special foods and entertainments, in order to distract the boy from his pain and to amuse the guests that gather to celebrate the occasion. Moreover, the boy's parents and other family members give him gifts and money. Turkish circumcision ceremonies usually take place in the autumn before the school year starts, or after the end of the school year.

In Malaysia families also celebrate the circumcision of their sons by hosting parties with special foods and music. Indonesian families also throw a party. It takes place three days after the circumcision and includes a lavish outfit for the boy, who is paraded in his finery through the streets, as well as a gift of money. In Uzbekistan the proud parents of a newly circumcised boy invite many family members and friends to a party with music, dancing, and large amounts of food. Alcohol is often served, in spite of the Muslim teaching that forbids it.

In recent years the king of Morocco has sponsored a national circumcision day. On this day doctors at public hospitals will circumcise boys for free. Afterwards family members celebrate with sweets and tea, and perhaps a festive meal.

A young boy and his father at prayer in a mosque in the Comoros Islands.

In countries where males are circumcised well into boyhood (as opposed to being circumcised as an infant), the operation often marks a turning point in their gender status. Afterwards, they are expected to join their father and the other men for prayer, rather than stay with their mothers. In cultures that maintain the custom of separate living rooms for men and women, the operation usually marks the boy's transition to the male spaces. Uncircumcised boys move more freely between these zones.

In recent decades, educated, middle- and upper-class Muslims have increasingly tended to have their sons circumcised by doctors in hospitals around the time of birth. This is also true of nearly all Muslims living in Europe and North America. For these groups, therefore, the operation doesn't tend to mark a change in the boy's use of social space.

Female Circumcision

Female circumcision—also called female genital mutilation—is not required in Islam. Nevertheless it is practiced in many African countries with high Muslim populations and is especially common in Djibouti, Eritrea, Ethiopia, Gambia, Mali, Somalia, Sierra Leone, Egypt, and Sudan. In Egypt, Coptic Christians as well as Muslims perform the operation on their daughters. It can also be found in Oman, Yemen, and the United Arab Emirates. Researchers believe that the practice dates back to pre-Islamic times and therefore is not Muslim in its origins. The procedure varies from country to country. In some places people practice a more moderate form of the operation, which entails removing a small amount of skin from or scarring the clitoris. In other places, however, tradition calls for the amputation of the clitoris, the removal of the labia, or other severe violations of female anatomy. These operations usually take place during girlhood, but may take place any time from infancy to adulthood. Some Muslim leaders have spoken out against the practice, having concluded that it is prohibited in Islam. While some religious experts openly disapprove of these operations, others find the practice acceptable or even commendable, despite the fact that it is not sanctioned in the Quran or reliable hadith traditions.

In recent years female genital mutilation has become the subject of international controversy. Many feminist groups believe the practice is inhumane and should be stopped everywhere.

Khatma or Ameen Ceremony

Muslim children around the world also begin learning Arabic and studying the Quran at a relatively young age. Many well-off Muslim parents send their children to special teachers to learn to read the text correctly and clearly. It usually takes the children around two years or less to work their way through the entire Quran. In many countries children complete these studies between the ages of four and seven. Parents often host a special celebration to commemorate the child's first complete reading of the Quran. The Arabic name for this celebration is *al-khatma* or *khatmi-Quran*, which means, "Sealing the Quran."

Parents often host a special celebration to commemorate the child's first complete reading of the Quran. The Arabic name for this celebration is al-khatma *or* khatmi-Quran, *which means, "Sealing the Quran."*

In Southeast Asia the event is called an ameen ceremony. In the American version of the ceremony, the family invites guests to a large, festive meal held in the child's honor. The child reads from the Quran and receives gifts to mark the occasion. In Iraq, a girl recites to her female relatives and friends, who give her gifts and prepare a lunch or tea in her honor. A boy's male relatives listen to him recite and host a party for him and his friends. In Oman, traditional celebrations begin with a procession through the village. The boy, his teacher, and his fellow students parade through the streets, stopping to recite verses from the Quran, prayers, and bits of religious poetry. The boy's family slaughters a sheep or goat and prepares a feast for the boy and his fellow students, as well as family members, friends, and neighbors. When the boy and his fellow students enter the house for the feast, the assembled guests throw money at him.

Puberty

In Muslim societies, the age at which boys and girls begin to change into men and women carries with it new rules and responsibilities. Muslims begin to learn the formal prayers and the required cleansing rituals during childhood,

The Koranic School for Girls in Nzwani (Anjouan), Comoros Islands, teaches its young students to read from the Quran.

but are not expected to pray five times daily until puberty. Children also learn the rules of modest dress, but will not be expected to conform to the adult standards until puberty. At this time girls who come from families that wear the hijab will often begin to wear the garment themselves. Children may also do a modified fast during Ramadan. After reaching puberty, however, they will be expected to fast the entire month of Ramadan.

Courtship

Islam encourages its followers to marry. Nevertheless, many—but not all—Muslims worldwide do not approve of American-style dating. So how do young people meet each other and decide to marry? Like many American couples, many young Middle Eastern couples meet for the first time while attending a university, through mutual friends, or in the workplace. Family members usually play a much greater role than is common in America in looking for prospective mates for their unmarried relatives. Depending on the beliefs of the family and the customs of the country, dating may be permitted as long as a chaperone accompanies the couple. The parents of the prospective bride and groom often have a great deal to say about whom their sons and daughters marry. In some countries, arranged marriages—that is, marriages in which the bride and groom's parents have selected their partners for them—are common. In most instances, this does not mean that the young people hand over all control to their parents. Often the parents present the young people with several possible marriage candidates and ask them to choose among them. If these are rejected, other suitable candidates will usually be sought. Islamic religious teachings forbid marrying a woman against her will.

According to certain schools of Islamic law, Muslim women must have a male representative, called a *wali*, to help them through the process of selecting a mate and to keep them from being bothered by unwanted suitors. The institution was established in centuries past to prevent sheltered teenage girls from being taken advantage of by unscrupulous men. A male relative usually performs the role of wali.

> *According to certain schools of Islamic law, Muslim women must have a male representative, called a* **wali**, *to help them through the process of selecting a mate and to keep them from being bothered by unwanted suitors.*

Local customs—and even one's access to modern technology—have a lot to say about how young Muslims find mates. In rural Somalia, young men seek out wives by hanging around the wells. Before fetching the water the young women dress in their finest clothes, as everyone knows that this task presents them with the possibility of attracting a suitor. The young men gallantly offer to fill their water jugs, which gives them a chance to chat with the young ladies. At Somalian weddings, only the young and unwed are expected to sing and dance. So weddings also furnish opportunities for young people to meet potential marriage partners. In Morocco, a yearly festival, called Imichil, has for centuries provided the Berber people with a kind of marriage fair. For three days eligible men and women stroll about the singles' area of the fair, stopping to briefly chat with whoever catches their eye. While looks and personality are important to both partners, the brides-to-be also size up each man's assets, as this will most likely determine the kind of lifestyle the couple will have together.

In the United States young Muslims interested in marriage may seek mates at Islamic events. These can be local events sponsored by mosques, Islamic centers, or Muslim student associations. They may also try regional and national events, such as conferences sponsored by the Islamic Society of North America and other Muslim organizations, at which matrimonial matchmaking services may be available. Computer literate Muslims from around the world may also take advantage of the many Muslim matrimonial web sites that have sprung up on the World Wide Web.

Marriage

Once the couple has indicated interest in marrying each other, a contract is drawn up. In Islam marriage is not a sacrament, as it is in some forms of Christianity, but rather a contractual arrangement between a man and a woman. Never-

theless, it is considered an important and blessed event. The marriage contract makes clear the obligations that each partner must fulfill. The groom must make a bridal gift, called a *mahr*, to his wife. The contract spells out what it is and when it will be delivered. It could be a relatively modest gift, or it could be something substantial, such as a house. If the husband later initiates a divorce, the wife is permitted to keep the mahr. In the Arab world husbands often acquire and furnish a home before the wedding, and, if they can afford it, give their prospective wives gifts of gold jewelry.

The traditional marriage ceremony, called a nikah, *centers around the signing of the marriage contract by the groom and the bride's* wali *in the presence of witnesses.*

The traditional marriage ceremony, called a *nikah,* centers around the signing of the marriage contract by the groom and the bride's wali in the presence of witnesses. Some Muslims do not consider it necessary for the bride to attend. Afterwards those present recite the opening chapter of the Quran. In some parts of the world, this takes place in a judge's office or a private home. In America, Muslim couples often marry in a mosque, where an imam offers a sermon on marriage after the signing of the contract. Readings from the Quran also take place.

After the ceremony the families and the guests of the bride and groom gather together for a party called a *walimah*. In very conservative Muslim environments, the men and women will hold two separate parties. The style of celebration will vary according to the local culture, but these parties usually involve food, gifts, and merrymaking, and sometimes also music and dance. In some countries bridal processions take place in which the groom rides through the streets accompanied by his friends and family members. In other types of bridal processions the gifts given to the bride are displayed, or the bride is carried to her new home in a litter or car. Among Arabs, family and friends typically give the bridal couple gifts of cash. Turkish brides traditionally receive gifts of gold coins.

Islam permits men to have up to four wives, but women may have only one husband. Nevertheless, this practice, known as polygyny, is relatively rare in the Muslim world. Most men simply cannot afford to house more than one wife and one set of children.

According to Islamic law, a Muslim man may marry a Jewish or Christian woman, but a Muslim woman must marry a man of her own faith. In recent times, however, a few Muslim women have broken with this tradition.

Death and Preparation for Burial

According to custom, when a Muslim feels death approaching he or she recites the *shahada*, the Muslim declaration of faith. If he or she is unable to speak, someone else whispers these words into his or her ear. These are the same phrases that are whispered into the ears of newborns. Thus life ends as it began, grounded in the teachings of Islam. Often relatives will read the 36th chapter of the Quran to a dying person. When hearing of a recent death, some Muslims will quote from the Quran, saying, "to Allah we belong and to Him is our return" (Quran 2:156).

The wedding document has already been signed and witnessed earlier in the legally binding ceremony. Now the families and the guests of the bride and groom gather together for a party called a walimah.

After death has occurred the corpse is prepared for burial without delay. Muslims do not use an embalming process. Instead, they wash the body and the hair and scent it with a non-alcoholic perfume. Women wash female corpses, and men wash male corpses. Spouses may wash one another's corpse and parents may wash the dead bodies of their children, however. The corpse is washed three times, the right side of the body preceding the left. Prayers accompany this process. If three washings do not seem sufficient, additional washings may take place, but such that the total number of cleansings equals an uneven number. The body is then wrapped up in a clean, white cotton shroud. Expensive materials are not used to make shrouds; neither should expensive objects accompany the dead person into the grave. Men's shrouds are composed of three pieces of white cloth; women's, five. The deceased may be placed into a simple, wooden coffin, but often they are buried without one.

A hadith of the Prophet Muhammad instructs Muslim bystanders who witness a funeral procession to rise to their feet, whether the dead person was a Muslim or not.

Funerals

Muslim funerals vary in form and content according to local culture and tradition. For example, in many parts of the Muslim world women are not expected to or are even prohibited from attending funerals. They may also be discouraged from visiting the graves afterwards. Other Muslims disagree with these prohibitions, however, and accept women's participation in funerals and mourning customs.

The following description of a Muslim funeral offers a general outline of commonly observed customs. Muslim funerals take place on the day the deceased died, or on the following day. A brief prayer service, *salat al-janaza* (salat over the dead), generally precedes the burial. It may take place in a mosque, someone's home, or even in the graveyard, though this last is not recommended. The coffin or funeral bier is placed in front of the assembled mourners and the imam, or a male relative of the bereaved family, leads the group in prayer. This simple ceremony revolves around four declarations of the takbir, which are followed by either a recitation of the first chapter of the Quran or by informal prayers. Often the first takbir is followed by the Fatiha, the second by a prayer for the Prophet, the third by a prayer for the dead person, and the fourth by a prayer for the worldwide Muslim community. There are no prostrations during this service, during which the mourners stand. Afterwards they turn to those on their right and left and bid them peace.

The body of the deceased may be carried to the grave on a bier. A hadith of the Prophet Muhammad instructs Muslim bystanders who witness a funeral pro-

cession to rise to their feet, whether the dead person was a Muslim or not. Another custom teaches Muslim bystanders who encounter a funeral procession to offer to carry the funeral bier for a short while. Some Muslims believe that funeral processions should take place in silence, without music or loud exclamations of grief.

Mourners in Uzbekistan climb the steps of the mosque carring the funeral bier.

Graves are usually dug four to six feet deep. Grave markers are often simple, small, and low to the ground. Many times this teaching is not observed, however.

The corpse is laid on its right side in the grave, with its face pointing towards Mecca. Sometimes a green brick is placed under the deceased's head. Those who lower the body into the grave declare as they do so, "In the name of God and according to the Way of the Prophet." If the shahada was not recited during the dying process, it is said now. Then the mourners come forward and toss three handfuls of earth into the grave. After this has been done, one of the mourners makes a short speech, reminding the person in the grave of the truth of the central teachings of Islam. The Fatiha may be recited instead. Then the mourners leave the graveside. After walking 40 steps they stop and repeat the Fatiha. This custom is said to lend support to the deceased, who, according to traditional beliefs, is already being questioned by the angels about his or her religion.

The Afterlife

Islam teaches that sometime in the future—on a day and hour known only to God—there will come a Day of Judgment. On this day all the dead will rise out of their graves and will appear, body and soul, before God. Each will be judged according to how he or she lived life on earth. More specifically, each person will be measured against the teachings of his or her religion. Everyone's own actions while here on earth, each of which has been recorded in heaven in the Book of Deeds, will be used as evidence for and against them. Those whose good deeds outweigh their bad deeds will go to Paradise. Those whose bad deeds weigh more heavily than their good will go to hell, there to be tormented for all eternity by being cast into raging fires, scorching winds, and boiling waters. Paradise, on the other hand, rewards the good with an eternity spent in beautiful mansions surrounded by enchanting gardens, through which flow peaceful streams.

One traditional belief subscribed to by some Muslims suggests that men who go to Paradise will be given beautiful female companions known as *houris*. Some have translated this term as "perpetual virgins," but others suggest that its meaning is closer to "purified souls." Some Muslim terrorists have sought to motivate young Muslim men to participate in suicide bombings by promoting the idea that the bombings constitute acts of martyrdom in defense of Islam. Therefore, the terrorists argue, God will welcome suicide bombers into heaven and reward them with eternally beautiful virgins as their companions. It should be noted, however, that even in times of war Islam forbids the killing of non-combatants (people who are not soldiers). It also strongly condemns suicide.

Mourning

The first and most concentrated period of mourning lasts for three days after the burial. In some countries those in mourning do not wear jewelry, perfume, or fresh, clean clothes during this period. Some Muslim women will wear white head coverings (*hijab*) to indicate that they are in mourning. Custom encourages well-wishers to visit the bereaved family at this time to offer their condolences and bring gifts of food. In some cultures women express their grief through loud wailing and moaning. Women who are particularly good at wailing may even be hired to help the mourners express their grief. Muslim religious authorities generally disapprove of this folk custom, but have not been able to stamp it out everywhere.

In Indonesia, family members will not sleep until all the ceremonies surrounding the burial of their loved one have been concluded. Relatives, friends, neighbors, and business associates are expected to pay a condolence call on the family during the first three days of mourning after a death. So important are these calls that some people leave work immediately after hearing of a death in order to fulfill this duty. It is customary to bring a small gift of money in a plain white envelope, or some simple food items, like tea or sugar. In Uzbekistan, families in mourning will not cook a meal during the first three days after the death. Professional mourners may be invited into a family's home in order to amplify the expression of grief.

Women gather to commemorate a death at the Blue Mosque in Baku, Azerbaijan.

During the first 40 days after the funeral, special observances — including meals, prayers, and recitations of the Quran — may be held in memory of the dead person. Many Muslims practice some special rites on the 40th day after a death, which marks the close of the mourning period. In Turkey and Iran friends and family members bring food to the house of the bereaved family on the 7th and 40th days after the burial. Together the family and their well-wishers eat, pray, and read from the Quran. Muslims from the Indian subcontinent often participate in *chalismoh* ceremonies on the 40th day after a death. At these ceremonies people pray together and offer food to the deceased person's relatives. Another Indian custom involves the sponsoring of a ceremonial dinner, called a *fatiha*, every Thursday night during the first 40 days after a death. The bereaved family offers the meal as a charitable donation and as a petition for God's forgiveness and mercy on the deceased. At the end of the meal everyone recites the first chapter of the Quran, the Fatiha. In Malaysia families mourn on the 3rd, 7th, 14th, 40th, and 100th day after the death of a loved one. These gatherings generally revolve around recitation from the Quran.

Muslims may also practice mourning customs that spring from local folk belief or from the generally accepted practices of their culture. For example, in Java some Muslims leave offerings of food for the deceased person underneath his or her bed during the first 40 days of mourning. In the United States, some Muslims have adopted the practice of holding an open casket viewing, with the corpse's made-up face visible to the public, before the funeral and burial. Sudanese Muslims may arrange a design in pebbles on top of graves. Iranian Muslims sometimes wrap the deceased's body in a shroud inscribed with verses from the Quran.

"Al-Fatiha," the opening chapter of the Quran, is here depicted in an ornamented fragment from an early, undated manuscript.

During the mourning period some Muslims offer prayers for the dead after the conclusion of the formal prayers said at sunset on Thursday evenings. In India and East Africa, these prayers take the form of a *khane Quran* or a *khatm al-Quran*, that is, a congregational recitation of the entire Quran. This ceremony takes place at the mosque every Thursday night for the first 40 days after a death, and begins after the night (*isha*) prayer. Each person who stands up to recite tries to complete an entire chapter. Thursday evening marks the beginning of the Muslim holy day (Friday), as the Muslim calendar (like the Jewish calendar) reckons each new day to begin at sunset.

Conversion to Islam

Converting to Islam from another religion is a relatively simple affair. The new Muslim must first perform a full ablution. Then, in the presence of two witnesses, he or she repeats the *shahada*, the Muslim declaration of faith, with belief in his or her heart. This declaration may be rendered thus: "I witness that there is no God but God, and that Muhammad is the Messenger of God." These statements are contained in the Muslim call to prayer, and indeed lie at the core of Islamic religious belief. Formal acts of conversion usually take place in mosques. Afterwards the new convert is expected to live life according to the rules and teachings of Islam.

Muslims believe that an Islam-like monotheism was humanity's original religion. They trace their own faith back to the biblical figure Abraham, whom they view neither as a Jew nor as a Christian, but rather as a simple and devout monotheist. Therefore they often speak of those who convert to Islam from Christianity or Judaism as "reverts" rather than "converts." By this they mean that these people are coming back, or reverting, to the religion of their distant ancestors.

Conversion from Islam

Under Islamic law conversion from Islam to another faith is not permitted and is considered a punishable offense. Under the strictest interpretation of religious law, this act—called apostasy—carries the death penalty. Islam was traditionally conceived of as a way of life for an entire group of people, so apostasy carries overtones of treason because it means that the individual is abandoning the group's way of life and perhaps thereby raising doubts in the minds of others. In recent centuries the death penalty has rarely been enforced on apostates. Imprisonment or expulsion from the community have frequently been substituted instead. Today, in countries ruled by Islamic laws, significant legal penalties still apply. The *fatwa* (ruling) issued by Iran's Ayatollah Khomeini against the writer Salman Rushdie, condemning him to death for ideas expressed in his book *The Satanic Verses*, was based on the traditional penalty for apostates under Muslim law. Many Muslims around the world did not agree with Khomeini's opinion, however, and they refused to support such a harsh judgment.

> *Islam was traditionally conceived of as a way of life for an entire group of people, so apostasy carries overtones of treason because it means that the individual is abandoning the group's way of life and perhaps thereby raising doubts in the minds of others.*

Chapter 24
Symbols

Crescent Moon

Throughout the world, the crescent moon — usually with a five- or six-pointed star between its horns — is recognized as a symbol of Islam. Called the *hilal* in Arabic, this symbol was first used on Muslim coins in the 7th century. Historians have traced its use in religious architecture back to the 11th century, when Muslim artisans working to convert churches into mosques began to replace crosses with the crescent and star. The rulers of the Ottoman Empire used the crescent on their banners and flags. During the Ottoman era the crescent became a widely used and recognized symbol of Islam. Today Turkey, Mauritania, Algeria, Tunisia, Azerbaijan, Turkmenistan, Uzbekistan, Pakistan, Malaysia, and Comoros have incorporated the crescent into the design of their flags.

A crescent moon and star — the symbol of Islam — adorns the dome of the Fatimi Mosque in Pattani, Thailand.

A red crescent moon against a white background is one of the official symbols of the nonprofit organization most Americans know as the Red Cross. In predominantly Muslim societies this disaster and wartime relief organization is known as the Red Crescent and uses the red crescent moon as its symbol. The official name of the international federation that coordinates these national groups is the International Federation of Red Cross and Red Crescent Societies.

Quran

Like Jews and Christians, Muslims base their faith in the teachings contained in their holy book. The Quran contains the essence of Islam and most Muslims

Foreign words used in the text are defined in the Glossary, pages 423-40.

227

believe it to be the literal words of God. It therefore may serve as a symbol of Islam.

Kaba

The Kaba is the most important Muslim shrine in the world. It is an approximately cube-shaped building—45 feet high with sides of 33 and 50 feet—located in Mecca, Saudi Arabia. The word kaba means "cube." The building itself is made of stone, but it is kept covered with a beautiful black cloth upon which verses from the Quran have been embroidered with gold and silver threads.

Muslim tradition declares that Adam built the original Kaba, thus making it the very first temple ever built to God. Adam constructed the building as a copy of the heavenly temple that houses the throne of God, around which the angels circle singing God's praises. Tradition explains that it was destroyed in the Great Flood only to be rebuilt by Abraham. By Muhammad's time it had become a temple to the many tribal gods of Arabia. Muhammad put an end to polytheism in Arabia and restored the Kaba to its original use.

Five times a day, Muslims from around the world turn towards Mecca to pray. Those who live in Mecca turn towards the Kaba. Thus it stands quite literally at the heart of worldwide Muslim devotions. Its role in orienting the prayers of the faithful is mandated in the Quran, where Muslims are instructed to "turn towards the Holy Mosque, and turn towards it wherever you be" (Quran 2:144, Ali trans.). Furthermore, one of the Five Pillars of Islam stipulates that every Muslim who is financially able should make a pilgrimage to Mecca at least once in his or her lifetime. In Mecca the pilgrims circle seven times around the Kaba, in imitation of the angels' adoration of God in heaven. Certain Muslim teachings state that the Kaba was built by Abraham, whom Muslims view as an important prophet and a devout monotheist. Therefore the Kaba serves not only as a symbol of Islam, but also recalls the pure monotheism of the Muslim religion.

Colors

Green symbolizes the Prophet Muhammad and thus is taken to represent Islam itself. This association comes from the traditional teaching that Muhammad's banner, cloak, and turban were green, as was the clothing of Ali, Muhammad's son-in-law and the fourth caliph. In some places, descendants of the Prophet may identify themselves as such by wearing green in their turbans. According to the Quran, in Paradise the dead wear robes made of green silk and brocade (Quran 18:31) and lounge peacefully in beautiful green gardens. Green has come to represent peace, hope, and paradise to many Muslims. Many mosques, funeral draperies, home interiors, and family emblems are green in color. Furthermore, Islamic folklore tells many tales of the mysterious *al Khidr* ("the Green Man"), an immortal figure who brings wisdom and blessings to humankind. Although never mentioned by name in the Quran, some scholars believe that certain verses pertain to him. Finally, green also dominates the color schemes found on the flags of a number of Muslim nations. The flags of Saudi Arabia, Libya, Mauritania, Pakistan, Bangladesh, Turkmenistan, and Comoros fall into this category.

White is worn by pilgrims making the Hajj. The ihram they wear is a symbol of their equality.

White also has special significance in Islam. Traditional Muslim shrouds are pure white and in some Muslim countries mourners wear white. White is also worn by pilgrims making the Hajj. In addition, angels are associated with the color white. White has positive connotations for Muslims, and is said to be an important color in paradise. In some Muslim countries, the nights before, during, and after a full moon are referred to as the "White Nights." These nights are thought to be especially lucky.

Islamic folklore suggests that the color blue can help to ward off the evil eye. It is also used a great deal in the interior of mosques and in tile work.

Black is associated with Shia Muslims, especially with their clergy, many of whom wear black turbans. Historically black was symbolic of the Abbasid Caliphs. It may also signify mourning.

Odd Numbers

A number of Muslim customs give evidence of a preference for odd numbers. For example, the dead are washed an uneven number of times in preparation for burial. This preference for odd numbers is symbolic. Because Muslims believe in only one, all-powerful God, they associate the number one with God. One, of course, is an odd number. Odd numbers — like God — cannot be divided in two. All odd numbers, but especially the number one, evoke this recollection of the divine. Furthermore, according to a hadith, the Quran was revealed to Muhammad during the odd nights of the last ten days during Ramadan. This event, too, gives odd numbers a positive connotation in Islam.

Chapter 25
Animals

Dogs

Many Muslims consider dogs to be unclean. They trace this belief back to several sayings of Muhammad's. According to one of them Muhammad declared, "Angels do not enter a house in which there is a dog or a picture." Some commentators note that in Muhammad's day dogs were much more likely to be carriers of disease and insect pests than they are today. In spite of advances in veterinary medicine, many Muslims still abide by this saying and won't have dogs as household pets. If a dog should touch human food or eating utensils, these must first be ritually purified before being used by humans again. Ritual purifications must also be performed if a dog should enter the area surrounding a mosque. A person who has been licked by a dog must perform ritual washing before going to pray.

Hunting, herding, and watchdogs provide an exception to these rules. They are not considered unclean. In fact, desert Arabs breed a kind of greyhound known as a Saluki, which they prize highly. Humans may consume the prey caught by hunting dogs if the dog's keeper recites the *basmallah* before releasing the dog.

To call someone a dog is a grave insult among Muslims. The term is usually reserved for enemies and unbelievers. One common folk notion suggests that the devil often takes the form of a black dog.

Foreign words used in the text are defined in the Glossary, pages 423-40.

231

Cats

Muslims generally consider cats to be clean, good, spiritual animals. Muhammad was said to have a cat and his love of cats gave rise to these beliefs. A Muslim legend tells that a cat once saved Muhammad from a snake. In gratitude Muhammad stroked it on its forehead and back. In so doing he blessed all cats in such a way that they never fall on their backs. Many cats even have stripe marks on their foreheads, marking the touch of Muhammad's fingers. Another Muslim folktale declares that the first cats came into the world when the lion on board Noah's Ark sneezed. Yet another traditional story suggests that the cat is the lion's (or sometimes tiger's) aunt. The cat teaches the lion everything she knows, except her last, best trick: how to climb a tree.

Cats are traditionally considered so pure that people may use their drinking water to perform the ritual washing necessary before prayer.

It is said that the Sakinah, a manifestation of the peace of God, appeared to Muhammad in the form of a white cat. Folktales in which cats assume the form of saints (*wali*), sense the presence of divine grace, and wander in search of people at prayer express belief in the spiritual purity of cats. Many Sufis keep cats as their animal companions. Unlike dogs, cats are permitted to wander freely through mosques. Cats are traditionally considered so pure that people may use their drinking water to perform the ritual washing necessary before prayer.

Pigs

Pigs are considered unclean. Like Jews, Muslims are not permitted to eat pork and should cleanse themselves if they come into contact with pigs or pork products. Very observant Muslims may be wary of eating in non-Muslim homes or in restaurants for fear of being served something made with pork or alcohol, another forbidden substance.

Treatment of Animals

In general Muslims believe that God rewards those who are kind to animals, even those that are considered unclean. According to one hadith, God pardoned a prostitute because she went out of her way to give a drink of water to a thirsty dog. Similarly, cruelty to animals may bring on divine wrath.

Chapter 26
Dance, Music, Poetry,
and Story

Social Dancing

Many Muslims disapprove of European-style social dancing (e.g. ballroom dancing) because unmarried men and women may participate and in so doing touch one another. This touching is viewed as sexually provocative. American-style rock and roll dancing may also be frowned on as sexually suggestive. In many Muslim countries folk dances of various kinds, in which dancers of the same sex move in a line or circle with each other, have traditionally been performed at social functions such as weddings.

In Middle Eastern countries, Oriental dancing, a restrained, folk version of belly dancing, sometimes takes place at weddings. Oriental dancing is not a Muslim custom, however, and is performed by people of other religions as well. Outside the Middle East, Muslims from many different cultures also enjoy folk or traditional dances at weddings and other special occasions. In Afghanistan, men customarily perform a folk dance called *atan* at weddings and holiday celebrations. They wave sticks, guns, or swords in the air while shouting, stamping their feet, and whirling around in circles. In past times the Pashtun people of Pakistan and Afghanistan performed this dance before heading into battle. Many Kuwaitis celebrate Eid al-Fitr by watching men dance troupes perform a sword dance called *ardha*.

Foreign words used in the text are defined in the Glossary, pages 423-40.

233

Religious Dancing

The members of certain Sufi orders dance as a means of expressing love of God and cultivating spiritual insight. The Mevlevi Order is especially famed for its religious dances, which help its devotees come to a direct experience of the divine. Known as the "Whirling Dervishes" in the West, these devotees spin round and round in place, which causes the skirt that they wear over their trousers to flare out in a circular shape. Dancers train themselves to stay stationary while spinning by grasping a nail in the floor between the first and second toes of one foot.

These ritual dance sessions last about an hour and contain many symbolic elements. In one part of the dance, the disciples spin in circles around the *pir*, or Sufi master, who represents the eternal and unchanging center point of the universe around which all creation revolves. The master participates near the end of the dance. His appearance signals the beginning of the disciples' symbolic ascent to God. Chanted Sufi songs and instrumental music accompany the dancers. The *ney*, or reed flute, has special significance for the Mevlevi Order. Its founder, the poet Jelaluddin al-Rumi (1207-1273), described himself as a reed flute through which the breath of God made heavenly music.

Islamic Attitudes Towards Music

The Quran contains certain warnings against those who tell frivolous stories that mislead others and those who waste time with pleasantries (Quran 31:6, 53:59-61). Some Muslims have interpreted these verses as condemning music, especially those songs or musical styles that entice listeners towards foolish or sexual behavior. Certain conservative Muslims believe that Islam forbids some kinds of music, specifically sensual or romantic music. This ruling has colored Muslim attitudes towards other kinds of music as well, generating a certain overall suspicion of the art form among very conservative Muslims. Nevertheless, over the centuries Muslim societies have generated many different genres of music. A good number of them are religious in nature, but folk music as well as artistically composed kinds of music developed, too. Some forms of religious music, such as the call to prayer, Quran chanting, naat, and madh, have been previously discussed. Most Muslims embrace these art forms. It should be pointed out, however, that many Muslims do not view the call to prayer and Quran chanting as music, even though non-Muslims admire their musical qualities.

Sufi and Devotional Songs

Unlike ordinary Sunni and Shia Muslims, many Sufis sing songs as a regular part of their religious activities. Some organize musical prayer and meditation sessions, called *sama*, in order to raise members to higher levels of spiritual devotion and awareness. Members of the Mevlevi and Chishtiyya Orders are especially famed for their use of music. Other orders, however, teach that music distracts the seeker from God.

Certain Sufi groups assert that music making brings devotees to an experience of divine bliss. Their songs typically express devotion to the Prophet, love for God, and admiration for the saints, or they may describe the desired spiritual state of union with God. In Persia, Pakistan, Afghanistan, and India these kinds of songs are called *qawwali*. In Turkey they are known as *ilahis*, in Egypt as *inshad*, and in other Arab countries as *qasidahs*. Sufis may perform them when gathered together with their spiritual teacher, or at the tombs of saints.

Ordinary Muslims also enjoy and sing these kinds of devotional songs. They have an important place in many religious celebrations. For example, it is not uncommon for groups of pilgrims to sing devotional songs while en route to Mecca, or a particular saint's tomb. Saints' days, Ramadan, and other important days in the Muslim religious calendar also provide occasions for people to express their religious sentiments in song. Accomplished singers of these kinds of songs give concerts and make recordings that are popular with a wide range of people.

Ordinary believers as well as accomplished poets often try to express their devotion to God and admiration for Muhammad and the saints by composing lines of beautiful verse.

Poetry

In the early days of Islam, many Muslims looked upon poetry with suspicion, fearing that its persuasive power might somehow compete with and undermine Islam or the Quran. The Arab inclination to honor the good and the beautiful in poetry was difficult to deny, however. In the long run, the impulse to praise God, the Prophet, and the saints in verse proved stronger than this initial reluctance. Several hundred years after Muhammad's death, religious poetry had become an important art form in the Muslim world. It still is today. Ordinary believers as well as accomplished poets often try to express their devotion to God and admiration for Muhammad and the saints by composing lines of beautiful verse. Religious holidays and pilgrimages provide occasions for reading, reciting, and singing these poems. They are also recited or sung at religious gatherings, as a means of celebrating faith and inspiring greater devotion to God, the Prophet, or the saints.

Legends Concerning Saints, Prophets, and Famous People

Many ordinary Muslim people around the world have a great deal of respect for the holy men and women of Islam. Sometimes referred to as "saints," these men and women demonstrate deep religious faith, lead exemplary lives, and seem to possess unusual spiritual powers. Most Muslim saints have also been Sufis, that is, people who have pursued the mystical dimensions of Islam. Many stories about saints circulate throughout the Muslim world. These folktales inspire faith in God and the saints, and teach ethical behavior. They often revolve around the saint's uncanny knowledge of the motivation of others or small miracles that occur in the presence of the saint. The tale retold in the following paragraph provides a sample of these kinds of stories.

The following miracle tale is told about a woman called Rabi'a al-Adawiyyah, a famous Sufi saint of 8th-century Iraq. One day Rabi'a remarked upon the fact that she had no vegetables left in her cupboards. At that moment, a cluster of onions dropped down from the heavens. The people who witnessed this event began to chatter gleefully about the miracle, calling it a blessing from God. Their jabbering disturbed Rabi'a, who recognized that it reflected not true spiritual insight and deepened faith, but rather superficial emotional excitement. In their delight with the onions they were in danger of forgetting the greatness of God! In an effort to redirect their thinking she remarked, "This, a great miracle? Do you suppose that Allah runs an onion shop?"

Legends concerning the prophets and famous figures from the history of Islam also circulate throughout the Muslim world. These folktales, too, usually contain spiritual or moral teachings. One such story, which appears in the writings of the great 13th-century Persian mystic Farid ad-Din Attar, recounts an incident in the life of Jesus. One day, Jesus walked past a group of men who sneered at him and yelled insults after him. Instead of returning anger for anger, Jesus offered a prayer on their behalf. This response intrigued a bystander who asked, "Weren't you angry at those men? You should have cursed them and yet you prayed for them." Jesus replied, "I cannot spend a coin that I do not carry in my purse." (Shah 1969: 63).

Nasreddin Hodja earned the reputation of teaching wisdom through foolish acts and funny stories.

Folktales and Sufi Teaching Stories

The flicker of humor found in the Rabi'a story echoes throughout many other Muslim folktales and teaching tales. One famous body of humorous folktales that teach moral lessons concerns Nasreddin Hodja. Some writers believe that these stories are based around the deeds of a 13th-century Turkish imam called Nasreddin. They argue that during his lifetime Nasreddin Hodja earned the reputation of teaching wisdom through foolish acts and funny stories. His reputation, and the number of stories attributed to him, only grew after his death. Hundreds of them circulate throughout the Muslim world. Stories concerning the Hodja (a Turkish title meaning "religious teacher") are most popular in Turkey and lands once under Turkish rule. Yet other countries also claim Nasreddin as a native son. In these places he may go by a slightly different name, such as Mulla Nasruddin, or Juha. Many other variations of the name also exist. The following tale illustrates the way in which the Hodja stories often combine humor and moral teachings.

ර@

One day Nasreddin Hodja was invited to a fancy dinner at the home of a prosperous man. At the appointed hour the earnest Hodja did not bother to change into his best clothes, but rather hurried hungrily to the feast. He was admitted to the house, but found that the well-dressed guests ignored him, and that he was not offered any food. Excusing himself from the banquet he trudged home, where his wife helped to dress him in his finest turban, pants, and coat. Upon returning to the wealthy man's home, he resumed his place at the table, and found that at last the host bid him to eat. When a plate of soup was set before him, the Hodja waved his coat sleeve over the dish, beckoning the coat to consume its fill. "Eat, honored coat, eat!" he declared. His statement startled the other guests, who asked for an explanation. The Hodja said, "When I arrived in humble clothes, you paid no attention to me and passed no dish my way. When I came back in my best garments, you began to treat me as an honored guest. I can only conclude that it was the coat you wanted at the feast, not me!"

ර@

Sufi religious teachers often use stories to impart spiritual principles. Some of these stories concern saints, and others do not. Many have an element of humor in them. They often poke fun at hypocritical, conceited, or ignorant people, and reveal the illusory nature of material wealth, fame, intellectual knowledge, and political power. Other common themes include descriptions of spiritual blindness, and the role of the Sufi teacher in spreading spiritual insight. The following tale provides an example of this last set of themes.

One day a man journeyed some distance from his home and found himself in the fabled Land of the Foolish. As he wandered through the farmland belonging to a certain village, he spied a group of panicky people rushing away from a particular field. He flagged them down and asked what had happened. "We discovered a frightening fiend there among the stalks of wheat," they cried. The people pointed to an object at the center of the field that looked vaguely familiar to the stranger. Peering at it more closely, he realized that it was a watermelon plant, with a large ripe watermelon on the vine. Assuring them that there was nothing to be afraid of, the visitor offered to rid them of the troubling fruit. He strode into the field, took out his knife, cut the melon from the plant, prepared himself a slice, and began to eat it. The people wailed in their distress, "The lunatic stranger is even more frightening than the fiend! Surely he will use his knife against us, too, unless we stop him." So they drove the man away, threatening him with their pitchforks and other farm implements.

Not long afterwards, another outsider strayed into the Land of the Foolish. By this time, the watermelon plant had produced another ripe fruit. The second man, too, encountered the fearful farmers flying from what he knew to be a delicious melon. But the second stranger attempted to relieve their distress in quite a different manner. Agreeing with them in hushed tones that they were indeed facing a fearsome monster, he crept quietly away from the fields with them. This act assured them of his reasonableness. After thus establishing trust, he settled down to live among them, deepening his friendship with them over time. All the while he imparted to them a series of simple facts that, once digested, dissolved their fear of watermelons. In time they even began to plant and harvest watermelons themselves.

∽∾

The following Sufi teaching tale, penned by famous Persian poet and Sufi teacher Sa'adi (ca. 1213-1292), also revolves around the contrast between the behavior and character of two different men. It illustrates the difference between superficial religious conformity and deep religious conversion.

A gentle and wise young man journeyed to the Persian city of Darband. The young man's manner made a very good impression on everyone in the town, including the pious elder in charge of the mosque. Even though the mosque was already pretty clean, the mosque's guardian grandly bestowed upon the newcomer the task of sweeping the dust from the floor in preparation for worship services. When the older man returned the next day, he suspected that the job had not been done. He found the stranger outside the mosque and scolded him, telling him that he had failed the congregation and accusing him of being too proud to serve. Surprised by the reprimand, the young man assured him that he had taken the only rubbish he had found out of the mosque. Seeing that the older man did not understand, the deeply passionate youth explained his actions. He confided that when he found himself alone in the mosque, he realized that in his own insignificance and imperfection he himself could be compared to the dust and straw that he had been asked to remove. So great was the young man's humility that he concluded that his own presence polluted the purity of that holy space more than the few remaining grains of dust. So he fulfilled his job by leaving the mosque immediately. Sa'adi ends his story by reminding his listeners that those who wish to come close to God must cultivate the kind of humility demonstrated by this young man.

Additional Resources
(Including Web Sites and Videos)

Abdul Hakeem, Ahmed. *A Treasury of Favorite Muslim Names*. Chicago, IL: Pearl Publications, 1997.

Ahmed, Akbar S. *Islam Today: A Short Introduction to the Muslim World*. London, England: I. B. Tauris, 1999.

Al Hariri-Wendel, Tanja. *Symbols of Islam*. New York: Sterling, 2002.

Ali, Ahmed, trans. *Al-Qur'an: A Contemporary Translation*. Rev. definitive ed. Princeton, NJ: Princeton University Press, 1988.

Barks, Coleman, and Michael Green. *The Illuminated Prayer: As Revealed by Jellaludin Rumi and Bawa Muhaiyaddeen*. New York: Ballantine, 2000.

Bayat, Mojdeh, and Mohammad Ali Jamnia, eds. *Tales from the Land of the Sufis*. Boston, MA: Shambala, 1994.

Betteridge, Anne H. "Domestic Observances: Muslim Practices." In *The Encyclopedia of Religion*, edited by Mircea Eliade. Vol. 4. New York: Macmillan, 1987.

Bowen, Donna Lee, and Evelyn A. Early, eds. *Everyday Life in the Muslim Middle East*. 2nd ed. Bloomington: Indiana University Press, 2002.

Chebel, Malek. *Symbols of Islam*. New York: Assouline, 2000.

Denny, Frederick Mathewson. "The Great Indonesian Qur'an Chanting Tournament." *The World and I* 2, no. 6 (June 1986): 216.

Denny, Frederick Mathewson. *An Introduction to Islam*. 2nd ed. New York: Macmillan, 1994.

Denny, Frederick Mathewson. "Qur'anic Recitation." In *The Oxford Encyclopedia of the Modern Islamic World*, edited by John L. Esposito. Vol. 3. Oxford, England: Oxford University Press, 1995.

Above: The imposing eastern wall of the Great Mosque in Djenne, Mali. Each year townfolk stage a festival and replaster the mud walls.

Opposite page: A Djenne Marabout prepares a copyboard for tracing to teach his students to learn to read, write, and recite the Quran.

Devine, Elizabeth, and Nancy L. Braganti. *The Travelers' Guide to Middle Eastern and North African Customs and Manners*. New York: St. Martin's Press, 1991.

Draine, Cathie, and Barbara Hall. *Culture Shock! Indonesia*. Rev. ed. Portland, OR: Graphic Arts Center Publishing Company, 1990.

Emerick, Yahiya. *The Complete Idiot's Guide to Understanding Islam*. Indianapolis, IN: Alpha Books, 2002.

Esposito, John L. *What Everyone Needs to Know About Islam*. Oxford, England: Oxford University Press, 2002.

Esposito, John L., ed. *The Oxford Encyclopedia of the Modern Islamic World*. 4 vols. Oxford, England: Oxford University Press, 1995.

Fadiman, James, and Robert Frager, eds. *Essential Sufism*. San Francisco, CA: HarperSanFrancisco, 1997.

Frishman, Martin, and Hasan-Uddin Khan, eds. *The Mosque*. London, England: Thames and Hudson, 1994.

Gilsenan, Michael. *Recognizing Islam: Religion and Society in the Modern Middle East*. Rev. ed. London, England: I. B. Tauris, 2000.

Glassé, Cyril. *The Concise Encyclopedia of Islam*. San Francisco, CA: HarperSanFrancisco, 1991.

Gollaher, David L. *Circumcision: A History of the World's Most Controversial Surgery*. New York: Basic Books, 2000.

Gordon, Matthew S. *Islam: Origins, Practices, Holy Texts, Sacred Persons, Sacred Places*. Oxford, England: Oxford University Press, 2002.

Hasan, Asma Gull. *American Muslims: The New Generation*. New York: Continuum, 2000.

Jereb, James F. *Arts and Crafts of Morocco*. San Francisco, CA: Chronicle Books, 1995.

Lunde, Paul. *Islam: Faith, Culture, History*. London, England: D. K. Publishing, 2002.

Macleod, Calum, and Bradley Mayhew. *Uzbekistan: The Golden Road to Samarkand*. 4th ed. Hong Kong: Odyssey Publications, 2002.

Maloney, Clarence, ed. *The Evil Eye*. New York: Columbia University Press, 1976.

Matlins, Stuart M., and Arthur J. Magida, eds. *How to Be a Perfect Stranger*. Woodstock, VT: Skylight Paths Publishing, 2003.

Nanji, Azim A., ed. *The Muslim Almanac: A Reference Work on the History, Faith, Culture, and Peoples of Islam*. Detroit, MI: Gale, 1996.

Nasr, Seyyed Hossein. *Islam: Religion, History, and Civilization*. San Francisco, CA: HarperSanFrancisco, 2003.

Newby, Gordon D. *A Concise Encyclopedia of Islam*. Oxford, England: Oneworld, 2002.

The gold-capped minaret of Sultan Thakorotuan Mosque in Male, the capital of Maldives.

Padwick, Constance E. *Muslim Devotions: A Study of Prayer-Manuals in Common Use*. Oxford, England: Oneworld, 1997.

Patai, Raphael. "Folk Islam." In *The Encyclopedia of Religion*, edited by Mircea Eliade. Vol. 5. New York: Macmillan, 1987.

Renard, John, ed. *Windows on the House of Islam: Muslim Sources on Spirituality and Religious Life*. Berkeley: University of California Press, 1998.

Sakr, Ahmad H. *Feasts, Festivities, and Holidays*. Lombard, IL: Foundation for Islamic Knowledge, 1999.

Schimmel, Annemarie. "Cats." In *The Encyclopedia of Religion*, edited by Mircea Eliade. Vol. 3. New York: Macmillan, 1987.

Sells, Michael A. *Approaching the Quran*. Ashland, OR: White Cloud Press, 1999. (Includes a CD)

Shad, Adbur Rehman. *Do's and Do Not's in Islam*. 3rd ed. New Delhi, India: Adam Publishers, 1992.

Shah, Idries. *The Exploits of the Incomparable Mulla Nasrudin*. New York: Simon and Schuster, 1996.

Shah, Idries. *Learning How to Learn: Psychology and Spirituality the Sufi Way*. Reprint, New York: Penguin Arkana, 1996.

Shah, Idries. *Tales of the Dervishes: Teaching Stories of the Sufi Masters over the Past Thousand Years*. New York: E. P. Dutton, 1970.

Shah, Idries. *The Way of the Sufi*. New York: E. P. Dutton, 1969.

Smith, Jane I. *Islam in America*. New York: Columbia University Press, 1999.

Warrier, Shrikala, and John G. Walshe. *Dates and Meanings of Religious and Other Multi-ethnic Festivals*, *2002-2005*. London, England: Foulsham Educational, 2001.

Weiss, Walter M., and Kurt-Michael Westerman. *The Bazaar: The Markets and Merchants of the Islamic World*. London, England: Thames and Hudson, 1994.

The minaret of the Quba Mosque in Medina, Saudi Arabia.

Resources for Children

Husain, Sharukh. *What Do We Know About Islam?* New York: Peter Bedrick Books, 1995.

Kalman, Bobbie. *Afghanistan: The Culture*. New York: Crabtree Publishing, 2003.

Kalman, Bobbie. *Afghanistan: The People*. New York: Crabtree Publishing, 2003.

Kelsey, Alice Geer. *Once the Hodja*. New York: David McKay, 1945.

Knight, Khadijah. *Islam*. New York: Thompson Learning, 1996.

Morris, Neil. *The Atlas of Islam: People, Daily Life, Traditions*. Hauppauge, NY: Barron's Educational, 2003.

Rodseth, Lars, Sally Howell, and Andrew Shryock. *Arab World Mosaic: A Curriculum Supplement for Elementary Teachers*. Detroit, MI: ACCESS Cultural Arts Program, 1994.

Wilkinson, Philip. *Islam (The Eyewitness Guides)*. London, England: D. K. Publishing, 2002.

Web Sites

Dr. Clay Shotwell, a music professor at Augusta State University, hosts an informative site titled "Music of Islam." Visitors can listen to a recording of the adhan (call to prayer), a mawal, and a Sufi song:
http://www.aug.edu/~cshotwel/2001.Islam.htm

For more on music and chant in Islam consult the "Islamic Art, Music, and Architecture Around the World" page posted by Professor Alan Godlas of the University of Georgia's Department of Religion. Includes links to recordings of the call to prayer, Quranic chanting, Madh, Dhikr, Sufi songs, Qawwali music, and more:
http://www.uga.edu/islam/IslArt.html

Great Mosque door knocker from Damascus in Aleppo, Syria.

For more on how to perform salat see the Shadhiliyya Sufi Center of North America's explanation at: **http://suficenter.org/Practices/performsalat.html**

A slightly different version of salat is described at Islamicity.com:
http://islamicity.com/Mosque/salat/salat9.htm

The Islamic Affairs Department of the Royal Embassy of Saudi Arabia explains various aspects of Islam on its web site. Includes explanation of the call to prayer, instructions on how to perform wudu (ablutions) and salat, and furnishes program that calculates correct local prayer times in the United States and other countries: **http://www.iad.org/**

The Turkish Cultural Foundation maintains a web site that offers information on many aspects of Turkish culture, including women's and men's rights and roles, the customs surrounding weddings, funerals, birth, and circumcision, and descriptions of Turkish prayer beads, mosques, hospitality, home layout, and much more: **http://www.turkishculture.org/**

For a list of female Muslim names and their meanings see the following page, sponsored by Islam for Today, a site authored by Hussein Abdulwaheed Amin, an American convert to Islam, and dedicated to bringing information about the contemporary practice of Islam to the web:
http://www.islamfortoday.com/female_names.htm

For a discussion of female dress codes in Islam, and an argument against compulsory veiling, see "Is Hijab Compulsory?" and "Women in Islam: Hijab," articles by Dr. Ibrahim B. Syed, at: **http://www.islamfortoday.com/syed01.htm**
http://www.islamfortoday.com/syed06.htm

For the history of female dress in Islam see Lyn Reese's web article entitled "Historical Perspectives on Islamic Dress," posted at the Women in World History web site at: **http://www.womeninworldhistory.com/essay-01.html**

For more on the debate about the veil in Turkey see "Turkey: The Veil Is a Symbol of the Rise of Islamism," by Jolyon Naegele, on the Radio Free Europe web site at: **http://www.rferl.org/features/1998/08/F.RU.980804132001.asp**

For more on the symbolism of the color green see the page posted by Web-Exhibits.org at: **http://webexhibits.org/pigments/indiv/color/greens.html**

See also a web article by Muslim herbologist and natural healer Karima Burns, entitled "The Healing Colors of Friday Prayer," at: **http://www.islam-online.net/english/Science/2001/02/article15.shtml**

For more folktales concerning Nasreddin Hodja, see retired professor of folklore D. L. Ashliman's site at: **http://www.pitt.edu/~dash/hodja.html#nasreddin**

Videos

A Visit to a Mosque in America: Understanding Islam and the American Muslim Community. Willowbrook, IL: Astrolabe, 2002. (Presented by the Islamic Center of Greater Cincinnati.)

A tile panel above the front door of the al-Attaar Mosque in Tripoli, Lebanon.

Section Three

Calendar System, Holidays, and Other Days of Observance

Section Three:
Calendar System, Holidays, and Other Days of Observance

Overview

Most of the Muslim holidays and festivals discussed in this book are scheduled according to the Muslim calendar. The Muslim calendar differs significantly from the Gregorian calendar used in the United States (and in most of the rest of the world). Therefore this section of the book begins with an explanation of the history and workings of the Muslim calendar.

Opposite page: Faithful Muslims crowd into the Ethem Bey Mosque in Tirane, Albania, for Ramadan prayers.

It's important to point out that certain conservative Muslims recognize only three of the holidays and festivals presented in this book. They are the fast of *Ramadan*, *Eid al-Fitr*, and *Eid al-Adha*. Conservative Muslims accept these holidays because their origins can be traced back to teachings contained in the Quran. Indeed, these festivals are considered to be the three most important in Islam. Nevertheless, throughout the Muslim world, many people celebrate other holidays in addition to these three. Important among them are *Mulid al-Nabi* (Birthday of the Prophet), *Laylat al-Bara'ah* (Night of Forgiveness), *Laylat al-Miraj* (Night of the Ascension), *Laylat al-Qadr* (Night of Power), and *Ashura*.

Some festivals presented in this book take place in certain locales only. For example, *Hidrellez* is primarily a Turkish observance. Most saints' celebrations, too, are local observances. Thousands of saints' festivals take place in Muslim communities around the world. In addition to general descriptions of these kinds of events, the book profiles seven saint's day celebrations from different parts of the Muslim world: South Asia, Southeast Asia, the Middle East and Turkey, North Africa, and West Africa. These profiles not only tell a little bit about each saint, but also show some of the ways in which local culture, custom, and history color the practice of Islam in different parts of the world.

Finally, in addition to providing information on holidays and festivals, this section of the book also includes descriptions of regularly occurring religious observances. These include Friday, the Muslim holy day, and the *Hajj*, a religious pilgrimage scheduled each year during the Muslim month of Dhu al-Hijjah. The White Nights — good luck days according to Muslim folklore — are also covered here.

Section three begins with an explanation of the Muslim calendar. Descriptions of Muslim holidays and festivals follow, arranged in calendar order (according to the Muslim calendar). A description of Friday observances comes after that, succeeded by a discussion of Hidrellez, which is scheduled according to the Gregorian calendar. The Lamp Nights, a collection of holidays, and the White Nights, which fall on the middle days of each month, appear next. Finally, the book concludes with a look at Muslim saints, their shrines, and their festivals.

Chapter 27
The Muslim Calendar

Introduction

The world has known many different calendar systems since human beings first began to keep track of time. Each civilization's history, culture, dominant religion, and knowledge of the natural world has influenced its time-reckoning system. As a result, these systems define, measure, and divide the passing of time in different ways.

The calendar in use in the United States is called the Gregorian calendar. It is the most commonly used calendar system in the world. The Gregorian calendar emerged out of Western Europe. European scientists invented this calendar in the 16th century. It fixed several long-standing problems with Europe's ancient Roman calendar—called the Julian calendar. By the 16th century scholars were well aware that the Christian holidays were not occurring at the same time of year as they had in ancient times. The problem hinged on the fact that the actual solar year (the number of days it takes the earth to revolve around the sun) is slightly shorter than the makers of the ancient Julian calendar had supposed. So each year the Julian calendar moved ahead of the solar year by about 11 minutes. Christmas, which had originally been scheduled for the winter solstice, was now being celebrated about a week and a half after the solstice. The desire to fix the timing of religious holidays, especially Easter, prompted Pope Gregory XIII to authorize a new calendar system, which was named after him. After the Roman Catholic Church gave the new Gregorian calendar its blessing, the countries of Europe gradually began to adopt it.

Foreign words used in the text are defined in the Glossary, pages 423-40.

251

European colonization efforts spread the calendar across the globe during the 17th, 18th, and 19th centuries.

Today almost every country in the world uses the Gregorian calendar in government and business affairs. (Saudi Arabia and Ethiopia are notable exceptions to this rule.) In many nations and among many religious groups, however, religious matters are still regulated by traditional calendars. The Muslim calendar is one of the most influential of these traditional calendars, in that more than a billion Muslims consult it to determine the dates of their most important holidays.

Above and opposite page: Quba, the first mosque of Islam, was originally built by the Prophet Muhammad and his fellow emigrants in 622. That year marks the beginning of both the Muslim Era and the Muslim calendar.

The Christian Era, the Muslim Era, and the Founding of the Muslim Calendar

The Gregorian calendar assigns the year of Jesus' birth as the first year in its calendar system. According to the traditional way of thinking, Jesus' birth began the Christian Era. In recent years, however, some people have objected to the Christian bias in this calendar system, which they feel implicitly honors Christianity above other religions. In an attempt to correct this bias, some scholars have renamed the Christian Era the "Common Era." In recent years, the term "Common Era" has been coming into accepted usage.

In the Gregorian calendar system, years prior to Jesus' birth are noted as B.C., meaning "before Christ," although these days some people prefer the initials B.C.E., meaning "before the Common Era." Similarly, the years after Jesus' birth used to be designated as A.D. which stands for the Latin phrase *anno Domini*, meaning "year of (our) Lord." In recent years some people have begun referring to them as C.E., or Common Era.

Islam, too, declares a pivotal year in its history to be the starting date of its calendar and the beginning of the Muslim Era. The Muslim calendar establishes the year 622 C.E. as year one of the Muslim Era. In 622 Muhammad and a small band of his followers journeyed from Mecca to Medina, where they founded the first society run according to Muslim beliefs, rules, and values. Muslims call this event the *Hijrah*, or migration. Though Muhammad had begun receiving revelations from God years before the Hijrah, Muslims view the founding of an Islamic society as the event that really marks the beginning of Islam. The Muslim calendar designates 622 C.E. as 1 A.H. The A.H. stands for *anno Hegira*, which is Latin for "year of the Hijrah."

The basic shape of the Muslim month, year, and day is suggested in the Quran. Other details were worked out later by religious experts. Historians usually credit Umar Ibn al-Khattab (d. 644), the second caliph, with establishing the Muslim calendar about ten years after Muhammad's death. He reckoned that the Hijrah took place on July 16, 622 C.E., so he began the Muslim calendar on that date.

Until the establishment of the Muslim calendar, the Muslim community named the years, in accordance with ancient Arabian tradition. For example, the year after the Hijrah to the year of Muhammad's death are known as follows:

Permission	2 A.H.	(623 C.E.)
Order for Fighting	3 A.H.	(624 C.E.)
Trial	4 A.H.	(625 C.E.)
Congratulation on Marriage	5 A.H.	(626 C.E.)
Earthquake	6 A.H.	(627 C.E.)
Enquiring	7 A.H.	(628 C.E.)
Victory	8 A.H.	(629 C.E.)
Equality	9 A.H.	(630 C.E.)
Exemption	10 A.H.	(631 C.E.)
Farewell	11 A.H.	(632 C.E.)

Because the Muslim year is shorter than the Gregorian year by some 11 days, the two calendar systems do not run along at an even pace. For example, during the course of 100 Muslim years, only about 97 Gregorian years will have taken place:

100 A.H.	is roughly equivalent to	719 C.E.
200 A.H.	is roughly equivalent to	816 C.E.
1400 A.H.	is roughly equivalent to	1979 C.E.

The Gregorian year 2004 straddles two Muslim years: 1424 and 1425.

The Ancient Arab Calendar and the Muslim Calendar

The Muslim calendar is similar to the calendar that was in use in Arabia during Muhammad's day. Whereas the Gregorian calendar takes the earth's yearly orbit around the sun as its primary cycle, the ancient Arabian calendar was rooted in the cycles of the moon. In this regard it resembled a number of other important Middle Eastern calendar systems, including the Jewish calendar. The ancient Arabs found, however, that the months kept slipping behind the seasons, and so, inspired by the calendar used by the ancient Jews, they added extra days to their year in order to keep the lunar months abreast of the solar seasons. This addition was necessary because moon cycles, or months, do not divide evenly into sun cycles, or years. It takes the earth 365.2422 days to revolve around the sun, a period of time we know as a year. The moon completes its cycle of waxing, waning, disappearing, and reappearing in 29.53059 days. In the course of one year, the moon completes 12 full cycles, and moves 11 days into a 13th cycle. Thus in a calendar based solely on 12 moon cycles, the lunar months will slip backwards through the seasons by about 11 days a year. The addition of extra days, called intercalary days, kept the months of the Jewish and Arabian calendars occurring at approximately the same time of year.

The Muslim calendar resembles the ancient Arab calendar in that each month begins with the appearance of the new crescent moon. The Quran states:

> They ask you of the new moons.
> Say: "These are periods set for men (to reckon) time,
> and for pilgrimage" (Quran 2:189, Ali trans.).

Like the ancient Arab calendar, the Muslim calendar also divides the year up into 12 months. The Quran validates this division:

> The number of months with God is twelve in accordance with
> God's law since the day He created the heavens and the earth
> (Quran 9:36, Ali trans.).

The Muslim calendar also retains the ancient Arab names for these 12 months, most of which reflect the seasonal events that the pagan Arabs associated with that time of year:

Muharram ....sacred month
Safar..empty month
Rabi al-Awwal ....first rainy/grazing month
Rabi al-Thani (or Rabi al-Akhir) ....second rainy/grazing month
Jumada al-Ula...first dry month
Jumada al-Akhira (or Jumada al-Thaniyya) ......second dry month
Rajab..revered month
Shaban...month of dispersion
Ramadan..month of great heat
Shawwal ....hunting month
Dhu al-Qada...truce month
Dhu al-Hijjah...pilgrimage month

The third and fourth months are also referred to as first Rabi and second Rabi. The fifth and sixth months also go by the names first Jumada and second Jumada.

Islam retained the traditional four holy months of ancient Arabia: Muharram, Rajab, Dhu al-Qada, and Dhu al-Hijjah. Islamic teachings forbid warfare during these months, except when it is necessary to protect Islam and Muslims from attack.

Months in the Muslim Calendar

The Muslim calendar differs from that of ancient Arabia in that it dropped the extra intercalary days that the ancient Arabs used to anchor the months to specific seasons. The Quran itself commands Muslims to do so. It proclaims:

> Intercalating a month is adding to unbelief.
> The unbelievers are misguided by this,
> for they take the same month to be sacred one year
> and sacrilegious the next,
> thus making the number of months sanctified by God
> accord with theirs
> in order to make what God has forbidden, lawful.
> Attractive can seem to them their evil deeds;
> But God does not show the unbelievers the way
> (Quran 9:37, Ali trans.).

Therefore, in the Muslim calendar the months do slip backwards through the solar year. What's more, because the Muslim year consists solely of 12 lunar months, it is shorter than the Gregorian year by some 11 days. In the space of 32 Gregorian years, the followers of Islam will have completed 33 Muslim years. This means that if the holy month of Ramadan begins in the first week of January in a given Gregorian year, then 32 Gregorian years will pass before it begins again in that week. It also means Ramadan—and all other holidays and events scheduled according to the Muslim calendar—gradually rotate through all the months of the Gregorian year and seasons of the solar year. Therefore, Muslim holidays do not generally have strong seasonal themes, as do some Christian and many folk European holidays. Finally, it is possible for an annual Muslim holiday to fall twice within a single Gregorian year. For instance, in 1943 Islamic New Year's Day (the First of Muharram) occurred once on January 8, and again on December 28.

According to Muslim tradition, a month begins when at least two reliable observers spot the new crescent moon in the sky. In the past, religious scholars usually undertook the duty of scanning the night skies for the new moon. Even though astronomers can now predict the cycles of the moon, many Muslims believe that it is necessary to wait until the moon is sighted to proclaim the beginning of a new month. For this reason it is often difficult to obtain a Muslim calendar that has been printed in advance. What's more, local weather conditions may prevent a new moon from being sighted in one locale, but not another. To complicate matters further, Muslims living in non-Muslim lands may follow the moon sightings made in Saudi Arabia, or by Islamic experts in other Muslim countries. Therefore it sometimes occurs that the various Muslim countries decide to start the month on different days. Groups of Muslims living in the same country may even decide to start the month on different days.

In Malaysia, Indonesia, and Brunei, Muslim authorities scan the skies at sunset for the new moon. They declare the beginning of a new month when the moon is three degrees away from the sun and two degrees over the horizon. In Saudi Arabia, experts use calculations to determine on which day the new crescent moon appears. Many Muslims living in Europe follow Saudi Arabia's decision. Iraq, Syria, and Turkey often synchronize their calendar with that of Saudi Arabia or Egypt. Egyptian authorities declare the beginning of a new month when the new crescent moon sets at least five minutes after the sun goes down. While the Egyptians do not rely on moon sightings, a number of other Muslim countries do. These include Pakistan, India, and Bangladesh.

The Islamic Shura Council of North America (which represents the four largest Muslim organizations in North America) has recently decided to rely on moon sightings as well. Not all American Muslims accept this decision, however. Any Muslim living in North America may report a new moon sighting to headquarters of the Islamic Society of North America. If the astronomers there agree that the moon could be visible on this date, and find the description given by the caller to conform with the expected appearance of the new moon, then they declare that the new month has begun.

The new crescent moon can be seen over the skyline of Cairo, Egypt's, minarets and domes.

The Muslim calendar system also assigns lengths to each month:

Muharram	30 days	Rajab	30 days
Safar	29 days	Shaban	29 days
Rabi al-Awwal	30 days	Ramadan	30 days
Rabi al-Thani	29 days	Shawwal	29 days
Jumada al-Ula	30 days	Dhu al-Qada	30 days
Jumada al-Akhira	29 days	Dhu al-Hijjah	29 or 30 days

If sightings rather than calculations are relied on, however, the actual length of each month may vary from the number of days given above. Furthermore, the calculated calendar adds an additional day to Dhu al-Hijjah in 11 out of every 30 years. This addition brings the average length of the Islamic month to just three seconds short of the actual length of the lunar cycle, which scientists have calculated to be 29.53059 days.

Days in the Muslim Calendar

The Quran specifically states that the cycles of the sun as well as the moon are to be used for reckoning time.

> He [God] ushers in the dawn,
> and he made the night for rest,
> the sun and moon a computation.
> Such is the measure appointed by Him,
> the omnipotent and all-wise (Quran 6:96, Ali trans.).

In the Muslim calendar each new day begins at sunset and ends at sunset the following day. Therefore a Muslim day will straddle two dates on the Gregorian calendar. For example, according to the Muslim calendar, Friday—which Muslims observe as the weekly day of congregational prayer—begins on Thursday evening and ends Friday at sundown. Because it is seen as part of the weekly holy day, Thursday evening is a favorite time for all kinds of spiritual activities and gatherings.

The position of the sun in the sky also determines the correct hour for daily prayer. These times vary throughout the year, just as the hour of sunrise and sunset varies throughout the year.

Weeks in the Muslim Calendar

The Muslim week consists of seven days with Sunday designated as the first day of the week. The days are numbered rather than named, except for Friday and Saturday. Saturday is known as *Yawm al-Sabt*, the Day of Rest (Sabbath). The ancient Arabs borrowed this name from the Jews. Islam does not teach that Saturday should be observed as a day of rest, however.

Years in the Muslim Calendar

The Muslim year begins on the first day of Muharram. The year lasts 354 or 355 days, depending on whether or not an extra day was added to Dhu al-Hijjah. The fact that the year is about ten or eleven days short of the actual time it takes the earth to revolve around the sun accounts for the fact that, according to the Gregorian calendar, each year the Muslim months begin slightly earlier than they did the previous year.

Chapter 28
The First of Muharram

New Year's Day

Muharram is the first month in the Muslim calendar. Therefore, for Muslims the first of Muharram is New Year's Day. Muslims observe the first of Muharram with little fanfare. Pious men attend dawn prayers at the mosque. In some Muslim countries special evening services take place at the mosque. They may include prayers, *dhikr* sessions, and Quran recitations.

The first month of the very first Muslim year began with an important event in the history of Islam, that is, the Hijrah, or migration from Mecca to Medina. Muslims remember this event on the first of Muharram. They may spend some time thinking or reading about those who left the safety and stability of their old lives behind to form the first Muslim community in Medina.

In some Arab countries, the following dish is eaten on the second day of the Muslim new year. Some say that consuming the hundreds of broken vermicelli noodles increases the chances of having children. Others say the noodles represent the prolongation of one's employment or increase in income.

> *The first month of the very first Muslim year began with an important event in the history of Islam, that is, the Hijrah, or migration from Mecca to Medina. Muslims remember this event on the first of Muharram.*

Foreign words used in the text are defined in the Glossary, pages 423-40.

Rice with Vermicelli

1 cup vermicelli noodles, broken into one-inch pieces
2½ tablespoons olive oil
1½ cups rice
3½ cups hot chicken stock, or boiling water
1 chicken bouillon cube (optional)
2 tablespoons butter
salt

Over medium heat, fry the noodles in the olive oil until they turn a golden brown. Stir with a wooden spoon to keep the noodles moving. Be careful not to let them burn. Add the rice. Keep stirring until the rice grains are coated with oil. Add the water or stock (if using water you may want to add a cube of chicken boullion) and sprinkle with salt. Cover and cook over low heat for about 20 minutes. Then take off lid, stir in butter, and serve.

Chapter 29
Ashura
(Also called Muharram, Hosay, Tenth of Muharram)

Ashura commemorates the murder of the Imam Husayn and certain members of his family in the year 680 at Karbala, a city located in modern-day Iraq. Virtually all Muslims respect Husayn as the grandson of the Prophet Muhammad. Shia Muslims, however, also venerate him as one of the first 12 imams, or supreme Muslim spiritual leaders. Today Ashura is primarily a Shia Muslim observance. Nevertheless, some Sunni Muslims participate in Ashura processions and laments, or honor the death of Husayn in other ways. Sunnis may also focus their tenth of Muharram observances on other Muslim teachings associated with the day.

Ashura falls on the tenth day of Muharram, the first month of the Muslim year. The word Ashura means "tenth" in Arabic. Many Shias participate in observances that take place during the first ten days of the month, and others may stretch their observances throughout the entire month and into the following month (Safar). The grieving for Husayn ends on the 40th day after Ashura, following a traditional Muslim custom of observing a 40-day period of mourning for the dead. This holiday, which falls on the 20th day of Safar, is called *Arbaeen* (Arabic for "forty"). Indian Muslims call the same observance *Cahallum*.

The tomb of Husayn, grandson of the Prophet Muhammad, is located in Karbala, Iraq.

Foreign words used in the text are defined in the Glossary, pages 423-40.

The Example of the Prophet, Sunni Customs, and Muslim Lore

Decades before the murder of Husayn, the Prophet adopted the practice of observing the tenth of Muharram as an optional fast day. Some scholars believe that he borrowed this practice from local Jewish communities, who fasted on the tenth day of the first month of the Jewish calendar (Tishri). Jewish people call this holiday *Yom Kippur*, or the Day of Atonement. They dedicate the day to acknowledging their sins, asking forgiveness from God, and reconciling with others.

For Muslims, the tenth of Muharram has special historical significance that dates back even before the founding of Islam. Many Muslims believe (in accordance with a hadith of the Prophet) that God assisted Moses and the Jewish people to escape from Egypt on the tenth of Muharram. Traditional Muslim lore also affirms that, following the Great Flood, Noah's Ark came to rest on dry ground on the tenth day of the first month of the year. Other bits of lore associated with Ashura suggest that on the tenth day of the first month of the year Adam was introduced to Eve, Abraham escaped unscathed from the fire, and Joseph and Jacob were reunited. Today Sunni Muslims tend to view the tenth of Muharram as a day of special goodness and blessing. Some may fast, following the example set by the Prophet.

> *Today Sunni Muslims tend to view the tenth of Muharram as a day of special goodness and blessing.*

The Martyrdom of Husayn

In the years after Muhammad's death, disputes arose over who should lead the growing Muslim community. Some came to the conclusion that the supreme religious and political leader should always come from the household of the Prophet. These people became known as Shias. Others believed that the Muslim community should be guided by the example set by the Prophet as well as by a virtuous Muslim political leader, or caliph, selected by a council of learned and upright men. These people came to be called Sunni Muslims.

In 680, after the death of the Umayyad caliph Mu'awaiyah, Shia Muslims favored Husayn to become the next caliph. Instead, Mu'awiyah appointed his son Yazid to the title. Yazid was known to drink alcohol, chase women, and practice other vices. Many Muslims felt he was not worthy enough to be caliph. Yazid used the threat of violence to quell opposition to his reign, however. In great contrast to Yazid, Husayn was known to be a noble and virtuous man. Many Shias promised to support Husayn if he rose up against Yazid. So Husayn, his family, and a small band of followers set out from Mecca on a journey to Iraq in order to challenge Yazid. Yazid's soldiers soon tracked them down, however. Realizing that they were greatly outnumbered by the approaching army, Husayn gave permission to his followers to leave him and thereby save their own lives. A good portion of Husayn's followers deserted him, but a group of about 70 men, including many family members, stayed on.

A band of 4,000 soldiers loyal to Yazid surrounded Husayn and his followers at a place called Karbala. After a few days of negotiations, during which Husayn's party was cut off from all sources of water, Yazid's troops attacked. It was the tenth of Muharram. Husayn and his company were brutally massacred. Even male children and infants were not spared. After Husayn had been slain, mounted soldiers trampled his body and cut off his head. Husayn's head was later paraded through the streets of the Iraqi town of Kufa as a warning to anyone harboring thoughts of rebellion. His womenfolk were rounded up, unveiled, and marched to the city of Damascus as prisoners.

The story of Husayn's martyrdom is central to Shia Islam. Its influence is felt far beyond the month of Muharram. So powerful is this story in forming the Shia religious outlook that some scholars have described Shia Islam as a religion of lament. Over the centuries the story has also inspired Shia Muslims to stand up against injustice, however. In recent times, the story of Husayn's death was used to inflame the citizens of Iran to rise up against the Shah in the Iranian Revolution (1979) that brought the Ayatollah Khomeini (1902-1989) to power. During the Iran-Iraq war (1980-88), Iranian posters, radio and television announcements, and even postage stamps reminded the citizenry that, "every day is Ashura; every place is Karbala; every month is Muharram." This same slogan was used during the Revolution. Iranian soldiers sent to battle in the Iran-Iraq war had the mottos, "the epic makers of Ashura," or "Ashura is the epic of faith, the epic of blood," printed onto their helmets and uniforms.

> *The story of Husayn's martyrdom has inspired Shia Muslims to stand up against injustice.*

Over the centuries, a number of Sunni Muslim rulers have expressed uneasiness about the power that the story of Husayn's martyrdom has to inspire their Shia subjects to political revolt. This dynamic carried on into modern-day Iraq. Saddam Hussein's secular regime (1979-2003) outlawed many aspects of Ashura observances and severely limited pilgrimage to Karbala.

Mourning Ceremonies

Shia Muslims observe Ashura with a variety of mourning ceremonies. Some take the form of processions in which people carry banners or floats that represent elements of the story of Husayn's martyrdom. Other people in these parades

whip themselves with iron chains, cut themselves with knives, or harm themselves in other ways. These practices may seem strange to many Americans, but for pious Shia Muslims participating in these activities is a way of demonstrating the depth of their sorrow for Husayn and their profound religious devotion. These acts also express remorse for the fact that so many of Husayn's followers deserted him in his hour of need. Grieving for Husayn is an act of merit according to Shia belief. God confers favors and protection upon those who grieve and pray for Husayn and his family during Muharram. Shia Muslims view those who demonstrate little or no grief for Husayn as lacking in love for Muhammad and God.

Assemblies at which the story of Husayn is retold in song, verse, story, or folk drama are another important way in which Shia Muslims commemorate Ashura. Audience members respond to these performances with expressions of sorrow. In many places, special tents are assembled to host these events. Many permanent auditoriums have been built for this purpose, too. These permanent and temporary structures are given the name *husayniyahs* in Iran, Iraq, and Lebanon. Iranian Muslims may also refer to them as *takiyah*. In Bahrain and Oman they are known as *matam*. Indian and Caribbean Muslims call them *imambarah*. These informal stage settings encourage the audience to surround the performers. Many times the action moves out into the audience, and audience response and participation is usually expected or encouraged.

Iranian Muslims are noted for celebrating Ashura with folk plays called *taziyah*. The heroes often wear green and white, while the villains are usually dressed in red. The story told in these plays may unfold over the course of a week or more's daily performances.

There are two very important religious sites in Karbala, Iraq — the shrine of Husayn (opposite page) and the shrine of Husayn's half brother, al-Abbas ibn Ali (above).

Pilgrimage to Karbala

There are two very important religious sites in Karbala. The town not only boasts the shrine of Husayn, but also the shrine of Husayn's half brother, al-Abbas ibn Ali. Karbala is an important pilgrimage site throughout the year, but the number of pilgrims surges dramatically during Muharram and Safar. At this time of the year, Karbala may host as many pilgrims as there are permanent residents. These pilgrims come from all over Iraq, and also from Iran, India, Pakistan, and other countries with significant Shia populations. Many hope to take home a little tablet of clay from Karbala — which may be used as

a headrest during formal prayer—as a religious souvenir. Some of these Karbala pilgrims are extremely elderly. They come to Karbala hoping to die there, and so to gain entrance into heaven. The Quran states that there are several gates into Paradise that will open to the righteous. According to certain Shia teachings, one of those gates is located in Karbala.

In 2003, the year that U.S. military forces invaded Iraq and ousted Saddam Hussein, close to a million pilgrims converged on Karbala in the days leading up to Arbaeen. On the tenth of Muharram, Hussein's forces had held Karbala. After coalition forces established control over the city, a flood of pilgrims, many on foot, poured into Karbala. Some chanted and recited prayers as they marched. Others slashed their foreheads with knives or whipped their backs with chains. A great number of pilgrims expressed deep joy about having regained the freedom to participate in these traditional religious rituals.

The change in government has also inspired foreign pilgrims to journey to Karbala. Between August and October of 2003, American soldiers patrolling the border between Iran and Iraq struggled to hold back a tide of anywhere between 400 to 1,000 Iranian pilgrims a day. The mostly poor pilgrims have been attempting the dangerous illegal journey on foot, through deserts, mountain passes, and land-mine-strewn areas, because they don't have the necessary permits and papers to cross the border legally.

Karbala, Iraq, is an important pilgrimage site throughout the year, but the number of pilgrims surges dramatically during Muharram and Safar. Four Shia Muslims (opposite page and above) rest in one of the niches along the wall of the Shrine of Hassan (Husayn's brother).

Foods

In many Muslim countries a special, sweet grain dish made of many ingredients is served on Ashura. These dishes go by a variety of names, including Ashura and Noah's Pudding. Indeed, Muslim folklore traces the custom of preparing such a dish on the tenth of Muharram back to Noah. It is said that when the Ark came to rest on dry ground, Noah's family scooped up all the bits of the remaining food and threw it together into a pot. The result was a delicious pudding. In most countries, recipes for these dishes are based on some combination of grains, legumes, nuts, dried fruit, and a sweetener. In Turkey and the Balkan countries, tradition urges cooks to combine 40 different ingredients in their pudding, one for each day of the Great Flood.

ᎦᎧ

Ashura Around the World

Ashura is honored in many different countries, especially those with high concentrations of Shia Muslims. Widespread celebrations take place in Iraq, Iran, India, and Trinidad. In other countries, such as Turkey, more subdued holiday observations take place.

India

In India Muharram observances vary significantly from place to place. The celebrations draw many Shia Muslims, though in some places Sunnis participate in some of the festivities as well. The following description, however, gives an overview of the kinds of customs associated with the holiday in India.

Some Muharram processions feature a white horse draped with a bloody shroud, recalling Husayn's horse Zuljanah, which returned riderless after Husayn had been slain.

Indian Muslims celebrate Muharram with assemblies (*majalis*) during which people recite poems concerning the martyrs and sing dirges. In many locations an assembly takes place on each of the first ten days of Muharram. In this way a detailed account of Husayn's martyrdom is spread over ten installments. For example, on the first day the orators relate the demands of Yazid's henchmen that Husayn accept Yazid's leadership or be killed. On the second the crowd hears of Husayn's journey from Mecca to Iraq, etc. The kind of folk play popular with Iranian Muslims is much less important to Indian Ashura observances than are these assemblies.

Indian Muslims also take part in public processions that focus on large models of the martyrs' tombs that are carried, as parade floats, on the shoulders of many strong men. Whereas in Iran the word taziyah refers to a folk drama about Husayn, in India it refers to the model tombs. On the first of Muharram temporary shelters, called *imambaras*, are erected to house the taziyahs. They also serve as the site for mourning assemblies. The temporary imambaras are equipped with detachable standards (flags or banners mounted on a pole). The standards are removed and carried during processions. Worshipers adorn the standards with locks of hair, and colorful threads, or cloths. These offerings may be made in gratitude for, or in anticipation of, answered prayers. Many Indian towns with a significant population of Shia Muslims also boast large, permanent imambaras that can be used as auditoriums. Many come to the imambaras during the first ten days of Muharram to offer prayers.

Some Muharram processions feature a white horse draped with a bloody shroud. A blood-spattered coffin may also accompany the horse. The white horse, an important symbol of Ashura, calls to mind Husayn's horse Zuljanah, which returned riderless to Husayn's womenfolk after Husayn had been slain. Upon catching sight of the horse the women began to mourn, as they knew Husayn had fallen. During these processions, weeping bystanders often reach out to touch the coffin. Afterwards they touch themselves, thereby blessing themselves with the spiritual power or blessing (*barakah*) that radiates from Husayn and his martyrdom. In some locales the procession stops at the homes of well-to-do Shia families. The lady of the house comes out, asks about the horse's rider, and offers the horse a drink of milk. These processions, emotionally draining for the participants, may last all night.

Ashura observances intensify on the seventh of Muharram. More processions take place, featuring the standards of Fatimah, Husayn, and other martyrs. On the eighth of Muharram, the evening's processions feature the standards of both Abbas and Husayn. This night in particular, however, is dedicated to Husayn's half brother, Abbas. In some locations, especially Varanasi (Benares), worshipers practice firewalking on the ninth of Muharram. They ignite a bed of coals and wait until the flames have died down and the embers are red-hot. Then they walk across the glowing coals.

The hand is another symbol often seen in these processions. The five fingers of the hand represent the five holy people most revered by Shia Muslims: Muhammad, Fatima, Ali, Husayn, and Hassan.

The largest processions take place on the day of Ashura itself. On this day Muslims fast until the taziyahs are buried. First, however, the tombs are paraded through the town. The processions stop at many places along the parade routes. Orators sing or recite funeral songs in praise of the martyrs, and devotees slash or whip themselves, spattering their bodies and clothing with blood. Women carry their sick children underneath the floats, because this practice is believed to cure illness. As the processions move through the streets they pass through crowds that weep openly and beat their chests. Many processions include a riderless white horse. The hand is another symbol often seen in these processions. The five fingers of the hand represent the five holy people most revered by Shia Muslims: Muhammad, Fatima (Muhammad's daughter), Ali (Muhammad's son-in-law), Husayn (Muhammad's grandson), and Hassan (Muhammad's grandson and brother of Husayn). Often referred to as the "hand of Fatima," it is an important symbol of Shia Islam. At the end of the procession the tombs are taken to a special location, known as a Karbala, for burial. They are traditionally buried at noon, the hour of Husayn's death according to Indian beliefs.

Shia Muslims in India concentrate their observances in the first ten days of Muharram, but special rites also take place on Cahallum, the fortieth day after Ashura. Some continue mourning even longer, until the eighth day of Rabi al-Awwal, which traditional lore identifies as the day that Yazid released the prisoners taken at the battle of Karbala.

In India's multireligious society, the boundaries between the rites and practices of one religion and another have become slightly blurred. For example, many Hindus participate in Ashura observances in order to commemorate the death of Husayn. Sunni Muslims may do so as well, although they generally avoid the practice of inflicting physical harm on themselves. In addition, in some places in India Muslims immerse their taziyahs in water. Scholars note that immersing sacred images in water is a Hindu custom that Muslims have incorporated into their Ashura observances.

Iran

Muslims in Iran, the vast majority of whom are Shia, observe the first ten days of the month of Muharram as a time of grief and lament for the killing of Husayn.

Muslims in Iran, the vast majority of whom are Shia, observe the first ten days of the month of Muharram as a time of grief and lament for the killing of Husayn. Many pious Muslims wear black during this period to signify the depth of their mourning. During the first ten days of Muharram worshipers gather for assemblies at which a skilled orator recites the story of the Karbala martyrs. The crowds respond with chanting, crying, chest beating, and laments. Traveling storytellers also roam the town during these days armed with a backdrop painted with various scenes from the story of Husayn's martyrdom. The storytellers pitch camp in various locations, singing and reciting the story while pointing to the appropriate scenes in the painting.

A kind of folk play called a *taziyah*, in which the tragic events surrounding the murder of Husayn are acted out, also takes place during these days. In some locations the entire story is broken up into ten different plays, which are staged in sequence on the first ten days of Muharram. An additional play, which tells the fate of the women of Husayn's family, may be performed after Ashura. Special theaters have been built for the purpose of performing taziyahs. These auditoriums feature theater-in-the-round seating. The action takes place on stage in the center of the theater as well as in aisles. Thus the audience is drawn deeply into the drama and feels as if they, too, are participating in the story. Professional as well as amateur theater groups perform taziyah plays.

Children have their own part to play in these dramas. Some participate in an event called *Shaam-e Ghariban* (The Night of the Deserted), which retells the

story of the children orphaned at Karbala. The young people divide up into two groups that sing songs and recite poetry back and forth to each other. The songs and poems retell the story of the orphans. During these recitals family members encourage the children to cry, wail, yell, and even to strike themselves gently in imitation of adult mourning practices.

In addition to attending the folk plays, Iranians express their grief and love for Husayn and their commitment to their religious beliefs by taking part in processions. Religious processions may occur before Ashura, but the largest and most elaborate ones take place on the tenth of Muharram. Floats or live tableaux representing scenes from the story of Husayn's death often accompany these processions. Some of the marchers hold poles between which are strung banners, representing the standard that Husayn carried into battle. Others inflict wounds on themselves. They may beat themselves with their own hands or with rocks, strike their backs with chains, or gash themselves with knives. Worshipers view all of these painful acts as expressions of deep religious devotion. In recent years, however, religious officials in Iran have spoken out against these practices. Still, passion for Husayn runs deep and many people are unwilling to give up their traditions. In the year 2000, Ashura processions in the capital city of Tehran drew well over a million people into the streets.

An Iranian actor dressed up as the enemy of Husayn, rides a horse during a folk play, or taziyah, marking the annual Ashura ceremony in Tehran, Iran.

271

Shollehzard (Iranian Rice Pudding)

2½ cups rice
12 cups water
2 cups sugar
6 tablespoons butter
½ cup slivered almonds
½ cup raisins

¼ teaspoon saffron
1½ teaspoons cardamom
3 tablespoons rosewater
1½ teaspoons cinnamon
2 tablespoons roughly chopped almonds
2 tablespoons roughly chopped pistachios

Rinse the rice under cold running water. Combine rinsed rice and 12 cups water in a large pot. Bring to a boil and then turn heat to medium low. Cook for about half an hour, or until rice is completely soft. Add the sugar and cook for another 20 minutes, stirring occasionally to keep grains from sticking to the bottom of the pot. Then add butter, almonds, raisins, saffron, cardamom, and rosewater and stir until combined. Cook another 20 minutes, or until mixture thickens. Pour it into a serving dish and chill for about three hours. Garnish with cinnamon, chopped almonds and pistachios, and serve.

To celebrate Arbaeen and the close of the period of mourning for Husayn, many Iranian cooks prepare a kind of rice pudding known as *shollehzard*. A similar dish (*kheer*) is prepared in India. Iranians also make shollehzard in thanksgiving for answered prayers.

Trinidad

In the 19th century, the British imported East Indian laborers to work on their Caribbean sugar plantations. These workers, many of them Shia Muslims, brought Ashura with them to Trinidad. There they began to call the holiday Hosay, a word that evolved from the name Husayn.

In Trinidad as in India, both Sunni and Shia Muslims participate in the observances, as well as people from other religious and ethnic backgrounds. This mingling of people of different cultures and faiths has given rise to a distinctly Trinidadian Hosay. For example, little remains of the Indian (and Persian) customs whereby devotees inflict physical harm on themselves as a means of expressing their grief and love for Husayn. In fact, in observing the Trinidadian holiday one finds little evidence of the laments found in Indian and Persian Ashura observances. Trinidadian Hosay celebrations tend instead towards gaiety. Some scholars believe that the light-heartedness of Trinidad's Carnival celebrations has to some extent rubbed off on the island's Hosay observances. For example, some Hosay processions include drumming and dancing similar to that found in Carnival processions. Some of the spectators drink alcohol, too, which is strictly forbidden according to Muslim teachings.

A major element of Trinidad's Hosay celebrations is the preparation of model tombs similar to those used in India. In Trinidad they call the models *tadjahs*. They are built by a select group of dedicated men, headed by master craftsmen. They usually measure about 13 to 15 feet high and 7 to 9 feet at the base. It takes about 40 days to build them. During most of this time the men maintain themselves in a state of heightened purity by remaining celibate, refraining from smoking, and eating a limited diet (a partial fast). Many people who help build the tombs see this process as a solemn undertaking through which they express their devotion to Husayn. These people may look with disapproval on those who treat the processions as simply a frivolous opportunity for fun. Special drums are also constructed for the processions, as well as two large stylized moons, which are paraded through the streets as representations of Hassan and Husayn.

> *A major element of Trinidad's Hosay celebrations is the preparation of model tombs called* tadjahs, *which take about 40 days to build.*

The processions take place on the eighth, ninth, and tenth of Muharram. The evening of the eighth is called "Flag Night," because on that night the parades center on a float covered with flags. Some of the flags represent the battle standards carried by Husayn's men. Others stand for vows made by certain devotees, and still others are there solely for decorative purposes. Drummers accompany these processions. The following night, the ninth of Muharram, is known as "Small Tadjah Night" of "Small Hosay Night." Small tadjahs, two to three feet high, are wheeled out into the streets in procession, again accompanied by the drummers. This evening's activities are dedicated to remembering Hassan.

On the evening of the tenth of Muharram the processions feature the large tadjahs, the drum bands, and the moons. These processions do not begin until after midnight and end around 4:00 in the morning. During the parade the moons are made to brush each other, which represents the last meeting of Hassan and Husayn. They are also made to brush against each tadjah, at which gesture the crowd shouts, "Hosay!" The processions start again the next day at noon and wind down around 7:00 P.M. At 3:30 — the hour of Husayn's death according to Trinidadian Muslims — a local imam says a funeral prayer service in honor of Husayn. When the processions are over the families most closely associated with building the floats attend prayer services and share a special meal. After a day of rest the floats are destroyed and tossed into the ocean.

Ashure

1 cup whole wheat (use barley if you cannot find whole wheat)	$1/2$ cup raisins
$1/4$ cup chickpeas	1 cup sugar
1 cup walnuts	3 tablespoons rosewater
$2/3$ cups hazelnuts	2 tablespoons pine nuts
8 dried apricots	2 tablespoons currants
4 dried figs, cut into slices	2 tablespoons pomegranate seeds

Place the wheat, chickpeas, and hazelnuts in separate bowls of water. Soak overnight and drain. Squeeze the chickpeas out of their skins. Throw away the skins and reserve the chickpeas. Peel the hazelnuts. Discard the skins and reserve the nuts.

Boil 8 cups of water in a large pot and add wheat. Reduce heat and cook until grain is tender, about 50 minutes. Drain and reserve cooking water. Prepare the chickpeas separately. Bring them to a low boil and cook until tender, about one hour, then drain.

Chop the apricots and figs into small pieces. Coarsely chop hazelnuts together with half the walnuts. Reserve the remaining walnuts for garnish. Take half the cooked wheat and a dash of the cooking water, and put them in a food processor. Whir until smooth.

In a large pot add 5 cups of the reserved cooking water, the blended wheat, whole wheat, chickpeas, figs, apricots, raisins, chopped nuts, and sugar. Bring to a simmer and cook for 20 minutes, stirring from time to time. The mixture should acquire the consistency of a thick soup. Remove from heat and stir in rosewater. Pour into dessert bowls and garnish with currants, pine nuts, and pomegranate seeds and remaining walnuts.

Turkey

On Ashura, Turkish Muslims remember the massacre at Karbala. They prepare a special dish, called Ashure, in honor of the day. Although now associated with the death of Husayn, the dish has its origins in the story of Noah's Ark. According to Turkish folk belief, it was the last meal Noah and his family ate on the Ark before returning again to dry land.

Chapter 30
Mulid al-Nabi

(Also called the Birthday of the Prophet, Maulidi, Mevlud Kandili, Mawlid ah-Nabi)

Muslims celebrate the birth of Muhammad on the 12th day of Rabi al-Awwal. The Arabic name for this celebration is *Mulid al-Nabi*, which means, "the Birthday of the Prophet." Many Muslims think that Muhammad died on this day. According to some scholars, early generations of faithful believers assumed that he was born on this date as well, thereby enshrining it in Muslim folk belief. Many Muslims honor the birth of Muhammad by reading poems and singing songs praising the Prophet. They may also enjoy special foods and go to mosques for special recitations or lectures concerning the life and example set by the Prophet. Processions take place in some Muslim countries.

Conservative Muslims do not celebrate Muhammad's birthday. They criticize those Muslims who do for adopting a festival that is not authorized in the Quran or the hadith. Nevertheless, in much of the Muslim world, large numbers of believers mark the 12th of Rabi al-Awwal with recitations and festivities.

History

Joyful but low-key observance of the Prophet's Birthday dates back to early centuries of Muslim history. These observances grew larger and more complex

Foreign words used in the text are defined in the Glossary, pages 423-40.

275

over time. For example, the rulers of Egypt's Fatimid Dynasty (909-1171), who traced their own ancestry back to Muhammad, began to honor the Prophet's birthday by inviting religious scholars to speak and passing out sweets. The first evidence of major celebrations of Mulid al-Nabi comes from the city of Irbil (then Arabala), a town now located in the nation of Iraq. These celebrations took place in the year 1207. The town's Sufi community was very active in these festivities. Sufi missionaries are credited with spreading the festival to East Africa.

Poems

One of the main features of the holiday in many countries is the recitation of long poems or litanies that express gratitude towards God and Muhammad, and praise the Prophet in the highest possible terms. In fact, this practice gave rise to a special genre of poetry called *mawlud*. In Turkey and lands once under Turkish rule, a particular a poem called the *al-Burdah* ("The Mantle") is a tra-

Copied in Thuluth script and complemented by spare rondels of gold, this 15th-century manuscript is opened to the text of al-Burdah (The Mantle), by Muhammad ibn Said al-Busiri (1213-1295).

ditional favorite recited every year on Mulid al-Nabi. It was written by a Berber poet born in Cairo, Egypt, called Muhammad ibn Said al-Busiri (1213-1295). His inspiration came to him in a dream that occurred during a period in his life when he suffered from paralysis. In his dream Muhammad approached him and wrapped his own mantle, or cloak, around him. Upon waking, al-Busiri discovered that he had been cured. In gratitude, al-Busiri composed "The Mantle." The poem recounts the life story of the Prophet and attempts to describe his exquisitely beautiful nature and his profound spiritual gifts. A famous line from the poet asserts that he is:

> Like a flower in tenderness, and like the full moon in glory,
> And like the ocean in generosity, and like all Time brought into one point (Glassé: 80).

Another famous poem often recited on Mulid al-Nabi was written by the Turkish poet Sulayman Chelebi around the year 1410. In this poem, called *Mevlid-i-sherif* (Noble Birth), those who hear of the birth of the Prophet respond with a litany of praise:

> Welcome, O high prince, we greet you!
> Welcome, O mine of wisdom, we greet you!
> Welcome, O secret of the Book, we greet you!
> Welcome, O medicine for pain, we greet you!
> Welcome, O sunlight and moonlight of God!
> Welcome, O one who is not separated from God!
> Welcome, O nightingale of the garden of Beauty!
> Welcome, O friend of the Lord of Power!
> Welcome, O refuge of your nation!
> Welcome, O eternal soul, we greet you!
> Welcome, O cupbearer of the lovers, we greet you!
> Welcome, O darling of the Beloved!
> Welcome, O much beloved of the Lord!
> Welcome, O mercy for the worlds!
> Welcome, O intercessor for the sinner!
> Welcome, O prince of this world and the next! (Renard: 56-57)

Over the years, both gifted poets and ordinary devotees have written poems praising the Prophet. These poems, too, may be read or recited around the time of the Prophet's birthday.

ତତ

Mulid al-Nabi Around the World

Egypt

The biggest Mulid al-Nabi celebrations in the Middle East usually take place in Egypt. Official Egyptian celebrations can be traced back to the time of the Fatimid Dynasty (909-1171). In those days, the festivities began with prayers at the al-Azar mosque and concluded with readings from the Quran given in the royal palace. Poor people, mosque guardians, and religious officials who attended the palace event were given specially prepared sweets.

Egyptian families often honor the day quietly at home, by making gifts to the poor, saying additional prayers, and giving friends and neighbors gifts of peanut, pistachio, or hazelnut candy.

In the following century, the Mamluk sultans (1254-1517) expanded the Mulid al-Nabi celebrations. They ordered the streets be decorated with lamps and large swaths of silk cloth. They also hosted a festival at Cairo's Citadel, in which musicians, Sufi groups, and singers were invited to perform. In addition, poor people, soldiers, and government workers were given presents of clothes and money.

In the 15th century, the Sultan Qaitbey acquired an enormous outdoors tent that was erected every year to serve as headquarters for the festival. Sufi groups marching behind large banners converged on the tent, accompanied by drummers, singers, and other musicians. Army and government officials brought up the rear. Once assembled the crowd settled in to eat, listen to speeches, and to pray. As in previous generations, the sultan gave away money and gifts.

In the 16th century, the sultans got rid of the tent and tried to dismantle the celebrations. The Sufi groups continued their processions and celebrations, however, and invited the king to join them. They issued these invitations right up until the reign of the last king of Egypt, King Farouk (r. 1936-52).

Today's celebrations still contain elements of festivities that took place under the kings and sultans. Celebrations begin three days before the actual date of Mulid al-Nabi. Various Sufi groups erect large tents in Cairo's El Hussain Square. Food is prepared in the tents and offered to anyone who enters. Some devotees recite poems about the Prophet while others recite the Quran. Colored lights and other decorations festoon city streets, adding to the excitement of the events. On the day before Mulid al-Nabi, the Sufi leaders and all their followers form a huge parade led by musicians from the army. Each group marches behind its

An Egyptian girl holds a candy doll, made from hot, molten sugar in the shape of a female figure that she received in celebration of Mulid al-Nabi.

own large banner to the tents on El Hussain Square. Processions also take place the following day, on Mulid al-Nabi.

In addition to these public celebrations, Egyptian families often honor the day quietly at home, by making gifts to the poor, saying additional prayers, and giving friends and neighbors gifts of peanut, pistachio, or hazelnut candy. Children receive candy dolls, made from hot, molten sugar poured into special molds. Girls often get female figures, while boys usually receive the figure of a man seated on a horse.

Kenya

Mulid al-Nabi is an important holiday for many Kenyan Muslims. They call the festival Maulidi. In coastal Kenya women prepare delicious dishes, such as shrimp pilaf, curried eggplant, cassava with coconut sauce, mango chutney, and roasted red snapper. Mosques offer special lectures on the life and teachings of the Prophet, or important social issues, such as AIDS education, economic development, and conservation of the environment.

On the islands of the Lamu archipelago, regattas take place, as well as poetry recitations, donkey races, henna painting contests, and board game tournaments. Displays of traditional music are scheduled for the afternoon and evening. During the month of Rabi al-Awwal, each mosque in Lamu chooses a different day on which to honor the Prophet with special poetry recitations. Residents of the islands who work in other parts of the country will try to make it home for this holiday. With so many residents returning to Lamu, Rabi al-Awwal has become an important time of year in which to arrange marriages.

> *A long poem written by Muhammad al-Mahdi al-Majdhoub furnishes a description and conveys the joy and excitement of Mulid al-Nabi celebrations in Sudan.*

Sudan

The excerpt on the following page, from a long poem written by Muhammad al-Mahdi al-Majdhoub (1921-1982), praises God and the Prophet, and also furnishes a description of Mulid al-Nabi celebrations in Sudan. The Muslims of East Africa observe this holiday with a great deal of enthusiasm. In Sudan, people celebrate by holding nighttime dances, many led by the members of Sufi lodges and their shaykhs. The beating of drums accompanies the dancing. The translator of the poem left certain foreign words intact in the text. For example, a *nuba* is a very large drum that is played at festivals and also at Sufi ceremonies. A *karir* is another kind of drum that is played during Sufi chanting and dancing sessions. A *muqaddam* is a spiritual teacher in a Sufi order. A *jallaby* is a long robe that is worn in many Middle Eastern and African countries. This fragment of Al-Majdhoub's poem conveys the joy and excitement of Mulid al-Nabi celebrations in Sudan.

Turkey

In addition to reciting poems praising the Prophet, Turkish Muslims celebrate the holiday by passing out sweets, burning incense, wearing their best clothing, and lighting candles. In Turkey Mulid al-Nabi is called *Mevlud Kandili*, or the Lamp Feast of the Birth, and is one of the five holidays collectively referred to as the Lamp Nights.

Excerpt from "Birth (al-Maulid)" written by Muhammad al-Mahdi al-Majdhoub (1921-1982)

Maulid Night
secret of all nights, of all beauty,
spring enchanting me with virtue's charm
tonight my Muslim land burns bright
with the works of imagination
it circles the shaikh's pillar,
blossoming with cluster lights
like Pleides light,
unveils woman's magic luster
in countless ways,
her loveliness fashioned by light
light reveals.
On 'Abdul Mun'im's Square
(who loved the people —
rain fall on his grave and bless him!)
the thousand who meet here
only on this holy day rejoice,
their painted tents granted
this one passionate night.

For it's here an old man
rocks to and fro, circling,
pounding the *nuba* dancers
keep circling, bowing,
like waves, back, forth,
up, down, their leaping
filling the night
under the long banners
that float from tent poles
like a drunken ship
on the mountain sea.

They meet, join souls
hand on shoulder greeting, feasting
they dance! They dance!
finding they drink together
the taste of joy:

eager feet stepping in
treading out the dance!
so swift they move like birds,
kicking up *jallabies*,
dervishes turning,
never stopping spinning!
feet jerking, swaying
in the nets of their robes
like fires of flame!

Karir drum beats louder
than *nuba's* echo,
each dancer rippling, bubbling,
rising like a fountain!

Now a moment of peace
quells the ringing dance,
now body forgets self,
spirit radiant with light
relaxes, the old man's eyes
close on a universe still
dreaming its great dream

The *muqaddam*, that great *shaikh*
raises his voice in song,
drawing near he pounds the sweating drum,
from his mouth scattering
the holy words of the rites:
everywhere the circle of his dancing
bending where he bends,
his drum a fire on fire!

(From *Modern Arabic Poetry: An Anthology*, by Salma Khadra Jayyusi, Editor. New York: Columbia University Press, 1987. © 1987 Columbia University Press. Reprinted with permission of the publisher.)

Chapter 31
Laylat al-Miraj

(Also called Al-Isra wa al-Miraj, Isra, Laylat al-Isra, Miraj, Night of the Ascension, Night Journey, Night of the Night Journey)

On the 27th of Rajab, Muslims celebrate Muhammad's ascent into heaven as a living man and his return with sacred teachings. The Arabic name for this observance is *Laylat al-Miraj*. This phrase means "Night of the Ascension" in Arabic. Both the story behind the holiday and the observance itself are frequently referred to as *Miraj*. Some people refer to them as *Laylat al-Isra* (Night of the Night Journey) or *Isra* (Night Journey) instead. This name comes from the traditional belief that Muhammad journeyed from Mecca to Jerusalem on a winged beast before ascending into heaven. Accordingly, some people call the entire event *al-Isra wa al-Miraj*, or "The Night Journey and Ascension."

Laylat al-Miraj According to the Quran

The Quran contains several passages often interpreted as allusions to Muhammad's Night Journey and Ascension. For example, the opening lines of chapter 17 speak directly about the incident:

> Glory to Him who took his votary
> to a wide and open land from the Sacred Mosque (at Makkah)
> to the distant Mosque whose precincts we have blessed, that
> We may show him some of Our signs (Quran 17:1, Ali trans.).

Opposite page: The Dome of the Rock in Jerusalem, completed in 691, is one of Islam's oldest and holiest shrines. It stands above the rocky summit of Mount Moriah, from which the Prophet Muhammad ascended to heaven.

Foreign words used in the text are defined in the Glossary, pages 423-40.

The phrase "the distant mosque," sometimes translated as "the farthest mosque," is usually understood to refer to a site in Jerusalem that Muslims call the Sacred Enclosure and Jews and Christians call the Temple Mount. In Muhammad's time, the Temple Mount was covered with ruins, but in the first century it had been the very focal point of the Jewish religion and the site of their great temple. After the armies of the expanding Arab empire conquered Palestine, two famous mosques were built on the Temple Mount. One is called *al-Aqsa*, or "The Farthest" mosque. The other is called the Dome of the Rock, (*Qubbat as Sakhrah*.)

Chapter 53 of the Quran offers a brief description of what some interpret as Muhammad's heavenly encounter with God:

Every devout Muslim hopes to pray in al-Aqsa Mosque—also refered to as the distant or "Farthest" Mosque —built in 715 in memory of the Prophet Muhammad's Night Journey from Mecca to Jerusalem.

I call to witness the star of the Pleiades when it has dipped
That your companion is not confused,
nor has he gone astray,
Neither does he speak of his own will.
This is only revelation communicated,
Bestowed on him by the Supreme intellect,
Lord of power and wisdom.
So he acquired poise and balance,
And reached the highest pinnacle.
Then he drew near and drew closer
Until a space of two bow (arcs)
or even less remained,
When He revealed to His votary what He revealed.
His heart did not falsify what he perceived.
Will you dispute with him what he saw?
He saw Him indeed another time
By the Lote-tree [a fruit-bearing tree found in Arabia]
beyond which none can pass,
Close to which is the Garden of Tranquility,
When the Lote-tree was covered over
With what it was covered over;
Neither did sight falter nor exceed the bounds.
Indeed he saw some of the greatest signs of His Lord
(Quran 53:1-18).

The Folklore of the Night Journey and Ascent

Muslim tradition has added many more details to the sparse account of the Night Journey and Ascension found in the Quran. The tale is told with a number of variations, but the following summary covers the main points found in most versions of the story.

Muhammad's Night Journey began on an evening that Muhammad slept next to the Kaba, in Mecca. The angel Gabriel (Jibril) descended from heaven accompanied by a flying steed named Buraq. Gabriel bade the Prophet to mount Buraq and the three of them flew to Jerusalem. They alighted at the Temple Mount, where Muhammad found assembled many of the other prophets highly respected by Islam, for example, Moses, Abraham, and Jesus. Together the prophets offered prayers to God. Then Gabriel presented Muhammad with a vessel containing water and others containing milk, honey, and wine. Muhammad chose the one containing milk and Gabriel informed him that he would obtain his desire: guidance from God and the prayer for faith. Some interpret Muhammad's selection to mean that he had chosen the path of Abraham, who, according to Muslim belief, was neither a Jew nor a Christian but rather a devout monotheist who submitted his will to God in all things.

At this point Muhammad, Gabriel, and the prophets ascended into heaven. As Muhammad journeyed upwards he passed through seven levels of heaven. The prophets reappeared to Muhammad as he passed through the level of heaven to which they belonged. According to one account, Muhammad saw Adam in the first heaven; Jesus, Mary, and John the Baptist in the second heaven; Joseph in the third heaven; Idris (probably the same as the biblical Enoch) in the fourth heaven; Aaron in the fifth heaven; Moses in the sixth heaven; and Abraham in the seventh heaven.

> *As Muhammad journeyed upwards he passed through seven levels of heaven until he reached the uppermost limit of paradise — the "lote tree beyond which none can pass."*

At last Muhammad rose above even the seventh heaven and reached the uppermost limit of paradise, described in the Quran as the "lote tree beyond which none can pass." This brought him within "two bow arcs" of God himself. According to some Muslims, at this exalted spot Muhammad found himself able to look directly at God, without either staring disrespectfully or glancing away in sheer awe. The Quran records this moment by noting, "neither did sight falter nor exceed the bounds." The ability to look directly at God revealed Muhammad's purity and his worthiness to have been granted such an exalted experience. Other Muslims disagree with this reading of the text, however, arguing that God does not have a physical form and so it does not make sense to say that Muhammad was looking directly at Him.

Opposite page: Ascent of Muhammad to heaven on Buraq, guided by Gabriel and escorted by angels. Nizami, Khamsa. Ms. Or. 2265, fol. 195a. Made for Tahmasp. Safavid dynasty, 1539-43. The original is located in the British Library, London, Great Britain.

During this encounter, God commanded Muhammad to teach his people to pray 50 times each day. After receiving these instructions, Muhammad descended to one of the lower levels of heaven and saw Moses. He told Moses about the instructions he had been given. Moses related to Muhammad the difficulty he had in getting the Jewish people to conform to God's teachings. Moses convinced Muhammad that unruly humanity would rebel against the burdensome task of performing 50 prayers a day and urged him to go back to God and ask for fewer prayers. Muhammad did so and returned to Moses. Muhammad told Moses that the number of daily prayers had been reduced to 10. Moses cautioned that human laziness would cause people to reject the rigors of 10 prayer sessions each day. So Muhammad went back to God. He asked for and received a reduction to 5 daily prayers. When Muhammad descended once again to Moses, Moses expressed doubts that people would be willing to observe even 5 daily prayers. He recommended that Muhammad revisit God and plead for another

reduction. This time Muhammad overruled him, however, feeling that to return one more time would be disrespectful.

After receiving the final instructions from God, Muhammad descended back to the earth and began the journey from Jerusalem back to Mecca. Though he was flying over the darkened landscape at top speed, he noticed several caravans on their way to Mecca. When he woke up in the morning, he spoke of his marvelous adventure to several people. Eventually the pagan Arabians found out about his claims and began laughing at him. Muhammad told his close associates about the caravans that he had seen on their way to Mecca. When the caravans arrived just as Muhammad said they would, his close associates knew that Muhammad had been telling them the truth.

Impact and Interpretations

Sufi thinkers have compared the story of Muhammad's ascent to the maturation of a Sufi devotee, as he or she progresses to higher and higher levels of spiritual truth.

The story of Muhammad's Night Journey and Ascent has shaped Islam in a number of ways. On the most obvious level, Muslim law adopted the five daily sessions of formal prayer (*salat*) requested by God as a requirement for all Muslims. Reciting these formal prayers should be more than a mechanical repetition of memorized words and phrases, however. Instead, if undertaken with enthusiasm, each prayer session should lift the believer closer to God. Muhammad drew a parallel between his miraj experience and the daily prayers of all believers. He is reported to have said, "the salat is the miraj of the believer."

Over the centuries many Sufi thinkers have viewed the miraj as a model for spiritual growth. They have compared the story of Muhammad's ascent to the maturation of a Sufi devotee, as he or she progresses to higher and higher levels of spiritual truth. The description of the seven heavens has also been interpreted as a symbolic model of the human soul.

Celebrations

In many Muslim countries people do not have to go to work on Laylat al-Miraj. Men go to the mosques to say prayers, especially in the evening. Mosques may also hold special lectures or celebrations in honor of Laylat al-Miraj. People decorate their homes with lights, and many stay up all night on this special occasion. Most Muslims consider this evening a good time to say some extra prayers. In a number of Middle Eastern countries, people look forward to indulging in a fried pastry, called *mushabbak*. In some towns street vendors sell this sweet treat on Laylat al-Miraj.

Mushabbak (Middle Eastern Fried Pastry)

3 cups warm water
1½ tablespoons sugar
1½ teaspoons yeast
2⅓ cups flour
¼ teaspoon salt
½ cup cornstarch

Oil for deep-frying
Sugar syrup
Food coloring (optional)
Plastic squeeze bottle
   (an old mustard or ketchup bottle will do)

In a large bowl combine warm water, sugar, and yeast. Stir till sugar dissolves and then let rest five minutes. Using an electric mixer or an eggbeater, slowly add flour, salt, and cornstarch and beat at low speed until batter is smooth. Cover and let rise one-half hour to 45 minutes.

Heat oil in a deep, heavy skillet. Fill squeeze bottle with batter. Squeeze batter into hot oil in the shape of a circle about two to three inches in diameter. Fill the circle with smaller circles, forming a rosette or spiral shape. When rosettes are golden brown remove from oil and drain. Four or five may be cooked at once. Dip rosettes in sugar syrup and serve. If desired, food coloring may be used to dye the sugar syrup.

Chapter 32
Laylat al-Bara'ah

(Also called Fifteenth of Shaban,
Night of Forgiveness, Night of Deliverance,
Night of Record, Shab-i-Barat, Night of Destiny,
Night of Fate, Birthday of the Twelfth Imam)

Laylat al-Bara'ah means "Night of Forgiveness" in Arabic. It is also some-times translated as the "Night of Deliverance" or "Night of Record." In South Asia this holiday is called Shab-i-Barat. It falls on the 15th of Shaban. It is widely believed that one's fate for the coming year is set on this day. More specifically, God draws up lists of those who will be born, die, undertake the Hajj, and experience other important events in this year. Sunni Muslim lore declares that God shakes the Tree of Life on Laylat al-Bara'ah. Everyone in the world is represented by a leaf on this tree, upon which his or her name is writ-ten. The leaves that fall from the Tree of Life on the 15th of Shaban represent those people who are destined to die in the coming year.

Opposite page and above: Many Shias try to visit important pilgrimage sites on Laylat al-Bara'ah, such as the Tomb of Ali (Muhammad's son-in-law), in Najaf, Iraq.

Birthday of the Twelfth Imam

Many Shia Muslims add another theme to their Laylat al-Bara'ah observances. They celebrate the birthday of the 12th and last imam on the 15th of Shaban. Born in 869 and given the name Muhammad, this boy was a direct descendant of the Prophet Muhammad through his daughter Fatima. Shia Muslims believe

Foreign words used in the text are defined in the Glossary, pages 423-40.

291

that only direct descendants of Muhammad are capable of serving as the supreme Muslim religious and political leader. They call these leaders imams. The Twelfth Imam, also called the Hidden Imam, disappeared when he was only four years old. Nevertheless, devout Shia Muslims believe he will reappear on earth at the end of time, when he will be called the *Mahdi,* or "the Guided One." Sunni Muslims also believe in the coming of the Mahdi, but disagree about his identity.

Shia Muslims honor the birthday of the Twelfth Imam by illuminating their mosques with special nighttime light displays. In addition, mosques host lectures and other educational events. Many Shias try to visit important pilgrimage sites on this date, such as the shrine of Husayn in Karbala, Iraq.

Sunni Muslims do not celebrate the birthday of the Twelfth Imam. They concentrate their 15th of Shaban observances on the themes associated with the Night of Forgiveness.

The Night of Forgiveness

On the evening of the 15th of Shaban, many Muslims attend religious gatherings where prayers are said and the Quran is recited. Many stay up late into the night, or even all night, praying for the forgiveness of their sins and asking for blessings in the year to come. In this way they hope to win God's pardon and a good fate in the year to come. These customs are recommended in a hadith of the Prophet.

In many towns in India, Bangladesh, and Pakistan, fireworks light up the night sky and children set off firecrackers on the Night of Forgiveness.

Ali reported God's messenger as saying, "When the middle night of Sha'ban comes, spend the night in prayer and fast during the day, for in it God most high comes down at sunset to the lowest heaven and says, 'Is there no one who asks forgiveness so that I may forgive him? Is there no one who asks provision so that I may provide him? Is there no one afflicted so that I may relieve him?'" (Renard: 14)

Many Muslims will also read the Quran, especially chapter 36 (called *Ya Sin*), which is strongly associated with this day. This chapter deals with the themes of death and judgment. In one verse in this chapter, God speaks of having advance knowledge of what people will do and of the careful records kept of everyone's deeds:

It is We indeed who bring back the dead to life,
And write down what they send ahead (of their deeds),

And traces that they leave behind.
We keep an account of all things in a lucid register
(Quran 36:12, Ali trans.).

In many countries, Muslim women prepare and serve special sweets on Laylat al-Bara'ah. In some countries people have the day off from work.

India, Bangladesh, and Pakistan

Muslims from India, Bangladesh, and Pakistan use the Persian name for this holiday, Shab-i-Barat, which means "Night of Destiny" or "Night of Fate." On this important holiday many Muslims stay up most or all of the night. They spend the hours in prayer for themselves and their family and in reciting the Quran. Fireworks light up the night sky in many towns and children set off firecrackers. Many families visit the graves of their relatives and pray for the dead. Those who are comfortably off give money and food to the poor, and neighbors exchange gifts of sweets. Children look forward to receiving coins from adults and eating the sweets prepared by older family members. In India and Pakistan, carrot halvah is a favorite Shab-i-Barat dish.

Carrot Halvah

4 cups grated carrots	1 cup ground, blanched almonds
4 cups milk	4 tablespoons butter
2 cups cream	½ teaspoon cardamom
1½ cups sugar	½ cup slivered, blanched almonds

Place the carrots, milk, and cream in a large saucepan and bring to a boil. While the mixture is heating stir it constantly to avoid scorching or sticking to the pan. Reduce heat to medium-low and cook for about one and one-half hours, stirring frequently. When the liquid is reduced about one-half in volume and will coat a spoon, add sugar. Stir and let cook for ten minutes. Then add ground almonds, butter, and cardamom. After mixing, let the halvah cook for another ten minutes. When the halvah begins to shrink away from the sides of the pan and achieves the consistency of thick pudding, remove from heat. Spoon it into a serving dish and sprinkle slivered almonds over the top. Serve warm or at room temperature.

Poem about the Month of Shaban
by Jelaluddin al-Rumi (1207-1273)

The medieval poet Jelaluddin al-Rumi (1207-1273) wrote a poem about the month of Shaban. The poem employs many beautiful images to describe the joy of growing closer to God during the month of Shaban.

Rajab has gone out and Sha'ban has entered; the soul has quit the body, and the Beloved has entered.

The breath of ignorance and the breath of heedlessness have gone forth; the breath of love and the breath of forgiveness have entered.

The heart is sprouting roses and eglantine and basil, since from the cloud of generosity rain has arrived.

The mouths of all the sorrowful ones are laughing because of this candy which has entered the teeth.

Man is wearing gold brocade like the sun, since that gold-scattering moon-faced one has entered.

Clap hands and speak, minstrel of love, for that ringleader of trouble has entered stamping feet.

If yesterday has gone, may today remain forever, and if 'Umar has departed, 'Uthman has entered.

All the past life is returning, since this eternal prosperity has entered.

If you are drunk[1] and asleep in the ship of Noah, why should you worry if the Flood has arrived?

The earth of Tabriz has become lit up like the sky, since Shams al-Din[2] has entered that maidan[3].

(From *Mystical Poems of Rumi: First Selection, Poems 1-200,* by Jalal Al Din Rumi. Translated by A. J. Arberry. © 1968 by A. J. Arberry. Chicago, IL: University of Chicago Press, 1968. Reprinted with permission.)

Editor's Note:
1. For Sufi poets like Rumi, drunkenness often serves as a metaphor for the kind of spiritual joy that comes from feeling very close to God.
2. Shams al-Din, who was from Tabriz, was the poet's beloved mentor.
3. Maidan is a Persian word meaning "square" or "field."

The Month of Shaban

Shaban is the eighth month of the Muslim calendar, the ninth month being Ramadan, the month of fasting. Some Muslims observe Shaban by giving in to their food cravings, knowing that 30 days of fasting lay just ahead. Others observe optional fast days during Shaban. According to a hadith, Muhammad observed more optional fast days in Shaban than in any other month. The last day of Shaban on which he fasted, however, was the 15th. Devout Muslims follow Muhammad's example by fasting for a handful of days during Shaban. Some find that this practice prepares them for Ramadan.

Muhammad believed it meritorious to fast during the month that heaven takes account of one's deeds and sets one's fate for the coming year. When asked about his tendency to fast during the month of Shaban, he replied:

> That is the month people neglect. It comes between Rajab and Ramadan. It is a month in which deeds are raised to the Lord of the Worlds. I love that my deeds be raised while I am fasting (Shakr: 32).

Chapter 33
Ramadan and Eid al-Fitr

What Is Ramadan?

Ramadan is the ninth month of the Islamic calendar. Observant Muslims fast throughout the entire month, refraining from eating and drinking during the daylight hours. This fast is considered one of the Five Pillars of Islam, that is, one of the five beliefs and practices agreed upon by all followers of the religion. Non-Muslims might assume that Muslims dread this difficult religious obligation, and may be surprised to find out that the reverse is true. All over the world, Muslims eagerly await the start of Ramadan. For many Muslims, Ramadan is the happiest time of year, similar to the December holiday season in the United States. A spirit of goodwill towards all and charity towards the less fortunate sweeps over the Islamic world. Religious devotion sets the tone of Ramadan, with increased attention paid to worship, prayer, meditation, and acts of kindness. Nevertheless, after the day's fast is over, many Muslims look forward to the distinctive pleasures that characterize the evenings of Ramadan. People eat special foods, enjoy nighttime light displays and entertainments, pass happy evenings with family and friends, and joyfully dedicate themselves to extra religious activities. At the close of Ramadan comes Eid al-Fitr, one of the biggest holidays of the Muslim year.

Through the quiet hours of the day, from dawn to sunset, observant Muslims fast throughout the entire month of Ramadan. In many Middle Eastern countries, when the sun is completely down, the booming cannon announces the end of the daily fast (opposite page).

The Origin of Ramadan

Ramadan was considered a holy month in Arabia before the start of Islam. Arabs observed it as one of the truce months during which the tribes pledged not to

Foreign words used in the text are defined in the Glossary, pages 423-40.

attack one another. The Prophet Muhammad was known to regularly leave Mecca in order to spend uninterrupted time in prayer and fasting in a cave on nearby Mt. Hira. Some say that his custom was to spend the entire month of Ramadan in this kind of solitary spiritual retreat. It was during the month of Ramadan in the year 610 C.E., while Muhammad was fasting and praying in the cave, that the Quran was first revealed to him. This event is commemorated on the 27th of Ramadan, in a holiday known as Laylat al-Qadr, "Night of Power." The Quran specifies that the fast of Ramadan was established to commemorate this event:

> Ramadan is the month in which the Quran was revealed
> As guidance to man and clear proof of guidance,
> And criterion (of falsehood and truth).
> So when you see the new moon you should fast the whole month . . .
> (Quran 2:185, Ali trans.).

The Month of Revelations

According to Muslim lore, the Quran was not the first holy scripture to be revealed during the month of Ramadan. God also sent the Torah (the first five books of the Bible), the Psalms, and the Christian gospels to humanity during the month of Ramadan. For that reason, Muslims also call it the "month of Revelations." Tradition teaches that Moses learned the Torah during the first week of the month, David acquired the Psalms during the second week, Jesus obtained the wisdom contained in the Gospels during the third week, and Muhammad received the Quran during the last week (or last ten days) of the month. For this reason, Muslims feel that the last days of Ramadan offer believers the potential for extremely close contact with the divine.

Sighting the New Moon

The date of Ramadan is calculated according to the Muslim calendar. Because the Islamic year doesn't contain the same number of days as does the Gregorian year, the month of Ramadan occurs a little earlier each year than it did the previous year. Muslim months begin when the new moon is visible in the sky. Some Muslim groups and countries determine this date with the use of astronomical calculations, while others rely on the traditional method of waiting until two reliable witnesses have sighted the new moon in the sky. The month of Ramadan is so special to Muslims, however, that even those who rely on astronomical calculations honor the tradition of scanning the skies for the first glimpse of the new crescent moon. They often cite a hadith of the Prophet that reads, "Do not fast until you see the crescent, and do not break your fast till

Important Historical Events Associated with Ramadan

Ramadan has been a very important month in the history of Islam.

- Muhammad led his followers in a successful battle against pagan Arabians from Mecca—the Battle of Badr (623 C.E.)—during the month of Ramadan.

- The Prophet became a widower on the 10th of Ramadan in 619 C.E., when his first wife Khadija died.

- In 624 he rejoiced when his grandson Husayn was born on the 6th of Ramadan.

- The Prophet and his forces rode victorious into Mecca and reclaimed the ancient Kaba as a shrine dedicated to Allah on the 19th of Ramadan in the year 630.

- Muhammad's son-in-law and successor, Ali, was born on the 22nd of Ramadan in 598 and died on the 21st of the month in 661.

- In 1973 Egypt and Syria launched the Arab-Israeli War, which the leaders of these countries viewed as a form of jihad, during the month of Ramadan. In Israel this war is known as the Yom Kippur War, because it began on the Jewish holiday Yom Kippur. In the Arab countries this war is often called the Ramadan War.

you sight the (following) crescent." In places where continually overcast skies may make it impossible to see the moon—northern Europe for example—Muslims rely on calculations or accept the starting date announced by a traditionally Muslim country, such as Saudi Arabia or Egypt. Ramadan ends when the next new moon appears, or when 30 days of fasting have been completed.

In Muslim countries, a great excitement arises on the 29th day of the month preceding Ramadan (Shaban). As the sun goes down, many people stand in the streets, climb up to their rooftops, hike up hillsides, or make their way to other good vantage points, hoping to be among the first to glimpse the new moon in the early evening sky.

People feel a surge of joy when the moon appears, signaling the start of Ramadan. Once the moon is sighted people start to offer each other Ramadan greetings. The most common greeting is *Ramadan Mubarak*, which means "Blessed Ramadan." Another greeting that may be used is *Ramadan Kareem,* which means "Generous Ramadan." Then everyone returns home for evening prayers and to prepare for the fast. In some Middle Eastern towns and cities, Muslim officials announce the sighting of the new Ramadan moon by firing off multiple cannon shots. Radio and television stations also announce the appearance of the new moon.

> *In some Middle Eastern towns and cities, Muslim officials announce the sighting of the new Ramadan moon by firing off multiple cannon shots.*

Nowadays many Muslims also use telephones and e-mail to deliver Ramadan greetings to friends and family members. In 2003, Saudi Arabians sent about 18 million mobile phone text messages offering Ramadan greetings at the start of the month.

Waking Up Early

The fast of Ramadan begins around sunrise on the morning following the sighting of the thin sliver of the new crescent moon. Traditionally, people held up a white thread and a black thread in front of them in the pre-dawn darkness. When they could distinguish the white thread from the black, they would begin their daily fast. In some Muslim countries groups of pious men, called *messaharatis*, hurry through neighborhoods before dawn, knocking on doors in order to wake people up in time to eat and drink before the beginning of the day's fast. Some trace the history of this custom back to 8th-century Baghdad. In other places the dawn criers play drums or other instruments, marching through the streets in the early morning darkness. In some Middle Eastern countries, the Ramadan dawn criers recite poems as they make their way through the dark streets. Some chant as they go, saying such things as:

> Wake up you sleepers
> And give praise to God
> Ramadan is a time for giving
> Wake up and give praises to God (Al-Gailani and Smith: 142).

Suhur

The early morning meal during the month of Ramadan is called *suhur*. People drink plenty of water with this meal. In the summer months, when nights are short and not much time has passed after the previous meal, a smaller amount

of food will be served at suhur than in the wintertime, when the nights are longer. The meal must occur before the light of dawn is visible in the sky. This requirement may place the meal as early as three in the morning. After the meal people listen for the call to prayer that announces the start of morning prayers and the beginning of the fast. In some places the firing of a cannon signals the beginning of the daylight hours. According to a hadith of the Prophet, suhur is a blessed meal and should not be skipped by those who will spend the day in fasting.

In the neighborhood of Bulaq al-Dakrour in Cairo, Eqypt, grandparents share a 2:00 A.M. suhur with their granddaughter.

Fasting

Each day of the month Muslims who observe the fast refrain from eating, drinking, smoking, and sex during the daylight hours. Observant Muslims specify in addition that those who fast may not take any substance into their body whatsoever during these hours. This includes cigarettes or any other kind of smoke, pills, injections, or even the slight amount of glue that touches the tongue when licking a postage stamp. Some Muslims will also deny themselves perfume or any other kind of scent during the fast. The day's fast ends when the sun is completely down. In many Middle Eastern countries, booming cannons announce the end of the daily fast.

The fast of Ramadan becomes more difficult when it falls during the long days of summer. It is especially difficult for those Muslims living in the far northern countries, where the summer days are especially long. A number of solutions to this problem have arisen. For example, some advocate ending the fast at the hour when the nearest predominantly Muslim country ends the fast.

Children and the very elderly are not expected to fast. Pregnant, breastfeeding, and menstruating women, as well as travelers and the sick, are also exempt from the fast. Nevertheless, they must make up the missed fast days at another time, or donate enough money to feed one or more poor people for every day of fasting missed. Some say that for every day of fasting missed, one must donate enough to feed 30 people.

> *Most Muslims believe that the obligation to fast for the entire month of Ramadan begins at puberty, around the age of 13.*

Muslim families disagree about the proper age for young people to begin observing the entire fast of Ramadan. Most believe that the obligation to fast for the entire month begins at puberty, around the age of 13. Some, however, believe that somewhat younger children should also fast during Ramadan. Parents often encourage elementary school children to fast for part of a day on several different days during Ramadan, as a means of allowing them to participate in the observance. The practice also helps to train youngsters in the self-discipline required for fasting. Muslim children are often eager to join in fasting with the rest of the Muslim community.

In predominantly Muslim countries, compliance with the official rules of fasting is widespread. In some countries, however, various kinds of external pressures also encourage Muslims to keep the fast. Some of the countries in the Persian Gulf region, for example, have passed laws forbidding people to eat, drink, or smoke in public during the daylight hours of Ramadan. Even non-Muslim foreigners must obey these rules or risk being fined or thrown in jail. In other Muslim countries, however, the decision on whether or not to break the fast in public is left up to the individual. In North Africa and the Levant, wily café owners sometimes invite flagging fasters to enjoy a cup of daytime coffee by covering over their windows during Ramadan, so the pious cannot see who may be breaking the fast within. In Beirut, Lebanon, which has long enjoyed the reputation of being the Arab world's most liberal city, some Muslims can be seen openly breaking the fast in cafés and restaurants, while others carefully observe it.

Daytime Activities

In predominantly Muslim countries, normal daytime activities are somewhat reduced during Ramadan. Restaurants and cafés often shut down completely during the day. Government offices usually keep shorter hours, as do many shops and businesses. Schools eliminate physical education and may shorten the length of the school day.

Some people, whose schedules permit, spend a good part of the day sleeping. Many go back to sleep after suhur and dawn prayers, for example. They may feel the need to catch up on their sleep since many people stay up very late during the nights of Ramadan, enjoying the evening festivities. The devout, however, stick closer to their normal daytime routines. Many of them spend any empty hours they may have due to relaxed work schedules with prayer and meditation, and by reading the Quran.

In the United States and other non-Muslims countries, few Muslims can shift their entire schedule for a month to accommodate the demands of Ramadan. So, they continue to work, go to school, and perform their normal round of activities while fasting. Sometimes Muslim parents will ask that their school-children be released from physical education classes during the month of Ramadan.

Visitors to Muslim countries may notice that people's tempers sometimes wear thin by the end of the day. Going without food and drink, especially when it is hot outside, can be a great challenge to one's ability to remain patient, calm, and polite. A rude awakening may result from discovering just how many of one's good traits disappear when one cannot satisfy one's hunger or thirst. Spiritually minded Muslims observe that making discoveries such as this is one of the main points of fasting. The humility that comes from such discoveries increases one's gratitude for the blessing of having enough to eat and one's devotion to God.

As sundown draws near, traffic jams begin to snarl in many towns and cities throughout the Muslim world. Everyone is rushing home at the same time to be with his or her family for the evening prayers and evening meal.

Breaking the Fast

The end of the day's fast coincides with the hour of sunset (maghrib) prayer. In some Muslim countries a cannon shot proclaims the end of the day's fast. In other places people listen for the call to prayer that announces the arrival of the time for sunset prayers.

A father and son from Holland pray together before breaking the daily Ramadan fast with dates and water.

A popular tradition calls for breaking the fast with a glass of water and a few dates. Muslims trace this tradition back to Muhammad, who ended his fast in this way. Some say that in so doing Muhammad was imitating something that Jesus had done before him. An old Muslim legend reports that when the baby Jesus and his parents fled from Bethlehem to the land of Egypt, they did not have the time to pack any food. As a result, they all went hungry for a little while. The first food that they came upon was a bunch of dates, and so the baby Jesus broke his fast with dates.

Many Muslims break their fast with dates and water, but some eat and drink other things instead, such as soup. After this snack Muslims prepare for and perform their evening prayers. Then they sit down to dinner. In this way, the empty stomach is not shocked by a sudden onslaught of food and is gradually prepared for the evening meal.

Iftar

During Ramadan the evening meal is called *iftar*. Iftar literally means "break-fast," which makes sense because Muslims are breaking their fast with this meal. Ramadan iftars often feature special, rich foods. In fact, some Muslims complain of gaining weight during Ramadan due to these rich meals. In many Muslim countries, tradition recommends beginning the meal with soup. Many countries and regions have their own special soup that is frequently eaten during Ramadan. Red lentil soup is popular in many Middle Eastern countries (see recipe on page 322). Tea, coffee, and fruit juice drinks also appear frequently on the iftar table.

The evenings of Ramadan are a time for eating, socializing, and celebrating with friends and relatives. In this regard, the month resembles the Christmas holiday season in the United States. Many families invite friends, neighbors, or extended family members over to share in their iftar. Well-to-do people may also enjoy fancy iftar banquets in hotels and restaurants.

The poor are not forgotten during Ramadan. Many mosques and charitable organizations hold free iftar banquets for those who could not otherwise afford to join in the celebrations. In Egypt these events are called the "tables of mercy."

Many mosques and charitable organizations hold free iftar banquets for those who could not otherwise afford to join in the Ramadan celebrations.

Evening Festivities

The evenings of Ramadan take on a festive tone in Muslim countries. Stores, cafes, and restaurants are open late. People often go out after dinner to shop, visit, attend religious events, or just to enjoy the special decorations that festoon the main streets of many towns. Colored light displays are popular in many Middle Eastern countries. In Egypt and other Middle Eastern countries, large food and entertainment tents are set up by hotels and other companies to entertain the crowds that mill about the streets during the evenings of Ramadan. In many places children's carnivals spring up during Ramadan and Eid al-Fitr, delighting youngsters with candy, games, and rides.

Quran Reading and Chanting

Many Muslims make a special effort to study the Quran during Ramadan. One popular practice involves reading or reciting 1/30th of the Quran each day of Ramadan. Over the course of the 30-day month one thereby recites the entire text.

Accomplished Quran chanters are in great demand during the month of Ramadan. They may perform publicly, or people hosting fancy evening get-togethers may hire them to recite at these private functions. Listening to their melodious chanting is a popular nighttime activity during Ramadan.

Pardons

In many Muslim countries, the government pardons a certain number of prisoners in honor of Ramadan. In Egypt this custom can be dated back to the 13th century.

> *Ramadan is a time for special prayers. At many mosques imams give extra religious talks and additional formal prayers called* taraweeh *are offered.*

Prayers

Ramadan is a time for special prayers. At many mosques imams give extra religious talks and additional formal prayers are offered. These extra prayers, called *taraweeh*, are said some time after the sunset prayers or night prayers and before the dawn prayers. Each prayer cycle, or rakah, may be repeated up to 20 or even 32 times. Many Muslims make an effort to attend the extra evening prayer sessions at their mosque. At home, worshipers may also spend more time in informal prayer, or supplications). Some beautiful supplications have been written down and are said by many Muslims during Ramadan. The following example reflects the earnest desire for increased virtue that underlines Ramadan devotions:

O God
In this month, make my being beautiful
With the adornments of modesty and chastity.
Clothe me with contentment and satisfaction.
Let me adhere to justice and equity in all my dealing.
Keep me safe from all that terrifies me.
I ask this through Your support,
O Supporter of those who are terrorized
(Safi, "The Essence of Ramadan" web article).

Some Muslims observe a kind of spiritual retreat, called *i'tikaf*, during the last ten days of Ramadan. This is not a mandatory practice but rather an optional one that those who are seeking deeper spiritual insights or greater contact with God may observe if they wish. The last ten days of Ramadan are thought to be especially full with spiritual power, as the Quran was revealed to Muhammad during this part of the month.

Muslim historians note that not only the Prophet Muhammad but also his wives regularly undertook the spiritual discipline of i'tikaf during Ramadan. The practice involves spending the last ten days of the month in a mosque, emerging only to eat (if this is not permitted inside the mosque), perform the required cleansing for prayer, take care of one's bodily needs, and to bathe. This seclusion permits the worshiper to dedicate himself or herself utterly to spiritual concerns. People who undertake this devotion spend their time in prayer and meditation. They also read and recite the Quran, and think deeply about their lives and their faith. In some countries women who wish to observe i'tikaf may be encouraged to do so at home rather than in the mosque.

Those who wish to make i'tikaf during Ramadan begin on the evening of the 20th or 21st of Ramadan and continue until the sighting of the new moon that announces the end of Ramadan. Muslims may also practice i'tikaf for short periods of time during the rest of the year. This practice is often undertaken in fulfillment of a vow.

At the Ramses Hilton Hotel in Egypt, employees of the Alfa Ceramics Company perform taraweeh prayers. Alfa is based in Port Said on the Mediterranean Coast, and the annual Ramadan iftar in Cairo affords employees a chance to visit family and friends in the city.

Zakat

Islam requires its followers to give 2.5 percent of their wealth to charity every year. This payment, called *zakat*, is one of the Five Pillars of Islam. Muslims traditionally pay their zakat during Ramadan, or during Eid al-Fitr, the festival that follows the close of the month. According to the Quran, this money should be used to sustain poor people, orphans, and widows, and to free slaves, pay debts, and spread the teachings of Islam. Muslims frequently give their zakat money to mosques and Islamic charities, or directly to poor people whom they know.

> *Muhammad once said, "If someone does not stop telling lies and promoting falsehoods during the fast, then know, Allah does not want a person simply to stop eating and drinking."*

The Spirituality of Ramadan

The fast of Ramadan involves more than going without food. Believers are supposed to refrain from lying, greed, envy, breaking promises, hostility, indecency, and speaking ill of others. Indulging in any one of these acts or sentiments is said to break the fast. Of course, Islam teaches that these behaviors should be avoided year-round. They are considered especially offensive during Ramadan, however. Muhammad once said, "If someone does not stop telling lies and promoting falsehoods during the fast, then know, Allah does not want a person simply to stop eating and drinking" (Ahmad: 409).

Even though it presents people with opportunities for enjoyment and celebration, Ramadan is a serious kind of holiday. Muslims experience the fast as a yearly spiritual training session. By fasting Muslims develop self-control, the kind of self-control that can later be brought to bear upon any situation when a person might be tempted to behave badly. It also teaches compassion for the suffering of the poor, who have to endure hunger throughout the year. One's gratitude to God for the good things in life often increases, too, when one temporarily abstains from indulging in them. Finally, by redirecting their attention away from their physical appetites, Ramadan challenges believers to focus their attention on spiritual things. Throughout the month Muslims strive to focus their minds on God. This focus on divine will and power helps them to persevere in the fast.

Muhammad taught that those who observe the fast of Ramadan find great favor with God. One hadith records a long proclamation that he made on the subject:

> Oh people, there comes upon you now a great month, a most blessed month, in which lies a night greater in worth than one thousand months. It is a month in which God has made compulsory that the

prescribed fasting should be observed by day; and He has made the Special Prayer (*taraweeh*) by night a Tradition. Whosoever tries drawing nearer to God by performing any virtuous deed in this month, for him/her shall be such reward as if he/she had performed a prescribed act of worship in any other time of the year. And whoever performs a prescribed act of worship for God, for him/her shall be the reward of seventy prescribed acts of worship in any other time of the year. This is indeed the month of patience, and the reward for true patience is paradise. It is the month of sympathy with one's fellow human beings; it is the month wherein a true believer's provisions are increased. Whosoever feeds a person performing the prescribed fast in order to end the fast at sunset, for him/her there shall be forgiveness of his/her sins and emancipation from hellfire, and for him/her shall be the same reward as for him/her whom he/she fed, without that person's reward being diminished in the least (Khandhlawi: 45-46).

Throughout the month Muslims strive to focus their minds on God. This focus on divine will and power helps them to persevere in the Ramadan fast.

Other teachings attributed to Muhammad assure Muslims that God listens to the prayers of those who fast during Ramadan and forgives them for their sins.

Ramadan in the Quran

The Quran itself links the Muslim fast to the fasting practices of the earlier, biblical religions. Moreover, it specifies that the purpose of fasting is to improve character:

> O believers, fasting is enjoined on you
> As it was on those before you,
> So that you might become righteous (Quran 2:183, Ali trans.).

The Quran also clearly establishes the rules for the fast:

> Fast a fixed number of days,
> But if someone is ill or is traveling
> (he should complete) the number of days (he had missed);
> and those who find it hard to fast
> should expiate by feeding a poor person.
> For the good they do with a little hardship is better for me.
> And if you fast it is good for you,
> If you knew.
> Ramadan is the month in which the Quran was revealed
> as guidance to man and clear proof of guidance,
> and criterion (of falsehood and truth).
> So when you see the new moon you should fast the whole month;
> but a person who is ill or traveling
> (and fails to do so) should fast on other days,
> as God wishes ease and not hardship for you,
> so that you complete the (fixed) number (of fasts),
> and give glory to God
> for the guidance, and be grateful.
> When My devotees enquire of you about Me,
> I am near, and listen to the call
> of every supplicant the moment he calls.
> It behooves them to hearken to Me
> and believe in Me
> that they may follow the right path.
> You are allowed to sleep with your wives
> on the nights of the fast:
> They are your dress as you are theirs.
> God is aware you were cheating yourselves,
> so He turned to you and pardoned you.
> So now you may have intercourse with them,
> and seek what God has ordained for you.
> Eat and drink until the white thread
> Of dawn appears clear from the dark line,

Then fast until night falls;
And abstain from your wives (when you have decided)
To stay in the mosques for assiduous devotion
(Quran 2:184-87, Ali trans.).

Ramadan Poems

For non-Muslims, reading the poetry written especially for and about Ramadan may be one of the best ways to grasp the spirit of the fast.

The 12th-century Persian poet Jelaluddin al-Rumi wrote a poem that describes the mysterious power of the Ramadan fast. Rumi argues that the fast enables believers to reach new spiritual heights by overcoming the downward pull of bodily pleasures that dull the mind and spirit:

> The month of fasting has come, the emperor's banner has arrived;
>   withhold your hand from food, the spirit's table has arrived.
>
> The soul has escaped from separation and bound nature's hands;
>   the heart of error is defeated, the army of faith has arrived.
>
> The army of *the snorting chargers* has put its hand to plunder, from
>   the fire of *the strikers of fire* the soul is brought to lamentation.
>
> The *Cow* was goodly, Moses son of 'Imran appeared; through him the
>   dead became living when it was sacrificed.
>
> Fasting is as our sacrifice, it is the life of our soul; let us sacrifice all
>   our body, since the soul has arrived as guest.
>
> Fortitude is as a sweet cloud, wisdom rains from it, because it was in
>   such a month of fortitude that the Koran arrived.
>
> When the carnal soul is in need, the spirit goes into Ascension; when
>   the gate of the prison is broken, the soul reaches the Beloved.
>
> The heart has rent the curtain of darkness and winged up to the sky;
>   the heart, being of the angels, has again arrived at them.
>
> Quickly clutch the rope out of this body's well; at the top of the well
>   of water cry, "Joseph of Canaan has arrived."
>
> When Jesus escaped from the ass his prayers became accepted; wash
>   your hands, for the Table has arrived from heaven.
>
> Wash your hands and mouth, neither eat nor speak; seek that speech
>   and that morsel which has come to the silent ones.

(From *Mystical Poems of Rumi: First Selection, Poems 1-200,* by Jalal Al Din Rumi. Translated by A. J. Arberry. © 1968 by A. J. Arberry. Chicago, IL: University of Chicago Press, 1968. Reprinted with permission.)

In 1996 American poet Daniel Moore, who converted to Islam as an adult, published a book of poems about the fast called *The Ramadan Sonnets.* In the following poem, entitled "Delight My Diet," Moore describes the beauty and strength he finds in fasting. Though hundreds of years of history and important cultural differences separate the two poets, Moore's perspective on the mysterious power of the fast echoes a theme found in Rumi's poem. For both poets, denying the appetites of the body encourages the spirit to rise to new levels of discovery and delight:

> Each year a segment of my time on earth turns dry
>   and takes me to the far edge of my life
> I turn from food and drink and lust of eye
>   (and making love in the daylight to my wife).
>
> Each time it comes the passage becomes clear
>   that thrusts me forward to that day of death,
> but there's a sweetness that's beyond compare
>   (greater than the rankness of my breath).
>
> A something that's like ease, a strength beyond my will
>   sustains the difficulty makes the day all right,
> creates a lake inside the heart that's still
>   and casts a golden glow upon the night.
>
> Each year it comes, my dread turns into quiet—
> Hardship becomes ease, delight my diet.

(Reprinted with permission from *The Ramadan Sonnets,* by Daniel Abdal-Hayy Moore, City Lights Books, 1996. © Daniel Abdal-Hayy Moore.)

About Daniel Moore

Daniel Moore was born in 1940 in Oakland, California. His first book of poems, *Dawn Visions,* was published in 1964 by Lawrence Ferlinghetti of City Lights Books, San Francisco, California. He became a Sufi Muslim in 1970, and changed his name to Daniel Abdal-Hayy Moore. He performed the Hajj in 1972 and has lived in Morocco, Spain, Algeria, and Nigeria. *The Ramadan Sonnets* was published in 1996 and his latest book of poems, *The Blind Beekeeper,* appeared in 2001. The poet currently lives in Philadelphia, Pennsylvania.

Eid al-Fitr

The close of the month of Ramadan ushers in a festival called Eid al-Fitr. The word Eid (also spelled "id") means "festivity" or "recurring happiness." Eid al-Fitr may be translated as "the feast of breaking fast." This holiday celebrates the successful completion of the holy month of Ramadan. It begins on the first day of Shawwal and lasts until the third day of that month. The holiday also goes by the nickname Eid al-Saghir, or "the Minor Festival." This name identifies it as one of the two major holidays celebrated by all Muslims. The other is Eid al-Adha, which carries the nickname Eid al-Kabir, or "the Major Festival."

When the new moon that marks the start of Shawwal is sighted, people greet each other with the phrase "Eid Mubarak," meaning "Blessed Eid!" On the first day of Eid al-Fitr, special morning prayers are offered after dawn. In many locales this prayer session, called "the prayer of the feast," takes place outside. In others the especially large crowds that gather for this well-attended service spill out of

At early-morning prayers on the Eid al-Fitr, the celebration that concludes the holy month of Ramadan, friends greet each other with a handshake outside the Al-Kulafah' al-Rashidin Mosque in central Asmara in Eritrea, Africa.

313

the mosques and spread out into the courtyard and streets. Like the noon prayers on Friday, the Muslim day of congregational worship, this prayer session includes a sermon.

Some Muslims take a different route on their way to and from the morning prayer service, a custom recorded as a hadith of the Prophet:

> Narrated by Jabir bin 'Abdullah: On the day of Id, the Prophet used to return (after offering the Id prayer) through a way different than that by which he went (Al Hariri-Wendel: 250).

Commentaries on this tradition suggest that the custom offers worshipers the opportunity to meet and greet twice the number of friends and neighbors. This custom is also practiced on Eid al-Adha.

Eid al-Fitr is a family holiday and most Muslims spend time visiting and celebrating with relatives.

In predominantly Muslim countries, schools and business close during the festival. Eid al-Fitr is a family holiday and most Muslims spend time visiting and celebrating with relatives. In many countries people look forward to enjoying special meals and sweets during Eid al-Fitr. They wear their very best clothes in honor of the festival. Those who can afford the expense buy new clothes especially for the holiday. Children often receive gifts of money and clothes from their parents. Those who successfully complete the fast feel spiritually cleansed, and the new clothes represent this state of spiritual renewal and cleanliness. Families who haven't yet paid their zakat tax pay it on the first day of Eid al-Fitr. Tradition specifies that it should be paid before morning prayers.

In many places fun fairs spring up for the holiday, providing children with plenty of opportunities to spend their money on sweets and games. Many families enjoy sending and receiving Eid greeting cards. Beautiful geometric designs or calligraphy grace the covers of these cards. Images of people, scenery, and animals less frequently appear, as traditional Islamic religious teachings disapprove of the use of representational art for religious purposes. Scholars trace the origin of Eid greeting cards back to Egypt in the 1950s. From there the custom spread throughout the Middle East. Nowadays people who own computers may also send electronic holiday greetings.

In the Middle East many people go to the movies during Eid al-Fitr, as theaters close in some countries during Ramadan. Women in the Gulf States celebrate by decorating their hands with henna. In many places people visit the graves of their relatives during Eid al-Fitr, as the emphasis on family celebrations during Eid al-Fitr inclines Muslims to think about relatives who have passed away.

Chapter 34
Ramadan and Eid al-Fitr
Around the World

The following profiles furnish country-specific information on Ramadan and Eid al-Fitr celebrations.

Egypt

In Cairo, Egypt, a cannon blast announces the start of the month of Ramadan. Each evening of the month the cannon roars again to announce the end of the daily fast. The cannon shot has become such an important symbol of Ramadan that it is broadcast on television.

During the first few evenings of Ramadan most people enjoy iftar dinners at home with family and extended family members. Then people begin to go out more. Some go to eat at cafés and restaurants, but many of the well-to-do prefer the special tents set up by the big hotels to entertain people during the evenings of Ramadan. Decorated to recall old Arabia, the tents feature tasty foods, traditional Egyptian music, sheeshas (water pipes), and other old-fashioned delights, along with more contemporary pleasures, such as promotional samples and information concerning new products. Sporting events provide another way to enjoy the evening. Soccer clubs arrange special Ramadan tournaments; in poorer neighborhoods children and teens play in the streets.

During the month of Ramadan many people stay up very late enjoying evening entertainments, visiting with friends, reading the Quran, or praying in the

Foreign words used in the text are defined in the Glossary, pages 423-40.

315

For centuries, Egypt's capital was known for its spectacular use of lanterns. Today, Cairo's children carry an age-old Ramadan tradition, swinging their lanterns and singing for treats.

mosque. Some stay up all night. Many people make up for these late hours by sleeping well into the morning.

Egyptian television stations offer their best programming during Ramadan. Families often gather around the television set in the evenings, watching dramas and game shows produced especially for Ramadan. These Ramadan shows are not usually religious, but rather are highly entertaining or dramatic. One favorite program, *Fawazir Ramadan*, revolves around the presentation of a daily riddle and gives prizes to those who solve it.

Ramadan nights sparkle with special light displays. Mosques are brightly illuminated after dark and colored lights festoon city streets. Furthermore, Egyptian children parade through the streets with their *fanus* (lanterns) after dark, singing songs, like the following:

> You have gone, O Sha'ban
> You have come O Ramadan.
> The Sultan's daughter is wearing a robe,
> Of red, yellow, and green (Abbas: 13).

Historians trace the custom of celebrating Ramadan with fanus back to the Fatimid era (909-1171). Traditional Ramadan lanterns are made from tin and colored glass and illuminated with a candle. Contemporary models may feature battery-operated electric lights.

Egyptian Muslims usually break their daily fast with some water and dates, following Muhammad's example. The iftar meal generally begins with juice, soup, tea, or broth. The rest of the meal varies depending on the preferences and income of the family, but those who can afford it may serve platters of rice and meat, as well as vegetable delicacies. These might include pickled vegetables, fried eggplant, and fried cauliflower. The less affluent may rely on *fuul* (fava beans), a staple of the Egyptian diet. Pudding or pastries often replace fruit for dessert during Ramadan. *Konafa*, a pastry resembling shredded wheat sweetened with raisins and sugar syrup or honey, is a popular Ramadan treat, as is *qatayef*, a pancake stuffed with cheese, nuts, and raisins, and drizzled with syrup. Many Eygptians prepare *khushaf* during Ramadan, a fruit cocktail made from dates, apricots, raisins, and black plums. *Qamar el-deen*, a thick apricot fruit drink or pudding made from reconstituted dried apricots, is another favorite treat. After dinner people snack on almonds and other nuts.

Wealthy Egyptians often sponsor iftar dinners for the less fortunate. It is considered an act of merit and a privilege to feed a fasting Muslim at this time of year.

In Egypt suhur differs little from a normal breakfast. Some combination of bread, tea, and white cheese, yogurt, fuul, or eggs is often served.

A striking example of a Cairo Ramadan lantern, crafted from strips of tin and pieces of hand-colored glass.

Egyptians prepare for Eid al-Fitr by painting or decorating their houses, sending greeting cards, and buying new clothes. When the morning of Eid arrives, men and boys get up and go to say their prayers at the mosque. Women and girls usually pray at home, but some also go to the mosque. Many families enjoy part of the day outdoors, along the Nile River, at parks or fun fairs. Parents often give children a few coins to buy candy and other small treats. Many families buy or bake a kind of cookie called *kahk* (literally "cake") as a special Eid treat. This cookie can be traced back to the palace ovens in 10th-century Egypt, where chefs stuffed the cookies with gold coins. Today they may be left plain or stuffed with mashed dates, nuts, or Turkish delight (a jelly-like candy). Qatayef is another popular Eid sweet. A nice meal with relatives rounds out the day's celebrations.

Kahk

1 cup clarified butter (ghee)	½ teaspoon cinnamon
½ cup lukewarm milk	½ teaspoon ginger
2 teaspoons sugar	¼ teaspoon cloves
2 cups plus 2 tablespoons flour	sesame seeds and powdered
1 tablespoon baking powder	sugar to garnish
½ teaspoon quick yeast	1 cup pureed dates (optional)

Sift together flour and spices. Put the butter in a pot and heat until close to boiling. Add the flour and spices, stirring with a wooden spoon until well blended. Or, you may add hot butter and flour mixture to a food processor and whir until combined.

Add the sugar and yeast to the milk and stir until dissolved. Add milk mixture to flour mixture and stir till combined. Turn dough out onto a floured board and knead it for about five minutes. Shape the dough into round balls and flatten them somewhat between the palms of the hands. Or, add a filling of mashed dates to the round balls before flattening. Place cookies on a greased sheet, sprinkle with sesame seeds, and let them rest in a warm area for about ½ hour. Preheat oven to 350 degrees. Bake cookies for about 15 minutes. Remove from oven and sprinkle with powdered sugar.

Indonesia

Indonesian Muslims often stay up late and rise early during Ramadan. Many take daytime naps to make up for lost sleep.

In Indonesia suhur usually includes milk or yogurt. Indonesians often break their daily fast with some water, several dates, and a kind of fruit salad made with melon, banana, and coconut. Main dishes made with coconut and meat or poultry often appear on the Ramadan and Eid al-Fitr dinner table.

Muslims living in big cities often try to visit their rural home villages during Ramadan, especially as the end of the month draws near. These trips may be funded by a special bonus, equal to one month's pay, given to many workers near the end of Ramadan. Indonesians call this the "thirteenth month" bonus. Many Muslims make charitable contributions in addition to their zakat tax during Ramadan. Beggars may be more visible on the streets of the big cities as they congregate along populated routes in order to receive the spontaneous charity of passersby. Many Muslims visit the graves of relatives in the last days during

Ramadan. There they clean the burial sites, place flowers, and pay their respects to the departed.

Indonesians refer to Eid al-Fitr as "Lebaran." The festivities begin on the evening of the last day of Ramadan (technically the first day of the next month, as Muslim days begin at sunset), with drumming, dancing, songs, prayers, and sermons. Many Muslims celebrate the start of Eid by cleaning their homes, taking a bath, splashing themselves with orange water or other kinds of perfume. Many also rise early the next day, don new clothes, and attend Eid prayers at a mosque or specially arranged outdoor location, such as a field, park, or central street. The rest of the day passes in visiting family members and friends and sharing festive meals with relatives. Ketupat, rice cakes steamed inside coconut leaves, is a favorite Lebaran dish.

Many Indonesians drop in at a friend's or neighbor's house on their way home from morning prayers. Often these brief visits involve asking forgiveness for any past offenses committed against them. Indeed, asking forgiveness from those relatives and friends one has injured or offended in the previous year is

A Ramadan feast meal from Bukittinggi (clockwise from top): red-snapper; a salad of lettuce, carrots, cucumbers and egg-yolk; "wedding" chicken; spiced beef cooked in coconut milk; lamb in a savory sauce; fern-tops; and in the center, steamed rice.

Gulai Ayam (Chicken in Coconut Milk)

10 macadamia nuts	1½ teaspoons coriander
4 cloves of garlic, crushed	½ teaspoon turmeric
½ cup chopped onion	1 teaspoon salt
1½ teaspoons chili flakes	1 bay leaf
3½ cups coconut milk	2 teaspoons ginger
2 tablespoons vegetable oil	6 pounds of small chicken pieces
1 tablespoon brown sugar	

Place the macadamia nuts, onion, garlic, chili flakes, and ½ cup coconut milk in a food processor or blender. Whir until blended. Heat oil in a large pot over medium heat and fry the blended paste for one minute. Then add the remaining coconut milk, spices, and sugar and stir till combined. Add the meat, making sure to coat each piece. Let the pot come to a boil and then reduce to a simmer, cooking for about an hour.

the hallmark of this holiday. In Indonesia the typical Lebaran greeting is *Selamat Idul Fitri: Ma'afkan Lahir Batin*, which means, "Happy Eid al-Fitr and forgive us for all our wrongdoings." Most Indonesian Muslims begin with visiting their parents and then their eldest relatives. It might take days for them to complete these rounds of family visits with their accompanying petitions for forgiveness. Other important Lebran activities include visits to parks and other outdoor areas where organized festivities are held.

Iran

In Iran, where the majority of Muslims follow Shia rather than Sunni customs, people remember the martyrdom of Ali (the Prophet's son-in-law) on the 21st day of Ramadan. According to Shia teachings, Ali was stabbed on the 19th of the month, and died on the 21st. Iranians sometimes refer to these three days as the "Nights of Revival." They are observed as a period of mourning. Some pious Muslims take to the streets, making great public displays of grief for Ali's suffering and death. Others mourn privately or gather with others at the local mosque, staying up late into the night praying, reading the Quran, and proclaiming their sorrow over Ali's death. Iranians also observe Laylat al-Qadr during these three days, unlike most other Muslims who celebrate it on the 27th of Ramadan.

Ramadan means extra time in the kitchen for many Muslim women, and Iranian women are no exception. Suhur often features some of the following foods: bread, eggs, cheese, jam, tea, *kofteh* (balls of meat, rice and herbs), and *kuku* (an omelet-like mixture of eggs, vegetables, and spices). Dinners often include a similar assortment of foods. Iranians break their fast with water, dates, bread, honey, tea, cheese, and halvah (a rose-water flavored candy). A full dinner follows. Some women prepare a different dish for every night of Ramadan.

Iraq

In Iraq the Ramadan early morning meal often includes bread, rice, eggs, cheeses, and drinks made out of reconstituted dried fruit. People break their daily fast with dates and yogurt. Lentil soup is a traditional iftar dish. After dinner, family visits, and night prayers, men often go out to coffee shops to spend time with their friends. Chess, dominoes, and backgammon are popular games at these get-togethers. The men might also enjoy listening to storytellers retell classic tales.

Kuwait

In Kuwait government offices open late and close early during Ramadan. The country comes alive at night, with food, festivities, and rounds of visits with family members and friends. Many people stay up all night.

Kuwaitis celebrate Eid al-Fitr by slaughtering a lamb and hosting large, festive meals. *Ardha*, a sword dance performed by men, is a traditional Eid entertainment.

Ardha, a sword dance performed by men, is a traditional Eid entertainment in both Kuwait and Saudi Arabia.

Lebanon

In Lebanese cities a cannon shot announces the end of the daily Ramadan fast. Lebanese Muslims break their fast with dates and a glass of water. The evening meal often features lentil soup, fresh fruit juices, *fattoush* (a salad made with cucumbers, tomatoes, lettuces, and bread), rice, and meat. Tea is served afterwards. When family and friends visit after dinner, they are offered sweets.

After dinner many Lebanese Muslims enjoy a stroll about the city streets, where they may shop, buy snacks from street vendors, or enjoy the displays of colored lanterns.

On the night people expect Ramadan to end, many go outside to see if they can spot the new moon. If it is sighted they rejoice and offer one another holiday greetings. Parents give children gifts of money on Eid al-Fitr. Sometimes girls will receive jewelry, too.

Shorabit Addas (Red Lentil Soup)

8 cups water
1½ pounds lamb meat and bones
2 cups red lentils
1 medium onion, chopped
1 cup chopped celery

1 cup chopped carrot
4 tablespoons olive oil
salt and pepper
chopped parsley and lemon
  wedges

In a large pot fry onions, celery, and carrot in olive oil over medium heat until onions begin to turn brown. Add water, lamb, and lentils. Bring to a simmer and cook over medium low heat for 1 ½ to 2 hours. The lentils will dissolve and create a thick broth. Take the bones out of the soup, remove the meat from the bones, cut into small pieces, and put the meat back in the soup. Season with salt and pepper. Ladle into bowls. Garnish with parsley and lemon wedges.

Mauritius

The island republic of Mauritius, located in the Indian Ocean east of Madagascar, boasts a multiethnic and multireligious population that lives harmoniously together. Radio stations honor Eid al-Fitr by playing *qawwalis* and other religious songs, and local television carries Islamic programming. Mauritius's Muslims, mostly descendants of settlers from the Indian subcontinent, take special pains to groom themselves on the morning of Eid al-Fitr. Men don white pants, long tunics, and prayer caps, and dab themselves with cologne. Women wear brightly colored pants, long tunics, and shawls. Many women decorate their hands with henna in honor of the occasion. A rich pudding called *sewiyan* or *sewiye* (see recipe on page 326) often appears on the breakfast table. Men attend special Eid prayer services, and then the family enjoys a day of visiting with relatives and friends, and savoring rich meals and snacks. *Biryani*, a blend of meat, vegetables, spices, and herbs, is a favorite Eid dish. Muslim families often invite their non-Muslim neighbors to join in their feast.

Morocco

In Morocco businesses and offices open late and close early during the month of Ramadan. As the sun nears the horizon everyone rushes for home, causing major traffic jams in urban areas. In many places a loud siren announces both the beginning and the end of the day's fast. Stores and restaurants reopen in the evening and restaurants often stay open past midnight. The streets are crowded during the evenings of Ramadan, with people shopping and socializing.

The iftar meal takes place in two stages. Most Moroccans break their fast by eating some dates, and then enjoying a bowl of *harira* (lamb and chickpea soup). Green tea, sweets, and cookies may accompany this small meal. One favorite Ramadan cookie, called *shebbakia*, is fried, dipped in honey, and sprinkled with sesame seeds. After this meal Moroccans perform the evening prayers, and later the night prayers. Then they have another, larger meal featuring platters of couscous cooked with vegetables and chickpeas, meat, or fish, and *pastilla* (a pastry stuffed with chicken, eggs, and almonds). Cake, custard, or fruit finish the meal.

Women decorate their hands with henna in honor of the start of Ramadan and also at the close of Ramadan. Visiting with family and extended family members is a favorite evening activity. The devout might choose instead to spend the hours reciting the Quran or blessings on the Prophet.

Above is Harira soup and lightly pickled lemons. Below is a simpler vegetable couscous.

Harira (Lamb and Chickpea Soup)

1 pound lamb cut into
  small pieces
1 teaspoon cinnamon
1 teaspoon turmeric
1 teaspoon ground pepper
1 teaspoon ginger
2 tablespoons butter
1 tablespoon olive oil
1 cup chopped celery
2 cups chopped onions

1/2 cup chopped parsley
2 (14 oz.) cans chopped tomatoes
  (separate juice from tomato pieces)
1 cup red lentils
8 cups water
1 cup chickpeas
1/2 cup vermicelli noodles
2 eggs, beaten together with the juice
  of 1/2 lemon
salt

Place lamb, butter, olive oil, celery, onions, parsley, and spices in a large pot. Cook over medium heat for 5 minutes. Add tomatoes and cook 5-15 minutes more. Salt to taste. Add tomato juice, 7 cups water, and lentils. Bring the pot to a boil. Then reduce heat to simmer for 2 hours.

Add noodles and chickpeas and cook an additional 5-10 minutes. Keeping soup at a simmer add egg and lemon mixture, stirring all the while so that it blends with and thickens the soup base. Once blended (1-2 minutes), ladle into bowls and garnish with extra parsley and lemon wedges.

Like the shops of Cairo, clothiers in Morocco also do a good business since new clothes are traditionally among the gifts that children receive for Eid al-Fitr, the celebration that follows Ramadan.

Nigeria

Nigerians call the festival at the end of Ramadan "Sallah" rather than Eid al-Fitr. In the northern Nigerian town of Katsina, Muslims celebrate Sallah with a colorful procession called Durbar. Durbar is a Persian word meaning "court" or "house." In the days when the British ruled Nigeria, the colonial governor served as the parade leader. These days, the local Muslim ruler, called the Emir, takes the top post. At the head of the parade come horsemen carrying decorated weapons and wearing colorful costumes, armor, red turbans, and copper helmets with feathery plumes. These riders are from the Hausa-Fulani ethnic group. They adorn their horses with brightly colored horse blankets, bridles, and decorations for their manes and tails. The Emir follows behind the horsemen, dressed in white and shaded by a parasol decorated with silver. Guards and wrestlers march behind the Emir. Drummers and other musicians take part in the parade, too. Spectators, also dressed in bright colors for the occasion, dance to the music.

Oman

Muslims in Oman eagerly await the sighting of the new moon that ends the month of Ramadan and begins the Eid al-Fitr festival. The people of Oman celebrate Eid al-Fitr for three days, as is common in many Muslim countries. On the evening that the new crescent moon is sighted, many Omanis stay up late preparing for the following day's activities. Men often take charge of cooking a special festival dish called *arsiyyah*, a mixture of lamb and mashed white rice. Women and children prepare fresh new clothes to be worn the next day and paint their hands with henna.

When the following day dawns, families put on new clothes, say their dawn prayers, and eat arsiyyah for breakfast. Children greet neighbors and elders, and receive coins from them in return. Then the men and boys of the family head out to special prayer services set up in outdoors locations used only during Eid. Afterwards everyone shakes hands with one another, as Eid al-Fitr is understood to be a blessed time of year for extending forgiveness and resolving conflicts. Then the men and boys follow the local shaykh to a large hall where a communal meal in served. This meal usually features arsiyyah, fruit, halvah, and coffee. Family visits and trips to bazaars that sell treats and toys for children fill out the rest of the day. Omanis also celebrate with folk music and dancing, and by firing guns off into the air.

> *After the special prayer services everyone shakes hands with one another, as Eid al-Fitr is understood to be a blessed time of year for extending forgiveness and resolving conflicts.*

The second day of Eid al-Fitr begins with the sacrifice of sheep, goats, or cows. In the afternoon preparation begins for a special dish of oven-roasted meat, called *tannur al-shwa*. The dish is prepared in communal oven pits, called *tannur*, that are dug into the ground. Community members clean out the pit, start firewood burning to create charcoal, and select the appropriate cuts of meat. Once marinated, each family's meat is placed in a burlap sack and placed on top of the heated charcoal. Then the oven is completely sealed and dirt is heaped on top, which prevents the sacks of meat from catching fire. Cheerful crowds form around the ovens as the preparations are made. The meat is left in the oven until the next day. On the second day of Eid al-Fitr, while the tannur al-shwa bakes, Omanis feast instead on bits of meat skewered on palms fronds and roasted over charcoal made from fragrant wood. Omanis call this shish kebab kind of dish *mashakik*. The second day of Eid al-Fitr is nicknamed *al-mashakik* in honor of this festival dish. Many Omanis also consume a dessert made from honey and eggs on this day.

Some Omanis call the third day of Id al-Fitr *al-shwa* day because the delicious slow-roasted meats are removed from the oven and eaten on this day.

Sewiyan di Kheer

½ cup butter
1½ cups fine soup noodles,
   broken up (vermicelli)
4 cups milk
1½ cups cream

½ teaspoon ground cardamom
½ cup raisins
½ cup sugar
¼ cup chopped pistachios

Heat butter in a heavy-bottomed pan over low heat. When it melts add the noodles, stirring them until they turn brown. Add the milk and raise heat to medium, bringing it to a boil while stirring. Do not allow it to scorch. Add the raisins, sugar, and cardamom, reduce heat to low, and cook, stirring for about 10 minutes. Add the cream and cook for 5 more minutes. Remove from pan and pour into serving dish. Garnish with chopped pistachios. Serve warm or refrigerate and serve cold.

Opposite page: In Islamabad, Pakistan, Eid al-Fitr crowds jam the Faysal Mosque's spacious grounds and worshipers fill the prayer hall for evening prayers.

Pakistan

In Pakistan employees receive special bonuses for Eid al-Fitr. This helps families celebrate the festival by giving gifts of new clothes and money to their children.

Pakistani men will often spend the evening before the first day of Eid al-Fitr traveling to one of the nation's bigger mosques. Once there the men start to form rows for prayer well before sunrise, spilling out into the courtyard, gardens, and streets because the crowds are so large.

On the morning of Eid al-Fitr many Pakistani families serve a rich pudding, *sewiyan di kheer,* for breakfast. After morning prayers Pakistanis spend the day visiting with friends and family and enjoying nice meals. Everyone dresses in new clothes; camel owners may even adorn their animals with decorated blankets and bridles.

Palestinian Territory

Palestinians break their fast with dates, water, and fruit juice. The evening meal often includes soup and ends with pastries, especially *Qatayef,* a sweet especially associated with Ramadan. So popular is this dessert that sidewalk stalls spring up during the month, to serve it up fresh to those who pass by. In Jerusalem, the markets of the old city are especially busy with shoppers and

strollers, and colored lamps are hung on the Damascus gate. In recent years many Ramadan customs, such as shopping and socializing after sundown, have gone into a steep decline due to curfews and other restrictions imposed upon Palestinians living in the West Bank and Gaza.

Palestinians observe Eid al-Fitr by visiting the graves of their relatives, where they recite verses from the Quran. Children celebrate the day with firecrackers and sparklers.

The evening meal often includes soup and ends with pastries, especially Qatayef, a sweet especially associated with Ramadan.

Qatayef (Sweet Pancakes with Ricotta Cheese Filling)

1 teaspoon yeast
1 teaspoon sugar
1 cup lukewarm water
³/₄ cup milk, room temperature
2 cups flour
Vegetable oil for frying
1 pound ricotta cheese
³/₄ cup sugar
1 pinch of cinnamon
¹/₂ cup ground pistachios

FOR SYRUP:
3 cups sugar
1¹/₄ cups water
3 tablespoons lemon juice
1 tablespoon rose water, or orange blossom water (optional)

Combine the yeast, 1 teaspoon sugar, and 1 cup lukewarm water in a large bowl. Let sit for 5-10 minutes, until the yeast is dissolved. Add the milk and flour and stir until a smooth batter forms. Heat a pan or griddle and coat with oil. Pour batter onto griddle, about ¹/₄ cup or less at a time. When pancake begins to bubble, turn over. Cook until batter sets. Remove from pan and set aside.

Mix together ricotta cheese, ³/₄ cup sugar, and cinnamon. When pancakes have cooled place about 2 tablespoons of this filling in the middle of each. Fold pancake in half and press to distribute filling. Set aside.

Prepare syrup by boiling the water and sugar together until they thicken, about 10 minutes. Add other ingredients and remove from heat.

Pour syrup over pancakes. Sprinkle with ground pistachio nuts and serve.

Qatar

In Qatar, daytime activities trickle to a near halt during Ramadan. When mid-afternoon prayers are finished, women enter their kitchens to begin preparing iftar. Favorite Ramadan dishes are *thareed*, a kind of meat stew served with flat, crispy bread, and *harees*, a puree of cooked wheat and lamb. Popular desserts are custard, rose-water flavored rice pudding, and *loqaimat*, fried dough dipped in honey. Many women make extra food to give as gifts to friends and relatives during Ramadan, or to distribute among the poor.

Many people spend some time praying at the mosque after iftar. Mosque attendance shoots up during Ramadan. In recent years, the government's religious affairs ministry has coped with this sudden yearly influx by repairing mosques and training new imams.

On the 14th day of Ramadan, Qataris celebrate a children's holiday called Garangaou. Children dress in costumes and go door to door, asking for treats.

After iftar and the evening prayers, many Qataris go out to shop and socialize with relatives, friends, and neighbors. In the capital city of Doha the first-class hotels have established special Ramadan tents in recent years, decked out to resemble the haunts of old Cairo, and well-stocked with food, entertainment, and water-pipes. Puffing on a water pipe is a popular amusement during Ramadan. Qataris eat a second dinner, called *ghabga*, around midnight. Guests are often invited home to partake of this late-night meal.

On the 14th day of Ramadan, Qataris celebrate a children's holiday called *Garangaou*. The holiday marks the halfway point in Ramadan. Children dress in costumes and go door to door, asking for treats and singing songs that assure generous givers of Allah's blessing. People offer the children candy, coins, or nuts, which the youngsters collect in a sack hanging round their neck.

In Qatar booming cannons or sirens announce the sighting of the new moon that ends Ramadan and begins the new month, Shawwal, and the Eid al-Fitr festival. Qataris celebrate Eid al-Fitr for three days. They prepare to welcome the holiday by adorning their bodies. Women have their bodies waxed and decorate their hands and feet with henna. In Qatar this custom is so common that the evening that the new moon is sighted in often referred to as "henna night." Women also wear new shoes and clothes, often caftans embroidered with beautiful designs in gold or silver thread. Men also pay special attention to their grooming. They apply perfume to their body or scent their clothes with incense.

The first morning of Eid begins with a special breakfast featuring *bulalit* (sweetened angel hair noodles covered with fried eggs), a sweet holiday bread, and other sweet foods. Children sing Eid songs and parents and elders give children money and treats. After prayers and breakfast, the rest of the day revolves around family visits. Visitors are offered coffee spiced with cardamom, rosewater-flavored tea, baklava, fruit, and other sweets. Relatives, friends, and neighbors frequently exchange baskets of sweet treats as gifts.

At lunchtime, extended family members gather at the home of an elder relative for a meal featuring freshly slaughtered lamb and rice. Often at these large gatherings, which might include 20 to 50 people, the food is placed on large tablecloths on the floor and people sit on the floor to eat. Men and women may be seated separately.

In the city of Doha, displays of sword dancing and drumming entertain crowds in public places. Fireworks, though a relatively recent addition to the celebrations, dazzle and delight onlookers in the evening.

Saudi Arabia

In Saudi Arabia during Ramadan many people stay up all night, or until the wee hours of the morning.

In Saudi Arabia, children's and adults' schedules change dramatically during Ramadan. Schools observe shortened hours. Offices open for the day in the afternoon, and stores and restaurants open after sunset and may stay open till two o'clock in the morning. Some stores feature all-night shopping. Businesspeople conduct deals long after the sun has gone down. In past generations, people did not change their schedules to such a degree. Before the oil boom brought tremendous wealth to Saudi Arabia, people often ate their iftar dinners at home and went to bed, rising in the early hours of the morning for suhur.

Nowadays many people stay up all night, or until the wee hours of the morning. After prayers are finished people enjoy socializing, shopping, having tea or coffee with their friends, or staying home and watching television serials. Many people stay up until it's time for suhur. Then they eat, say their dawn prayers, go to bed, and do not rise until noon. Deserted during the morning hours, important thoroughfares begin to stir in the afternoon. After a few hours of activity, the streets empty again as sunset draws near, as people rush home to break the fast with their families.

In Saudi Arabia suhur usually consists of rice, bread, and meat. At the end of the day Saudis break their fast with water, dates, and coffee. Iftar often begins with soup. One traditional recipe, *shorobat il-jereesh*, features cracked wheat, chopped tomatoes, and lamb or beef chunks. Red lentil soup is another Ramadan favorite. Other favorite Ramadan dishes include fried meat pies, fresh bread, salads, and beans. Apricot and other fruit juices, tea, and coffee are

usually served as well. Sweets, such as apricot pudding (*qamar el-deen pud-ding*), and various pastries, often round out the meal.

Saudis celebrate Eid al-Fitr by sharing elaborate meals with family members, and visiting friends and relatives for tea and sweets. Some families celebrate by roasting a whole lamb stuffed with noodles or rice, dried apricots and dates, and nuts. Going to a pleasant outdoors location to picnic or visiting a fun fair provides additional entertainment. Some families go on vacation at this time of year.

Saudis celebrate Eid al-Fitr by sharing elaborate meals with family members, and visiting friends and relatives for tea and sweets.

331

Apricot Pudding (Qamar el-Deen Pudding)

1 pound dried apricots or dried apricot paste
1 cup sugar
3 cups water
2 teaspoons cornstarch mixed with 2 tablespoons warm water
¼ teaspoon cardamom

Bring the water to a boil. Mince the apricots and put them into the boiling water. Transfer water to a bowl. Wait until apricot pieces dissolve, and then add the sugar. Transfer this mixture to a blender and whir until blended. Return the apricot mixture to a saucepan and heat to medium. Add the cardamom, cornstarch, and water. Stir until it thickens. If the mixture does not thicken add more cornstarch. Transfer the mixture to a baking dish or bowl. Refrigerate for several hours and serve.

Senegal

The people of Senegal call Eid al-Fitr "Korite." After the men and boys return from morning prayers at the mosque, the family celebrates with a special breakfast dish of millet cereal and curdled milk. After a large and festive lunch people spend the day socializing with friends and relatives. In Senegal, Muslims greet each other with the phrase "dewenati" on this holiday. It means, "may God give us life in the year to come." Girls and women dress in their best clothes and go door to door, receiving coins from householders.

Singapore

In the Republic of Singapore, Muslims eat a great variety of sweets during Ramadan. Shop windows dazzle potential buyers with a wide selection of pastries, candies, and cakes. As the end of the month draws near, Muslims give their homes a deep cleaning and visit the burial sites of relatives, where they wash and beautify the graves and recite verses from the Quran.

In Singapore Eid al-Fitr is known as Hari Raya Puasa. Muslims put on fresh, new clothes, visit their relatives, and enjoy special foods during this holiday. Custom encourages young people to ask their elders for forgiveness for any wrongdoing in the past year. Adults give children green packets containing money.

Syria

In Syria many Muslims sleep late into the day during Ramadan. Street life picks up around noon and peaks for the day just before sunset, as people rush to get home before the end of the fast. Syrians often break their fast with some dates or some dried fruit salad (*Khoshaf el Yameesh)*, water, and a cup of soup, such as *tirbiyali* (a meat broth thickened with barley flour) or lentil soup. Iftar dinners with family and extended family members are an important feature of Ramadan in Syria. The streets come alive again after dinner. Long evenings of socializing with friends and relatives characterize the holiday in Syria. In addition to chatting, people play card games, backgammon, and smoke water pipes. Many stay up until suhur and go to sleep after dawn prayers.

On Eid al-Fitr, Syrian children receive gifts of money, especially from their uncles. They often spend this money on rides and amusements at children's carnivals that appear in parks at the close of Ramadan.

Puffing on a water pipe and playing backgammon are popular amusements during Ramadan, not only in Syria but Lebanon as well.

Khoshaf el Yameesh (Dried Fruit Salad)

$1/2$ pound dried apricots
$1/2$ pound prunes
$1/4$ pound raisins
$1/4$ pound dried pitted sour cherries
$1/3$ cup almond halves
$1/3$ cup pistachio nuts (or pine nuts)
approximately $2/3$ cup sugar
1 tablespoon rose water
1 tablespoon orange blossom water

Wash dried fruit and place in bowl. Add nuts and cover with water. Add desired amount of sugar, rose water, and orange water.

Let the fruits soak for two days until they plump up and the remaining water becomes a light golden colored syrup.

Turkey

In Turkey the government sponsors Ramadan fairs that include free meals of rice and meat for those who cannot afford their own Ramadan iftars or for those workers who cannot get home to eat. The fairs also include entertainment for children. In Turkey the iftar meal often begins with appetizers, such as pieces of cheese and slices of preserved meats, pickled vegetables, and jams. After evening prayers it continues with soup, savory pies made with phyllo dough, vegetables, grain, and meat dishes. Fruit, pastries, puddings, candies, and coffee may be offered for dessert. One favorite Ramadan dish, eggs with caramelized onions, is said to have been eaten by the Ottoman sultans each year on the 15th day of Ramadan. They consumed this humble dish after coming home from viewing a cloak—housed in Istanbul—which many believe belonged to the prophet Muhammad.

After dinner many people enjoy an evening out on the town. Attending concerts, plays, shadow puppet shows, and strolling around plazas and parks are popular evening activities during Ramadan.

The three-day festival that follows Ramadan is called "Sekr Bayrami," or Sugar Festival, in Turkey, because so many sweets are served. Turkish women often spend long hours in the kitchen preparing a variety of sugary treats. Pastries — such as baklava, a sweet made from phyllo dough, clarified butter, nuts, spices, and sugar syrup — appear in abundance. So do candies, puddings, and cakes. Many Turks wrap little samples of holiday sweets as gifts and give them to their friends or relatives.

Turkish children offer adults holiday greetings, and show their respect by kissing the adult's hand and raising it to their forehead. Custom insists that adults greeted in this fashion give the children some money in return. Children have plenty of opportunities to greet adults during Sekr Bayrami, because Turks spend the holiday visiting with family, neighbors, and friends, enjoying delicious meals and treats, and exchanging gifts. Ten or more such visits may take place in a single day. Closer and more senior relatives are visited on the first day. Upon arriving young people first kiss the men's hands. Then the women are greeted in the same fashion. Hosts offer visitors coffee and sweets. The guests depart when a new batch of visitors arrives.

In some areas people celebrate by watching wrestling matches. In rural zones, villages host dances that attract participants from neighboring hamlets as well.

The puppets are cut from stiff, translucent camel leather, perforated, painted, then given stitched joints for mobility. The puppeteers use horizontal poles attached at critical points to animate the figures.

Eggs with Caramelized Onions

2 large purple or red onions
4 tablespoons butter
1/2 teaspoon salt
1/2 teaspoon mild tasting vinegar
1/8 teaspoon allspice

1/4 teaspoon cinnamon
1/2 teaspoon sugar
1/4 teaspoon black pepper
4 eggs
salt and pepper to taste

Cut the onions into quarters and then slice them very thin. Place butter in a heavy-bottomed skillet and melt. Add onions and salt and cook over very low heat for 40 to 50 minutes, stirring the onions every 4-6 minutes. As the onions dry out sprinkle them with water. Near end of cooking time add vinegar, spices, pepper, and sugar. Cook until the onions are crispy and reddish brown in color. Make 4 divots in the mound of onions and break an egg into each divot. Sprinkle the egg with salt and pepper. Cook until a film forms over the egg yolk, but the yolk is not fully solid. Divide into 4 portions and serve.

United States

American Muslims may find it more challenging to observe Ramadan than those Muslims who live in predominantly Muslim countries because work and public school schedules do not change to accommodate the holiday. For those Muslims who rely on moon sightings to begin and end the month of Ramadan, scheduling a day off to celebrate Eid al-Fitr presents a special difficulty, since one cannot know in advance on exactly which day it will fall. In addition, maintaining the fast for the entire day while coworkers and fellow students sip coffee and sodas, eat lunch, drink water, or nibble on snacks may add extra hardship for some. Yet in spite of the special difficulties it presents, some American Muslims feel that their Ramadan observance — especially because the wider community does not change its habits to make it easier for them — sets a shining example for Muslims everywhere.

In 2001, the U.S. Postal Service issued a special commemorative stamp that bears the phrase "Eid Greetings" (Eid Mubarek) in both English and Arabic calligraphy. A fifth-grade boy, Muhib Beekum, dreamed up the idea in 1996.

The parents of Muslim children attending American public schools sometimes ask the school administrators to make certain accommodations for Muslim children who have reached the age of fasting. For example, they might ask to have their children excused from physical education during the month of Ramadan, or they might ask that a room be set aside for Muslim students during lunchtime, so that they have a place to go where no one will be eating or drinking in front of them.

The North American Muslim community is very ethnically diverse, so it is difficult to identify foods and customs that are particular to them. Many events and traditions found among North American Muslims can be found in other parts of the world as well.

American mosques and Muslim community centers often hold special iftar dinners throughout Ramadan, some organized as potlucks for members and others as a free meal donated to a set number of people as a charitable gift. These institutions also offer extra spiritual and educational activities during Ramadan, such as lectures, study circles, Quran readings, and taraweeh prayers. Finally, some mosques organize i'tikaf nights for those members who wish to spend the entire night in the mosque. Special activities are often scheduled throughout the evening, especially for children and teens.

Like their counterparts in other countries, American Muslim children often receive money and gifts on Eid al-Fitr. They also look forward to special cookies and desserts prepared for the occasion.

336

September/October 2001

Saudi Aramco world

EID
34 USA
GREETINGS

NEW STAMP
CELEBRATES 'ID

In 2001, the U.S. Postal Service issued a special commemorative stamp that bears the phrase "Eid Greetings" (*Eid Mubarek*) in both English and Arabic calligraphy. A fifth-grade boy, Muhib Beekum, dreamed up the idea in 1996. Muhib, an avid stamp-collector, realized one day that although the U.S. Postal Service had issued stamps honoring many other holidays, no stamp yet existed to mark any Muslim observance. So Muhib got the ball rolling, along with his mother, Nadiah, and a family friend, Aminah Assilimi. Together they collected thousands of signatures on a petition submitted to the Citizen's Stamp Advisory Committee. The committee approved the idea of an Eid stamp and then commissioned well-known Muslim artist Mohamed Zakariya to design it. Finally, on September 1, 2001, the United States issued the Eid stamp, the first ever to recognize Islam in America.

As Muslim communities continue to grow, more mainstream businesses compete for their business. In 2003 Hallmark cards, one of America's leading greeting card manufacturers, offered Eid cards for sale for the first time. Though produced in limited numbers, the cards sold well in every location that carried them. Hallmark asserts that the decision to begin a line of Eid cards (as well as a line of cards for the Hindu holiday Diwali) was based on business principles, but admits that calls and letters from consumers requesting the cards alerted them to this unfilled need.

Another popular fast-breaking dish is shafoot.

Yemen

In Yemen children greet the arrival of Ramadan with songs about the glories of the holy month. Yemenis usually break their fasts with water, coffee, dates, and soup. *Shafoot*, a dish of bread pieces soaked in yogurt, is another popular fast-breaking dish. After prayers another meal is eaten. In some parts of the country, *rwani*, a honey covered cake, is a special Ramadan treat. Throughout the month, men gather to listen to or to sing religious songs, recite the Quran, or attend evening prayers and special religious talks given in mosques. Socializing in cafés and other public places are also popular evening activities for men. Women are more likely to stay home, watching television, listening to the radio, or socializing with friends.

Chapter 35
Laylat al-Qadr

(Also called Night of Power, Night of Destiny, Night of Determination, Precious Night)

Laylat al-Qadr is an Arabic phrase meaning "Night of Power" or "Night of Destiny." Muslims have also translated the phrase as "Night of Determination," or "Precious Night." It refers to a yearly holiday that commemorates the transmission of the Quran from God to the Prophet Muhammad. Some Muslims believe that the Prophet received it into his heart, in its entirety, in a single night. Others believe the angel Gabriel (Jibril) brought it down from heaven on that night, but transmitted it to Muhammad little by little. In any case, Sunni Muslims agree that the Quran came down from heaven to earth on a single evening that occurred during the last ten days of Ramadan in the year 610. On that night Muhammad heard the angel Gabriel speak to him for the first time. Therefore the date marks the beginning of the Prophet's God-given mission to transmit Islam to humanity. Most Muslims celebrate Laylat al-Qadr on the 27th of Ramadan, though no one can say for sure on which date the event occurred.

Ten Days of Prayer

Because the Night of Power is believed to have happened during the last ten days of Ramadan, this segment of the holy month is thought to be especially full of divine grace. Heaven lavishes rewards on those who perform special

Foreign words used in the text are defined in the Glossary, pages 423-40.

339

Devout Muslims sometimes spend the last ten days of Ramadan in a spiritual retreat called i'tikaf.

devotions during these days. Devout Muslims sometimes spend these ten days in a kind of spiritual retreat called i'tikaf. Muslim historians note that not only the Prophet Muhammad but also his wives regularly undertook the spiritual discipline of i'tikaf during Ramadan. The practice involves spending the last ten days of the month in a mosque, emerging only to eat (if this is not permitted inside the mosque), perform *wudu*, take care of one's bodily needs, and to bathe. This seclusion permits the worshiper to dedicate himself or herself utterly to spiritual concerns. People who undertake this devotion spend their time in prayer and meditation. They also read and recite the Quran, and think deeply about their lives and their faith. In some countries women who wish to observe i'tikaf may be encouraged to do so at home rather than in the mosque.

Those who wish to make i'tikaf during Ramadan begin on the evening of the 20th or 21st of Ramadan and continue until the sighting of the new moon that announces the end of Ramadan. Muslims may also practice i'tikaf for short periods of time during the rest of year. This practice is often undertaken in fulfillment of a vow.

Laylat al-Qadr in the Quran and in Muslim Folklore

Laylat al-Qadr is so full of grace that the Quran itself proclaims the night "better than a thousand months." It further explains that angels descend to earth to do the will of God. Some Muslims believe that God sets the events that will occur in the coming year on Laylat al-Qadr. These beliefs have their basis in chapter 97 of the Quran, which is devoted to the Night of Power:

> Truly We revealed it
> on the Night of Determination.
> How will you know what the Night
> of Determination is?
> Better is the Night of Determination
> than a thousand months.
> On (this night) the angels and grace descend
> by the dispensation of their Lord,
> for settling all affairs.
> It is peace
> Till the dawning of the day (Quran 97, Ali trans.).

An allusion is also made of the Night of Power in chapter 44, which affirms that the purpose of sending the Quran was to warn humanity of the standards by which God will judge them:

> The perspicuous Book is witness
> (that) We sent it down on a night of blessing—
> so that We could warn—
> on which all affairs are sorted out and decided
> as commands from us (Quran 44:2-5, Ali trans.).

According to Muslim lore, the veil separating heaven and earth thins on Laylat al-Qadr and great blessings disperse over the earth. Traditional beliefs assert that on this night all prayers are heard with sympathy. Islamic folklore teaches that the night skies are brighter and lighter on Laylat al-Qadr and the dawn breaks more brilliantly than on any other day of the month. Those who doubt that the 27th of Ramadan is the actual date of Laylat al-Qadr may scan the skies during the last ten days of Ramadan, seeking the telltale light that marks the real event.

A Night of Prayer

Devout Muslims often spend the night of the 27th of Ramadan in prayer at home or at the mosque. A hadith of the Prophet recommends this devotion:

> Whoever establishes the prayers on the night of Qadr out of sincere faith and hoping to attain Allah's rewards (not showing off) then all his past sins will be forgiven (Al Hariri-Wendel: 230).

In addition to favors and the forgiveness of sins, Muslims seek guidance, insight, and glimpses of the pure light of God on this night.

The following prayer was written especially for Laylat al-Qadr. On this holy night Muslims may recite composed prayers, such as the one given below, or simply place their own needs before God in their own words:

> In the name of Allah, the Beneficent the Merciful
> O Allah bless Muhammad and the family of Muhammad.
> O Allah, let it be that when You decree and ordain
> from the matters which are certain,
> That when You distinguish in the matters which are wise on the
>   night of Qadr,
> In the decree which cannot be reversed nor changed,
> That You write me amongst those who will go
> For pilgrimage (Hajj) to Your holy house,
> Whose Hajj is approved,
> Whose efforts are appreciated,
> Whose sins are forgiven,
> Whose evil deeds have been pardoned.
> And from what You decree and ordain,
> Let my life be lengthened,
> And increase my sustenance,
> And . . . [here the worshiper adds his or her own petition]
> (Kassamali: 79).

Iran and Shia Muslims

In Iran—where most people follow Shia rather than Sunni Islam—Muslims observe Laylat al-Qadr for three days, from the 19th to the 21st of Ramadan. They also commemorate the martyrdom of Ali (the Prophet's son-in-law) on these days, making this a very holy and spiritual time of year for Persian Muslims. According to Shia teachings, Ali was attacked on the 19th and died of his wounds on the 21st of Ramadan.

Persians sometimes refer to the Night of Power as the Precious Night. Prayers offered on these nights are said to be worth a thousand performed on other days, so many Iranians stay up late into the night in prayer. Some follow the custom of saying one hundred *rakat* of formal prayers on each of the three nights, in addition to many informal prayers of the kind given above.

Chapter 36
Hajj: Pilgrimage to Mecca

Every adult Muslim who has the financial means is expected to make at least one pilgrimage in his or her lifetime. The destination of this pilgrimage, which Muslims call *Hajj*, is Mecca, a city in Saudi Arabia. Mecca was the birthplace of Muhammad and is home to the most important shrine in Islam, the Kaba. In Mecca and the surrounding area pilgrims must perform specific ritual acts that recall the story of Abraham, Hagar, and Ishmael as it is recorded in the Quran and in traditional Muslim beliefs. Unlike many pilgrimages in other religions, the Hajj pilgrimage only takes place at a certain time of year, more specifically, the second week of the Muslim month Dhu al-Hijjah. The ceremonies begin on the eighth day of the month and continue for six days. Certain acts must be performed in certain places on certain days in order for the pilgrimage to be valid. Muslims generally view the journey as an expression of their faith in and submission to God, and a confirmation of their commitment to Islam. Those who complete the pilgrimage are accorded an extra degree of respect in the Muslim community. They are permitted to add the title "Hajji" (masculine) or "Hajjah" (feminine) to their name.

Opposite page: For nearly 14 centuries the Hajj, a pilgrimage to Mecca, has been one of the most impressive religious gatherings in the world. Mecca was the birthplace of Muhammad and is home to the most important shrine in Islam, the Kaba.

Abraham, Hagar, and Ishmael

The story of Abraham (Ibrahim), his second wife, Hagar (Hajirah), and their son, Ishmael (Isma'il), that appears in the Quran and is retold in Muslim lore differs somewhat from that found in the Bible. Both versions agree that Abraham first married a woman called Sarah. The two grew into old age with-

Foreign words used in the text are defined in the Glossary, pages 423-40.

345

out having children, so Abraham also married Hagar, Sarah's maidservant. Hagar bore a son called Ishmael. Sarah was jealous of Ishmael and Hagar, and urged Abraham to turn them out of the house. God gave his assent to this plan, so Abraham took them to a dry, desolate area and left them there with a single skin of water, which they quickly drank. Then Hagar prayed to God for water to keep her son alive, and God revealed to her a hidden spring. Islam agrees with this story so far, but adds more details. For example, Muslim teachings specify that Abraham left Hagar and Ishmael in the place that would later become Mecca. Two hills in that area, named Safa and Marwah, still stand today. Desperate for water to keep her baby alive, Hagar ran between these two hills seven times. In spite of her apparent panic, Hagar felt sure in her heart that if God had directed Abraham to leave them there, then God would take care of them. God answered Hagar's prayers by sending an angel to reveal to her the location of a nearby hidden spring called Zamzam. Thanks to this spring, Hagar and her son lived.

> *The Hajj is understood as a kind of sacrifice offered to God. Many pilgrims report feeling closer to God on the Hajj than at any other time of their life.*

According to Muslim tradition, Abraham returned to visit Hagar and Ishmael some years later. Muslims believe that the events narrated in chapter 37 of the Quran took place at this time. Chapter 37 relates that God spoke to Abraham in a dream, asking him to sacrifice his son. While the Bible teaches that Abraham planned to sacrifice Isaac (born from Sarah as Abraham's second son), the Quran does not specify the name of the son to be sacrificed. Muslim tradition teaches that Abraham intended to sacrifice Ishmael, the first-born son, not Isaac, the second-born. According to the Quran, Abraham's son, who was also devoted to the Lord, encouraged his father to carry out God's will. Although he loved his son more than anything on earth, Abraham took him to a deserted place and prepared him for sacrifice. At the last minute, God, pleased with Abraham's obedience, intervened to spare the boy's life. He sent the angel Gabriel (Jibril) with a ram that Abraham was to substitute for his son. Abraham rejoiced, and slew the sheep. The Eid al-Adha festival commemorates this event. Muslims tend to believe that Isaac was born after this incident. They see his birth as a reward for Abraham's willingness to sacrifice Ishmael.

According to the teachings of Islam, Abraham left Hagar and Ishmael again, but returned some time later, after Hagar's death. Together father and son built the Kaba, a shrine that they dedicated to the worship of the one God. They built it near the place where the sacrifice of the ram had occurred. Muslim tradition asserts that the very first temple in the world once stood on this spot. Adam and Eve built the first house of worship at this location, but it had long since fallen into ruin. Muslim lore suggests that after they completed construction of the Kaba, Abraham and Ishmael performed the rites of the Hajj pilgrimage.

When faced with situations in which they were about to lose all, Abraham, Hagar, and Ishmael demonstrated tremendous faith in God. Abraham wanted his son to live, but when God commanded the sacrifice of Ishmael, Abraham faithfully obeyed. Ishmael witnessed his faith by giving assent to the sacrifice. Circumstances forced Hagar to depend entirely on God to sustain her and her son in the wilderness. She responded with prayers and faith.

The story of Abraham, Hagar, and Ishmael also illustrates God's faithfulness to those who put all their trust in him. He intervened at the last minute to save Ishmael, and he delivered Hagar and Ishmael from almost certain death in the desert.

Belief in and worship of the one, all-powerful God is the most important component of the Muslim religion. The story of Abraham, Hagar, and Ishmael is very important to Islam because these three lived according to this teaching. They persevered even when things got difficult for them and it would have been easy to lose faith. In performing the Hajj pilgrimage, Muslims visit sites where the events in these stories took place. There they remember Abraham, Hagar, and Ishmael, and dedicate themselves to achieving the same level of faith. Because of all the difficulties and the expense involved, the Hajj is understood as a kind of sacrifice

In performing the Hajj pilgrimage, Muslims visit sites where the events in the stories of Abraham, Hagar, and Ishmael took place. There they remember and dedicate themselves to achieving the same level of faith.

offered to God. In performing this important act of worship pilgrims renew and revitalize their relationship with God. Many pilgrims report feeling closer to God on the Hajj than at any other time of their life.

The Founding of the Hajj According to the Quran

The Quran traces the history of the pilgrimage back to Abraham. It names Abraham and Ishmael as the builders of the Kaba, and notes that God charged them with establishing it as a temple to God and a place of spiritual retreat:

> Remember, when his Lord tried Abraham
> by a number of commands which he fulfilled,
> God said to him: "I will make you a leader among men."
> And when Abraham asked: "From my progeny too?"
> the Lord said: "My pledge
> does not include transgressors."
> Remember, We made the House (of Ka'bah) a place
> of congregation and safe retreat,
> and said: "Make the spot where Abraham stood
> the place of worship;" and enjoined
> upon Abraham and Ishmael
> to keep Our House immaculate for those
> who shall walk around it and stay in it
> for contemplation and prayer,
> and for bowing in adoration (Quran 2:124-25).

A later passage elaborates on this idea, and predicts that people will someday come to worship at the temple from far away lands:

> When We chose the site of the House for Abraham
> (We said) "Associate no one with Me,
> and clean My House for those who will circumambulate it,
> stand (in reverence), and bow in homage.
> Announce the Pilgrimage to the people.
> They will come to you on foot and riding along distant roads
> on lean and slender beasts,
> in order to reach the place of advantage for them,
> and to pronounce the name of God on appointed days
> Over cattle He has given them for food;
> then eat of the meat and feed the needy and poor.
> Let them then attend to their persons
> and complete the rites of pilgrimage,
> fulfill their vows and circuit round the ancient House"
> (Quran 22:26-29, Ali trans.).

The History of the Hajj

At the time of Muhammad's birth, Mecca was already the site of the most important pilgrimage in Arabia. Each year, during the months that the warring Arab tribes agreed to respect as a time of truce, a steady stream of pilgrims trouped towards Mecca and its most important shrine, the Kaba. The Kaba held stone idols of many gods and goddesses important to the pagan Arabians. The pilgrims came to pray and make offerings to these gods and goddesses. They also brought valuable trade to the city's merchants, so most of the people of Mecca were angered by Muhammad's attempts to banish the idols from the Kaba. Years later, when the Prophet and his army conquered the city, Muhammad did order the destruction of the stone idols, but maintained the shrine. He taught that the Kaba had been built by Abraham as a temple to the one God worshipped by Muslims and other monotheists. After restoring the Kaba to its original function as the "House of God," he encouraged Muslims to make a pilgrimage to the Kaba as a testimony of their faith. Shortly before his death Muhammad established a sequence of acts that Muslims should perform at the Kaba and nearby locations. This is the same series of rituals that Muslim pilgrims perform today.

The Hajj has never been an easy journey. In spite of the difficulties and dangers involved, historical accounts that date back to the Middle Ages reveal that pilgrims made the trip from all corners of the Muslim world. In so doing they risked becoming the victims of bandits, tricksters, battling armies, disease, unscrupulous guides, mercenary government officials, and even slave traders. These risks merely added to the grueling hardships that travel over long distances posed in those days. In the 9th century C.E. conditions improved somewhat for pilgrims traveling from Baghdad. Zubaydah, the wife of the famous Abassid Caliph Harun al-Rashid, commanded the building of a road from Baghdad to Mecca. At her command wells were sunk along the way to provide the parched pilgrims with water along the dusty route. The road and cisterns still exist today.

'Abd al-Ghaffar, al-Sayyid, a physician of Mecca, took this photograph between 1885 and 1889 of Muslims praying around the Kaba during the Hajj.

Some of the dangers facing pilgrims increased as they drew closer to Mecca, namely, banditry. As late as the 1920s the Banu Utayba, Banu Harb, and other Bedouin tribes of Arabia routinely attacked bands of pilgrims traveling by camel caravans. If they refused to pay the sum demanded of them, the tribes simply plundered the caravans and took what they wanted by force. Even so, historians estimate that about 10,000 pilgrims a year made the dangerous journey to Mecca during the first two decades of the 20th century.

349

Muslims from all over the world gather in the plaza before Mecca's Sacred Mosque.

In the decades that followed modern transportation and improved law enforcement made the trip easier. These advancements attracted greater numbers of pilgrims. In 1941, authorities estimate that 80,000 pilgrims made the trip. Five short years later, in 1946, some 150,000 pilgrims came to Mecca for the Hajj. In 1952, half a million devotees completed the trek. Three quarters of a million pilgrims undertook the journey in 1960.

The numbers of pilgrims continued to increase throughout the 20th century. In 2003, Mecca hosted about two million Hajj pilgrims. The massive crowds that currently converge on Mecca carry with them their own dangers. In 1997 more than 340 pilgrims died in a fire that started in a crowded tent encampment near Mina. Over 1,300 people were injured. Stampedes and outbreaks of disease have also plagued the event in recent years. In 2003, 14 pilgrims fell and were trampled to death in Mina, when two large masses of pilgrims moving in opposite directions collided with one another in an area where passage was partially blocked by baggage and bundles left on the ground. In 2004, 224 people died in a stampede that occurred during the stoning ritual in Mina.

The Saudi government and the people of Arabia have responded to the challenges posed by an ever-expanding number of pilgrims with new safety and hospitality measures. Fireproof tents have been installed at the pilgrim encampments. Some 60,000 security officers patrol the pilgrimage routes, trying to spot trouble before it happens. Civil defense officers, their motorcycles equipped with fire extinguishers, patrol the tent cities. Hospitals and clinics insure that doctors and other medical staff are on duty round the clock. Boy Scouts do their part by offering directions to pilgrims who have lost their way. Finally, vendors of food and drink, as well as charitable organizations that provide cold water for the pilgrims, disperse themselves along the pilgrim route.

The Hajj has been called the most extraordinary pilgrimage in the world. Each year it gathers together one of the largest and most culturally diverse groups of people in the world that assemble in the same place for the same religious purpose. Somewhat less than half of those who attend the Hajj are Saudi Arabians, or guest workers in Saudi Arabia. The remaining pilgrims come from all over the globe. In 2003, about 1.4 million foreign pilgrims entered Saudi Arabia to perform the Hajj. Although Arabs constitute only about 15 percent of the worldwide Muslim population, they represent about 50 percent of foreign Hajj pilgrims. This difference may be explained by the fact that the Hajj takes place in the center of the Arab world, thus making it easier for Arabs to attend. Differences in the distribution of wealth throughout the Muslim world also determine who attends the Hajj. The second largest group of foreign attendees, Asian Muslims, makes up about 35 percent of the pilgrims. Ten percent come from sub-Saharan Africa and only about 5 percent from Europe and the Americas.

> *Each year the Hajj gathers together one of the largest and most culturally diverse groups of people in the world that assemble in the same place for the same religious purpose.*

Preparations for the Hajj

Pilgrims must begin the Hajj with a clean slate, financially, ethically, and spiritually. For example, the Hajj may not be performed with borrowed money or with money earned in illegal or unethical endeavors. Nor may anyone perform the Hajj if in so doing they would jeopardize their family's livelihood. Moreover, pilgrims should repay all their old debts before they put aside money to pay for their pilgrimage expenses. Potential pilgrims should also make every effort to repair their relationships with friends, family, and community members, and to ask forgiveness from those whom they have offended. In addition, would-be pilgrims often undertake special courses of study that help them learn and memorize all the rituals and prayers associated with the Hajj. Finally, pilgrims should draw up a will before they depart for Mecca. This act not only represents their total submission to whatever God has in store for them, but also insures that their families will be provided for in the event of their death.

Hajj pilgrims are often viewed as representatives of their particular community. Friends and relatives will often make small donations to help them defray the costs of the journey and ask the pilgrim to pray for them when they reach the Plain of Arafat. In this way, one pilgrim can spread blessings on the whole community.

Nearly all pilgrims who undertake the Hajj do so in groups. This habit not only reflects the communal orientation of Islam, but also serves to assist foreigners in completing what could otherwise be a confusing set of rituals in a strange, new place. Once inside Saudi Arabia, these groups usually hire Arabian guides to lead them through the pilgrimage. Women have special restrictions placed on them in this regard. The government of Saudi Arabia requires that they travel with a male guardian (*mahram*) of some kind, usually a father, brother, husband, or son. This requirement is viewed as a safeguard for their protection.

> *When a Muslim intent on performing the Hajj approaches Mecca, he or she must enter into a state of ritual purity called* ihram.

Before Entering Mecca

The Hajj begins when the pilgrims prepare to cross over into the sacred precinct of Mecca. This zone is considered so holy that non-Muslims are not permitted to enter. When a Muslim intent on performing the Hajj approaches Mecca, he or she must enter into a state of ritual purity called *ihram*. Ihram means "consecration" or "sanctity" and it involves bathing, putting on certain clothes, and forming a clear intention to remain in a spiritually elevated state of mind throughout the Hajj. More specifically, Muslims entering into a state of ihram for the pilgrimage must perform the more thorough of the two kinds of ceremonial baths before prayer, called *ghusl*. Then they state their intention and recite the *ta'awwudh* and the *basmallah*. Next they put on their Hajj clothes and humbly ask God to accept their pilgrimage as an act of worship. In addition, they repeat the phrase, "Here I am at your service, O Allah."

There are several stations on the outskirts of Mecca that provide facilities for pilgrims to enter into ihram. Travelers may make use of these stations, called *miqat*, or enter into ihram before arriving in Mecca.

All male pilgrims must wear a special kind of clothing also called an ihram. An ihram looks like a simple white robe. Actually it is made out of two pieces of white cloth, which the pilgrim wraps around the left shoulder and the lower parts of his body. The ihram represents the humility of the worshiper before God. It strips away all the worldly trappings of wealth, status, and rank. Seeing hundreds of thousands of pilgrims all dressed alike and looking alike reminds the worshiper of one of Islam's most important teachings — that all people are equal before God. In addition, since the ihram resembles the plain and simple Muslim burial shroud, pilgrims are constantly reminded of the reality of death and the need to do God's will and to ask for his blessing before that time. After they return home, most pilgrims keep their ihram. Some save it to use as their burial shroud.

A man's ihram may not be stitched together in any way. In a similar vein, instead of regular shoes pilgrims are required to wear unstitched sandals. Because many mass-produced sandals are stitched, pilgrims often rely on plastic sandals. Other modern accommodations include money belts and identification cards, often worn with a cord around the neck.

Women are not required to wear the ihram. They may wear whatever they wish, as long as it is sufficiently modest, which means that it must cover the body, legs, arms, neck and head. Some choose to wear the dress of their native country. Others fashion a plain white robe for themselves, which may also be called an ihram.

Rules While on Pilgrimage

After crossing over into Mecca, all pilgrims must follow certain rules. These rules will maintain them in a state of purity (*ihram*) necessary to complete the Hajj. They must not fight or quarrel with one another. They cannot hunt or kill animals, or cut down a living tree. They must refrain from cutting their hair and nails and from sexual intercourse. Finally, they may not use perfume, wear jewelry, or adorn themselves in any way.

Men don a garment of two seamless pieces of white cloth called an ihram, *which they wear for the duration of Hajj. Women wear modest and unobtrusive dress of any color, and cover their heads.*

Some of these rules are given in the Quran. It states:

> Known are the months of pilgrimage.
> If one resolves to perform the pilgrimage in these months,
> let him not indulge in concupiscence, sin or quarrel.
> And the good you do shall be known to God.
> Provide for the journey,
> and the best of provisions is piety (Quran 2:197, Ali trans.).

The Prayer of the Pilgrim

Throughout the pilgrimage, the devotee repeats a special prayer attributed to Abraham. Called the *talbiyah*, the prayer announces the worshiper's willingness to undertake the required pilgrimage and affirms the basic tenets of Islam:

> Here am I, O Allah, here am I in Thy presence; there is no associate with Thee, here am I; surely all praise is Thine and all favors are Thine and the kingdom is Thine, there is no associate with Thee (Al Hariri-Wendel: 233).

Before the Pilgrimage Starts

After entering the Great or Holy Mosque of Mecca, pilgrims perform the first ritual called the tawaf—*the circling around the Kaba seven times.*

Most pilgrims arrive in Mecca one or more days before the pilgrimage starts. There is a set of sacred rituals for them to perform at this time, which is referred to as the *umrah*, or "lesser pilgrimage." Upon entering the sacred city of Mecca, the pilgrims make their way to the Kaba. An enormous mosque has been built around the site, capable of holding about one million people. This mosque, called the Great Mosque or Holy Mosque of Mecca, is built around a huge courtyard, at the center of which stands the Kaba. The Kaba is a roughly cube-shaped stone structure, about 50 feet high, 40 feet wide, and 33 feet deep. It is covered with a dark silk ceremonial cloth (called a *kiswa*) onto which verses from the Quran have been embroidered in gold thread. The kiswa is replaced each year, before it can become damaged or soiled. The replacement takes place on the second day of the pilgrimage, called the Day of Arafat, which is considered the most important day of the Hajj. Some 200 employees work year round fashioning the new covering for the sacred building, the cost of which runs about 4.5 million dollars.

The first ritual that the pilgrims must perform is called the *tawaf*. It requires the pilgrims to enter the courtyard of the Great Mosque and circle seven times around the Kaba. Circling the Kaba echoes the angels' adoration of God in heaven. According to popular Muslim teachings, the angels in heaven express their adoration for God by circling round His throne. The Kaba symbolizes the very heart of Islam on earth. The world's Muslims turn toward Mecca when they offer their daily prayers. In the city of Mecca, Muslims turn towards the Kaba when they pray. Inside the Kaba, it doesn't matter which direction one faces, since one cannot be any closer to God on earth. Hence for Muslims, the circling of the Kaba is an act of intense devotion.

> *In the* tawaf *ritual, pilgrims enter the courtyard of the Great Mosque and circle seven times around the Kaba, echoing the angels' adoration of God in heaven.*

The pilgrims circle in a counter-clockwise direction around the Kaba, beginning each circle at the corner of the Kaba in which is set the famous black stone. Contained by a sparkling silver setting, the stone, which measures just about eight inches across, is embedded in the wall of the Kaba six and one-half feet above the ground. According to Muslim legend, this stone fell from heaven. It was originally white, but since it absorbs the sins of those who touch it, it has turned black over the years. In Muhammad's day the pagan Arabs venerated the black stone. Muhammad recognized the stone's true significance, however, and so permitted it to remain in the Kaba after he cleansed it of idols. Muhammad is said to have kissed the stone in order to show his love for and gratitude to God. Some pilgrims believe that they must actually touch the black stone during the tawaf. A portion of these pilgrims fight the crowds in order to get close enough to brush against or kiss the black stone. These days, with thousands of pilgrims circling the Kaba at the same time, it is clear that not everyone can touch the black stone. So most pilgrims gesture towards the corner of the Kaba that contains the black stone when they pass by. The gesture represents their love for the Prophet and their sense of being one family with all those who have kissed the stone since Muhammad.

As they circle the Kaba, the pilgrims say prayers. Some simply repeat the words, "Here I am at your service, O Allah." Others recite declarations of faith. During the seventh and the last circling of the Kaba, many recite prayers like the following:

> O Allah! I ask of You perfect faith,
> True conviction and a heart full of devotion to you
> A tongue busy remembering You
> Vast provision, and lawful and clean earning,
> Sincere repentance and repentance before death,
> Peace at the time of death
> And your forgiveness (Is'harc 1997: 97).

After pilgrims make an informal prayer called dua, *they go to a special kiosk that contains a stone said to bear the imprint of Abraham's foot. Here the pilgrims say two* rakat *of formal prayers.*

After completing the seven circuits of the Kaba, the pilgrims make an informal prayer (*dua*) while facing the door of the Kaba. Then they go to a special kiosk that contains a stone said to bear the imprint of Abraham's foot. Here the pilgrims say two *rakat* of formal prayers.

After completing these duties many pilgrims make their way to the lower level of the mosque for a drink of Zamzam water. The source of the spring is now located underneath the mosque. The icy cold water is not only very refreshing after the day's heat, but also has a special spiritual significance for Muslims. Many believe that God will bless them through this water, just as He blessed Hagar and Ishmael. Containers of Zamzam water are available in many locations around the mosque. Large numbers of pilgrims fill their canteens with this water, in order to refresh themselves on the journey to come. Before leaving Saudi Arabia many pilgrims will fill up bottles with Zamzam water to share with friends and family at home.

Pilgrims put their shoes back on after having a drink of water from the Well of Zamzam located underneath the mosque.

After leaving the mosque the pilgrims begin another ritual, called the *sa'y*. The sa'y requires them to go to the nearby hills called Safa and Marwah and run back and forth between them seven times, a total distance of 3.5 kilometers (about 2.25 miles). This rite recalls Hagar's desperate search for water in the desert. The Saudi government has paved the path between the hills in marble. There are several lanes, one for travel from Safa to Marwah, another for travel in the reverse direction, and two inner lanes reserved for those with mobility problems or those in ill health. The healthy and the young jostle along in the outer lanes. In memory of Hagar's desperate search, one is supposed to hurry along for a good portion of the trip.

Once these ceremonial acts have been completed, the pilgrims may trade their ihrams for streets clothes and put aside the behavioral rules that keep them in a state of heightened purity. In this way, early arrivals may take advantage of the time to do some sightseeing in Mecca. They must, however, cleanse them-

selves again, resume their ihram, and once again adopt the purity rules before continuing with the Hajj. Alternatively, pilgrims may perform the umrah right before the Hajj and continue directly into the pilgrimage maintaining unbroken their state of ceremonial purity.

First Day

If pilgrims have not completed the *tawaf* in the Great Mosque before the eighth of Dhu al-Hijjah, they do so on this day. The main task facing the pilgrims, however, on this, the first day of the pilgrimage, is to journey from Mecca to Mina. Mina lies about seven miles away from Mecca. In spite of the heat, many people walk to Mina. The huge number of pilgrims creates enormous traffic jams that many prefer to avoid. Great numbers of pilgrims take

On the first day of Hajj, pilgrims gather in the flat valley of Mina, about three miles east of Mecca. Meditating and praying in preparation for the next day, most spend the night in tents.

off on foot, prayer rug in one hand and duffel bag in the other. Some even carry a parasol, to protect them from the blazing Arabian sun. In this flowing sea of people, most of whom are dressed exactly alike, the danger of losing one's companions is great. To that end, many groups march behind a national flag, or pin signs or other insignia to their clothing. Some groups form a large square, with stronger individuals at the edges and weaker people at the center. Shuffling along in lockstep they ensure that no member gets lost, and that the frailer members are protected.

To accommodate the pilgrims in Mina, the government of Saudi Arabia has set up a huge number of fireproof tents, furnished with air conditioning, electric lamps, and fire extinguishers. This tent city is also equipped with bathrooms. Once settled, pilgrims spend their time resting, praying, reading the Quran, and making friends with fellow pilgrims. So many pilgrims are gathered here on this day that the mosques cannot contain them all and so many say their daily prayers outside.

> *Many pilgrims savor the opportunity to reflect on their life and their faith while encamped at Mina.*

The first day of the Hajj has a special name. It is called the "Day of Reflection." Many pilgrims savor the opportunity to reflect on their life and their faith while encamped at Mina.

Second Day

The second day of the Hajj is called the "Day of Standing Together Before God" or the "Day of Arafat." On the second day of the pilgrimage (the ninth of Dhu al-Hijjah), the first task facing the pilgrim is to get from Mina to the plain of Arafat, a journey of about five miles. The pilgrims leave after dawn prayers. Traffic may slow them down to such an extent that it may take those traveling in motor vehicles the better part of the morning to reach their destination. Those who walk must take care not to be overcome by heat exhaustion or dehydration. To this end the Saudi government has installed machines that spray water across the road at intervals. According to the Prophet, the time spent on the plain of Arafat is the high point of the Hajj. He is believed to have said, "The Hajj is Arafat." Many Muslims believe that God is never closer to earth than on this day at this place. Pilgrims must arrive by sundown or their whole pilgrimage is considered invalid.

Another tent city has been established at Arafat, in order to give the pilgrims some degree of shelter from the heat of the sun. At Arafat the pilgrims spend the time between noon and sunset in prayer, recitation of the Quran, and supplication, asking God to forgive their sins and bless their family and friends. On this day at Arafat, everywhere one looks one finds people engaged in deep self-examination, confession of sins, and earnest devotions of all kinds. It is said that if a

Muslim prays with great humility and earnestness at Arafat, God will forgive his or her sins and grant his or her requests. So powerful are these prayers that pilgrims whose sins have destined them for hell may turn their fate around on this day. Another saying affirms that God releases more people from the fire on this day than on any other. Indeed, Muslim commentators have interpreted the standing at Arafat as a preview of the Day of Judgment.

The Plain of Arafat has a special significance for Muslims. Islam teaches that Adam and Eve were separated after they were expelled from the Garden of Eden. They wandered, lonely, for years, until they finally encountered one another on the plain of Arafat. In fact, Arafat means "recognition" in Arabic. Here they beseeched God in prayer to pardon their sin. And here God forgave them.

At one end of the Plain of Arafat there is a small hill called the Mount of Mercy. Ambitious pilgrims scale these heights and attempt to spend the day there. The Prophet Muhammad delivered the very last sermon he gave before his death from this hill. Each year a special sermon is delivered to the Hajj pilgrims assembled at Arafat.

On the second day, from noon prayers until sundown, pilgrims stand or sit — some for minutes, some for hours — and before God reflect on their lives and pray for mercy and renewal. Some make their way to the Mount of Mercy, a rocky hill at the foot of which the Prophet Muhammad delivered his last sermon.

When the sun sets on the ninth of Dhu al-Hijjah, the pilgrims do not ready themselves for the sunset prayer. Instead, according to the rituals demanded of the pilgrims, they promptly depart Arafat and head for the Plain of Muzdalifah. Here they say a combined version of the sunset and night prayers and prepare to spend the night. There are fewer accommodations in Muzdalifah, and many spend the night sleeping in the open air. Some choose not to sleep at all but rather to pass the night in prayer. The pilgrims also busy themselves in collecting 49 pebbles. The stones must be about the size of a bean or a chickpea and will be used in the days to come.

Third Day

The third day of the Hajj is called the "Day of Sacrifice." Throughout the world, Muslims celebrate this day, the tenth of Dhu al-Hijjah, as the Feast of the Sacrifice. The pilgrims leave Muzdalifah for Mina after dawn prayers. After arriving again at Mina, the pilgrims find the three, large stone pillars that represent Satan's tempting Abraham and Ishmael to turn aside from doing God's will. Then they cast seven of the pebbles collected at Mina at the largest of the three pillars. This gesture signifies their own rejection of the Devil and his temptations. They will throw the rest of the stones in the following days.

From this day until the twelfth of the month pilgrims may offer an animal for sacrifice. This sacrifice recalls God's command to Abraham to sacrifice his son, Abraham's joyful obedience, and God's substitution of the ram at the last minute. Not all pilgrims make the sacrifice, and some actually substitute ten days of fasting (three of which take place during the pilgrimage). This practice was authorized by the Quran, which states:

After spending the day at Arafat, two pilgrims wait atop their bus for the sunset cannon to signal them to move to Muzdalifah. There, they will collect 49 pebbles that they will throw at the three pillars of Jamarat over the next three days.

> Perform the pilgrimage and holy visit (Umra, to Makkah)
> in the service of God.
> But if you are prevented, send an offering
> which you can afford as sacrifice,
> and do not shave your heads until
> the offering has reached the place of sacrifice.
> But if you are sick or have ailment of the scalp
> (preventing the shaving of hair),
> then offer expiation by fasting
> or else giving alms or a sacrificial offering.
> When you have security, then those of you who wish
> to perform the holy visit along with the pilgrimage,
> should make a sacrifice according to their means.
> But he who has nothing,
> should fast for three days on the pilgrimage
> and seven on return, completing ten (Quran 2:196).

On the third day of the Hajj is the stoning at Jamarat and the start of the three-day Eid al-Adha — the "Feast of the Sacrifice" — which is commemorated by sacrificing a sheep. After throwing stones at the first pillar, men shave their heads, and women cut off a lock of their hair. Using their remaining 42 pebbles, pilgrims pass through Jamarat again on the fourth and fifth day, stoning each of the three pillars with seven pebbles.

Very few of the sacrifices offered by Hajj pilgrims are carried out by the pilgrims themselves. These days the Islamic Development Bank organizes and carries out the mass sacrifice of animals for Hajj pilgrims. Pilgrims buy coupons to have an animal sacrificed in their name. Many band together and offer an animal jointly. The Islamic Development Bank has built a number of large slaughterhouses in the town of Mina, each capable of processing tens of thousands of animals a day. The meat is then frozen and later sent to needy people and communities in Muslim nations around the world. In the year 2003 about 30,000 employees worked nearly nonstop for three days to complete the killing and butchering of approximately 700,000 animals.

Up until recently, much of the meat from the sacrificial animals was simply buried in the ground. Since the development of adequate technology and facilities to preserve it, the meat has been shipped to the needy. Twenty-seven Muslim nations worldwide receive shipments of the sacrificial meat. Greater emphasis has been placed on the charitable aspect of the sacrifice since the development of the means to preserve and distribute the large quantities of meat.

After stoning the pillar at Mina, men have their hair cut. Some shave their hair off completely. Women cut only a lock of their hair. This task accomplished, the pilgrims may take off their ihram. They must observe the pilgrimage rules that maintain them in a state of purity until they leave Mina, however.

361

On the sixth day, or the 13th of Dhu al-Hijjah, pilgrims return to the Holy Mosque in Mecca to make a third, final, "farewell" circum-ambulation called tawaf al-ifadhah. At this point, pilgrims are deconsecrated, and the state of ihram is ended.

Fourth, Fifth, and Sixth Days

The pilgrims stay in Mina for the 11th, 12th, and 13th days of Dhu al-Hijjah. On each of these days, the pilgrims throw seven stones at each of the three pillars. Over the course of these three days, more and more of the pilgrims take off their ihram. Thus begins their gradual return to everyday life.

Next the pilgrims return to Mecca. Here they may perform the tawaf and s'ay rituals again. For many pilgrims the last act of the Hajj is to return to the Kaba and perform the tawaf. After that the pilgrims leave Mecca, though many take advantage of the opportunity to visit other historic sites in Saudi Arabia, such as Medina, the town in which the very first Muslim community was formed.

Chapter 37
Eid al-Adha

*(Also called Feast of the Sacrifice,
Festival of the Sacrifice, the Major Festival,
Eid al-Kabir, Tabaski, Kurban Bayram,
Baqar Eid)*

All three monotheistic faiths—Judaism, Christianity, and Islam—revere the figure of Abraham. His story can be found in the Bible's Book of Genesis and in the Quran. Eid al-Adha commemorates the willingness of Abraham to sacrifice his son Ishmael to God as told in the Quran. The Arabic word *eid* means "festivity" or "recurring happiness." The phrase "Eid al-Adha" means Festival of the Sacrifice. The holiday begins on the tenth day of the Islamic month of Dhu al-Hijjah and in many places is celebrated for three days.

Other Names

Eid al-Adha goes by a variety of names. It is also called Eid al-Kabir, or "the Major Festival." This name distinguishes it from Eid al-Fitr, which is sometimes called Eid al-Saghir, or "the Minor Festival." Turkish Muslims call the festival Kurban Bayram, which means, "Feast of the Sacrifice" in Turkish. Indian Muslims refer to the holiday as Baqar Eid, or "Cow Festival." In West Africa, Muslims know the feast as "Tabaski."

Foreign words used in the text are defined in the Glossary, pages 423-40.

363

Abraham

Islam views Abraham—Ibrahim in Arabic—as an early champion of monotheism. Muslims revere him for his faithfulness to God and his defense of his beliefs in the face of persecution. According to the Quran, Abraham broke with his parents and his people, rejecting the worship of stone idols for the fervent belief in one, all-powerful God. The Quran tells that the break came during a festival, during which Abraham destroyed some of the idols, but left the largest statue untouched. The people accused Abraham of the deed, but he suggested that the

large idol had himself committed the crime, and said that they should ask the statue for the truth about what had happened. The people replied that the idol was not capable of speech. Catching them in their own illogic, Abraham then asked why they bowed down to mute statues and turned away from the one, all-powerful God. Abraham's response angered the people, who then cast the young man into a fire. But God protected Abraham by turning the fire cold, and so the youth survived the ordeal unscathed (Quran 21:52-71).

This incident was neither the last, nor the most dramatic, demonstration of Abraham's faith in a unique, all-powerful God. Abraham married a woman called Sarah. The two grew into old age without having children, so Abraham also married Hagar, Sarah's maidservant. Hagar bore a son called Ishmael (Isma'il). Chapter 37 of the Quran relates that one day, God spoke to Abraham in a dream, asking him to sacrifice his son. He shared his dream with his son, who encouraged him to carry out God's will. Although he loved his son more than anything on earth, Abraham took him to a deserted place and prepared him for sacrifice. At the last

Abraham is shown about to sacrifice his son as the angel Gabriel, at the right holding a ram, descends from heaven.

minute, God, pleased with Abraham's obedience, intervened to spare the boy's life. He sent the angel Gabriel (Jibril) with a ram to substitute for Abraham's son. Abraham rejoiced, and slew the sheep in place of his son. The Eid al-Adha festival commemorates this event.

The Bible also contains an account of Abraham's sacrifice. According to the Bible, Abraham intended to sacrifice Isaac, his son by Sarah, and not Ishmael. Although the Quran does not specify which son was the intended victim, most Muslims assert that it would have been Ishmael. They believe that after Abraham proved his faithfulness, God then rewarded him with another son, Isaac.

According to the Muslim teachings, Abraham and Ishmael later rebuilt the Kaba—an ancient temple—and consecrated it to the worship of the one, true

God. By Muhammad's time, the people had slipped back into the worship of many gods and idols. Muhammad, like Abraham, called people back to the worship of the one, all-powerful God.

The Origin of the Holiday

At the time that Muhammad was born, the Kaba, located in the town of Mecca, was an important site of pilgrimage. The pagan Arabs had installed stone idols representing many tribal gods in the shrine. During the yearly time of truce between Arabia's warring tribes, many people made pilgrimages to the Kaba to worship at this important temple. Muhammad instructed his people to maintain the tradition of pilgrimage, but to rededicate the observance to the worship of Allah. The Prophet first called upon Muslims to observe Eid al-Adha in the second year of the Muslim era, after he and his followers had all moved to Medina. The Muslim people of Medina found themselves in conflict with the pagan people of Mecca, and so were unable to make a pilgrimage to the Kaba. Instead they honored the faith of Abraham by performing sacrifices in their new hometown. The sacrifices performed by the Medina Muslims paved the way for the yearly Eid al-Adha festival still observed today by the world's Muslim communities.

Unlike the pagan Arabs, Muslim pilgrims reenacted elements of Abraham's experience with the sacrifice of Ishmael, thereby expressing their own dedication to carrying out the will of the one, true God.

After the Muslim forces under Muhammad's command conquered Mecca, Muhammad urged his followers to keep up the Arab tradition of the yearly pilgrimage to Mecca. Unlike the pilgrimages of the pagan Arabs, however, the Muslim pilgrimage honored the one God of monotheism. Moreover, Muslim pilgrims reenacted elements of Abraham's experience with the sacrifice of Ishmael, thereby expressing their own dedication to carrying out the will of God. This pilgrimage, called the Hajj, takes places on the same dates of the Muslim calendar each year, from the eighth to the thirteenth of Dhu al-Hijjah. Hajj pilgrimages celebrate Eid al-Adha in Saudi Arabia. For many it is the high point of the pilgrimage.

Religious Observances

Eid al-Adha celebrations begin with a morning prayer service. This special service, which takes place at mosques or specially arranged outdoor locations, usually follows the dawn prayers. It was established by the Prophet. According to a hadith, Muhammad once proclaimed, "The first thing we begin with on

At sunrise during the Eid al-Adha, which commemorates Abraham's faithful willingness to sacrifice his son, worshipers fill a suburban square in Mohandiseen, Cairo, Egypt.

this day of ours (the Feast) is to pray. Then we return to perform the sacrifice. Whoever does this has acted correctly according to our Sunna (practice)" (Martin: 171). In many Muslim countries the girls and women generally stay at home while the men and boys attend the prayer service. This service includes a sermon, as does the morning prayer service on Eid al-Fitr.

Muslim families commemorate Abraham's faithfulness and God's mercy by slaughtering a sheep or another animal, such as a cow, camel, or goat. Not every nuclear family unit has to provide an animal for sacrifice, however. The sacrifice made by wealthier relatives or even other community members, is often considered sufficient to cover the poor. In predominantly Muslim countries, large livestock fairs are set up just outside cities and towns in the days preceding the festival. These fairs cater to urbanites who don't raise their own livestock and need to buy a sheep or other animal to participate in the sacrifice.

The Eid al-Adha sacrifice must be offered according to Islamic law. The person who performs the killing must be an adult male of sound mind. Animals selected for sacrifice must be without blemish. The animal to be killed must face in the direction of Mecca while the man who performs the sacrifice cuts its throat, severing the windpipe and jugular vein. Certain prayerful phrases must accompany the killing. One such Islamic prayer formula combines the *basmallah* and the *takbir*. The family consumes about one-third of the meat, gives some to neighbors and relatives, and donates the rest to charity.

In pre-Islamic times blood sacrifices were thought to appease the gods. The Quran reminds Muslims that the sheer act of sacrificing an animal itself is not sufficient and that God does not actually benefit in any way from the slaughtered animals. Instead it is the faithfulness of those who perform the sacrifice that reaches God:

> It is not their meat or blood that reaches God:
> It is the fealty of your heart that reaches Him.
> That is why He has subjugated them to you
> That you may glorify God for having shown
>   you the way (Quran 22:37, Ali trans.).

> *According to a hadith, Muhammad once proclaimed, "The first thing we begin with on this day of ours (the Feast) is to pray. Then we return to perform the sacrifice."*

Foods and Customs

Some Muslims take a different route on their way to and from the morning prayer service on Eid al-Adha, a custom recorded as a hadith of the Prophet. Commentaries on this tradition suggest that the custom offers worshipers the opportunity to meet and greet twice the number of friends and neighbors. This custom is also practiced on Eid al-Fitr.

Many Eid al-Adha customs honor God's mercy to Abraham in human acts of kindness, generosity, and good will. Many Muslim families visit the graves of relatives on Eid al-Adha. Governments often arrange to pardon prisoners and commute sentences. Adults often give gifts to children, and sometimes exchange gifts among themselves as well. In Muslim countries people offer each other holiday greetings and well wishes. A kindly holiday spirit fills the air.

Other Eid customs are more festive in nature. For example, Muslims try to wear new clothes in honor of the day. Other popular holiday activities include visiting extended family members and sharing large, rich meals. These meals usually feature tasty lamb dishes. North African Muslims often enjoy *mrouzia*, a lamb stew prepared with honey and raisins.

Mrouzia

5 pounds lamb meat with bones	1/4 teaspoon ground cloves
1 teaspoon cinnamon	1/2 cup olive oil
1 teaspoon salt	1/4 cup butter
3/4 teaspoon pepper	1 cup whole almonds, blanched
3/4 teaspoon turmeric	4 cups water
1/2 teaspoon ginger	2/3 cup honey
1/2 teaspoon cardamom	1 1/3 cups raisins
1/4 teaspoon cayenne pepper	2 teaspoons orange water
1/4 teaspoon nutmeg	

Blend the oil and the spices together and cover the lamb meat with the mixture. Let the meat marinate from 1 hour to overnight. Melt butter in a large pot and add marinated meat. Cook over medium heat until slightly browned. Pour water into pot, add almonds, and bring to a simmer. Cook for about 1 hour, until meat is tender. Put honey and raisins into the pot and, over low heat, cook about 1/2 hour, stirring often. When the sauce becomes thick, add orange water and serve.

៦៩

Many Muslim families not only make good use of the meat from the sacrificial lamb, they also use the bones to make soup. The following recipe for lamb soup, called *shorbet el-fata*, comes from Egypt and is very popular around the time of Eid al-Adha.

Shorbet el-Fata

2 lamb marrow bones (washed)	1/2 cup rice, washed and drained
1 pound lamb cut into small pieces	2 round pita breads
2 quarts water	3 cloves garlic, crushed
1/2 teaspoon salt	3 tablespoons olive oil
1/4 teaspoon pepper	4 tablespoons wine vinegar
	4 tablespoons chopped parsley

Put bones into a pot of boiling water and cook for 8-10 minutes. Throw out the water and reserve the bones. Add 2 quarts of fresh water to the pot, along with the lamb meat and bones. Allow the pot to come to a boil. Skim off any scum that rises to the top. Add the salt and pepper and reduce the pot to a simmer. Cook until meat softens, about 2 hours. Add more water if level becomes too low.

Add rice and continue to simmer for about 20 minutes. Toast and split pita breads. Place one piece of bread each in the bottom of four bowls. Heat oil and fry garlic until light golden brown. Add vinegar. Pour this mixture over the pita bread slices in each bowl. Ladle a serving of soup into each bowl and garnish with parsley. Serves four.

&c.

Sweets, such as candy, pastries, puddings, and cookies, are also very popular during Eid al-Adha. In Syria and other Arab countries, housewives bake *Ma'amool*, buttery date-filled cookies, to serve to their families and guests. Middle Eastern Christians serve a similar cookie at Easter time.

Ma'amool

3 cups farina (cream of wheat)	2 tablespoons vegetable oil
1 cup clarified butter (ghee)	2 tablespoons water
1 teaspoon yeast	1/2 teaspoon cinnamon
1/2 cup lukewarm water	1/4 teaspoon ginger
8 oz. pitted, chopped dates	1/3 cup chopped almonds or walnuts

Blend together the farina and clarified butter. Let this mixture rest for at least 6 hours. Add yeast to the 1/2 cup warm water and stir until yeast dissolves. Begin to add the water and yeast mixture to the farina butter mixture, blending them to make soft dough. You may not have to use all of the water. Let the resulting dough sit for five minutes.

Mix vegetable oil, 2 tablespoons water, and chopped dates together in a saucepan over low heat. Cook, stirring, until blended and thick. Take the pan off the stove and stir in spices and nuts.

Roll a ball of dough about one inch in diameter and use your finger or thumb to make a deep indentation in it. Fill with about a teaspoon of date filling and close the dough over it. Press dough ball between the palms of your hand to flatten somewhat.

Preheat oven to 350 degrees. Place dough balls on an ungreased cookie sheet and bake for about 20 minutes, until golden brown.

Children's Customs in Bahrain and Countries of the Persian Gulf

In Bahrain and the Persian Gulf countries, children celebrate Eid al-Adha with *gufas*. A gufa is a round basket woven from palm fronds. Children buy these baskets on the first day of Dhu al-Hijjah and fill them with soil. They bury the seeds of fast-growing plants, such as wheat, lentil, or parsley, in the soil, and water them. Then they place the baskets in a string net and hang them on the wall. As the days go by, each child boasts that his or her plants have grown the most. The children care for the gufas until the tenth day of the month. On that day, families walk together to the sea and the children toss their gufas into the water. Before parting with their baskets the children say little rhymes and sing songs, asking the plants to go on the pilgrimage to Mecca in their place. They also watch to see who was able to throw their gufa the farthest. This basket, they believe, has the best chance of making it to Mecca.

Hajj Pilgrims

Eid al-Adha falls during the time of the Hajj pilgrimage. Indeed, for pilgrims the festival serves as the celebratory conclusion of their stay in Arabia. Most pilgrims, too, sacrifice an animal during the festival. Up until recently, much of this meat went to waste because adequate technology and facilities did not exist to preserve it so that it could be shipped to the needy. These days the Islamic Development Bank organizes and carries out the mass sacrifice of animals for Hajj pilgrims. Pilgrims buy coupons to have an animal sacrificed in their name. Many band together and offer an animal jointly. The Islamic Development Bank has built a number of large slaughterhouses in the town of Mina, each capable of processing tens of thousands of animals a day. The meat is then frozen and later sent to needy people and communities in 27 primarily Muslim nations around the world. In the year 2003 about 30,000 employees worked nearly nonstop for three days to complete the killing and butchering of approximately 700,000 animals.

Controversies

Muslims living in countries where they are not the majority have found that others sometimes object to their manner of celebrating Eid al-Adha. In Europe, for example, animal rights activists have criticized the mass slaughter of animals. In India, some Hindus—who consider the cow to be a sacred animal—have objected to the sacrifice of cows.

Chapter 38
Friday

(Also called Day of Assembly,
Day of Congregation, Yawn al-Juma)

Like observant Jews and Christians, observant Muslims assemble for congregational worship once a week. Friday is the Muslim day of communal worship. In Arabic it is called *Yawm al-Juma*, the Day of Congregation, or Day of Assembly. It was not traditionally thought of as a day of rest, that is, a Sabbath day on which all work should cease. This stance can be traced back to the Quran's account of the creation of the world, which differs somewhat from the story told in the Bible. The Bible's Creation story states that God made the world in six days and rested on the seventh, thus setting the precedent for the observance of the Jewish Sabbath. By contrast, the Quran insists that God had no need to rest after creating the world in six days (Quran 50:38). So Muslims do not insist on the need to cease all productive work on this day. Nevertheless, in some Muslim countries Friday has become one of the weekend days off from work.

Faithful Muslims assemble at the Friday mosque for midday prayers. A Friday mosque, or congregational mosque, is a large mosque built to accommodate the Friday congregation of a particular town or part of a city. During the week people may attend prayer services at smaller, neighborhood mosques, but on Fridays the congregation comes together at the larger mosque. Men are expected to attend the noon prayer service. Women may join as well, but they are not required to do so.

Foreign words used in the text are defined in the Glossary, pages 423-40.

Thursday and Thursday Evenings

Because days start at sunset in the Muslim calendar, Thursday evening is technically considered part of Friday. Thus it is a suitable evening to attend religious events or say extra prayers. Some Muslims view Thursday as a good day on which to fast.

In some Muslim countries, especially India and Pakistan, religious assemblies called *majalis* are held on Thursday evenings. At these events religious texts are read to the assembly, and the group sings or engages in various forms of *dhikr*. Dhikr (also spelled Zikr) is a collection of practices aimed at cultivating a constant remembrance of God. The poem on the following page, by the famous Persian poet Hafiz (c. 1320-1389), speaks of the spiritual illumination that many Muslims find in the practice.

Friday Prayer Service

Historians point out that Muhammad and his followers first observed Friday as a day of assembly during their stay in Medina. Some speculate that Muhammad chose Friday as the Muslim day of communal worship in order to distinguish the Muslims from Medina's Jewish population, which assembled for group worship

Zikr

Remembrance lowers the cup into
His luminous sky-well.

The mind often becomes plagued and can deny
The all-pervading beauty
Of God

When the great work of *zikr*
Is forgotten.

I have changed my every dancing atom
Into a divine seat in the Beloved's Tavern.

What I have learned
I am so eager to share:

Every ill will confess
It was just a lie

When the golden efforts of your love
Lift the precious wine
To your mouth.

Remembrance of our dear Friend
Lowers the soul's chalice
Into God.

Look, my sweet efforts and His Sublime Grace
Have now turned Creation into a single finger on my hand

And from the vast reservoirs
In my heart and palms

Hafiz offers
God.

EDITOR'S NOTE: Sufi poets like Hafiz sometimes write metaphorically about wine drinking and its effects to describe the exhilaration that comes from experiencing God's presence.

on Saturdays. It should also be noted that the Quran specifically requires a weekly day of congregational prayer. In chapter 62 God speaks to Muslims, saying:

> O you who believe, when the call to prayer is made
> On the day of congregation, hasten to remember God,
> Putting aside your business.
> This is better for you if you can understand.
> And when the service of prayer is over
> Spread out in the land, and look for the bounty of God.
> And remember God a great deal,
> That you may prosper (Quran 62:9-10, Ali trans.).

The Muslim congregational worship service follows a simple format. The service takes place at midday and begins with a sermon, called a *khutba*. This sermon usually lasts from about 15 minutes to half an hour. It is a special feature of the Friday prayer service, and does not occur at the prayer sessions that take place throughout the week, though special sermons are given on some holidays. An imam, or prayer leader, usually delivers it, but any knowledgeable Muslim may do this job. The speaker often begins with a quote from the Quran, which serves as the inspiration for his speech. After the sermon the congregation performs two rakat of formal prayer instead of the four rakat customarily performed at noon prayers.

Worshipers descend the main steps of Djenne's Great Mosque in Mali after Friday prayers.

Other Friday Activities and Beliefs

In some Muslim countries, people get Fridays or Friday afternoons off from work. This gives them more time for their devotions and for the leisure activities that make up their weekends. Some families make a point of enjoying an especially nice lunch or dinner on Friday evenings.

In spite of the fact that Islam does not consider Friday to be a holy day of rest, Muslims do view it as a special day, the best and most blessed day of the week. According to Muslim tradition, Muhammad once proclaimed:

> The best day on which the sun rises is Friday. On it Adam was created, on it he was expelled [from paradise], on it his contrition was accepted, on it he died, and on it the Last Hour will take place. On Friday every animal is on the lookout from dawn to sunrise in fear of the Last Hour, but not jinn and men, and it contains a time at which no Muslim prays and asks anything from Allah but He will give it to him (Emerick: 238).

Chapter 39
Hidrellez
(Also called Khidr Festival)

Turkish Muslims celebrate a holiday called Hidrellez on May 6. Unlike many other Muslim festivals, this one was assigned a date on the Gregorian calendar rather than the Muslim calendar. This observance marks the beginning of summer. It is dedicated to a mysterious folk figure whose name is Khidr in Arabic and Hizir in Turkish. He is said to come to the aid of those who call upon him. Khidr is known throughout the Muslim world. Not all Muslims approve of the folk customs connected to Hidrellez, however. Some Muslims reject these customs and celebrations because they think that they violate the strict monotheism that lies at the heart of Muslim religious belief. They fear that these activities will distract people from offering prayers and praise to God.

Khidr in the Quran

A variety of stories about Khidr circulate throughout the Muslim world. "Khidr" means "the Green One" in Arabic. Many Muslims believe that certain verses in the Quran refer to him, although he is not mentioned there by name. Chapter 18 offers a detailed description of an encounter between Moses and a person described simply as one of God's votaries. It further states that this devotee received his knowledge directly from God. Recognizing the votary as a great sage, Moses asks the stranger to accompany him on his travels. The votary agrees, on

Foreign words used in the text are defined in the Glossary, pages 423-40.

the condition that Moses will not question his behavior. The mysterious figure expresses doubt, however, that Moses will be able to abide by this request. Sure enough, Moses cannot resist asking about the meaning of the votary's seemingly unjust actions:

> So they set out till they (came to the quay)
> And went on board a ship
> In which he had made a hole, (and Moses said:)
> "You have done a strange thing!"
> "Did I not tell you," he replied,
> "that you will not be able to bear with me?"
> (Moses) said: "Do not hold me for having forgotten,
> and do not reprove me and make my task difficult."
> The two went on till they came to a boy, who he killed.
> Moses exclaimed: "You have killed an innocent soul
> Who had taken no life. You have done a most abominable thing!"
> He said: "Did I not tell you
> You will not be able to bear with me?"
> Moses said: "If I ask you any thing again
> Then do not keep me with you. You have my apology."
> The two went on till they came upon some villagers,
> and asked the people for food,
> But they refused to entertain them.
> There they found a wall that was crumbling,
> which he repaired. Moses remarked:
> "You could have demanded wages for it if you liked."
> "This is the parting of our ways," he said.
> "But I will now explain the things you could not bear:
> That boat belonged to poor people
> Who used to toil on the sea.
> I damaged it because there was a king after them
> who used to seize every ship by force.
> As for the boy, his parents were believers,
> but we feared that he would harass them
> With defiance and disbelief.
> We hoped their Lord would give them a substitute
> better than him in virtue and goodness.
> As for that wall, it belonged to two orphan boys
> Of the city, and their treasure was buried under it.
> Their father was an upright man. So your Lord
> willed that on reaching the age of maturity

They should dig out their treasure as a favor from their Lord.
So, I did not do that of my own accord.
This is the explanation of things
you could not bear with patience" (Quran 18:71-83, Ali trans.).

This story illustrates Khidr's intuitive knowledge of God's reasoning and thus his close connection with the Divine.

Khidr in Folklore

Muslim tradition asserts that Khidr is a prophet who in ancient times became immortal because he drank the Water of Life. Possessed of deep wisdom and supernatural power, he wanders the world righting wrongs, enlightening spiritual seekers, and aiding those in distress. He is sometimes described as the patron saint of travelers. His name, the Green One, has special significance. In Islam green symbolizes peace, hope, spirituality, and paradise. Khidr may have acquired his name because he, too, is associated with these things, or because he often turns up in green places, such as woods or fields. The color green is also closely associated with Muhammad and thus is sometimes used to represent Islam itself.

> *Possessed of deep wisdom and supernatural power, Khidr wanders the world righting wrongs, enlightening spiritual seekers, and aiding those in distress.*

Hidrellez in Turkey

In Turkey Hidrellez is also called *Ruz-I Hizir*, or Day of Hizir. Turkish folklore asserts that two prophets, Hizir and Ilyas (Elijah), met on this day. Over the years the names Hizir and Ilyas have merged together to form the word Hidrellez. It is also interesting to note that May 6 corresponds to April 23 in the old Julian calendar traditionally used by Orthodox Christians. Before the Turks conquered their current homeland, Orthodox Christians populated the land now known as Turkey. Many continued to live there after Turkish rule was established. Both Orthodox and Catholic Christians celebrate April 23 as St. George's Day. Some scholars believe that Hidrellez came into being when Khidr celebrations joined with and later took over earlier St. George's Day celebrations.

In Turkey, where the folk calendar divides the year into two seasons, summer and winter, May 6 marks the beginning of the summer season. Turkish folklore has assigned Hizir some special powers associated with spring and the coming of warmer weather. For example, he is reputed to help crops to grow and to bless animals with fertility. He also works miracles of increase, such as adding to food stores, or multiplying coins in purses.

The folk customs surrounding Hidrellez are practiced more often by rural than by urban Turks. One popular custom encourages people to give their homes a spring cleaning in preparation for Hidrellez. It is said that Hizir will only visit clean dwellings. People also honor the day by wearing new clothes and new shoes. In addition, some fast, make charitable contributions, or sacrifice an animal.

Turkish folklore also records a number of charms associated with Hidrellez. For example, the water in which one has boiled plants and flowers picked on Hidrellez is said to cure illness and restore beauty. Other spells are said to increase people's luck. Many of them claim to increase the chances that unmarried women will find husbands.

Chapter 40
Lamp Nights
(Also called Kandil Geceleri, Candle Feasts)

Turkish Muslims honor five religious holidays associated with events in the life of the prophet Muhammad by keeping their mosques lit all night. Taken together these special evenings are called the Kandil Geceleri. The word kandil means "candle," and the name of this observance is translated as Candle Feasts or Lamp Nights. This manner of observance dates back to the times of the Ottoman Empire. In the 16th century Sultan Selim II ordered candles or lamps placed in mosque minarets to announce these important dates to the public. Nowadays electric light displays, including strings of lights hung between minarets, keep the mosques beautifully illuminated at night. Some strict Muslim scholars dislike these displays, believing that the Turks copied the idea of nighttime illuminations celebrating the birth of the Prophet from Orthodox Christian Christmas celebrations.

The five Lamp Nights are the Birthday of the Prophet Muhammad (*Mulid al-Nabi*, celebrated on the 12th of Rabi al-Awwal), the Conception of the Prophet Muhammad (celebrated on the 1st of Rajab), Muhammad's Night Journey and Ascension (*Laylat al-Miraj*, celebrated on the 27th of Rajab), the Night of Forgiveness (*Laylat al-Bara'ah*, celebrated on the 15th of Shaban), and the Night of Power (*Laylat al-Qadr*, celebrated on the 27th of Ramadan). Turkish Muslims feel that these evenings have an especially holy air about them. Many attend prayer service at the mosques and engage in other devotional activities,

Foreign words used in the text are defined in the Glossary, pages 423-40.

such as reciting or singing poems written about the Prophet Muhammad. In past generations, young people paid visits to their elders as a sign of respect on these evenings. These days a phone call may suffice.

Turks associate a special biscuit, called *kandil simidi*, with the Lamp Nights. These ring-shaped, crispy biscuits appear in local bakeries on these days and hawkers carry basketfuls through the city streets, selling them to passersby. *Lokma*, fritters drenched in a sweet syrup, are also frequently prepared on the Lamp Nights.

Kandil Simidi (Sesame Rings)

1³/₄ cups flour
1 teaspoon yeast
¹/₂ teaspoon sugar
¹/₄ cup warm water
¹/₂ teaspoon salt
¹/₂ cup plus 2 tablespoons butter, room temperature

1 egg
1 egg yolk
1 teaspoon ground mahclep (ground black cherry kernels, available in Middle Eastern markets)
1 tablespoon milk
sesame seeds

Make a sponge by combining water, yeast, and sugar in a small bowl and let sit in warm area until it becomes frothy. Stir in ¼ cup flour, cover, and put aside for one-half hour.

To make dough, sift the remaining flour and salt together and place in a heap on your work surface. Create a well in the center and add the sponge, butter, mahclep, and egg. Use fingers to mix wet ingredients with dry ingredients near the center, gradually incorporating more and more flour into the dough until it all comes together. Knead dough until smooth. Transfer the dough to an oiled bowl and cover. Let sit for 20 minutes.

Divide dough into ten sections. Form dough into balls and then cover and let sit for 20 minutes. Roll dough balls into ropes about one foot long and join ends to form a ring. Put dough rings on a greased baking sheet. Beat together the egg yolk and milk. Brush this mixture onto the tops of the dough rings. Sprinkle with sesame seeds. Let dough rings sit in a warm place for about 15 minutes. Then bake in a 375-degree oven for about 25 minutes.

Chapter 41
White Nights

The White Nights fall on the days before, after, and during the full moon. On these nights the full or nearly full moon lights up the night skies with silvery moonbeams, making these nights "white." In the Islamic calendar months begin on the first day of the new moon and last for 29 or 30 days. Hence the White Nights will generally occur on the 13th, 14th, and 15th of each month. Islamic folklore hints that these nights are likely to be especially lucky or blessed. Many Muslims consider them a good time to observe optional fast days. Shia Muslim authorities recommend extra prayers on the White Nights that fall during the months of Rajab, Shaban, and Ramadan. Some believe that extra blessings will come to those who observe this teaching.

Foreign words used in the text are defined in the Glossary, pages 423-40.

381

Chapter 42
Saints and Their Festivals

Saints in Islam

The holy men and women of Islam are often referred to as saints. This term can be somewhat misleading if one assumes—as in Roman Catholic Christianity—that some body of clerical authorities proclaims who is and who is not a saint. In Islam believers decide for themselves who is a saint. Muslims deem someone a saint when their encounters with that particular holy person, the knowledge of his or her deeds, or the depth of his or her writings convinces them that the holy person has reached a level of spiritual insight beyond that achieved by the ordinary person. Typically these holy men and women demonstrate deep religious faith. They lead exemplary lives, possess deep spiritual understanding, and sometimes demonstrate unusual spiritual powers or uncanny knowledge of others. Muslims call such a holy individual a *wali Allah*, which means "one who is near God." Sometimes they are simply referred to as *wali* (plural *awliya*), a term which is often translated as "friend." Thus Muslim saints are the friends of God. Many Muslim saints have been Sufis, that is, explorers of the mystical dimension of Islam.

Many Shias hold in great esteem the Iranian cities of Mashhad—burial site of the eighth Shia imam, Ali ibn Musa al-Rida—and Qom — the town where the eighth imam's sister, Fatima the sinless, is buried (opposite page).

Devotion to the Saints

The strict monotheism of Islam prohibits the actual worship of saints. It teaches that only God is worthy of veneration and that prayers should be addressed to God, who alone has the power to answer them. Many Muslims worldwide

Foreign words used in the text are defined in the Glossary, pages 423-40.

383

feel that the admiration, study, imitation, and celebration of saints offer no conflict with these religious principles. They point to certain verses from the Quran to support this belief. For example, they argue that chapter 62 verse 10, which reads, "Remember, there is neither fear nor regret for the friends (awliya) of God," indicates the existence of a special, saintly class of people.

Other Muslims go beyond the study of the saints. They ask favors, protection, prayers, healings, and blessings from them. During the 20th century interest in the saints declined somewhat, due to the influence of Wahhabi teachings that oppose the veneration of saints. Nevertheless, many Muslims worldwide still love and honor the saints. Those Muslims whose spirituality includes devotion to saints feel that it draws them closer to God. They point to another verse from the Quran, which states, "None can intercede with Him except by his leave" (Quran 10:3, Ali trans.), to support the idea that certain people are permitted by God to intercede on behalf of others.

Pilgrimages to visit a saint or a saint's tomb offer devotees a chance to absorb some of the divine grace that flows to earth through the saint.

Many Muslims hold to the idea that certain people, places, and things are channels for *barakah*. Barakah may be translated as God's "grace" or "blessing." Holy people and their tombs are often considered sources of barakah. Therefore pilgrimages to visit a saint or a saint's tomb offer devotees a chance to absorb some of the divine grace that flows to earth through the saint.

Some saints acquire a reputation for being especially good at granting certain kinds of favors, much like the Christian patron saints. Devotees may become attracted to them because their particular need matches the saint's special powers. Other devotees may become attached to a certain saint out of their admiration for his or her deeds. Many Muslim saints have a large following in the area in which they lived their life, but are relatively unknown elsewhere.

Rejection of the Saints

Some Muslims completely reject devotion to the saints, however. They, too, can point to verses from the Quran to back up their view. For example, chapter 9, verse 116, states:

> Verily God's is the kingdom of the heavens and the earth.
> He alone is the giver of life and death;
> And none do you have besides God as friend and helper.

These conservative Muslims feel that devotion to the saints inevitably leads the devotee into the gravest sin a Muslim can commit, that is, worshiping something other than God (*shirk*). Wahhabi Muslims are particularly strong proponents of this viewpoint, though other Muslims may hold it, too. In fact, under the leadership of Muhammad ibn Abd al-Wahhab (1703-1792), Wahhabi forces attacked the tomb of the Prophet and his companions in Mecca and Medina. What's more, they successfully eradicated saints' shrines throughout much of the Arabian peninsula. Some years later, Wahhabi forces destroyed the shrine of Husayn in Karbala, Iraq.

Shrines

Saint celebrations take their most intense form at the shrines that house the saint's earthly remains. Many of these shrines consist of a simple building, constructed especially to house the saint's tomb. These buildings are often topped with a dome or cupola. The tomb itself is usually shaped like a rectangular box, and is often covered with a cloth. Cages or fences are sometimes erected around the tombs of especially famous saints. Sometimes shrines are located inside cemeteries. Other shrines are located next to or inside of mosques. In some Muslim countries, shrines are built in beautiful, but sometimes hard to reach, natural settings.

North African Muslims have built an especially large number of shrines to house the remains of their saints. In this part of the world saints are sometimes referred to as *marabouts*, a French term that comes from the Arabic *murabitun*, which means, "those who reside in Ribat fortresses." In western Morocco, experts have estimated that there is one shrine for every 150 people. Other Muslim countries, where reverence for saints is less intense, have considerably fewer shrines.

Interior of the mausoleum with the shrine of Sayyida Zaynab, Muhammad's granddaughter. Mosque of Zaynab in Damascus, Syria.

Urs and Mulids

Festivals honoring a saint often take place on the day of the saint's birth or the day of his or her death. The birth festivals are called *mulids*, which means "birth" in Arabic. The most important mulid is the Birthday of the Prophet Muhammad, Mulid al-Nabi.

The word *urs* can be translated as "wedding celebration." Muslims also use the word to refer to festivals marking the death anniversaries of holy men and women. Rather than viewing the death of these people as sad events, their devotees understand the event to signify a unification, or "wedding," with God.

Some saint festivals take place on dates unassociated with the birth or death of the saint. The mulid of the famous Egyptian saint Ahmad al-Badawi, for example, takes place in the second half of October. This time of year corresponds with neither his birth nor his death anniversary, but rather represents the season when the majority of his devotees, many of whom are farmers, have the greatest amount of free time. During this period, thousands and thousands of devotees travel to al-Badawi's native town of Tanta.

Pilgrimage to Shrines

Saints' shrines are year-round pilgrimage sites. The number of pilgrims increases dramatically around the time of the saint's annual festival, however. Pilgrims undertake the journey to saints' shrines to make religious vows, to offer their gratitude to the saint for favors received, to ask for healings or other forms of help, to absorb the spirituality of the place, or simply to express their admiration and love for the holy person. In many Muslim countries, women are well represented among the shrine-goers. A number of scholars have noted that in some of these places, local custom excludes women from other forms of Islamic worship and from the means and power to redress their grievances. Therefore, they believe, many women both express their spirituality and seek help with life's difficulties by visiting the shrines and asking the saints for assistance.

> *Pilgrims undertake the journey to saints' shrines to ask for help, to absorb the spirituality of the place, or simply to express their admiration and love for the holy person.*

When visiting a shrine it is important to observe proper etiquette. Often a walled courtyard surrounds the shrine. In many places beggars surround the entrance to the courtyard, in the hopes that pilgrims are in a generous mood. They may also be attracted by the free food that is sometimes distributed at saints' shrines. Before entering the walled compound, the pilgrim removes his or her shoes. Some pilgrims enjoy resting or chatting quietly in the courtyard.

When entering the shrine itself, one steps across the threshold with one's right foot first. Pilgrims avoid stepping on the threshold itself, as many visitors stoop to kiss it. Once inside, pilgrims walk in a circle around the tomb. It is also important to offer a greeting to the saint, and to recite some verses of the Quran as well as some blessings on the Prophet. It is commonly believed that barakah emanates from the saint's grave and the goal of many pilgrims is to say prayers before it. Some also leave offerings there. These offerings usually consist of small cash donations, but pilgrims may instead leave small objects, oil for the shrine's lamps, food, or flowers. Some pilgrims offer grave cloths,

beautifully decorated pieces of fabric that that are thrown over the tomb. In some locales, pilgrims buy and burn incense at the tomb. One popular custom is to tie a ribbon or lock a padlock around the rungs of the fence or the cage surrounding the saint's tomb. This act is believed to ensure that the devotee's request receives the saint's attention. Some Muslims plead for the saint's assistance by making a vow. For example, they may ask the saint to pray for the healing of one of their family members and vow that if their relative is healed, they will sacrifice a lamb. Vows made at a saint's shrine are considered especially binding.

Many other activities also occur in shrines. Some pilgrims will sit quietly in the shrine, reading from the Quran. Some Sufi visitors perform spiritual practices associated with their order—such as various forms of chanting, or dhikr—at shrines. When a visitor is ready to leave, he or she asks for the saint's permission to go, then backs away respectfully from the tomb.

Pilgrims at tomb of the eighth Shia imam, Ali al-Rida (Reza) located in Mashhad, Iran.

387

Saints' Festivals

A saint's feast day draws many pilgrims and fun seekers to the saint's shrine. Usually these festivals take place over a couple of days, but climax on one particular day. Most devoted pilgrims who attend the festival seek to perform at least some of the pilgrimage rituals described above. During a saint's festival, however, many other activities are also available to them. For example, processions are a common feature of saints' festivals. If the saint belonged to a particular Sufi order, then members of that order often play a large role in organizing and participating in the procession. Some processions are led by one of the saint's descendants. Festival organizers may also arrange for religious talks and discussion sessions to take place. Sufi orders often play a large role in the religious activities that take place at saints' festivals. In addition to marching in the procession, they may also organize exuberant dhikr sessions, or give demonstrations of spiritual practices associated with their order. They may also host gatherings dedicated to the enjoyment of or participation in religious music and dance.

> *At most saints' festivals, a kind of miniature fairgrounds springs up next to the shrine, complete with food stalls, trinket sellers, vendors of religious goods, and amusements.*

Saints' festivals often are composed of both religious and festive elements. At most festivals, a kind of miniature fairgrounds springs up next to the shrine, complete with food stalls, trinket sellers, vendors of religious goods, and amusements. In India and Pakistan, some celebrations that accompany a saint's day are major, circus-like attractions that include bumper cars or other amusement park rides, acrobatic and daredevil kinds of performances, and large screen televisions available for public viewing. Major saint's day celebrations in Egypt are also accompanied by large fairs.

Chapter 43
A Closer Look at a Few
Saints' Festivals

Thousands of saint's day celebrations take place across the Muslim world. Some of the saints are relatively well known, while others are known and loved only in the part of the world in which they lived. The distinguishing features of a few of these festivals have been described in some detail below in order to give the reader an idea of the local flavor of these events.

৬৫

Mulid of Shaykh Yusuf Abu el-Haggag
Place: Luxor, Egypt
Date: Middle of Shaban

Yusuf Abu el-Haggag is one of upper Egypt's well-known and well-loved saints. He was born in Tunisia in the 12th century to a family that traced its lineage back to Muhammad. After studying with a well-known Sufi, he moved to Egypt. He settled in Luxor, which at that time was primarily Christian. Not long after he arrived in town, Abu el-Haggag asked Tharzah, the female, Christian ruler of the city, to grant him the amount of land that he could cover with a camel's hide. She agreed. Abu el-Haggag set about cutting his camel hide into thin strips and tying them together end to end. He created a long strand that enabled him to encircle

Foreign words used in the text are defined in the Glossary, pages 423-40.

389

the entire city. Under the influence of Abu el-Haggag, Tharzah agreed to convert to Islam and the two of them were married. Abu el-Haggag organized the construction of a mosque in the center of the ruins of the ancient Egyptian Temple of Amon at Luxor. Both the temple and mosque still stand today. Abu el-Haggag is buried inside the mosque.

The festival opens with a speech inside the mosque given by the current patriarch of the Haggagi family. Members of Sufi orders set up tents in the week preceding the procession, an event that signals the high point of the festival. There they host Sufi dances. These dances serve as a physical means of expressing one's devotion to God. Displays of horsemanship also take place in the nearby fields. Street vendors hawk toys, trinkets, food, and amusements. On the evening before the procession, the Haggagi clan hosts an evening of religious lectures open to men only. Free meals are given to the needy as well.

The mosque of Abu el-Haggag, built inside the Luxor Temple centuries before exacavation began in 1892, is visible in the temple walls. The mosque's entrance now opens more than seven meters above floor level.

The procession in honor of Abu el-Haggag takes place on the middle day of Shaban. The parade route through Luxor is said to be the same route which Abu el-Haggag traced with his strip of camel hide. At the head of the procession ride the men of the Haggagi family, with the elderly patriarch riding in a carriage. Then comes a line of camels, each of which bears a model of one of the tombs inside the mosque (several prominent people are buried inside this mosque). Next appears a series of six boats, set in wagons. Some speculate that the use of boats in the procession symbolizes a miracle worked by the saint. According to legend, when Abu el-Haggag was returning to Egypt after making the Hajj, he saved the boat that was carrying him from sinking and all its passengers from drowning. Others suspect, however, that the boats echo an ancient Egyptian festival custom. Groups of tradesmen also march in the procession. For example, Nile boatmen, carriage drivers, restaurant workers, and others take part, each carrying a symbol or the tools of their trade.

ꙮ

The Urs of Data Ganj Bakhsh
Place: Lahore, Pakistan
Date: Third Week of Safar

The saint that Pakistanis often call "Data Ganj Bakhsh," meaning, "the master bestower of treasure," was born in Gazna, Afghanistan, in the late 10th or early 11th century. His given name was Ali ibn Uthman al-Jullabi al-Hujwiri (d. 1070). He grew up to be a mystic and a writer. Many claimed that Data Ganj Bakhsh had the power to work miracles. He produced the first book on Sufi spirituality to be written in the Persian language. The saint never married and taught that celiba-

cy was best for those who wished to pursue the Sufi path. He traveled throughout the Muslim world in his lifetime, and is buried in Lahore, a town that lies inside the modern nation of Pakistan.

Pilgrims have been visiting the shrine of Data Ganj Bakhsh for over 900 years. Devotees often gather there on Thursday evenings, to read the Quran and to pray. His shrine has also become the site of one of Pakistan's most popular festivals. The festival takes place during the third week of Safar. It attracts more than half a million pilgrims, as well as national television, radio, and live Internet coverage. Politicians, scholars, activists, businessmen, and other prominent members of Pakistani society attend the event, and some try to promote their viewpoint, cause, or enterprise by linking it to the popular festival.

Some visitors spend a large percentage of their time praying, listening to professional Quran reciters, and performing dhikr in the shrine compound. They may also join the Sufi-led discussion groups (*halaqa*) that form to study the

The tomb of Data Ganj Bakhsh — one of the many Sufis who brought Islam to Asia by peaceful means — is located in Lahore, Pakistan.

saint's major work, a treatise on spiritual development. The largest crowds, however, are to be found surrounding the stages where devotional music, called *qawwali*, is performed. The event organizers hire the nation's best qawwali groups for the festival. It is customary for each group to begin with a song praising God and a song praising the Prophet. The following songs praise Data Ganj Bakhsh and other saints. If spectators are deeply moved by the performance, they offer sweets and money to musicians.

ᘒᘒᘒ

The Urs of Baba Farid Shakar Ganj
Place: Pak Patan, Pakistan
Date: Fifth of Muharram

Fariduddin Masud, who later became known as the saint Baba Farid Shakar Ganj, was born on the 29th of Shaban near Lahore, Pakistan, in the year 1179. According to legend, the child displayed amazing spiritual powers at an early age. It is said that his mother usually placed a few sweets under his prayer rug, in order to encourage him to pray. One day she forgot to put them there. Nevertheless, when the boy rolled up his rug, a heap of sweets was lying there. Some say that the title by which he was known later in life, Shakar Ganj, meaning "heap of sweets," comes from this tale. Others say it grew out of the following story, which takes place after Baba Farid had joined the Chishtiyya order of Sufis and become a well-known holy man.

> *During his lifetime, Baba Farid acquired a far-flung reputation for miracle working.*

Everyone who had ever met Baba Farid knew he was fond of sweets. One day Baba Farid greeted a man carrying a sack that contained sugar. The saint asked the man, "What's in the bag?" The man realized that if he told the truth, he would feel compelled to share some sugar with Baba Farid. His greed to possess all the sugar urged him to lie to the saint. So, the man declared, "The bag is full of salt." "So be it," replied Baba Farid with a twinkle in his eye. When the man got home and opened the bag, he found that the sugar had changed into salt. Humbled by the realization that he had not been able to fool the saint about the sugar or his desire for it, he returned to Baba Farid and apologized for his actions. Then the saint graciously turned the salt back into sugar.

Baba Farid was known to live a very austere life and to practice many physically taxing spiritual exercises. During his lifetime he acquired a far-flung reputation for miracle working. Although Baba Farid spent most of his life as a celibate, he married three wives late in life and had ten children. He died in 1256 and was buried in the Punjab at Pak Patan, a town that lies in the modern nation of Pakistan. Over the years followers of the great saint have showered him with many titles, which today's devotees sometimes recite as a kind of spiritual exercise. His titles, which resemble those listed as the 99 names of God or the titles of the Prophet Muhammad, include "the Patient," "the Great," "the Present," "the Praised," "the Perfect," "the Secret of God," and "the Spirit of God."

The Urs of Baba Farid Shakar Ganj falls on the fifth of Muharram. Devotees gather at his shrine in Pak Patan to celebrate the saint's reunion with God. For many believers the highlight of the festival comes when a special door to the shrine is opened and pilgrims pour into the shrine through this door. This entryway, called the "Door of Paradise," is only opened on the fifth of Muharram. It acquired its name from a vision received by Baba Farid's successor some time after the saint's death. This man, called Nizamuddin, was meditating at the shrine when he had a vision of the Prophet Muhammad, who pointed to the door and said, "O Nizamuddin, whosoever shall enter this door shall be saved." Many pilgrims believe that special spiritual benefits come to those who enter the shrine through this door. In 2001, a delay in opening the door led to the death of 44 people, who were trampled to death by an eager crowd when the doors finally opened. This event, though very tragic, illustrates the great enthusiasm shared by the crowds that attend this festival.

☙☯❧

Pilgrimage to the Shrine of Sunan Bayat

Place: Tembayat, Java, Indonesia
Date: A mulid festival takes place on the 21st day of the Javanese month of Mulud

Some Indonesians count Sunan Bayat as one of the nine Sufi saints responsible for converting the people of the Indonesian island of Java to Islam. (Others include him as an honorary tenth member of this illustrious group.) This 16th-century saint began life as a king and a non-Muslim. He converted to Islam after a Muslim holy man recognized in him the seeds of spiritual greatness. The holy man convinced Sunan Bayat to leave his palace, power, and wealth to become a man of God. After some initial reluctance, Sunan Bayat abandoned his privileged life and began a new life of prayer, meditation, and preaching. He founded a religious school and is said to have performed many miracles.

The tomb of Sunan Bayat is the site of year-round pilgrimage. There are a number of dates, however, on which the people of Java find it especially beneficial to make a pilgrimage to the tomb. Thursday evenings and Monday evenings (which would be considered Friday evenings and Tuesday evenings according to the Muslim calendar) are considered specially blessed times to make the pilgrimage.

Although some auspicious dates to visit the tomb are based on the Muslim calendar, others are based on the traditional Javanese calendar, or on a combination of the Javanese and Muslim calendars. The Javanese week lasts only five days. The names of these days are Kliwon, Legi, Paing, Pon, and Wage. As in the Muslim calendar, days begin at sunset. When important dates in the Javanese calendar line up with important dates or days of the week in the Muslim calendar, the Javanese deem it a good opportunity for a pilgrimage to the tomb. For example, many pilgrims visit on the evening of a Friday-Kliwon or a Friday-Legi. This preference may be explained by the fact that the great saint was born on a Legi and died on a Kliwon. Moreover, in Java, Friday-Kliwon is considered a good time to visit graves. New Year's Eve in the Javanese calendar is also believed to be a blessed date on which to visit the saint. Finally, since 1973, a mulid festival has been celebrated yearly at the tomb on the 21st day of the Javanese month of Mulud.

> *The tomb of Sunan Bayat is located on top of a mountain, as were many important indigenous religious sites.*

Islam is Indonesia's predominant religion. As Islam spread, however, it borrowed customs and took over religious sites from Indonesia's other major faiths — Hinduism, Buddhism, Christianity, and indigenous Indonesian religion. In fact, in Indonesia it can be difficult to completely separate Hindu, Muslim, Buddhist, Christian, and indigenous Indonesian religious sites and customs. For example, though the tomb of Sunan Bayat is said to house a Muslim saint, many Christians and Confucian Chinese visit the tomb to ask for the saint's intercession. The tomb is located on top of a mountain, as were many important indigenous religious sites. Some elements of the shrine's architecture are clearly Hindu in origin. The tomb of the saint itself, however, is modeled on Islam's most holy shrine: the Kaba. Though this kind of religious blending has a long history in Indonesia, certain conservative Muslims have become uncomfortable with it in recent decades. Some of these people have lobbied other Muslims to observe only orthodox Muslim religious practices.

Pilgrims to the shrine of Sunan Bayat begin the last leg of their journey in a modern car park. This car park was recently built at the foot of the stairway leading up the mountainside where the saint is buried. Here modern facilities permit devotees to complete the ritual washing necessary to perform Islam's formal prayers. Here also pilgrims buy a ticket that permits them to enter the burial complex. They may also take the opportunity to buy flowers or incense from parking lot vendors that cater to the needs of pilgrims.

Halfway up the winding staircase to the shrine, pilgrims take off their shoes, a gesture of respect and cleanliness that Muslims also perform before stepping into the prayer hall of a mosque. In case they should grow physically or spiritually fatigued on their journey up the mountainside, little stands along the way offer food, drinks, souvenirs, and religious items. These stalls are a relatively new addition to the pilgrimage scene, having sprung up in the 1990s. At the top of the staircase pilgrims pay an additional fee to enter the shrine. Those who want to sleep overnight near the grave must pay an extra fee. The added cost is worth it for many pilgrims, however, as they believe that sleeping next to the saint's tomb is the best way to absorb his barakah.

The attendant who sits in the antechamber to the shrine prays aloud to the saint on the pilgrims' behalf, sandwiching these petitions in between recitations of the Fatiha in Arabic.

The attendant who sits in the antechamber to the shrine performs an important function for the pilgrims. He prays aloud to the saint on their behalf, sandwiching these petitions in between recitations of the Fatiha (first chapter of the Quran) in Arabic. Then the pilgrims proceed into the shrine itself, where they may offer their own, silent prayers. Like the Kaba, on which it was modeled, it contains no lighting fixtures, so pilgrims enter and absorb the atmosphere of the tomb in complete darkness. Sunan Bayat's two wives are buried on either side of him. Each tomb is covered with a white cloth that is replaced each year. The old grave cloth is cut into small pieces and distributed to devotees as amulets. Pilgrims bring flowers for the saint, but also remember flowers for his wives. In addition, many will place flowers on the graves of his helpers, who are buried elsewhere in the shrine complex. Once inside the saint's tomb they place the flowers on the graves and, as it is too dark to see these offerings, begin to feel the stems and blossoms with their fingers. According to local custom, the saint signifies his willingness to answer their prayers or to confer blessings on them by causing new buds to suddenly appear on the stalks.

After paying their respects to the saint and his wives the pilgrims visit the other graves contained in the shrine complex. Many Javanese Muslims believe that the saint's barakah is strongest in evenings. They make a point of visiting the shrine after dark and staying until at least midnight, a time when unseen powers are believed to be at their highest potency. Some stay overnight, sleeping alongside the tombs. Those who feel uncomfortable with the gender mixing that takes place near the tombs may sleep in recently constructed male and female sleeping pavilions.

⊗⊙

Moussem of Moulay Idriss
Place: Moulay Idriss, Morocco
Date: September

Many moussems feature amazing displays of horsemanship called "fantasias."

Moroccans generally refer to a saint's festival as a "moussem." This word comes from *mawsim,* the Arabic word for season. In Morocco saints' festivals that draw large numbers of attendees are accompanied by fairs, making the event as much an opportunity for worship as for commerce. The fair also attracts storytellers, musicians, and other entertainers. Pilgrims come from locations near and far to take advantage of all that a moussem has to offer, setting up housekeeping in makeshift tents. Many moussems feature amazing displays of horsemanship called "fantasias," which involve armed men riding horses at top speed, firing rifles, and wheeling their horses about with great skill.

The Moussem of Moulay Idriss commemorates a saint of the same name, who was known to be a descendant of Muhammad. He is sometimes called Moulay Idriss I, in order to distinguish him from his son, Moulay Idris II. In the 8th century the father united Morocco's Berber tribes, founded the city of Fez, and established the nation's first Muslim ruling dynasty. Folklore portrays Moulay Idriss as a highly competent and energetic man, assigning him 500 wives, 1,000 children, and 12,000 horses. After his death, a small town called Moulay Idriss grew up around his shrine and tomb.

One of Morroco's most important moussems takes place in the town of Moulay Idriss during the month of September. The moussem lasts several weeks, but the religious high point may be considered the procession of the Sufi brotherhoods to the shrine, in which a large carpet is carried over the heads of the marchers. Musicians play and march alongside the brothers, some of whom slip into a trance state in the highly charged religious environment. Among the fair's varied forms of secular entertainments, an elaborate fantasia stands out as the most spectacular.

Moroccans consider Moulay Idriss to be a holy city and non-Muslims are not permitted to stay the night there. Many Moroccans are uncomfortable with the presence of non-Muslims in Moulay Idriss. Therefore, non-Muslims would do well to keep a low profile at any religious events that they are allowed to attend.

After the death of Moulay Idriss I, a small town called Moulay Idriss, also known as the Holy City of Zerhoun, grew up around his shrine and tomb.

ↄ◌

The Grand Magal of Shaykh Amadou Bamba
Place: Touba, Senegal
Date: The 18th of Safar

The city of Touba houses the remains of Senegal's most revered marabout (or saint), Shaykh Amadou Bamba (1850-1927). All year round religious pilgrims come to the city to visit his tomb. The greatest influx of pilgrims, however, arrives on the 18th day of Safar, when the Senegalese celebrate his feast day. This event is often referred to as the "Grand Magal" or great pilgrimage. It is celebrated neither on the date of the saint's birth, nor on his death anniversary, but rather on the date in 1895 on which he departed for seven years of exile abroad.

Shaykh Bamba began building a mosque in the town of Touba in 1926. He is buried inside the mosque.

Shaykh Bamba was the son of a marabout. He grew up to be a mystic and spiritual leader himself, one that radiated personal charm as well as barakah. Like other marabouts, he taught the Quran and made amulets for people, but he distinguished himself from other Muslim spiritual leaders by rejecting violence and refraining from waging war on pagan Africans. He attracted such a great following that the French colonial authorities feared he might be plan-ning to challenge their rule, so in 1895 they forced him into exile in Gabon. This only increased his popularity. Today many legends claim that the French subjected him to harsh restrictions and in some cases even torture. In the face of all these hardships, so the stories say, Bamba displayed amazing supernatural powers. For example, one tale proclaims that French authorities forbade the shaykh from praying while traveling on a ship to Gabon. As an observant Muslim, Bamba felt that he could not put the rules of his French captors above God's rules. So he simply broke the chains that shackled him and leapt overboard. A prayer rug materialized underneath the saint and held him up above the waves. He performed the prayers and returned to the ship.

Bamba spent much of his time while in prison writing poetry and meditating on God. These poems are still popular with his devotees. In 1902 the French authorities permitted the shaykh to return to Senegal, but French fears led to another foreign exile in 1903, this time to Mauritania.

The Grand Magal attracts anywhere between one and three million pilgrims each year.

By 1907 the French had come to the conclusion that Bamba had no intention of overthrowing French rule, so they permitted him to return to Senegal. Nevertheless they kept him under closer surveillance until 1913. Shaykh Bamba began building a mosque in the town of Touba in 1926. He is buried inside the mosque. Bamba also founded a Sufi order called Mouride. The name comes from the Arabic word *murid*, meaning "aspirant," or "student." Shayhk Bamba's descendants still head up the Mouride Brotherhood.

The Grand Magal attracts anywhere between one and three million pilgrims each year. So many Senegalese journey to Touba at this time of year that the streets of the capital city, Dakar, look somewhat deserted. It can be difficult to find public transport around the time of the Grand Magal, since so many vehicles are pressed into service to ferry pilgrims back and forth from Touba. Members of the Mouride Brotherhood will return to Senegal for this event, even if they are living as far away as Europe or North America.

In addition to offering prayers at the Shaykh's tomb, pilgrims visit with respected spiritual leaders from the Mouride Brotherhood from whom they seek spiritual guidance. They also look forward to the public address offered by the current head of the Mouride Brotherhood. Once these religious duties have been completed they can wander the streets of the town, where thousands of vendors have set up shop selling food, drink, religious paraphernalia, jewelry, and traditional crafts, as well as cell phones and other contemporary gadgets.

ගය

The Urs of Jelaluddin al-Rumi
(Also called Whirling Dervish Festival, Sheb-i-Arus)
Place: Konya, Turkey
Date: Week leading up to December 17

The Life of Jelaluddin al-Rumi

The poet and Sufi mystic Jelaluddin al-Rumi was born in the year 1207 in Balkh, a city which lies in modern-day Afghanistan. Jelaluddin's family left the area when he was still a child in order to escape the advancing Mongol army. They wandered the world for many years, visiting Mecca and Medina, and then living in Baghdad. According to legend, they also spent time in Nishapur, where the famous Persian mystic and writer Farid ad-Din Attar met the boy and his father. The stories say that Attar blessed the boy and recognized him as a future saint. The family finally settled down in Konya, located in today's central Turkey. Though he lived the rest of his life in what is now Turkey, Rumi was an ethnic Persian and wrote most of his famous poetry in Farsi, the language of Persia. His *nisbah*, or place name, however, indicates his adopted homeland. Rumi means "Roman." At that time, many Muslims referred to Asia Minor (Turkey) as Rome because it was still ruled — at least in part — by the last vestiges of the eastern Roman Empire (also known as the Byzantine Empire).

> **When Rumi was 37 years old, he met a wandering Sufi dervish called Shams ad-Din at-Tabrizi. Shams became Rumi's spiritual teacher and dearest friend.**

Rumi's father was a noted scholar and religious teacher. He transmitted this knowledge to his son, who took over his father's job as head of a religious school upon his father's death. The school taught theology and various devotional practices, music, poetry, agriculture, animal husbandry, cooking, and other subjects designed to facilitate spiritual growth. Rumi's reputation as a pious man and excellent spiritual teacher grew to the point where the school boasted thousands of students. In addition to his school duties, Rumi also adopted the spiritual disciplines of Sufism.

When Rumi was 37 years old, he met a wandering Sufi dervish called Shams ad-Din at-Tabrizi. The meeting with Shams changed Rumi's life. Shams became Rumi's spiritual teacher and dearest friend. Rumi's soul flowered in Shams' company. The insights that Rumi experienced with Shams inspired the poet to write verses that offer blissful glimpses of the divine and impart profound spiritual wisdom in everyday language.

According to legend, the relationship was equally important to Shams. Tales tell that he had longed for someone whose insight was advanced enough to understand his teachings and to join him in spiritual friendship. When asked by the Divine what he would give for such a friendship, he said, "my head." Shams then received guidance from God suggesting that the friend he was looking for was Jelaluddin of Konya, so he journeyed to Turkey to find Rumi. A number of stories describe the nature of the relationship between the two men. Several tales illustrate how Shams pushed Rumi further along the mystical path and away from his more traditional scholarly activities. In one of them Shams spots Rumi discussing some learned books with some of his advanced students. Sham strides up to Rumi and tosses his book and the others beside it into the water. He declares, "From now on you must live this rather than read about it." Rumi glances back at the books. Shams reaches into the water and draws out a book. To everyone's astonishment, the book is completely dry. From this day forward, the story says, Rumi followed Shams without hesitation.

The relationship between Rumi and Shams lasted only a few years (1244-47). During that period Shams disappeared from Konya twice. After the first disappearance Rumi ordered that a search be made. Some say Shams turned up about two years later of his own accord; others say Rumi's son Sultan Veled found him in Damascus, Syria, and brought him back. The second disappearance was permanent. Scholars suspect that this time Shams may have been murdered by some of Rumi's students or family members, who were jealous of the time that Rumi spent with Shams. Rumi grieved deeply for the loss of his friend and never ceased to miss his company. Much of Rumi's poetry was dedicated to his teacher and friend, Shams of Tabriz.

Rumi died on the evening of December 17, 1273. He admonished his followers not to grieve for him, as he saw the end of his earthly life as his wedding night with God. He left his devotees with this couplet concerning his grave:

> When I am dead, seek not my tomb in the earth,
> But find it in the hearts of men.

Rumi's Poetry and the Mevlevi Order

With his unquenchable gift for poetry, Rumi composed about 40,000 verses in his lifetime. The following poem offers a sample of Rumi's work. It describes the difference between the knowledge acquired by scholars and the kind of inner knowing cultivated by mystics such as himself, but available to every human being.

> There are two kinds of intelligence: One acquired,
> as a child in school memorizes facts and concepts
> from books and from what the teacher says,
> collecting information from the traditional sciences
> as well as from the new sciences.

> With such intelligence you rise in the world.
> You get ranked ahead or behind others
> in regard to your competence in retaining
> information. You stroll with this intelligence
> in and out of fields of knowledge, getting always more
> marks on your preserving tablets.

> There is another kind of tablet, one
> already completed and preserved inside you.
> A spring overflowing its springbox. A freshness
> in the center of the chest. This other intelligence
> does not turn yellow or stagnate. It's fluid,
> and it doesn't move from outside to inside
> through the conduits of plumbing-learning.

> This second knowing is a fountainhead
> from within you, moving out.

(From *This Longing* by Rumi, Versions by Coleman Barks and John Moyne. © 1988 by Coleman Barks. Reprinted by arrangement with Shambhala Publications, Inc., Boston, www.shambhala.com.)

Some trace the dance ritual of the whirling dervish back to a personal habit attributed to Rumi. It is said that he expressed his grief for Shams by walking round and round a pole in his garden, speaking his now famous poems as they came into his mind.

After Rumi's death his son, Sultan Veled, founded a Sufi order around his father's teaching. Rumi's two great collections of verse, *The Works of Shams of Tabriz* and the *Masnavi*, serve as the main teaching material for the order. Rumi's students called him *mevlana*, "our lord" or "our master" in Arabic. The name of the order rooted in the teachings of the great saint and poet comes from that word. It's called Mevlevi in Turkish and Malawi in Arabic.

The use of music and dance as a means of experiencing spiritual ecstasy is a distinctive feature of the Mevlevi Order. Its members have been called the "Whirling Dervishes" in reference to their dance rituals, in which the devotees spin in place for extended periods of time. Some trace this ritual back to a personal habit attributed to Rumi. It is said that he expressed his grief for Shams by walking round and round a pole in his garden, speaking his now famous poems as they came into his mind. Others suggest another origin for the whirling dances. They say that Rumi frequently browsed through Konya's marketplace. According to these stories, the poet-saint would sometimes come across a goldsmith pounding precious metals or a blacksmith hammering out a new copper pot. Captivated by the rhythmic tapping of the hammer, Rumi would begin to twirl in place to the beat.

Rumi's fame soon spread far beyond the bounds of the Mevlevi Order, however. His poetry won him many admirers across the Muslim world. So great was the respect for the beauty and wisdom of the *Masnavi* among Persian-speakers that they nicknamed the book the "Persian Quran." New translations have made Rumi's poetry widely accessible to English-speakers as well.

The Festival

The city of Konya, Turkey, hosts a festival that honors Rumi on December 17. Actually the celebrations begin a week earlier on December 10. Merchants decorate their shop windows with posters advertising the festival and many stock little whirling dervish and musician figurines, and other mementos of interest to tourists. Special nighttime light displays bejewel the town, which fills up with hundreds of tour buses during this week. The town may also host exhibits that showcase the history of the Mevlevi Order and conferences on Rumi and his legacy. In recent years around 25,000 people have attended the festival. Most hail from Turkey, but a good number of foreigners, both Muslims and non-Muslims, also come to pay their respects to the master. The celebrations reach a climax on December 17, known as Sheb-i-Arus, or the Nuptial Night.

Festivalgoers often stop first at the saint's tomb. Rumi's devoted followers established the shrine in the 13th century on land donated for the purpose from the Seljuk Palace rose garden. Over the centuries a Mevlevi compound grew up around the spot, which includes a mosque, dance hall, schoolrooms, Quran chanting chamber, kitchen, living quarters for members of the order, and the tombs of its leaders and well-known members. Construction finally came to a halt in the 19th century.

Rumi's mausoleum and the entire Mevlevi complex is one of the most popular museums in Turkey. Visitors linger near the tomb to offer prayers, meditate, or simply to enjoy the beauty and peace of the shrine.

A beautiful green tower tops the room where Rumi lies entombed. Visitors linger near the tomb to offer prayers, meditate, or simply to enjoy the beauty and peace of the shrine. This room contains two of the oldest copies of Rumi's great books —*The Works of Shams of Tabriz* and the *Masnavi*— known to be in existence.

Two famous quotes from the poet's work — written in calligraphy — that grace walls of the room summarize Rumi's spiritual teachings. The first, written in Turkish, states:

> Either seem as you are
> Or be as you seem.

The second, written in Persian, reflects the universal spirit of Rumi's religious teachings:

> Come, come, come again whoever you are.
> An unbeliever, a fire-worshiper, come.
> Our lodge is not a lodge of despair.
> Even if you have broken your vows a hundred times,
> Come, come, come again.

In 1925 the government of the new Republic of Turkey forbade Sufi ceremonies and meetings, and closed down the Sufi lodges and shrines, effectively outlawing Sufism in Turkey. In 1927, the Mevlevi complex in Konya became a state-run museum. In 1953, the state permitted the remaining Mevlevis to resurrect their dance ceremony once a year — as a cultural event of interest to tourists — on the date of Rumi's death. In 1973, in honor of the 700th anniversary of the saint's death, the Turkish government authorized a troupe of dancers to tour outside of Turkey, bringing the famous dance of the Whirling Dervishes to international audiences. In spite of the official ban on Sufism, Rumi's mausoleum and the entire Mevlevi complex is one of the most popular museums in Turkey.

Opposite page: Members of the Mevlevi Order have been called the "Whirling Dervishes" in reference to their dance rituals, in which the devotees spin in place for extended periods of time.

In keeping with the government's promotion of the festival as a cultural rather than a religious event, today's festival dancers perform in Konya's enormous sports stadium rather than the museum or some other religious site. The dances are scheduled during the evenings. They are preceded by an hour of Turkish band music and punctuated by speeches. The proceedings are slightly more elaborate on the evening of December 17, the anniversary of Rumi's death.

The Dance of the Whirling Dervishes

Though other Sufi orders hold musical prayer and meditation sessions, called *sama*, the Mevlevis developed a distinctive form of dancing as well. They whirl round and round in place which causes the white skirt they wear over their trousers to stand out around them like a hoop skirt. In addition to their white pants, overskirt, jacket, and black cloak, the dancers wear tall cylindrical hats. These items of clothing, like the movements of the dance itself, symbolize specific things to the Sufi dancers. The hat represents the gravestone of the dancer's ego, his cloak stands for his ego's coffin, and the billowing white skirt symbolizes his ego's shroud. The dance itself symbolizes the ascent of the dancer's spirit, as he dies to his own selfishness and conceit and turns towards love and truth.

A group of musicians accompanies the dancers. The band always includes a drum and a *ney* (reed flute). Sometimes other instruments appear as well, such as the *kanun* (similar to a zither), *oud* (similar to a lute), *rebab* (like a violin) and *tambur* (also like a lute).

Mausoleum of Jelaluddin al-Rumi in Konya, Turkey. The beautiful green tower tops the room where Rumi lies entombed.

For many visitors to Konya, witnessing the dance of the dervishes is the highlight of their festival experience. The ceremony is composed of seven sections, each of which has a particular meaning. Before it begins some of Rumi's poems are read aloud, and prayers are offered. During the first section of the ceremony the dervishes meditate while listening to the shaykh recite a *naat*. The second and third sections of the ceremony are musical in nature. The second section features the drum, which represents the voice of God uttering the word "Be!" when he created the universe. The third section features the ney, which stands for the life-giving breath of God. The dervishes move in a circular pattern in the fourth section of the ceremony, offering greetings to one another. Their actions represent the soul's recognition and greeting of other souls. The whirling begins in the fifth segment of the ceremony, in which the dervishes salute four stages of spiritual ascent. As the dervishes begin to whirl in place, they stretch their arms open to the left and right. The right hand faces up, meaning that the dervish opens himself up to God's goodness, and the left hand faces down, meaning that the dervish radiates that goodness to all humankind and to all creation. The sixth section features a reading from the Quran. It generally includes this verse: "To God belong the East and the West. Wherever you turn the glory of God is everywhere. All-pervading is He and all-knowing" (Quran 2:115). During the seventh and last section of the ceremony, the dervishes offer a prayer for all the prophets and all departed believers.

The dances of the Mevlevi Order help its members to remember God, and thus they constitute a form of *dhikr*. The ceremony contains many other symbolic elements in addition to the ones discussed above. For example, when the dancers cross their arms over their chests they are acknowledging the unity of God. The whirling itself is said to represent the circular movement of creation, from the rotation of the particles of an atom to rotation of the stars and planets. It also stands for the cycle of life: growth, decline, death, and new life.

Pilgrimage

Many Muslims and non-Muslim admirers of Rumi make pilgrimages to his mausoleum in Konya, Turkey, throughout the year. More than two million pilgrims and tourists visit the site each year.

Another Rumi Festival

In 1997 the Rifa'i Ma'rufi Order of America, an American branch of an established Sufi order, began hosting a yearly Rumi festival in Chapel Hill, North Carolina. This festival takes place in September, in order to mark the date of Rumi's birth. Festival organizers changed the date in order to honor the birth of Rumi's popularity in the United States, and the rebirth of his popularity abroad.

Additional Resources
(Including Web Sites and Videos)

The Muslim Calendar

Blackburn, Bonnie, and Leofranc Holford-Strevens. *The Oxford Companion to the Year: An Exploration of Calendar Customs and Time-Reckoning.* Oxford, England: Oxford University Press, 1999.

Denny, Frederick Mathewson. *An Introduction to Islam.* 2nd ed. New York: Macmillan, 1994.

Glassé, Cyril. *The Concise Encyclopedia of Islam.* San Francisco, CA: Harper-SanFrancisco, 1991.

Reingold, Edward M., and Nachum Dershowitz. *Calendrical Calculations.* Cambridge, England: Cambridge University Press, 2001.

Richards, E. G. *Mapping Time: The Calendar and Its History.* Oxford, England: Oxford University Press, 1998.

Schubel, Vernon. "Islamic Calendar." In *The Oxford Encyclopedia of the Modern Islamic World,* edited by John L. Esposito. Vol. 2. Oxford, England: Oxford University Press, 1995.

Web Sites

WebExhibits.org, in collaboration with various educational, cultural, and scientific organizations, has produced a site explaining the world's calendar systems: **http://webexhibits.org/calendars/calendar-islamic.html**

While on Hajj (opposite page and above), pilgrims are not required to visit Medina, but most do. There they visit the first mosque of Islam — Quba.

The government of Singapore posts that nation's Islamic calendar online at: **http://www.muis.gov.sg/english/islamic_matters/Taqwim/Taqwim2003.aspx? pMenu=4**

The Royal Embassy of Saudi Arabia in Washington, D.C., posts its yearly calendar on its information page. Click on calendar: **http://www.saudiembassy.net/InfoMain.asp**

Khalid Shaukat, a Washington, D.C., scientist and consultant to the Islamic Society of North America and Shura Council of North America, maintains a web site covering many aspects of the Muslim calendar and tracking monthly moon sightings: **http://www.moonsighting.com**

Zurich University's Institute of Oriental Studies offers a web site that will convert Muslim to Gregorian dates, and Gregorian dates to Muslim dates: **http://www.ori.unizh.ch/hegira.html**

Ashura

Shia Muslims observe Ashura by visiting the Shrine of Husayn in Karbala, Iraq.

Chelkowski, Peter. "Ashura." In *The Oxford Encyclopedia of the Modern Islamic World*, edited by John L. Esposito. Vol. 1. Oxford, England: Oxford University Press, 1995.

Esposito, John L., ed. *The Oxford Encyclopedia of the Modern Islamic World*. 4 vols. Oxford, England: Oxford University Press, 1995.

Hossain, Shakeel. "Muharram Celebrations in India: A Case Study." In *The Muslim Almanac: A Reference Work on the History, Faith, Culture, and Peoples of Islam*, edited by Azim A. Nanji. Detroit, MI: Gale, 1996.

Korom, Frank J. *Hosay Trinidad: Muharram Performances in an Indo-Caribbean Diaspora*. Philadelphia: University of Pennsylvania Press, 2002.

Pinault, David. *Horse of Karbala: Muslim Devotional Life in India*. New York: Palgrave, 2001.

Sakr, Ahmad H. *Feasts, Festivities, and Holidays*. Lombard, IL: Foundation for Islamic Knowledge, 1999.

Resources for Children

Rajendra, Vijeya, and Gisela Kaplan. *Iran (Cultures of the World)*. New York: Marshall Cavendish, 1993.

Web Sites

For more on foods associated with Ashura see "Serving the Guest: A Sufi Cookbook," by Kathleen Seidel, at: **http://www.superluminal.com/cookbook/essay_ashura.html**

For more on Muharram celebrations in Iran see writer Massoume Price's web site, entitled "Culture of Iran.Com," at:
http://www.cultureofiran.com/muharram.php

Videos

Bishop, John, and Frank Korom. *Hosay Trinidad*. Watertown, MA: Documentary Educational Resources, 1998. 45 minutes.

Eid al-Adha

Esposito, John L., ed. *The Oxford Encyclopedia of the Modern Islamic World*. 4 vols. Oxford, England: Oxford University Press, 1995.

Glassé, Cyril. *The Concise Encyclopedia of Islam*. San Francisco, CA: Harper-SanFrancisco, 1991.

Schubel, Vernon. "The Islamic Calendar." In *The Oxford Encyclopedia of the Modern Islamic World*, edited by John L. Esposito. Vol. 2. Oxford, England: Oxford University Press, 1995.

Resources for Children

Ahsan, M. M. *Muslim Festivals*. Vero Beach, FL: Rourke Enterprises, 1987.

Al-Gailani, Noorah, and Chris Smith. *The Islamic Year: Surahs, Stories, and Celebrations*. Stroud, England: Hawthorn, 2002.

Web Sites

Britain's Channel 4 maintains a page titled "Day of Sacrifice," which is part of its larger site on the Hajj:
http://www.channel4.com/life/microsites/H/hajj/gend_three_sacrif.html

The kids' section of the Peace Corps web site furnishes a short descriptive article on Tabaski in Mali at:
http://www.peacecorps.gov/kids/like/mali-celebration3.html

Muslims join in celebration of Eid al-Adha, the Feast of Sacrifice, at a mosque in London, England.

First of Muharram

Glassé, Cyril. *The Concise Encyclopedia of Islam*. San Francisco, CA: Harper-SanFrancisco, 1991.

Resources for Children

Ahsan, M. M. *Muslim Festivals*. Vero Beach, FL: Rourke Enterprises, 1987.

Al-Gailani, Noorah, and Chris Smith. *The Islamic Year: Surahs, Stories, and Celebrations*. Stroud, England: Hawthorn, 2002.

Friday

Chebel, Malek. *Symbols of Islam*. New York: Assouline, 2000.

Emerick, Yahiya. *The Complete Idiot's Guide to Islam*. Indianapolis, IN: Alpha Pearson, 2002.

Esposito, John L. *What Everyone Needs to Know About Islam*. Oxford, England: Oxford University Press, 2002.

Glassé, Cyril. *The Concise Encyclopedia of Islam*. San Francisco, CA: HarperSanFrancisco, 1991.

Peters, F. E. *Islam: A Guide for Jews and Christians*. Princeton, NJ: Princeton University Press, 2003.

Sakr, Ahmad H. *Feasts, Festivities, and Holidays*. Lombard, IL: Foundation for Islamic Knowledge, 1999.

Worshipers attend Friday noon prayers at the Friday Mosque in Moroni, the capital of the Comoros Islands.

Hajj

Bianchi, Robert. "Hajj." In *The Oxford Encyclopedia of the Modern Islamic World*, edited by John L. Esposito. Vol. 2. Oxford, England: Oxford University Press, 1995.

Chebel, Malek. *Symbols of Islam*. New York: Assouline, 2000.

Denny, Frederick Mathewson. *An Introduction to Islam*. 2nd ed. New York: Macmillan, 1994.

Eickelman, Dale F., and James Piscatori, eds. *Muslim Travellers: Pilgrimage, Migration, and the Religious Imagination*. Berkeley: University of California Press, 1990.

Esin, Emel. *Mecca the Blessed, Medina the Radiant*. New York: Crown, 1963.

Glassé, Cyril. *The Concise Encyclopedia of Islam*. San Francisco, CA: HarperSanFrancisco, 1991.

Is'harc, Istafiah. *Islam and Its Festivals*. London, England: Ta-Ha, 1997.

Kamal, Ahmad. *The Sacred Journey, Being Pilgrimage to Makkah*. New York: Van Rees Press, 1961.

Lunde, Paul. *Islam: Faith, Culture, History*. London, England: D. K. Publishing, 2002.

Nomachi, Ali Kazuyoshi, and Seyyed Hossein Nasr. *Mecca the Blessed, Medina the Radiant: The Holiest Cities of Islam*. New York: Aperture, 1997.

Parker, Ann, and Avon Neal. *Hajj Paintings: Folk Art of the Great Pilgrimage*. Washington, D.C.: Smithsonian Institute Press, 1995.

Sakr, Ahmad H. *Feasts, Festivities, and Holidays*. Lombard, IL: Foundation for Islamic Knowledge, 1999.

Wolfe, Michael. *The Hadj: An American's Pilgrimage to Mecca*. New York: Atlantic Monthly Press, 1993.

Wolfe, Michael, ed. *One Thousand Roads to Mecca*. New York: Grove, 1997.

Resources for Children

Al-Gailani, Noorah, and Chris Smith. *The Islamic Year: Surahs, Stories, and Celebrations*. Stroud, England: Hawthorn, 2002.

Husain, Shahrukh. *Mecca*. New York: Dillon Press, 1993.

Web Sites

Britain's Channel 4 television station maintains a site on the Hajj which outlines the main events of the pilgrimage, discusses preparations, offers maps, gives prayers, and more: **http://www.channel4.com/life/microsites/H/hajj/index.html**

Those interested in the Saudi Arabian government's rules and regulations for Hajj pilgrims can find them on the web at: **http://saudiembassy.net/Travel/Hajj.asp**

The Saudi Embassy web site also carries press releases on events related to the Hajj: **http://saudiembassy.net**

Malaysian pilgrims in Malacca prepare for their Hajj by practicing the tawaf — the circling of the Kaba — around a scale model of the building.

Hidrellez

Glassé, Cyril. *The Concise Encyclopedia of Islam*. San Francisco, CA: Harper-SanFrancisco, 1991.

Omar, Ifran. "Khidr in Muslim Tradition." *Muslim World* 83, no. 3-4 (July 1993): 279-93.

Owadally, Mohamad Yasin. *Khidr: The Mysterious Wandering Green Man*. Kuala Lumpur, Malaysia: A. S. Noordeen, 1997.

Walker, Warren S., and Ahmet E. Uysal. "An Ancient God in Modern Turkey: Some Aspects of the Cult of Hizir." *Journal of American Folklore* 86, no. 341 (September 1973): 286-89.

Resources for Children

Halman, Hugh Talat. *Al-Khidr: The Green One*. Chicago, IL: Iqra, 2001.

Web Sites

Turkey's Ministry of Culture and Tourism maintains a web page on "Hidrellez Traditions" at: **http://www.kultur.gov.tr/portal/kultur_en.asp?belgeno=5659**

Lamp Nights

Schimmel, Annemarie. "Islamic Religious Year." In *The Encyclopedia of Religion*, edited by Mircea Eliade. Vol. 7. New York: Macmillan, 1987.

Laylat al-Bara'ah

Glassé, Cyril. *The Concise Encyclopedia of Islam*. San Francisco, CA: Harper-SanFrancisco, 1991.

Grunenbaum, G. E. von. *Muhammaden Festivals*. London, England: Curzon, 1988.

Padwick, Constance. *Muslim Devotions: A Study of Prayer-Manuals in Common Use*. Reprint, Oxford, England: Oneworld, 1997.

Sakr, Amad H. *Feasts, Festivities, and Holidays*. Lombard, IL: Foundation for Islamic Knowledge, 1999.

Schimmel, Annemarie. "Islamic Religious Year." In *The Encyclopedia of Religion*, edited by Mircea Eliade. Vol. 7. New York: Macmillan, 1987.

Laylat al-Miraj

During the ten days of Laylat al-Qadr, devout Muslims sometimes spend it in a kind of spiritual retreat called i'tikaf.

Ali, Ahmed, trans. *Al-Qur'an: A Contemporary Translation*. Rev. definitive ed. Princeton, NJ: Princeton University Press, 1988.

Chittick, William. "Miraj." In *The Oxford Encyclopedia of the Modern Islamic World*, edited by John L. Esposito. Vol. 3. Oxford, England: Oxford University Press, 1995.

Glassé, Cyril. *The Concise Encyclopedia of Islam*. San Francisco, CA: Harper-SanFrancisco, 1991.

Sakr, Ahmad H. *Feasts, Festivities, and Holidays*. Lombard, IL: Foundation for Islamic Knowledge, 1999.

Resources for Children

Al-Gailani, Noorah, and Chris Smith. *The Islamic Year: Surahs, Stories, and Celebrations*. Stroud, England: Hawthorn, 2002.

Laylat al-Qadr

Glassé, Cyril. *The Concise Encyclopedia of Islam*. San Francisco, CA: Harper-SanFrancisco, 1991.

Is'harc, Istafiah. *Islam and Its Festivals*. London, England: Ta-Ha, 1997.

Sakr, Ahmad H. *Feasts, Festivities, and Holidays*. Lombard, IL: Foundation for Islamic Knowledge, 1999.

Schimmel, Annemarie. "Islamic Religious Year." In *The Encyclopedia of Religion*, edited by Mircea Eliade. Vol. 7. New York: Macmillan, 1987.

Web Sites

For more on Ramadan in Iran see the following site, compiled by writer and researcher Massoume Price: **http://www.cultureofiran.com/ramadan.php**

Mulid al-Nabi

Gearhart, Rebecca. "Four Days for the Prophet: Kenya's Maulidi Festival Celebrates the Birth of Muhammad." *The World and I* 13, no. 9 (September 1998): 218-24.

Glassé, Cyril. *The Concise Encyclopedia of Islam.* San Francisco, CA: HarperSanFrancisco, 1991.

Is'harc, Istafiah. *Islam and Its Festivals.* London, England: Ta-Ha, 1997.

Schimmel, Annemarie. "Islamic Religious Year." In *The Encyclopedia of Religion*, edited by Mircea Eliade. Vol. 7. New York: Macmillan, 1987.

Resources for Children

Abbas, Jailan. *Festivals of Egypt.* Cairo, Egypt: Hoopoe Books, 1995.

Ahsan, M. M. *Muslim Festivals.* Vero Beach, FL: Rourke Enterprises, 1987.

Al-Gailani, Noorah, and Chris Smith. *The Islamic Year: Surahs, Stories, and Celebrations.* Stroud, England: Hawthorn, 2002.

Web Sites

An essay touching on the controversy over whether and how to celebrate Mulid al-Nabi, written by Dr. Sulayman Nyang, can be found on the web site of the Islamic Supreme Council of America at:

http://www.islamicsupremecouncil.org/bin/site/ftp/Mawlid-Nyang.pdf

Ramadan and Eid al-Fitr

Ahmed, Akbar S. *Islam Today: A Short Introduction to the Muslim World.* London, England: I. B. Tauris, 1999.

Ahsan, M. M. *Muslim Festivals.* Vero Beach, FL: Rourke Enterprises, 1987.

Alhinai, Abdulrahman Bin Ali. *Ceremonies and Celebrations of Oman.* Reading, England: Garnet Publishing, 1999.

Ambrust, Walter. "The Riddle of Ramadan: Media, Consumer Culture, and the 'Christmasization' of a Muslim Holiday." In *Everyday Life in the Muslim Middle East*, edited by Donna Lee Bowen and Evelyn A. Early. 2nd ed. Bloomington: Indiana University Press, 2002.

Bakhtiar, Laleh. *Ramadan: Motivating Believers to Action.* Chicago, IL: Kazi Publications, 1995.

Early, Evelyn A. "Syrian Television Drama: Permitted Political Discourse." In *Everyday Life in the Muslim Middle East*, edited by Donna Lee Bowen and Evelyn A. Early. 2nd ed. Bloomington: Indiana University Press, 2002.

Esposito, John L., ed. *The Oxford Encyclopedia of the Modern Islamic World.* 4 vols. Oxford, England: Oxford University Press, 1995.

Copied in Thuluth script and complemented by spare rondels of gold, this 15th-century manuscript is a page of text from al-Burdah (The Mantle), *by Muhammad ibn Said al-Busiri (1213-1295).*

Glassé, Cyril. *The Concise Encyclopedia of Islam*. San Francisco, CA: Harper-SanFrancisco, 1991.

Grunenbaum, G. E. von. *Muhammadan Festivals*. Reprint, London, England: Curzon, 1992.

Hajar, Rachel. "Recurring Happiness: Qatar Celebrates Eid al-Fitr." *The World and I* 14, no. 1 (January 1999): 202.

Is'harc, Istafiah. *Islam and Its Festivals*. London, England: Ta-Ha, 1997.

Kerven, Rosalind. *Id-ul-Fitr*. Austin, TX: Raintree Steck-Vaughn, 1997.

Martin, Richard C. "Id al-Fitr." In *The Oxford Encyclopedia of the Modern Islamic World*, edited by John L. Esposito. Vol. 2. Oxford, England: Oxford University Press, 1995.

Ramdoyal, Ramesh. *Festivals of Mauritius*. Stanley, Rose-Hill, Mauritius: Edition de l'Océan Indien, 1990.

Roden, Claudia. *The New Book of Middle Eastern Food*. New York: Alfred A. Knopf, 2000.

Sakr, Ahmad H. *Feasts, Festivities, and Holidays*. Lombard, IL: Foundation for Islamic Knowledge, 1999.

Schimmel, Annemarie. "Islamic Religious Year." In *The Encyclopedia of Religion*, edited by Mircea Eliade. Vol. 7. New York: Macmillan, 1987.

Weiss-Armush, Anne Marie. *The Arabian Delights Cookbook*. Los Angeles, CA: Lowell House, 1993.

Throughout many Middle Eastern countries, when the sun is completely down, the booming cannon announces the end of the daily fast during the month of Ramadan.

Resources for Children

Abbas, Jailan. *Festivals of Egypt*. Cairo, Egypt: Hoopoe Books, 1995.

Al-Gailani, Noorah, and Chris Smith. *The Islamic Year: Surahs, Stories, and Celebrations*. Stroud, England: Hawthorn, 2002.

Berg, Elizabeth. *Egypt*. Milwaukee, WI: Gareth Stevens, 1997.

Ghazi, Suhaib Hamid. *Ramadan*. New York: Holiday House, 1996.

Griffin, Robert, and Ann H. Shurgin. *Junior Worldmark Encyclopedia of World Holidays*. Vol. 4. Detroit, MI: U.X.L., 2000.

Hoyt-Goldsmith, Diane. *Celebrating Ramadan*. New York: Holiday House, 2001.

Layton, Leslie. *Singapore (Cultures of the World)*. 2nd ed. Tarrytown, NY: Marshall Cavendish, 2002.

MacMillan, Dianne M. *Ramadan and Eid al-Fitr*. Hillside, NJ: Enslow, 1994.

Marchant, Kerena. *Id-Ul-Fitr*. Brookfield, CT: Millbrook Press, 1996.

McCarthy, Kevin M. *Saudi Arabia: A Desert Kingdom*. Parsippany, NJ: Dillon Press, 1997.

Mirpuri, Gouri, and Robert Cooper. *Indonesia (Cultures of the World)*. 2nd ed. Tarrytown, NY: Marshall Cavendish, 2002.

Nigeria (Fiesta!). Danbury, CT: Grolier Educational, 1997.

O'Shea, Maria. *Saudi Arabia (Festivals of the World).* Milwaukee, WI: Gareth Stevens, 1999.

O'Shea, Maria. *Turkey (Festivals of the World).* Milwaukee, WI: Gareth Stevens, 1999.

Rajendra, Vijeya, and Gisela Kaplan. *Iran (Cultures of the World).* New York: Marshall Cavendish, 1993.

Rodenbeck, Christine. *Egypt: A Portrait of the Country Though Its Festivals and Traditions.* Danbury, CT: Grolier, 1999.

Rodseth, Lars, Sally Howell, and Andrew Shryock. *Arab World Mosaic: A Curriculum Supplement for Elementary Teachers.* Dearborn, MI: ACCESS Cultural Arts Program, 1994.

Sheehan, Sam. *Pakistan (Cultures of the World).* New York: Marshall Cavendish, 1994.

South, Coleman. *Syria (Cultures of the World).* New York: Marshall Cavendish, 1995.

Turkey (Fiesta!). Danbury, CT: Grolier Educational, 1997.

Walker, Richard Kennedy. *Lebanon: A Portrait of the Country Through Its Festivals and Traditions.* Danbury, CT: Grolier, 1999.

A young boy prays before breaking the daily Ramadan fast with dates and water.

Web Sites

Safi, Omid. "The Essence of Ramadan," December 3, 2002, an editorial published through the Progressive Media Project and available on the web at:
http://www.progressive.org/Media%20Project%202/mpod302.html

Bledsoe, Helen Wiemen. "The Festival of Ramadan." *Calliope.* January-February 1997. This article, which is written for children ages nine through fourteen, is available on the web at:
http://www.cobblestonepub.com/pages/FACALLRamadan.html

Marlowe, John. "Islam's First U.S. Postage Stamp for Muslim Eid Holiday," an article originally published in *Saudi Aramco World*, and posted to the web by the U.S. State Department:
http://usinfo.org/usia/usinfo.state.gov/usa/islam/a112101.htm

The Kuwait Information Office offers information on Ramadan and Eid al-Fitr celebrations at: **http://www.kuwait-info.com/sidepages/festivals_ram.asp**
http://www.kuwait-info.com/sidepages/festivals_eid.asp

For more on Muslim holidays in Senegal see the following page, sponsored by Lewis and Clark University:
http://www.lclark.edu/~nicole/SENEGAL/HOLIDAYS.HTM

The Republic of Turkey's Ministry of Culture and Tourism posts a page on religious holidays in Turkey at:
http://www.kultur.gov.tr/portal/kultur_en.asp?belgeno=5657

The government of Yemen offers information on Ramadan observances in that country at: **http://www.yemeninfo.gov.ye/ENGLISH/panorama/Celebrations.htm**

See also, "Ramadan in Yemeni Cities," an article from *The Yemen Times*, volume 10, issue 50, December 11 through December 17, 2000. Available on the web at: **http://www.yementimes.com/00/iss50/culture.htm**

See Kathleen Seidel's web cookbook, *Serving the Guest: A Sufi Cookbook*, for recipes from Muslim lands, especially those associated with religious figures and observances: **http://www.superluminal.com/cookbook**

For more on Ramadan in Iran see the following site, posted to the web by writer and researcher Massoume Price: **http://www.cultureofiran.com/ramadan.php**

"Wahawi, ya wahawi iyyahah," chant the children of Cairo, their faces aglow in Ramadan lantern light.

Saints and Their Festivals

Atia, Tarek. *Mulid! Carnivals of Faith*. Cairo, Egypt: American University in Cairo Press, 1999.

Biegman, Nicholaas, H. *Egypt: Moulids, Saints, Sufis*. The Hague, The Netherlands: SDU Publishers and Kegan Paul International, 1990.

Denny, Frederick Mathewson. *An Introduction to Islam*. 2nd ed. New York: Macmillan, 1994.

Esposito, John L., ed. *The Oxford Encyclopedia of the Modern Islamic World*. 4 vols. Oxford, England: Oxford University Press, 1995.

Friedlander, Shems. *Rumi and the Whirling Dervishes*. New York: Parabola Books, 2003.

Glassé, Cyril. *The Concise Encyclopedia of Islam*. San Francisco, CA: HarperSanFrancisco, 1991.

Henderson, Helene, and Sue Ellen Thompson, eds. *Holidays, Festivals, and Celebrations of the World Dictionary*. 2nd ed. Detroit, MI: Omnigraphics, 1997.

Huda, Qamar-ul. "Celebrating Death and Engaging in Texts at Data Ganj Baksh's Shrine." *Muslim World* 90, no. 3-4 (fall 2000): 337-55.

Lewis, Franklin D. *Rumi, Past and Present, East and West: The Life, Teachings, and Poetry of Jalal al-Din Rumi*. Oxford, England: Oneworld, 2000.

Renard, John. *Seven Doors to Islam: Spirituality and the Religious Life of Muslims*. Berkeley: University of California Press, 1996

Robinson, David. "Muridiyah." In *The Oxford Encyclopedia of the Modern Islamic World*, edited by John L. Esposito. Vol. 3. Oxford, England: Oxford University Press, 1995.

Schreibman, Jane. "At the Shrine of the Pir: India's Healing Saints." *The World and I* 5, no. 8 (August 1990): 642.

Schubel, Vernon James. "Devotional Life and Practice." In *The Muslim Almanac: A Reference Work on the History, Faith, Culture and Peoples of Islam*, edited by Azim A. Nanji. Detroit, MI: Gale, 1996.

Subhan, John A. *Sufism: Its Saints and Shrines*. New Delhi, India: Cosmo Publications, 1999.

Van Doorn, Nelly, and Kees de Jong. "The Pilgrimage to Tembayat: Tradition and Revival in Indonesian Islam." *Muslim World* 91, no. 3-4 (fall 2001): 325-53.

Waschsmann, Shelley. "Sailing into Egypt's Past." *Archeology* 6, no. 4 (July/August 2002): 36-40.

Wines, Leslie. *Rumi: A Spiritual Biography*. New York: Crossroads, 2000.

Zak, Susannah. "Whirling Before Allah: Mevlevis Dance to an Old World Song." *The World and I* 9, no. 5 (May 1994): 250.

The green tower tops the room in the mausoleum of Jelaluddin al-Rumi, a famous poet and Sufi mystic, who is buried there in Konya, Turkey.

Web Sites

For more on the city of Touba see "Sacred Sites," a web site put together by writer, researcher, and photographer Martin Gray at:
http://www.sacredsites.com/africa/senegal.html

UCLA's Fowler Museum of Cultural History web exhibit, "Passport to Paradise: Sufi Arts of Senegal and Beyond," offers photos and information on the life of Shaykh Amadou Bamba and the folk art created by members of the Mouride Brotherhood: **http://www.fmch.ucla.edu/paradise/main001.htm**

For information about Rumi, his mausoleum, and the Mevlevi Order, see the following site, posted by the family of Dr. Celaleddin B. Celebi, an expert on the Mevlevi Order and a descendant of Rumi. Includes links to sites featuring Rumi's poetry: **http://www.mevlana.net**

For more on Konya's Mevlana festival see the following site, posted by the Republic of Turkey's Ministry of Foreign Affairs:
http://www.mfa.gov.tr/grupc/ca/caa/uu/orta%20anadolu/mevlana.htm

Turkey's Ministry of Culture and Tourism offers information on Rumi's life at:
http://www.kultur.gov.tr/portal/ARKEOLOJI_en.asp?belgeno=788

For more information on Rumi's life, his recent popularity in the United States, and the Mevlevi Order see the following page, posted by the Islamic Supreme Council of America:

**http://www.islamicsupremecouncil.org/bin/site/wrappers/
default.asp?pane_2=content-spirituality-mevlevi**

Turkey's Ministry of Culture and Tourism provides a detailed description of the Mevlana Museum (Dervish Lodge) at: **http://www.kultur.gov.tr/portal/ARKEOLOJI_en.asp?belgeno=709**

Travel writer Kamin Mohammadi's description of the Whirling Dervish festival can be found at: **http://www.travelintelligence.net/wsd/articles/art_2418.html**

For more on the Chapel Hill, North Carolina, Rumi festival see: **http://www.rumifest.com**

A holy man contemplating at a shrine in Lahore, Pakistan.

White Nights

Grunenbaum, G. E. von. *Muhammaden Festivals*. London, England: Curzon, 1988.

Schimmel, Annemarie. "Islamic Religious Year." In *The Encyclopedia of Religion*, edited by Mircea Eliade. Vol. 7. New York: Macmillan, 1987.

Glossary

The glossary includes most of the foreign words that have been mentioned in the text. (Most place names and proper names do not appear here.) It also includes certain English words that refer to Islamic concepts (e.g., "minaret" and "mosque"). Foreign words appear in italics.

A Note on Spellings

The Arabic alphabet differs significantly from the Roman alphabet. Over the years, scholars have employed a number of different Arabic transliteration systems in order to transcribe Arabic words and phrases into English. Each system results in slightly different English language spellings. The situation is made more complicated by the fact that the pronunciation of Arabic words differs throughout the Arab world. As a result, English spellings vary also, as they attempt to capture these differences. These circumstances have created an English language literature on the Middle East that encompasses a wide variety of spellings for the same Arabic words and phrases. What's more, some spellings of Arabic words, now deemed incorrect by today's scholars and native speakers, have become established in the English language. The name of the city where Muhammad was born provides an example. Some Muslims and contemporary scholars would prefer to spell it "Makkah," but the old spelling, "Mecca," has already rooted itself in the English language.

Yet there are other examples in which old English conventions are changing in favor of more precise spellings. For example, the old, inaccurate term "Moham-madan" was changed in the middle of the 20th century to "Moslem," which has now been replaced by the most correct form of the word, "Muslim." Another example is the word Quran, which has come to be accepted as the more precise way to refer to the holy scripture that is sometimes spelled "Koran." Just as the Chinese city that was once called Peking in English is now Beijing, the English language has been slowly changing to reflect more accurate spellings of Arabic terms.

The spellings chosen for this book are among the simplest in common usage. Diacritical marks have been omitted. Readers who know Arabic may find that

In Muslim countries, the call to prayer issues from the minaret of local mosques five times each day.

these spellings oversimplify the Arabic words they are intended to represent. Nevertheless, these simple spellings were chosen to help the vast majority of readers — whom we assumed would not know Arabic — understand a text that of necessity includes many foreign words.

A

abaya — A loose, long-sleeve, full-length robe worn by some Muslim women when they go out in public. See also *burqa* and *chador.*

Abbasid — Name of the most illustrious caliphate in the history of Islam. The *Abbasid* caliphs reigned from their capital in Baghdad, Iraq, between the years 749 and 1258.

abd — Arabic for "servant." A common component of many Muslim names, such as Abdullah, meaning "servant of God."

abu — From the Arabic word *Ab,* meaning "father." Followed by a name, *abu* means "father of."

adhan — Call to prayer. In Muslim countries, the call to prayer issues from the minaret of local mosques five times each day.

A. H. See *anno Hegira.*

Allah written in Thuluth, a soft cursive style of Arabic calligraphy.

al-hamdu Lillah — Means "Thanks be to God" or "Praise be to God." Referred to as the *hamdallah.* The full phrase, *al-hamdu Lillahi Rabb il-Alameen,* means "Praise be to Allah, the Lord of the Worlds." After the *basmallah,* it is the first sentence in the first chapter of the *Quran.*

Allah — God. Literally, "the God" in Arabic.

Allahu akbar — Arabic for "God is greater. . . ." The implication is that no matter what one places at the end of the sentence, God is greater than that thing. Also translated as "God is Great," and "God is greater than all." Referred to as the *takbir.*

Allah umma salli ala an-Nabi — An Arabic phrase meaning "God's blessing and grace upon the Prophet."

al-Quds — "The Holy" in Arabic. Refers to the city of Jerusalem.

ameen — Arabic for "truly" or "so be it." The equivalent of the English "amen." Said at the end of prayers.

ameen **ceremony** — Party held to celebrate a child's first complete reading of the *Quran* in Arabic.

anno Hegira — Means "Hegira Year." Abbreviated A.H. The Muslim calendar begins in 1 A.H., the first year after the Hegira, that is, the migration of Mecca's original Muslim community to Medina.

ansar — "Helpers" or "allies" in Arabic. Muslims use the term to refer to the first converts at Medina who helped Muhammad and the Muslims from Mecca establish themselves in that city.

aqiqah — Naming ceremony.

Arab — Person who speaks Arabic and whose heritage is linked to Arab culture.

arabesque — Swirling designs found in Islamic art, based on stylized renditions of twining vines, leaves, and flowers.

arbaeen — Means "forty" in Arabic. In terms of the Muslim calendar, it can stand for the 40th day after *Ashura*, marking the end of the period during which devout *Shia* Muslims mourn for Husayn, grandson of the Prophet Muhammad. This holiday, called *Arbaeen*, falls on the 20th day of *Safar*. Indian Muslims call the same observance *Cahallum*.

ardha — A sword dance performed by Kuwaiti men.

Ashura — From the Arabic word for "ten," this refers to the tenth day of *Muharram*, a holiday observed by *Shia* Muslims as a day of mourning for Husayn, grandson of the Prophet Muhammad. *Sunni* Muslims also remember Husayn but in addition recall blessed events from scripture associated with this day.

asr — Mid-afternoon prayers.

as-salam alaykum — Arabic phrase meaning "peace be upon you." Greeting offered from one Muslim to another. Response is *wa-alaykum as-salam*, "peace be upon you, too."

atan — An Afghani dance customarily performed by men at weddings. The dance includes waving sticks, swords, or guns in the air, while stamping one's feet and whirling. Shots are often fired into the air as part of the dance.

awliya — Literally "ones who are close." Often translated as "friends [of God]." Singular form is *wali*. Muslims use the term to refer to holy men and women, sometimes called saints.

azza wa jall — "Great and majestic" in Arabic. An honorific phrase that devout Muslims insert after speaking or writing the word *Allah*.

Masons embellished many domes and minarets with elaborate arabesque patterns.

B

barakah — God's blessing or grace.

barakallah — Arabic phrase meaning literally "the blessing of God," but often used to say, "God bless you."

basmallah — Name for the longer Arabic phrase, *bismallah ir-Rahman ir-Rahim*, which means "In the name of God, the merciful, the compassionate." This phrase comes at the beginning of nearly every chapter of the *Quran*. The *basmallah* is said throughout the day as a means of blessing ordinary activities as well as religious acts. Also used as a grace before meals.

Muslims from Uzbekistan during asr or mid-afternoon prayers.

A Bedouin woman wearing a burqa. This is similar to a niqab.

Bedouin — Nomadic Arab tribes living in the rural, desert regions of the Middle East. Today only about 1 percent of Arabs are Bedouins.

ben — See *bin*.

bin — Arabic for "son of," a shortened form of the word *ibn*. In some Arabic dialects it is written as *ben*.

bint — Arabic for "daughter." When followed by a proper name it means "daughter of."

burqa — A garment worn by some conservative Muslim women in India and Afghanistan. It covers them from head to toe, with a meshwork grill or a narrow opening over the eyes to permit vision. The word *burqa* also refers to veils that cover the neck, head, and face, except for the eyes. See also *chador*.

C

Cahallum — See *arbaeen*.

caliph — From *khalifa*, Arabic for "successor" or "representative." The caliphs served as political leaders and defenders of the faith after the time of Muhammad's death.

caliphate — The lands ruled by a caliph or the reign of a particular caliph or series of caliphs. Also used to refer to the office of the caliph.

chador — Persian word for a long, black cloak and head covering worn by some conservative Muslim women in Iran and other countries.

chalismoh — A mourning ceremony observed by Muslims from the Indian subcontinent. Held on the 40th day after a death. Features prayers and gifts of food to the deceased's relatives.

Chishtiyya — *Sufi* order popular in India and Pakistan.

D

Some people refer to the dancers of the Mevlevi Order of Sufis as "dervish dancers" or the "whirling dervishes."

darud — Blessings on the prophet Muhammad.

dervish — From the Persian for "poor." Refers to *Sufis*, especially members of those *Sufi* orders that expect their followers to embrace poverty and live on money given to them by others. Also spelled *darwish*. Some people refer to the dancers of the *Mevlevi* order of *Sufis* as "*dervish* dancers" or the "Whirling *Dervishes*."

dhikr — "Remembrance" in Arabic. Also spelled *zikr*. Refers to the devotional practice of chanting phrases that praise or thank God, such as *Allahu akbar*, "God is greater than all." May also be practiced silently, by focusing one's mind on God.

426

dhimmi—Arabic for "protected people." Refers to non-Muslims—especially Jews, Christians, and Zoroastrians—living under Muslim rule.

Dhu al-Hijjah—The 12th month of the Muslim calendar. The month during which the *Hajj* pilgrimage takes place.

Dhu al-Qada—The 11th month of the Muslim calendar.

dhuhr—Noon prayers.

dua—Informal prayer. From the Arabic for "plea" or "call." In informal prayer Muslims lay out their personal concerns before God. By contrast, the five-times-daily formal prayers, *salat*, affirm belief in and offer praise to God.

durud—Formulaic blessings on Muhammad, inserted after speaking or writing his name.

E

Eid al-Adha—Arabic for "festival of the sacrifice." The holiday takes place on the tenth of *Dhu al-Hijjah* and commemorates Abraham's willingness to sacrifice his son Ishmael.

Eid al-Fitr—The festival that occurs at the end of Ramadan.

F

fajr—The prayers said at dawn. Must be said before sunrise. Also called *subh*.

fanus—Lanterns used as Ramadan decorations.

Fatiha—Arabic for the "opening." Refers to the first chapter of the *Quran*. Used in daily formal prayers. In India, it is also the name of a ceremonial dinner held every Thursday night during the first 40 days after a person's death, during which the Fatiha is recited.

Fatima—The most famous daughter of Muhammad, the one who married Ali and became the matriarch of the *Shia* imams. Especially revered by *Shias*.

Fatimid—An important Muslim caliphate that lasted from 909 to 1171. *Fatimid* caliphs founded the city of Cairo, Egypt, and made it their capital.

fatwa—An opinion given by a religious authority who is an expert in Islamic law.

Five Pillars of Islam—The five pillars are the five most important religious beliefs and practices required of Muslims. They are: 1) belief in one God and Muhammad as the prophet of God (*shahada*); 2) prayer five times a day (*salat*); 3) giving 2.5 percent of one's wealth annually to charity (*zakat*); 4) fasting during the month of *Ramadan* (*sawm*); 5) making a pilgrimage to Mecca at least once in one's lifetime, if financially feasible (*Hajj*).

Friday—Muslims observe Friday as the day appointed for congregational prayer. Called *Yawm al-Juma*, Day of Congregation, in Arabic.

Fatiha—the first chapter of the Quran.

G

Garangaou — In Qatar, a children's holiday celebrated on the 14th of *Ramadan*.

ghabga — In Qatar, a second dinner eaten during *Ramadan* nights.

ghusl — The more complete ritual washing required before participating in formal prayer, consisting of something like a shower or bath accompanied by a thorough scrubbing of the body. Women who have completed menstruation or childbirth, and anyone who has had sex or touched a dead body, must perform *ghusl* before praying or attending services at the mosque. The less thorough form of ritual washing before prayer is called *wudu*.

gufas — Small tightly woven baskets that children in Bahrain and the Persian Gulf countries plant with wheat, lettuce, or parsley as an *Eid al-Adha* custom.

The Grand Mosque in Mecca, Saudi Arabia, is the starting and ending point of the Hajj.

H

hadith — An account, report, or speech concerning the words or deeds of the prophet Muhammad. Often translated as "tradition." The hadith are important sources of religious wisdom for Muslims, second only to the *Quran* in their importance and authority.

hafiz — From the Arabic root for "memorize" or "preserve." Title given to a person who has succeeded in memorizing the *Quran*.

Hajj — Pilgrimage to Mecca, a city in Saudi Arabia. One of the Five Pillars of Islam.

Hajjah — Title given to a woman who has completed the *Hajj*.

Hajji — Title given to a man who has completed the *Hajj*.

halal — Arabic for "permitted" or "clear." Used most commonly to distinguish those foods permitted to Muslims from those foods forbidden to them.

halaqa — An event in which a group of listeners forms a circle around a teacher and listens to him or her speak.

hamdallah — Name for the Arabic phrase *al-hamdu Lillah*, which means "Praise be to God" or "Thanks be to God." See also *al-hamdu Lillah*.

hammam — Public bathhouse.

Hanafi — School of Islamic Law. Popular in Turkey, regions formerly under Turkish rule, and the Indian subcontinent.

A basin from a hammam in Damascus, Syria.

Hanbali — One of the stricter schools of Islamic law, adhered to in Saudi Arabia and Qatar.

hanif — Monotheist, that is, a person who believes there is only one God. Some *hanifs* lived in Arabia before the founding of Islam.

haram — Arabic for "forbidden." Muslims sometimes use this word to refer to those things forbidden them by their religion. Other times they use the word to refer to places that are especially sacred, such as the area surrounding the *Kaba*, or the women's quarters in a traditional home. It is from this last meaning that the English concept of "harem" derives.

harim — A part of the house reserved only for women and girls. Found in traditional Muslim homes in some parts of the world.

Hejaz — Region of Arabia. The historically important cities of Mecca and Medina are located in this area. Also spelled "Hijaz."

henna — An herb that can be used to dye the skin or the hair red. In some countries it is used to decorate women's hands and feet on Muslim holidays. Henna designs also adorn brides on their wedding day and boys on the day of their circumcision in some Muslim cultures.

Hidrellez — A festival observed in Turkey on May 6. It honors the Muslim folk figure known as *Hizr*, or *Khidr*.

hijab — "Screen," "separation," "cover," or "partition" in Arabic. Has come to refer to the large scarf that some Muslim women use to cover their head, neck, and hair. May also refer to female dress codes or compliance with those codes.

A hijab is a large scarf that some Muslim women use to cover their head, neck, and hair.

Hijrah — The migration of Muhammad and his fledgling Muslim community from Mecca to Medina in 622 c.e. This year marks the beginning of the Muslim calendar, in which it is denoted as 1 a.h.

hilal — Crescent moon symbol, often with a star between its horns. A symbol used to represent Islam.

hodja — A Turkish term for a religious teacher. "The *Hodja*" refers to a famous wise fool, who is the subject of many folk tales. *Hodja* is also known as *Nasreddin, Mulla Nasruddin,* or *Juha.*

houris — Beautiful female companions given to men who go to heaven after they die. Some describe the *houris* as "perpetual virgins," while others believe they are "purified souls."

Husayn — Grandson of the Prophet Muhammad. Revered by *Shia* Muslims as the first of the *imams*, great spiritual leaders descended from the Prophet.

husayniyahs — A word used in Iran, Iraq, and Lebanon to refer to a tent, assembly hall, or other location at which the story of Husayn's martyrdom is retold.

I

Ibadis — Descendants of the ancient *Kharijites*, a small group of Muslims who believed that any exemplary Muslim man, regardless of birth, could serve as caliph. Today's *Ibadis* constitute less than 1 percent of the world's Muslims.

ibn — Arabic for "son." When followed by a proper name, it means "son of." See also its shortened form, *bin*.

An iman leads midday prayer at a Uighur mosque in Turpan, China.

iftar — The meal with which Muslims break their daily fast during the month of *Ramadan*.

ihram — Arabic for "consecration." Refers to a state of purity that Muslims must enter into before performing the *Hajj*. Also refers to the special clothing worn by *Hajj* pilgrims.

ilahi — Sufi religious song (Turkey).

imam — A Muslim prayer leader. Among *Shia* Muslims the word not only refers to prayer leaders and current religious authorities, but also to important early spiritual leaders who were descendants of Muhammad through his daughter Fatima and her husband Ali.

imambarah — A word used by Indian and Caribbean Muslims to refer to a tent, assembly hall, or other location at which the story of Husayn's martyrdom is retold.

inshad — Sufi religious song (Egypt).

inshallah — Arabic phrase meaning "If God wills." Often recited when making plans for the future. Also spelled *in sha Allah*.

iqamah — The words recited by the *imam* just before prayer begins. Essentially the same text as the *adhan* (call to prayer), except that the words "prayer has started" are added to the end.

isha — Last prayers of the day, said after the fall of darkness.

Islam — The religion followed by Muslims. Comes from the Arabic term for submission, surrender, and/or obedience. See also *salam*.

Islamic law — *Sharia* in Arabic. The rules for religious and everyday conduct. Defined and interpreted somewhat differently by each of the schools of Islamic law.

i'tikaf — A spiritual retreat practiced at home or at the mosque. The devotee gives up his or her normal round of activities and focuses on prayer, reflection, and the *Quran*. Associated with the last ten days of *Ramadan* but may also be performed at other times of the year.

J

Jafari — Term used for the most important school of Islamic law for *Shia* Muslims. *Shia* Muslims are most numerous in Iran and Iraq, but smaller communities exist in other countries.

jalla jalaluhu — "Great is his majesty" in Arabic. An honorific phrase that devout Muslims insert after speaking or writing the word *Allah*.

jihad — Arabic for "struggle" or "striving." Muslims are encouraged to struggle against their own weaknesses and for the good of the community. Sometimes translated as "holy war." The term has been used by some Muslims to refer to warfare against non-Muslims.

jilbab — A loose, full-length, long-sleeve robe worn by some Muslim women when they go out in public.

jinn — Good and bad spirits, often attached to particular places in nature. The English word "genie" derives from the Arabic term *jinn*.

juma — Congregation. Muslims refer to the Friday congregational prayer service as *salat al-juma*. In Arabic, Friday is *Yawm al-Juma*, or "Day of Congregation."

Jumada al-Akhira — The sixth month of the Muslim calendar.

Jumada al-Ula — The fifth month of the Muslim calendar.

K

Kaba — "Cube" in Arabic. A building in the center of the Grand Mosque in Mecca, built roughly in the shape of a cube. The Kaba existed before the start of Islam. Muslims believe it was built by Adam and rebuilt by Abraham. Today it is Islam's holiest shrine.

Islam's holiest shrine is the Kaba, located in the center of the Grand Mosque in Mecca.

keffiyah — A large scarf that some Middle Eastern men use to cover their heads.

khane Quran — A congregational recitation of the *Quran*. In some parts of the Muslim world these recitations, usually scheduled on Thursday evenings, take place during the 40 days of mourning that follow a death. Also called *khatm al-Quran*.

Kharijites — A small group of early Muslims who believed that any Muslim man of exemplary character could become caliph. Today their descendants are called *Ibadis*.

khatm al-Quran — See *khane Quran*.

khatmi-Quran — Literally, "sealing the Quran." Arabic phrase for the celebration held in honor of a child who has completed his or her first reading of the *Quran*. Also called an *ameen* ceremony, or party.

Khidr — The "green man" of Islamic folk legends.

khutba — Sermon delivered at a mosque's Friday noon congregational prayer service.

kiswa — Beautifully embroidered cloth covering placed over the *Kaba*.

Koran — See *Quran*.

kunya — A name that identifies a man or a woman through their offspring. Example: *umm Kulthum*, "mother of Kulthum." See also *umm*.

kursi — A stand made especially to hold a copy of the *Quran*.

The Quran is placed on a stand called a kursi.

miswak—A twig from a special kind of tree used for cleaning the teeth in Muhammad's day. Also called *siwak*.

Mogul—See *Mughal*.

monogamy—System of marriage in which a man may have only one wife and a woman only one husband.

monotheism—Belief in only one God.

mosque—Islamic house of worship. Comes from the Arabic word *masjid*, meaning "place of prostration."

moulay—French form of the Arabic term *mawlay*.

moulid—See *mulid*.

Mouride—The name of the West African *Sufi* brotherhood founded by Shaykh Amadou Bamba. From the Arabic word *murid*, meaning "aspirant," or "student."

moussem—The word that Moroccans and other North Africans use to describe a saint's festival. Comes from *mawsim*, the Arabic word for "season."

mu'adhdhin—See *muezzin*.

muezzin—Man who performs the *adhan*, or call to prayer. Called *mu'adhdhin* in Arabic.

Mughal—North Indian dynasty whose rule lasted from 1526 to 1858. The Taj Mahal was built by a Mughal emperor. Also spelled "Mogul."

Muhammad—The prophet who delivered the *Quran* to humanity, thereby laying the foundation for the Muslim religion. Muslims consider Muhammad to have been the last and most important of all the prophets recognized by Islam, but they do not consider him in any way divine.

Muharram—The first month of the Muslim calendar.

mulid—Arabic for "birthday" or "anniversary." Often spelled *moulid* or *mawlid*. The birthdays of local holy men and women are celebrated throughout the Muslim world. The Prophet's Birthday, *Mulid al-Nabi*, is celebrated by many Muslims worldwide on the 12th of *Rabi al-Awwal*.

Mulid al-Nabi—"The Birthday of the Prophet." A Muslim holiday celebrated on the 12th of *Rabi al-Awwal*.

mulla—From the Arabic word for "master." Central Asians and Persians use the word as a title for religious scholars and officials.

muqri—A professional Quran chanter.

musallah—Arabic term for the large room set aside for prayer in each mosque.

Muslim—A person who follows the religion of Islam. In Arabic a male Muslim is called a *Muslim* and a female Muslim is called a *Muslima*. English-speakers do not make this distinction.

Muslim law—See *sharia*.

A Muslim student from Cairo reading from a small pocket-size Quran.

N

naat — A poem written to honor Muhammad or one of his family members.

Naqshbandiyyah — *Sufi* order that has many adherents in Central Asia and the Caucasus region.

nasab — That part of someone's name that indicates the name of his or her mother or father.

ney — Reed flute.

nikah — Muslim marriage ceremony. Revolves around the signing of the marriage contract, the bride's (or her *wali*'s) reception of the marriage gift (*mahr*), and the recitation of the *Fatiha*.

Ninety-Nine Names of Allah — Ninety-nine titles given to God in the *Quran,* or derived from traditional Muslim names for God. Recitation of the 99 names from memory is a Muslim devotion.

niqab — Face veil worn by very conservative Muslim women. Attached to a head scarf so that only the eyes are showing.

nisbah — That part of someone's name that tells where he or she is from.

niyyah — Arabic for "intention." A clear intention to perform a devotional act must be formed before proceeding to the act.

O

Ottoman — Name of a Turkish empire and its ruling dynasty that lasted from the late 13th to the early 20th century.

P

PBUH — Abbreviation for the phrase "Peace be upon him," a blessing that devout Muslims traditionally insert after each mention of Muhammad's name.

pir — Title given to *Sufi* teachers and heads of *Sufi* orders in Turkey, Iran, India, and parts of Central Asia. Arabic speakers call these men *shaykh*.

polygyny — System of marriage in which a man may have more than one wife. Contrary to popular belief polygyny differs from polygamy, which is a system whereby either a man or a woman may have more than one spouse.

polytheism — Belief in the existence of more than one god and/or goddess.

prayer rugs — Small (about three feet by five feet) rugs that provide a clean surface on which to pray.

Prophet — Islam recognizes many different prophets, including Moses, David, and Jesus. When Muslims refer to the Prophet (with a capital "P"), however, they are referring only to Muhammad, whom they believe to be the last and most important of God's prophets.

A page from a 17th-century Ottoman copy of the Quran.

435

Q

qari — Arabic term for a professionally trained *Quran* reciter.

qasidah — Means "poem" in Arabic. Word also used for *Sufi* religious songs in some Arab countries.

qawwali — Word for *Sufi* religious songs in Iran, Pakistan, Afghanistan, and India.

Quran — The holy scripture of Islam (also spelled *Koran* or *Qur'an*). In Arabic the word means "recitation." The *Quran* is a collection of the recitations that Muhammad delivered over his lifetime. Muslims believe that God inspired Muhammad with the exact words contained in these recitations.

R

Rabi al-Awwal — The third month of the Muslim calendar.

Rabi al-Thani — The fourth month of the Muslim calendar.

Rajab — The seventh month of the Muslim calendar.

rakah — Arabic for "a bowing." Refers to one complete cycle of the words and physical movements that make up formal prayer. The plural of the word is *rakat*. Each session of prayer consists of two or more *rakat*.

Ramadan — The ninth month of the Muslim calendar. Observed as a month of fasting.

S

Safar — The second month of the Muslim calendar.

Safavid — A Persian empire that lasted between 1501 and 1732. The *Safavid* rulers established Twelve Imam Shiism as the dominant branch of Islam in Iran.

saint — Arabic speakers used the word *wali* to refer to a saint. Sometimes called *wali Allah*, or "one who is near God." For Muslims a saint is a man or woman who leads an exceptionally virtuous life, achieves a deep understanding of God, and demonstrates uncanny knowledge of others or extraordinary spiritual powers. There is no body of religious officials that determines who is and who is not a saint.

sala-Allahu 'alayhi wa-sallam — An Arabic phrase meaning "God's blessing and peace be upon him." Devout Muslims insert this phrase after speaking or writing Muhammad's name.

salam — Arabic for "peace." Often spelled "salaam." Directly related to the Hebrew word "shalom." Shares the same root as the word "Islam."

salat — Formal, composed prayers affirming belief in and praising God. Performed five times a day by devout Muslims. Praying in this fashion is the second of the five pillars of Islam.

A Muslim completes a rakah on a prayer rug.

Worshipers from Uzbekistan perform salat.

salat al-janaza — Funeral prayer service.

salat al-juma — Friday congregational prayer service.

sama — *Sufi* prayer and meditation sessions in which music plays a primary role.

sawm — Fasting. Muslims are required to fast during the entire month of *Ramadan*, by refraining from eating and drinking during the daylight hours. This is the fourth of the five pillars of Islam.

sa'y — A ritual performed by those who come to Mecca to perform the *Hajj* or the *umrah*. It requires them to run seven times between the hills of Safa and Marwah, a distance of about 2.25 miles.

sayyid — Arabic for "lord" or "master." A number of English spellings, such as *seyyed*, are in use. Title given to the descendants of Muhammad. Also used as a form of address, like the English "sir" or "mister." Other titles given to the descendants of Muhammad include *sharif, shah, moulay,* or *mawlay.*

seyyed — See *sayyid.*

Shaam-e Ghariban — "The Night of the Deserted." A children's *Ashura* observance in Iran.

Shaban — The eighth month of the Muslim calendar.

Shadhiliyyah — *Sufi* order with many adherents in North Africa and the Middle East.

Shafii — School of Islamic law predominant in Indonesia, Malaya, and the Philippines.

shah — Persian for "king" or "ruler." Also title given to descendants of Muhammad. Other titles include *sayyid, sharif, moulay,* or *mawlay.*

shahada — From the Arabic for "testify" or "witness." The *shahada* is the Muslim declaration of faith and serves as the first pillar of Islam. It consists of proclaiming in public with sincerity and conviction, "I witness that there is no God but God, and that Muhammad is the messenger of God."

sharia — From the Arabic for "path to the spring." Religious rules for personal behavior addressing everything from crimes such as theft and murder, to marriage and inheritance, clothing, and dress. Often called Muslim or Islamic law.

sharif — Arabic for "honored" or "highborn." Title given to descendants of Muhammad. May be incorporated into formal names. Other titles for those related to Muhammad include *sayyid, shah, moulay,* or *mawlay.*

Shawwal — The tenth month of the Muslim calendar.

shaykh — Arabic for "old man." Alternative spelling: *sheikh.* A title given to the head of a village, the elder of a particular tribe, or a person who is in charge of a spiritual or political endeavor due to his superior knowledge. May also be used to refer to spiritual teachers, for example, *Sufi* elders and heads of *Sufi* orders. *Pir* is the title given to these *Sufi* teachers in Turkey, Iran, India, and parts of Central Asia.

Shaykh Al-Amin Osman Al-Amin, mufti of Eritrea, Africa, is the spiritual leader of his country's Muslims.

Shia Muslims at the Khadinain Mosque in Iraq.

Shia — Muslims who follow a branch of Islam that teaches that the descendants of Muhammad should serve special political and religious functions. About 15 percent of Muslims worldwide are *Shias*. Sometimes called *Shi'ites*. Also spelled *Shi'ah*.

shirk — Associating anything or anyone with God. Belief in the unity, completeness, power, and reality of God is central to Islam. To associate anyone or anything with God denies the unity and completeness of God and therefore casts doubt on the truth of Islam. *Shirk* is considered the root of all sin, and the most serious sin in Islam.

siwak — A twig from a special kind of tree used for cleaning the teeth in Muhammad's day. Still used by pious Muslims today. Also called *miswak*.

subh — The prayers said at dawn. Must be said before sunrise. Also called *fajr*.

subha — Related to the Arabic word for "praise." Used to refer to prayer beads. Also called *misbaha. Tespih* in Turkish.

subhana-Allah — An Arabic phrase meaning "Glory to you O God our Lord." Often used as meditative chant *(dhikr)*.

subhanahu wa ta'ala — An Arabic phrase meaning "He is glorified and exalted." Pious Muslims insert this phrase after every mention of the word *Allah* or God. Abbreviated in English with the letters "SWT."

Sufi — Muslim who follows a mystical path, seeking direct experiences of God through various spiritual disciplines. There are many *Sufi* orders throughout the Muslim world. These orders were founded by different spiritual teachers and use somewhat different methods to bring disciples to higher levels of spiritual insight and awareness.

suhur — A very early breakfast meal eaten before dawn during the month of *Ramadan*.

sultan — Arabic for "authorized ruler." A king.

sunna — Arabic for "custom" or "usage." Used to refer to the customs, thoughts, words, and deeds of the Prophet Muhammad, which Muslims take as a guide for their own behavior. The adjective *Sunni*, which describes the majority of the world's Muslims, comes from this term.

Sunni — The main body of the world's Muslims, comprising about 85 percent of believers. Unlike *Shia* Muslims, *Sunni* Muslims do not believe that Muhammad's descendants should necessarily serve special religious and political functions. Therefore they call themselves *Sunni*, claiming to follow the correct example, or *sunna*, of the Prophet.

sutra — An object that a worshiper places in front of herself or himself while at prayer. The space between the worshiper and the sutra should not be crossed by another person during the time of prayer.

SWT — Stands for the Arabic phrase *subhanahu wa ta'ala*, meaning "He is glorified and exalted." Inserted after speaking or writing the word *Allah*.

T

ta'awwudh — Name for a long phrase in Arabic that means "I take refuge in God from Satan the stoned one." Often voiced before reciting from the *Quran* or performing other religious acts.

tadjah — Word used by Caribbean Muslims to refer to a model of Husayn's tomb used in *Ashura* celebrations (see also *taziyah*).

takbir — Name for the Arabic phrase *Allahu akbar*.

takiyah — A word used by Iran Muslims to refer to a tent, assembly hall, or other location at which the story of Husayn's martyrdom is retold.

talbiyah — A prayer beginning "Here I am, Lord" (*labayka Allahumma*), associated with the *Hajj* and said frequently by *Hajj* pilgrims.

taraweeh — Extra prayers offered during *Ramadan*.

tashahhud — "Testimony" in Arabic. A summation of the central teaching of Islam — that there is only one God and Muhammad is his Prophet—said at the end of each session of formal prayer.

tawaf — "Circumambulation," a ritual whereby pilgrims to Mecca enter the Grand Mosque and circle seven times round the *Kaba*.

taziyah — In Iran, a folk play that dramatizes the martyrdom of Husayn. In India, a model of Husayn's tomb (see also *tadjah*). Accompanies *Ashura* observances.

tespih — Turkish for prayer beads. Called *subha* or *misbaha* in Arabic.

Talbiyah can be heard by these Hajj pilgrims.

U

Umayyad — The first great Islamic caliphate (661-750). An empire ruled by the *Umayyad* caliphs from their capital in Damascus, Syria.

umm — Arabic for "mother." When followed by a proper name, it means "mother of."

umma — The worldwide community of Muslims. All believers belong to the *umma*.

umrah — The "lesser pilgrimage." The rites of this pilgrimage take place within or nearby Mecca's Grand Mosque. They may be performed at any time of year. *Hajj* pilgrims often add these rites to their pilgrimage experience.

urs — A wedding celebration, but when used to describe a festival dedicated to a *Sufi* saint it refers to the saint's death anniversary, the day when he or she was united with God.

Tespih is the Turkish word for prayer beads.

W

wa-alaykum as-salam—Arabic phrase meaning "Peace be upon you, too." Response to the peace greeting (see *as-salam alaykum*) that Muslims offer to one another.

Wahhabism—A strict school of Islamic law and thought. Dominant in Saudi Arabia with adherents in other countries as well.

wali—Arabic for "to be near," often translated as "friend." Plural: *awliya*. Muslims use the term to refer to a saint, and also to the man who serves as the bride's guardian in marriage negotiations.

walimah—Party that follows a marriage ceremony.

White Nights—The three days before, during, and after a full moon. Some consider them to be especially lucky or blessed.

wudu—The less thorough form of ritualized washing required before formal prayer. The more complete washing is called *ghusl*.

A Muslim marabout from Djenne, Mali, performs wudu.

Y

Ya Latif—Literally, "O Beneficent One." Phrase used to refer to a composed prayer recited in times of trouble.

Yathrib—See Medina.

Yawm al-Juma—See *juma*.

Yawm al-Sabt—"Saturday" in Arabic. Literally, "Day of Rest."

Z

zakat—A yearly 2.5 percent tax of one's income and goods. The money is given to charities. The third of the Five Pillars of Islam.

zikr—See *dhikr*.

Zoroastrianism—Monotheisistic faith that developed in ancient Persia (Iran). There were a fair number of Zoroastrians in Arabia and Persia in Muhammad's day, but their numbers have decreased significantly since then.

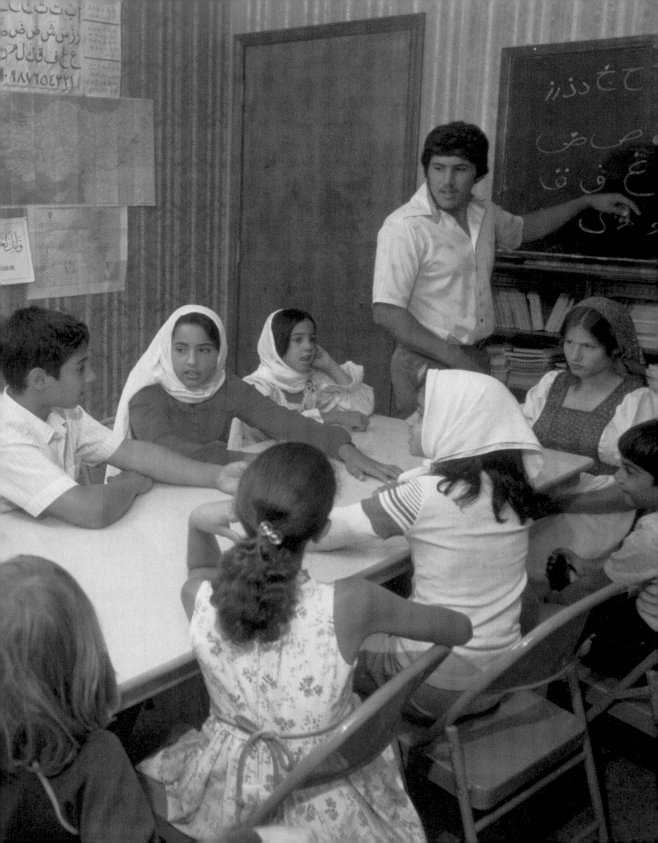

Topical Bibliography
(Including Web Sites and Videos)

☾☾

A Brief Introduction to Islam

The Teachings of Islam

AbuKhalil, As'ad. "Jihad Organizations." In *The Oxford Encyclopedia of the Modern Islamic World*, edited by John L. Esposito. Vol. 2. Oxford, England: Oxford University Press, 1995.

Ahmed, Akbar S. *Islam Today: A Short Introduction to the Muslim World*. London, England: I. B. Tauris, 1999.

Ahmed, Akbar S. *Living Islam: From Samarkand to Stornoway*. New York: Facts on File, 1994.

Ali, Ahmed, trans. *Al-Qur'an: A Contemporary Translation*. Rev. definitive ed. Princeton, NJ: Princeton University Press, 1988.

Al-Shiekh, Abdallah. "Zakat." In *The Oxford Encyclopedia of the Modern Islamic World*, edited by John L. Esposito. Vol. 4. Oxford, England: Oxford University Press, 1995.

Bowker, John. *What Muslims Believe*. Oxford, England: Oneworld, 1995.

Braswell, Jr., George W. *Islam: Its Prophet, Peoples, Politics, and Power*. Nashville, TN: Broadman and Holman, 1996.

Chittick, William C. "Sufism: Sufi Thought and Practice. In *The Oxford Encyclopedia of the Modern Islamic World*, edited by John L. Esposito. Vol. 4. Oxford, England: Oxford University Press, 1995.

Cleary, Thomas F., trans. *The Essential Koran: The Heart of Islam: An Introductory Selection of Readings from the Qur'an*. 2nd ed. San Francisco: HarperSanFrancisco, 1993.

Denny, Frederick Mathewson. *An Introduction to Islam*. 2nd ed. New York: Macmillan, 1994.

Esposito, John L. *Islam: The Straight Path*. 3rd ed. New York: Oxford University Press, 1998.

Muslims gather outside the Cedar Rapids Islamic Center in Iowa after Sunday prayers (above). The children are being taught Arabic during a Sunday morning class at the Islamic Center (opposite page).

Esposito, John L. *What Everyone Needs to Know About Islam*. Oxford, England: Oxford University Press, 2002.

Glassé, Cyril. *The Concise Encyclopedia of Islam*. San Francisco, CA: HarperSanFrancisco, 1991.

Gordon, Matthew S. *Islam: Origins, Practices, Holy Texts, Sacred Persons, Sacred Places*. Oxford, England: Oxford University Press, 2002.

Kepel, Gilles. *Jihad: The Trail of Political Islam*. Cambridge, MA: Harvard University Press, 2002.

Nanji, Azim A., ed. *The Muslim Almanac: A Reference Work on the History, Faith, Culture, and Peoples of Islam*. Detroit, MI: Gale, 1996.

Nasr, Seyyed Hossein. *The Heart of Islam: Enduring Values for Humanity*. San Francisco, CA: HarperSanFrancisco, 2002.

Nasr, Seyyed Hossein. *Islam: Religion, History, and Civilization*. San Francisco, CA: HarperSanFrancisco, 2003.

Newby, Gordon D. *A Concise Encyclopedia of Islam*. Oxford, England: Oneworld, 2002.

Peters, F. E. *Islam: A Guide for Jews and Christians*. Princeton, NJ: Princeton University Press, 2003.

Peters, Rudolph. "Jihad." In *The Oxford Encyclopedia of the Modern Islamic World*, edited by John L. Esposito. Vol. 2. Oxford, England: Oxford University Press, 1995.

Renard, John. *Seven Doors to Islam: Spirituality and the Religious Life of Muslims*. Berkeley: University of California Press, 1996.

Sells, Michael. *Approaching the Quran*. Ashland, OR: White Cloud Press, 1999. (Includes a CD)

Woodward, Mark R. "Popular Religion: An Overview." In *The Oxford Encyclopedia of the Modern Islamic World*, edited by John L. Esposito. Vol. 3. Oxford, England: Oxford University Press, 1995.

Zepp, Jr., Ira G. *A Muslim Primer: A Beginner's Guide to Islam*. 2nd ed. Fayetteville: University of Arkansas, 2000.

Children leaving a Quran class file across the courtyard of Dargah Mosque—built by the Mughal emperor Akbar at his short-lived capital of Fatehpur Sikri in India.

☾☾

The Middle East Institute, located in Washington, D.C., offers the entire text of M. Cherif Bassiouini's *Introduction to Islam* on its web site at:
http://www.mideasti.org/indepth/islam/index.html

To view a searchable version of the Quran and a compilation of hadiths visit al-islam.com, sponsored by Harf Information Technology:
http://www.al-islam.com/Default.asp

Professor Alan Godlas, of the University of Georgia's Department of Religion, has compiled a comprehensive and well-regarded web site on all aspects of Islam: **http://www.uga.edu/islam/**

Scholars from three universities, members of the Carolina-Duke-Emory Institute for the Study of Islam, have put together Islamweb, an Islamic Studies Internet Guide: **http://www.unc.edu/depts/islamweb/index.html**

The History of Islam

Al-Faruqi, Ismail R. *A Cultural Atlas of Islam*. New York: Macmillan, 1986.

Ali, Ahmed, trans. *Al-Qur'an: A Contemporary Translation*. Rev. definitive ed. Princeton, NJ: Princeton University Press, 1988.

Armstrong, Karen. *Muhammad: A Biography of the Prophet*. San Francisco, CA: HarperSanFrancisco, 1992.

Bogle, Emory C. *Islam: Origin and Belief*. Austin: University of Texas Press, 1998.

Braswell, Jr., George W. *Islam: Its Prophet, Peoples, Politics, and Power*. Nashville, TN: Broadman and Holman, 1996.

Cleary, Thomas F., trans. *The Essential Koran: The Heart of Islam: An Introductory Selection of Readings from the Qur'an*. San Francisco, CA: HarperSanFrancisco, 1993.

Denny, Frederick Mathewson. *An Introduction to Islam*. 2nd ed. New York: Macmillan, 1994.

El Fadl, Khaled Abou, ed. *The Place of Tolerance in Islam*. Boston, MA: Beacon Press, 2002.

Esposito, John L. *Islam: The Straight Path*. 3rd ed. New York: Oxford University Press, 1998.

Esposito, John L. *What Everyone Needs to Know About Islam*. Oxford, England: Oxford University Press, 2002.

Esposito, John L., ed. *The Oxford History of Islam*. Oxford, England: Oxford University Press, 1999.

Glassé, Cyril. *The Concise Encyclopedia of Islam*. San Francisco, CA: HarperSanFrancisco, 1991.

Glubb, Sir John. *The Life and Times of Muhammad*. New York: Stein and Day, 1970.

Gordon, Matthew S. *Islam: Origins, Practices, Holy Texts, Sacred Persons, Sacred Places*. Oxford, England: Oxford University Press, 2002.

Jordan, Michael. *Islam: An Illustrated History*. London: Carlton Books, 2002.

Lewis, Bernard. *The Crisis of Islam: Holy War and Unholy Terror*. New York: Modern Library, 2003.

A Muslim woman reads an article on the history of Islam while visiting the library at Darat al-Funun in Amman, Jordan.

Lewis, Bernard. *Music of a Distant Drum: Classical Arabic, Persian, Turkish, and Hebrew Poems*. Princeton, NJ: Princeton University Press, 2001.

Lunde, Paul. *Islam: Faith, Culture, History*. London, England: D. K. Publishing, 2002.

Nanji, Azim A., ed. *The Muslim Almanac: A Reference Work on the History, Faith, Culture, and Peoples of Islam*. Detroit, MI: Gale, 1996.

Nasr, Seyyed Hossein. *The Heart of Islam: Enduring Values for Humanity*. San Francisco, CA: HarperSanFrancisco, 2002.

Nasr, Seyyed Hossein. *Islam: Religion, History, and Civilization*. San Francisco, CA: HarperSanFrancisco, 2003.

Nettler, Ronald L. "Dhimmi." In *The Oxford Encyclopedia of the Modern Islamic World*, edited by John L. Esposito. Vol. 1. Oxford, England: Oxford University Press, 1995.

Newby, Gordon D. *A Concise Encylopedia of Islam*. Oxford, England: Oneworld, 2002.

Newby, Gordon D. "Muslims, Jews, and Christians: Relations and Interactions." In *The Muslim Almanac: A Reference Work on the History, Faith, Culture, and Peoples of Islam*, edited by Azim A. Nanji. Detroit, MI: Gale, 1996.

Robinson, Francis. *Cambridge Illustrated History of the Islamic World*. Cambridge, England: Cambridge University Press, 1996.

Schimmel, Annemarie. "Calligraphy and Epigraphy." In *The Oxford Encyclopedia of the Modern Islamic World*, edited by John L. Esposito. Vol. 1. Oxford, England: Oxford University Press, 1995.

Sweitochowski, Maire Lukens. "Iconography." In *The Oxford Encyclopedia of the Modern Islamic World*, edited by John L. Esposito. Vol. 2. Oxford, England: Oxford University Press, 1995.

Swisher, Clarice, ed. *The Spread of Islam*. San Diego, CA: Greenhaven, 1999.

Zepp, Jr., Ira G. *A Muslim Primer: A Beginner's Guide to Islam*. 2nd ed. Fayetteville: University of Arkansas, 2000.

Inscribed with much of the text of the Quran, this 18th-century linen Shiite Muslim battle tunic also bears inscriptions in praise of the Prophet Muhammad and of his son-in-law, Ali. It is an eloquent testimony to the place of religious commitment in all aspects of life in the Islamic world. Across the shoulders is inscribed verse 13 of Surah 61 ("al Saff," or Battle array): "Help from God and a speedy Victory. So give the Glad Tidings to the Believers."

ᴏꞏᴏꞏ

Professor Barbara R. von Schlegell, a professor in the department of religious studies at the University of Pennsylvania, has posted a web site that gives maps of the Arab conquests and the expansion of the Muslim world. The maps come from W. C. Brice's *An Historical Atlas of Islam* (1981) and R. Roolvink et al *Historical Atlas of the Muslim Peoples* (1957):
http://ccat.sas.upenn.edu/~bvon/pages/maps.html

The Middle East Institute, located in Washington, D.C., offers the entire text of M. Cherif Bassiouini's *Introduction to Islam* on its web site at:
http://www.mideasti.org/indepth/islam/index.html

For an explanation of the different styles of Arabic calligraphy see "The Art of Arabic Calligraphy," by Mamoun Sakkal, professional architect, designer, and graphic artist: **http://www.sakkal.com/ArtArabicCalligraphy.html**

Muslims Today

Abdallah, Anouar et al. *For Rushdie: Essays by Arab and Muslim Writers in Defense of Free Speech*. New York: George Braziller, 1994.

Afkhami, Mahnaz, ed. *Faith and Freedom: Women's Human Rights in the Muslim World*. New York: Syracuse University Press, 1995.

Ahmed, Akbar S. *Islam Today: A Short Introduction to the Muslim World*. London, England: I. B. Tauris, 1999.

Ahmed, Akbar S. *Living Islam: From Samarkand to Stornoway*. New York: Facts on File, 1994.

Altorki, Soraya. "Women and Islam: Role and Status of Women." In *The Oxford Encyclopedia of the Modern Islamic World*, edited by John L. Esposito. Vol. 4. Oxford, England: Oxford University Press, 1995.

Armstrong, Sally. *Veiled Threat: The Hidden Power of the Women of Afghanistan*. New York: Four Walls Eight Windows, 2002.

Benard, Cheryl. *Veiled Courage: Inside the Afghan Women's Resistance*. New York: Broadway Books, 2002.

Braswell, George W. *Islam: Its Prophet, Peoples, Politics, and Power*. Nashville, TN: Broadman and Holman, 1996.

Burke, Alison. "Women for Women." *The World and I* 18, no. 6 (June 2003): 122.

Council on Islamic Education. *Teaching About Islam and Muslims in the Public School Classroom*. 3rd ed. Fountain Valley, CA: Council on Islamic Education, 1995.

Easwaran, Eknath. *Nonviolent Soldier of Islam: Badshah Khan, a Man to Match His Mountains*. Tomales, CA: Nilgiri Press, 1999.

El Fadl, Khaled Abou, ed. *The Place of Tolerance in Islam*. Boston, MA: Beacon Press, 2002.

Esin, Emel. *Mecca the Blessed, Madinah the Radiant*. New York: Crown Publishers, 1963.

Esposito, John L. *Islam: The Straight Path*. 3rd ed. New York: Oxford University Press, 1998.

Esposito, John L. *What Everyone Needs to Know About Islam*. Oxford, England: Oxford University Press, 2002.

Fernea, Elizabeth W. "The Veiled Revolution." In *Everyday Life in the Muslim Middle East*, edited by Donna Lee Bowen and Evelyn A. Early. 2nd ed. Bloomington: Indiana University Press, 2002.

A caravan of Muslims stop and pray during one of the five prayer periods of the day.

Findley, Paul. *Silent No More: Confronting America's False Image of Islam.* Beltsville, MD: Amana Publications, 2001.

Ghada, Talhami. "Jerusalem in the Muslim Consciousness." *Muslim World* 86, no. 3-4 (July 1996): 229-42.

Ghazal, Jen'nan. "Challenging Myths of Muslim Women: The Influence of Islam on Arab-American Women's Labor Force Activity." *Muslim World* Vol. 92, no. 1-2 (spring 2002): 19-37.

Glassé, Cyril. *The Concise Encyclopedia of Islam.* San Francisco, CA: Harper-SanFrancisco, 1991.

Goodstein, Laurie. "Stereotyping Rankles Silent, Secular Majority of American Muslims." *The New York Times*, December 23, 2001, 1A20.

Hasan, Asma Gull. *American Muslims: The New Generation.* New York: Continuum, 2000.

Henderson, Carol E. *Culture and Customs of India.* Westport, CT: Greenwood, 2002.

Hermansen, Marcia K. "Women, Men, and Gender in Islam." In *The Muslim Almanac: A Reference Work on the History, Faith, Culture, and Peoples of Islam*, edited by Azim A. Nanji. Detroit, MI: Gale, 1996.

Jordan, Michael. *Islam: An Illustrated History.* London, England: Carlton Books, 2002.

Lawrence, Bruce B. *Shattering the Myth: Islam Beyond Violence.* Princeton, NJ: Princeton University Press, 1998.

Lewis, Bernard. *The Crisis of Islam: Holy War and Unholy Terror.* New York: Modern Library, 2003.

Lunde, Paul. *Islam: Faith, Culture, History.* London, England: D. K. Publishing, 2002.

Majaj, Lisa Suhair. "Who Are the Arab Americans?" *Cobblestone* 23, no. 5 (May 2002): 3-7.

Mernissi, Fatima. *The Veil and the Male Elite.* Reading, MA: Addison-Wesley, 1991.

Miller, John, and Aaron Kenedi, eds. *Inside Islam: The Faith, the People, and the Conflicts of the World's Fastest Growing Religion.* New York: Marlow and Company, 2002.

Morris, Neil. *The Atlas of Islam.* Hauppauge, NY: Barron's, 2003.

Mozzafari, Mehdi. "Rushdie Affair." In *The Oxford Encyclopedia of the Modern Islamic World*, edited by John L. Esposito. Vol. 3. Oxford, England: Oxford University Press, 1995.

Three young boys perform salat with their teacher after a Quran class at the Shah Jehan Mosque in London, England.

Nanji, Azim A., ed. *The Muslim Almanac: A Reference Work on the History, Faith, Culture, and Peoples of Islam*. Detroit, MI: Gale, 1996.

Nasr, Seyyed Hossein. *The Heart of Islam: Enduring Values for Humanity*. San Francisco, CA: HarperSanFrancisco, 2002.

Nasr, Seyyed Hossein. *Islam: Religion, History, and Civilization*. San Francisco, CA: HarperSanFrancisco, 2003.

Nimer, Mohamed. *The North American Muslim Resource Guide*. New York: Routledge, 2002.

Reese, Lyn. *Women in the Muslim World: Personalities and Perspectives from the Past*. Berkeley, CA: Women World History Curriculum, 1998.

Rogers, Patrick, Liz Corcoran, Nina Biddle, and Joanne Fowler. "Lifting the Veil: Sima Samar Fights to Bring Much Needed Education and Medicine to Afghan Women." *People* 59, no. 25 (December 26, 2002): 147-48.

Safi, Omid, ed. *Progressive Muslims: On Justice, Gender, and Pluralism*. Oxford, England: Oneworld, 2003.

Shaheen, Jack G. "Reel Bad Arabs: How Hollywood Villifies a People." Special issue, *Islam: Enduring Myths and Changing Realities*, edited by Aslam Syed. *The Annals of the American Academy of Political and Social Science* 588 (July 2003): 171-93.

Smith, Jane I. *Islam in America*. New York: Columbia University Press, 1999.

Uddin, Zaheer. "Muslims in America: Muslims Live in Every Part of the United States, Adding Greatly to the American Mosaic." *The World and I* 17, no. 3 (March 2002): 32.

Wolfe, Michael. *Taking Back Islam: American Muslims Reclaim Their Faith*. New York: Rodale and Beliefnet, 2002.

Zepp, Jr., Ira G. *A Muslim Primer: A Beginner's Guide to Islam*. 2nd ed. Fayetteville: University of Arkansas Press, 2000.

The call to prayer from the Derone Bay Mosque.

❀❀❀

The web site of the Arab American Institute offers a wealth of information on Arab Americans, and also some material on Islam in America: **http://www.aaiusa.org**

Professor Alan Godlas, a professor of religion at the University of Georgia, offers his insights on women, Islam, and feminism (includes many links to other important sites for those interested in the position of women in Islam): **http://www.arches.uga.edu/~godlas/Islamwomen.html**

The Muslim Women's League web site furnishes information on women's roles and rights in Islam: **http://www.mwlusa.org/**

For more on the history of women's dress in Islam see Lyn Reese's article, "Historical Perspectives on Islamic Dress," posted at: **http://www.womeninworldhistory.com/essay-01.html**

The *Detroit Free Press* maintains a page dedicated to debunking common Arab stereotypes: **http://www.freep.com/jobspage/arabs/arab10.html**

"Hollywood Widens Slur Targets to Arab and Muslim Americans Since September 11," an article by Jack Shaheen, professor of mass communications at Southern Illinois University, is available at the Pacific News Service site: **http://news.pacificnews.org/news/view_article.html?article_id=819**

This PBS Global Connections site gives a page on common American stereotypes about Islam and the Middle East, and contrasts them to common stereotypes about Americans: **http://www.pbs.org/wgbh/globalconnections/mideast/questions/types/**

The book-shaped mihrab in the Faysal Mosque in Islamabad, Pakistan, displays the 99 attributes of God.

"The Muslim Mainstream," a *U.S. News & World Report* article by Jonah Blank, describes mainstream American Muslims that defy the commonly held stereotypes about Islam: **http://www.islamicity.com/recognitions/usnews/20isla.htm**

"Islam: Stereotypes Still Prevail," an article by Rick Blasing, is available through the National Council for the Social Studies web site listed below. Also available in print form: *Social Education,* volume 60, number 2, 1996: **http://www.ncss.org/resources/moments/600208.shtml**

The Saudi Embassy posts articles from the magazine *Saudi Arabia* on its web site. For more on Mecca and Medina see the articles entitled "Makkah the Blessed" (spring 1997, volume 14, number 1) and "Al-Madinah Al-Munawwarah, the City of the Prophet" (spring 1998, volume 15, number 2) at: **http://saudiembassy.net/**

The CIA's *World Factbook* provides up-to-date information on the geography, government, economies, and populations of foreign countries: **http://www.odci.gov/cia/publications/factbook/index.html**

For a discussion of female dress codes in Islam, and an argument against compulsory veiling, see "Women in Islam: Veiling," an article by Dr. Ibrahim B. Syed, at: **http://www.islamfortoday.com/syed01.htm**

For a 2003 study by the Pew Forum on Religion and Public Life documenting an increase in the percentage of Americans who believe that Islam encourages its followers to violence see: **http://pewforum.org/docs/index.php?DocID=26**

For more information on Women for Women see its web site at: **http://www.womenforwomen.org**

"The Islamic Mind, with Seyyed Hossein Nasr," in the series *A World of Ideas with Bill Moyers* [videorecording]. Alexandria, VA: PBS Video, 1991. 30 minutes.

Religious Customs and Folklore

Abdul Hakeem, Ahmed. *A Treasury of Favorite Muslim Names*. Chicago, IL: Pearl Publications, 1997.

Abdullahi, Mohamed Diriye. *Culture and Customs of Somalia*. Westport, CT: Greenwood Press, 2001.

Ahmed, Akbar S. *Islam Today: A Short Introduction to the Muslim World*. London, England: I. B. Tauris, 1999.

Ahmed, Akbar S. "Mosque: The Mosque in Politics." In *The Oxford Encyclopedia of the Modern Islamic World*, edited by John L. Esposito. Vol. 2. Oxford, England: Oxford University Press, 1995.

Algar, Hamid. "Imam." In *The Oxford Encyclopedia of the Modern Islamic World*, edited by John L. Esposito. Vol. 2. Oxford, England: Oxford University Press, 1995.

Al Hariri-Wendel, Tanja. *Symbols of Islam*. New York: Sterling, 2002.

Ali, Ahmed, trans. *Al-Qur'an: A Contemporary Translation*. Rev. definitive ed. Princeton, NJ: Princeton University Press, 1988.

Al-Qaradawi, Yusuf. *The Lawful and the Prohibited in Islam*. Translated by Kamal El-Helbawy, M. Moinuddin Siddiqui, and Syed Shukry. Plainfield, IN: American Trust Publications, 1994.

Barks, Coleman, and Michael Green. *The Illuminated Prayer: As Revealed by Jellaludin Rumi and Bawa Muhaiyaddeen*. New York: Ballantine, 2000.

Bayat, Mojdeh, and Mohammad Ali Jamnia, eds. *Tales from the Land of the Sufis*. Boston, MA: Shambala, 1994.

Betteridge, Anne H. "Domestic Observances: Muslim Practices." In *The Encyclopedia of Religion*, edited by Mircea Eliade. Vol. 4. New York: Macmillan, 1987.

Bierman, Irene A. "Architecture: Traditional Forms." In *The Oxford Encyclopedia of the Modern Islamic World*, edited by John L. Esposito. Vol. 1. Oxford, England: Oxford University Press, 1995.

Birch, Nicholas. "Turkey's Republic Day Party Dress Code: No Head Scarves." *Christian Science Monitor,* October 31, 2003, 08.

Bogle, Emory C. *Islam: Origin and Belief*. Austin: University of Texas Press, 1998.

Bowen, Donna Lee, and Evelyn A. Early, eds. *Everyday Life in the Muslim Middle East*. 2nd ed. Bloomington: Indiana University Press, 2002.

Budge, E. A. Wallis. *Amulets and Talismans*. 1930. Reprint, New York: Collier, 1970.

Muslims of every nationality come to pray at the Faysal Mosque in Islamabad, Pakistan. It has room for 10,000 worshipers.

Campo, Juan Eduardo. "Houses." In *The Oxford Encyclopedia of the Modern Islamic World*, edited by John L. Esposito. Vol. 2. Oxford, England: Oxford University Press, 1995.

Chebel, Malek. *Symbols of Islam*. New York: Assouline, 2000.

Danielson, Virginia. "Devotional Music." In *The Oxford Encyclopedia of the Modern Islamic World*, edited by John L. Esposito. Vol. 1. Oxford, England: Oxford University Press, 1995.

Davis, Susan Schaefer. "Growing Up in Morocco." In *Everyday Life in the Muslim Middle East*, edited by Donna Lee Bowen and Evelyn A. Early. 2nd ed. Bloomington: Indiana University Press, 2002.

Denny, Frederick Mathewson. "Funerary Rites: Modern Practice." In *The Oxford Encyclopedia of the Modern Islamic World*, edited by John L. Esposito. Vol. 2. Oxford, England: Oxford University Press, 1995.

Denny, Frederick Mathewson. "The Great Indonesian Qur'an Chanting Tournament." *The World and I* 2, no. 6 (June 1986): 216.

Denny, Frederick Mathewson. *An Introduction to Islam*. 2nd ed. New York: Macmillan, 1994.

Denny, Frederick Mathewson. "Qur'anic Recitation." In *The Oxford Encyclopedia of the Modern Islamic World*, edited by John L. Esposito. Vol. 3. Oxford, England: Oxford University Press, 1995.

Devine, Elizabeth, and Nancy L. Braganti. *The Travelers' Guide to Middle Eastern and North African Customs and Manners*. New York: St. Martin's Press, 1991.

Doumato, Eleanor Abdella. "Marriage and Divorce: Modern Practices." In *The Oxford Encyclopedia of the Modern Islamic World*, edited by John L. Esposito. Vol. 3. Oxford, England: Oxford University Press, 1995.

Draine, Cathie, and Barbara Hall. *Culture Shock! Indonesia*. Rev. ed. Portland, OR: Graphic Arts Center Publishing Company, 1990.

Dubin, Lois Sherr. *The History of Beads, from 30,000 B.C. to the Present*. New York: Harry N. Abrams, 1987.

El Guindi, Fadwa. "Hijab." In *The Oxford Encyclopedia of the Modern Islamic World*, edited by John L. Esposito. Vol. 2. Oxford, England: Oxford University Press, 1995.

Emerick, Yahiya. *The Complete Idiot's Guide to Understanding Islam*. Indianapolis, IN: Alpha Books, 2002.

Ernst, Carl W. "Spiritual Life and Institutions in Muslim Society." In *The Muslim Almanac: A Reference Work on the History, Faith, Culture, and Peoples of Islam*, edited by Azim A. Nanji. Detroit, MI: Gale, 1996.

Esposito, John L. *What Everyone Needs to Know About Islam*. Oxford, England: Oxford University Press, 2002.

A Muslim street vendor prays by his wares in Urumqi, China

Esposito, John L., ed. *The Oxford Encyclopedia of the Modern Islamic World*. 4 vols. Oxford, England: Oxford University Press, 1995.

Fadiman, James, and Robert Frager, eds. *Essential Sufism*. San Francisco, CA: HarperSanFrancisco, 1997.

Fernea, Elizabeth W. "The Veiled Revolution." In *Everyday Life in the Muslim Middle East*, edited by Donna Lee Bowen and Evelyn A. Early. 2nd ed. Bloomington: Indiana University Press, 2002.

Frishman, Martin, and Hasan-Uddin Khan, eds. *The Mosque*. London, England: Thames and Hudson, 1994.

Gaffney, Patrick D. "Mosque: The Mosque in Society." In *The Oxford Encyclopedia of the Modern Islamic World*, edited by John L. Esposito. Vol. 2. Oxford, England: Oxford University Press, 1995.

Gibb, H. A. R., and J. H. Kramers. "Kalb (Dog)" and "Turban." In *Shorter Encyclopedia Of Islam*. Leiden, The Netherlands: E. J. Brill, 1965.

Gilsenan, Michael. *Recognizing Islam: Religion and Society in the Modern Middle East*. Rev. ed. London, England: I. B. Tauris, 2000.

Glassé, Cyril. *The Concise Encyclopedia of Islam*. San Francisco, CA: HarperSanFrancisco, 1991.

Gollaher, David L. *Circumcision: A History of the World's Most Controversial Surgery*. New York: Basic Books, 2000.

Gordon, Matthew S. *Islam: Origins, Practices, Holy Texts, Sacred Persons, Sacred Places*. Oxford, England: Oxford University Press, 2002.

Hasan, Asma Gull. *American Muslims: The New Generation*. New York: Continuum, 2000.

Hoffman-Ladd, Valerie J. "Women and Islam: Women's Religious Observances." In *The Oxford Encyclopedia of the Modern Islamic World*, edited by John L. Esposito. Vol. 4. Oxford, England: Oxford University Press, 1995.

Jereb, James F. *Arts and Crafts of Morocco*. San Francisco, CA: Chronicle Books, 1995.

Kalman, Bobbie. *Afghanistan: The Culture*. New York: Crabtree Publishing, 2003.

Kalman, Bobbie. *Afghanistan: The People*. New York: Crabtree Publishing, 2003.

Kelsey, Alice Geer. *Once the Hodja*. New York: David McKay, 1945.

Knight, Khadijah. *Islam*. New York: Thompson Learning, 1996.

Kolstad, Katherine C. "Puberty Rites." In *The Oxford Encyclopedia of the Modern Islamic World*, edited by John L. Esposito. Vol. 3. Oxford, England: Oxford University Press, 1995.

Lunde, Paul. *Islam: Faith, Culture, History*. London, England: D. K. Publishing, 2002.

Mosque inside the Islamic Center in Washington, D.C.

Macleod, Calum, and Bradley Mayhew. *Uzbekistan: The Golden Road to Samarkand*. 4th ed. Hong Kong: Odyssey Publications, 2002.

Maloney, Clarence, ed. *The Evil Eye*. New York: Columbia University Press, 1976.

Matlins, Stuart M., and Arthur J. Magida, eds. *How to Be a Perfect Stranger*. Woodstock, VT: Skylight Paths Publishing, 2003.

Mozzafari, Mehdi. "Rushdie Affair." In *The Oxford Encyclopedia of the Modern Islamic World*, edited by John L. Esposito. Vol. 3. Oxford, England: Oxford University Press, 1995.

Naik, Gautam. "The Mating Game Is a Three-Day Event For Moroccan Berbers." *The Wall Street Journal*, September 10, 2003, A1.

Nanji, Azim A., ed. *The Muslim Almanac: A Reference Work on the History, Faith, Culture, and Peoples of Islam*. Detroit, MI: Gale, 1996.

Nasr, Seyyed Hossein. *Islam: Religion, History, and Civilization*. San Francisco, CA: HarperSanFrancisco, 2003.

Nelson, Kristina. "The Sound of the Divine in Daily Life." In *Everyday Life in the Muslim Middle East*, edited by Donna Lee Bowen and Evelyn A. Early. 2nd ed. Bloomington: Indiana University Press, 2002.

Newby, Gordon D. *A Concise Encyclopedia of Islam*. Oxford, England: Oneworld, 2002.

Nurbakhsh, Javad. *The Path: Sufi Practices*. New York: Khaniqahi Nimatullahi Publications, 2003.

Padwick, Constance E. *Muslim Devotions: A Study of Prayer-Manuals in Common Use*. Oxford, England: Oneworld, 1997.

Patai, Raphael. "Folk Islam." In *The Encyclopedia of Religion*, edited by Mircea Eliade. Vol. 5. New York: Macmillan, 1987.

Racy, Ali Jihad. "Music." In *The Oxford Encyclopedia of the Modern Islamic World*, edited by John L. Esposito. Vol. 2. Oxford, England: Oxford University Press, 1995.

Reese, Lyn. *Women in the Muslim World: Personalities and Perspectives from the Past*. Berkeley, CA: Women World History Curriculum, 1998.

Reinhart, A. Kevin. "Birth Rites: Traditional Practice." In *The Oxford Encyclopedia of the Modern Islamic World*, edited by John L. Esposito. Vol. 1. Oxford, England: Oxford University Press, 1995.

Renard, John, ed. *Windows on the House of Islam: Muslim Sources on Spirituality and Religious Life*. Berkeley: University of California Press, 1998.

Rodseth, Lars, Sally Howell, and Andrew Shryock. *Arab World Mosaic: A Curriculum Supplement for Elementary Teachers*. Detroit, MI: ACCESS Cultural Arts Program, 1994.

The elevated pulpit, called a minbar, provides a place from which to deliver a sermon or speech.

Sakr, Ahmad H. *Feasts, Festivities, and Holidays*. Lombard, IL: Foundation for Islamic Knowledge, 1999.

Sanders, Paula. "Cliteridectomy." In *The Oxford Encyclopedia of the Modern Islamic World*, edited by John L. Esposito. Vol. 1. Oxford, England: Oxford University Press, 1995.

Schimmel, Annemarie. "Cats." In *The Encyclopedia of Religion*, edited by Mircea Eliade. Vol. 3. New York: Macmillan, 1987.

Schimmel, Annemarie. "Devotional Poetry." In *The Oxford Encyclopedia of the Modern Islamic World*, edited by John L. Esposito. Vol. 1. Oxford, England: Oxford University Press, 1995.

Schimmel, Annemarie. "Islamic Religious Year." In *The Encyclopedia of Religion*, edited by Mircea Eliade. Vol. 7. New York: Macmillan, 1987.

Schubel, Vernon. "Devotional Life and Practices." In *The Muslim Almanac: A Reference Work on the History, Faith, Culture, and Peoples of Islam*, edited by Azim A. Nanji. Detroit, MI: Gale, 1996.

Sells, Michael A. *Approaching the Quran*. Ashland, OR: White Cloud Press, 1999. (Includes a CD)

Sells, Michael A. "Dhikr." In *The Oxford Encyclopedia of the Modern Islamic World*, edited by John L. Esposito. Vol. 1. Oxford, England: Oxford University Press, 1995.

Shad, Adbur Rehman. *Do's and Do Not's in Islam*. 3rd ed. New Delhi, India: Adam Publishers, 1992.

Shah, Idries. *The Exploits of the Incomparable Mulla Nasrudin*. New York: Simon and Schuster, 1996.

Shah, Idries. *Learning How to Learn: Psychology and Spirituality the Sufi Way*. Reprint, New York: Penguin Arkana, 1996.

Shah, Idries. *Tales of the Dervishes: Teaching Stories of the Sufi Masters over the Past Thousand Years*. New York: E. P. Dutton, 1970.

Shah, Idries. *The Way of the Sufi*. New York: E. P. Dutton, 1969.

Smith, Jane I. *Islam in America*. New York: Columbia University Press, 1999.

Taylor, Abdulkader I. "Purification." In *The Oxford Encyclopedia of the Modern Islamic World*, edited by John L. Esposito. Vol. 3. Oxford, England: Oxford University Press, 1995.

Warrier, Shrikala, and John G. Walshe. *Dates and Meanings of Religious and Other Multi-ethnic Festivals, 2002-2005*. London, England: Foulsham Educational, 2001.

Waugh, Earle H. "Birth Rites: Modern Practice." In *The Oxford Encyclopedia of the Modern Islamic World*, edited by John L. Esposito. Vol. 1. Oxford, England: Oxford University Press, 1995.

Worry beads is in fact a misnomer— the "misbaha" is most commonly used in prayer, but it has social functions as well.

Waugh, Earle H. "Circumcision." In *The Oxford Encyclopedia of the Modern Islamic World*, edited by John L. Esposito. Vol. 1. Oxford, England: Oxford University Press, 1995.

Waugh, Earle H. "Names and Naming." In *The Oxford Encyclopedia of the Modern Islamic World*, edited by John L. Esposito. Vol. 2. Oxford, England: Oxford University Press, 1995.

Weiss, Walter M., and Kurt-Michael Westerman. *The Bazaar: The Markets and Merchants of the Islamic World*. London, England: Thames and Hudson, 1994.

Witton, Patrick et al. *Indonesia*. Melbourne, Australia: Lonely Planet Publications, 2003.

Yusuf, Imtiyaz. "Rites of Passage." In *The Oxford Encyclopedia of the Modern Islamic World*, edited by John L. Esposito. Vol. 3. Oxford, England: Oxford University Press, 1995.

"Say: He is God, the One" (Sura 112:1), done in the calligraphic style of Tughra.

⊕⊙⊙

Dr. Clay Shotwell, a music professor at Augusta State University, hosts an informative site titled "Music of Islam." Visitors can listen to a recording of the adhan (call to prayer), a mawal, and a Sufi song: **http://www.aug.edu/~cshotwel/2001.Islam.htm**

For more on music and chant in Islam consult the "Islamic Art, Music, and Architecture Around the World" page posted by Professor Alan Godlas of the University of Georgia's Department of Religion. Includes links to recordings of the call to prayer, Quranic chanting, Madh, Dhikr, Sufi songs, Qawwali music, and more: **http://www.uga.edu/islam/IslArt.html**

For more on how to perform salat see the Shadhiliyya Sufi Center of North America's explanation at: **http://suficenter.org/Practices/performsalat.html**

A slightly different version of salat is described at Islamicity.com: **http://islamicity.com/Mosque/salat/salat9.htm**

The Islamic Affairs Department of the Royal Embassy of Saudi Arabia explains various aspects of Islam on its web site. Includes explanation of the call to prayer, instructions on how to perform wudu (ablutions) and salat, and furnishes program that calculates correct local prayer times in the United States and other countries: **http://www.iad.org/**

The Turkish Cultural Foundation maintains a web site that offers information on many aspects of Turkish culture, including women's and men's rights and roles, the customs surrounding weddings, funerals, birth, and circumcision, and descriptions of Turkish prayer beads, mosques, hospitality, home layout, and much more: **http://www.turkishculture.org/**

For a list of female Muslim names and their meanings see the following page, sponsored by Islam for Today, a site authored by Hussein Abdulwaheed Amin, an American convert to Islam, and dedicated to bringing information about the contemporary practice of Islam to the web:
http://www.islamfortoday.com/female_names.htm

For a discussion of female dress codes in Islam, and an argument against compulsory veiling, see "Is Hijab Compulsory?" and "Women in Islam: Hijab," articles by Dr. Ibrahim B. Syed, at : **http://www.islamfortoday.com/syed01.htm http://www.islamfortoday.com/syed06.htm**

For the history of female dress in Islam see Lyn Reese's web article entitled "Historical Perspectives on Islamic Dress," posted at the Women in World History web site at: **http://www.womeninworldhistory.com/essay-01.html**

For more on the debate about the veil in Turkey see "Turkey: The Veil Is a Symbol of the Rise of Islamism," by Jolyon Naegele, on the Radio Free Europe web site at: **http://www.rferl.org/features/1998/08/F.RU.980804132001.asp**

For more on the symbolism of the color green see the page posted by WebExhibits.org at: **http://webexhibits.org/pigments/indiv/color/greens.html**

See also a web article by Muslim herbologist and natural healer Karima Burns, entitled "The Healing Colors of Friday Prayer," at:
http://www.islam-online.net/english/Science/2001/02/article15.shtml

For more folktales concerning Nasreddin Hodja, see retired professor of folklore D. L. Ashliman's site at: **http://www.pitt.edu/~dash/hodja.html#nasreddin**

A Visit to a Mosque in America: Understanding Islam and the American Muslim Community [videorecording]. Willowbrook, IL: Astrolabe, 2002. (Presented by the Islamic Center of Greater Cincinnati.)

A man reading the Quran on a rooftop in Hunza, China. Hunza is hidden among the towering, ice-clad peaks of the Karakorum Mountains, astride the ancient Silk Road to China. It is the highest outpost of Islam in the world.

The Muslim Calendar

Blackburn, Bonnie, and Leofranc Holford-Strevens. *The Oxford Companion to the Year: An Exploration of Calendar Customs and Time-Reckoning.* Oxford, England: Oxford University Press, 1999.

Denny, Frederick Mathewson. *An Introduction to Islam.* 2nd ed. New York: Macmillan, 1994.

Glassé, Cyril. *The Concise Encyclopedia of Islam.* San Francisco, CA: HarperSanFrancisco, 1991.

Newby, Gordon D. *A Concise Encyclopedia of Islam.* Oxford, England: Oneworld, 2002.

Reingold, Edward M., and Nachum Dershowitz. *Calendrical Calculations.* Cambridge, England: Cambridge University Press, 2001.

Richards, E. G. *Mapping Time: The Calendar and Its History*. Oxford, England: Oxford University Press, 1998.

Schubel, Vernon. "Islamic Calendar." In *The Oxford Encyclopedia of the Modern Islamic World*, edited by John L. Esposito. Vol. 2. Oxford, England: Oxford University Press, 1995.

Warrier, Shrikala, and John G. Walshe. *Dates and Meanings of Religious and Other Multi-Ethnic Festivals, 2002-2005*. London, England: Foulsham Educational, 2001.

A fragment of a carved, gilt, and painted wooden panel from the original Dome of the Rock, now preserved in Jerusalem's Islamic Museum.

☟☟

WebExhibits.org, in collaboration with various educational, cultural, and scientific organizations, has produced a site explaining the world's calendar systems: **http://webexhibits.org/calendars/calendar-islamic.html**

The government of Singapore posts that nation's Islamic calendar online at: **http://www.muis.gov.sg/english/islamic_matters/Taqwim/Taqwim2003.aspx? pMenu=4**

The Royal Embassy of Saudi Arabia in Washington, D.C., posts its yearly calendar on its information page. Click on calendar: **http://www.saudiembassy.net/InfoMain.asp**

Khalid Shaukat, a Washington, D.C., scientist and consultant to the Islamic Society of North America and Shura Council of North America, maintains a web site covering many aspects of the Muslim calendar and tracking monthly moon sightings: **http://www.moonsighting.com**

Zurich University's Institute of Oriental Studies offers a web site that will convert Muslim to Gregorian dates, and Gregorian dates to Muslim dates: **http://www.ori.unizh.ch/hegira.html**

Ashura

Algar, Ayla. *Classical Turkish Cooking: Traditional Turkish Food for the American Kitchen*. New York: HarperCollins, 1991.

Associated Press. "Iranians Mourn Revered Shiite Muslim Saint." *The Dallas Morning News*, April 16, 2000, 19A.

Ayoub, Mahmoud M. "Husayn ibn Ali." In *The Oxford Encyclopedia of the Modern Islamic World*, edited by John L. Esposito. Vol. 2. Oxford, England: Oxford University Press, 1995.

Chelkowski, Peter. "Ashura." In *The Oxford Encyclopedia of the Modern Islamic World*, edited by John L. Esposito. Vol. 1. Oxford, England: Oxford University Press, 1995.

Collier, Robert. "Religious Frenzy and Anger on Once-Banned Pilgrimage; Power of Ancient Ritual Suggests Shiites' Importance in Iraq's Future." *San Francisco Chronicle*, April 23, 2003, A1.

Esposito, John L., ed. *The Oxford Encyclopedia of the Modern Islamic World*. 4 vols. Oxford, England: Oxford University Press, 1995.

Fisher, Ian. "Resolute Iranian Pilgrims Meet Awed G. I.'s." *New York Times*, October 7, 2003, A1.

Grunenbaum, G. E. von. *Muhammadan Festivals*. Paperback ed. London, England: Curzon, 1988.

Hossain, Shakeel. "Muharram Celebrations in India: A Case Study." In *The Muslim Almanac: A Reference Work on the History, Faith, Culture, and Peoples of Islam*, edited by Azim A. Nanji. Detroit, MI: Gale, 1996.

Kifner, John. "Iraqi Shiites Show Their Fervor in City They Hold Holy." *New York Times*, April 23, 2003, A13.

Korom, Frank J. *Hosay Trinidad: Muharram Performances in an Indo-Caribbean Diaspora*. Philadelphia: University of Pennsylvania Press, 2002.

Peterson, Scott. "Shiite Pilgrims to US: 'Thanks. Please Go Now.'" *Christian Science Monitor*, April 23, 2003, 01.

Pinault, David. *Horse of Karbala: Muslim Devotional Life in India*. New York: Palgrave, 2001.

Rajendra, Vijeya, and Gisela Kaplan. *Iran (Cultures of the World)*. New York: Marshall Cavendish, 1993.

Sachedina, Abdulaziz. "Karbalah." In *The Oxford Encyclopedia of the Modern Islamic World*, edited by John L. Esposito. Vol. 2. Oxford, England: Oxford University Press, 1995.

Sakr, Ahmad H. *Feasts, Festivities, and Holidays*. Lombard, IL: Foundation for Islamic Knowledge, 1999.

Schubel, Vernon. "Muharram." In *The Oxford Encyclopedia of the Modern Islamic World*, edited by John L. Esposito. Vol. 3. Oxford, England: Oxford University Press, 1995.

Smith, Craig S. "Elated Shiites, on Pilgrimage, Want U.S. Out." *New York Times*, April 22, 2003, A1.

Thais, Gustav. "Husayniyah." In *The Oxford Encyclopedia of the Modern Islamic World*, edited by John L. Esposito. Vol. 2. Oxford, England: Oxford University Press, 1995.

Entrance to the shrine of Abbas, Karbala, Iraq.

     ೧ೕ೧

For more on foods associated with Ashura see "Serving the Guest: A Sufi Cookbook," by Kathleen Seidel, at:

http://www.superluminal.com/cookbook/essay_ashura.html

For more on Muharram celebrations in Iran see writer Massoume Price's web site, entitled "Culture of Iran.Com," at:

http://www.cultureofiran.com/muharram.php

Bishop, John, and Frank Korom. *Hosay Trinidad* [videorecording]. Watertown, MA: Documentary Educational Resources, 1998. 45 minutes.

Eid al-Adha

In 2001, the U.S. Postal Service issued a special commemorative stamp that bears the phrase "Eid Greetings" (Eid Mubarek) in both English and Arabic calligraphy. A fifth-grade boy, Muhib Beekum, dreamed up the idea in 1996.

Ahsan, M. M. *Muslim Festivals*. Vero Beach, FL: Rourke Enterprises, 1987.

Al-Gailani, Noorah, and Chris Smith. *The Islamic Year: Surahs, Stories, and Celebrations*. Stroud, England: Hawthorn, 2002.

Esposito, John L., ed. *The Oxford Encyclopedia of the Modern Islamic World*. 4 vols. Oxford, England: Oxford University Press, 1995.

Glassé, Cyril. *The Concise Encyclopedia of Islam*. San Francisco, CA: Harper-SanFrancisco, 1991.

Martin, Richard C. "Id al-Adha." In *The Oxford Encyclopedia of the Modern Islamic World*, edited by John L. Esposito. Vol. 2. Oxford, England: Oxford University Press, 1995.

Moosa, Ebrahim. "Sacrifice." In *The Oxford Encyclopedia of the Modern Islamic World*, edited by John L. Esposito. Vol. 3. Oxford, England: Oxford University Press, 1995.

Roden, Claudia. *The New Book of Middle Eastern Food*. New York: Alfred A. Knopf, 2000.

Schubel, Vernon. "The Islamic Calendar." In *The Oxford Encyclopedia of the Modern Islamic World*, edited by John L. Esposito. Vol. 2. Oxford, England: Oxford University Press, 1995.

Weiss-Armush, Anne Marie. *The Arabian Delights Cookbook*. Los Angeles, CA: Lowell House, 1993.

৩৩

Britain's Channel 4 maintains a page titled "Day of Sacrifice," which is part of its larger site on the Hajj:

http://www.channel4.com/life/microsites/H/hajj/gend_three_sacrif.html

The kids' section of the Peace Corps web site furnishes a short descriptive article on Tabaski in Mali at:

http://www.peacecorps.gov/kids/like/mali-celebration3.html

First of Muharram

Ahsan, M. M. *Muslim Festivals*. Vero Beach, FL: Rourke Enterprises, 1987.

Al-Gailani, Noorah, and Chris Smith. *The Islamic Year: Surahs, Stories, and Celebrations*. Stroud, England: Hawthorn, 2002.

Glassé, Cyril. *The Concise Encyclopedia of Islam*. San Francisco, CA: HarperSanFrancisco, 1991.

Friday

Ali, Ahmed, trans. *Al-Qur'an: A Contemporary Translation*. Rev. definitive ed. Princeton, NJ: Princeton University Press, 1988.

Chebel, Malek. *Symbols of Islam*. New York: Assouline, 2000.

Emerick, Yahiya. *The Complete Idiot's Guide to Islam*. Indianapolis, IN: Alpha Pearson, 2002.

Esposito, John L. *What Everyone Needs to Know About Islam*. Oxford, England: Oxford University Press, 2002.

Glassé, Cyril. *The Concise Encyclopedia of Islam*. San Francisco, CA: HarperSanFrancisco, 1991.

Peters, F. E. *Islam: A Guide for Jews and Christians*. Princeton, NJ: Princeton University Press, 2003.

Sakr, Ahmad H. *Feasts, Festivities, and Holidays*. Lombard, IL: Foundation for Islamic Knowledge, 1999.

The Islamic Center of Italy in via Casella (Rome) during the prayer of Friday.

Hajj

Adawi, Hassan. "14 Killed in Mina Stampede." *Arab News*, February 12, 2003. Available online at: http://www.arabnews.com.

Al-Gailani, Noorah, and Chris Smith. *The Islamic Year: Surahs, Stories, and Celebrations*. Stroud, England: Hawthorn, 2002.

Al-Ghalib, Essam. "Millions of Pilgrims Mass at Mina." *Arab News*, February 10, 2003. Available online at http://www.arabnews.com.

Al-Ghalib, Essam, and Hassan Adawi. "Pilgrims Seek Forgiveness at Pinnacle of Haj." *Arab News*, February 11, 2003. Available online at: http://www.arabnews.com.

Al Hariri-Wendel, Tanja. *Symbols of Islam*. New York: Sterling, 2002.

Ali, Ahmed, trans. *Al-Qur'an: A Contemporary Translation*. Rev. definitive ed. Princeton, NJ: Princeton University Press, 1988.

Bianchi, Robert. "Hajj." In *The Oxford Encyclopedia of the Modern Islamic World*, edited by John L. Esposito. Vol. 2. Oxford, England: Oxford University Press, 1995.

Carlson, Charles. "Hajj Pilgrims Converge to Hear Warning of 'Enemies of Islam.'" *Radio Free Europe*, February 10, 2003. Available online at:

http://www.rferl.org/nca/features/2003/02/10022003171151.asp.

Chebel, Malek. *Symbols of Islam*. New York: Assouline, 2000.

Denny, Frederick Mathewson. *An Introduction to Islam*. 2nd ed. New York: Macmillan, 1994.

Eickelman, Dale F., and James Piscatori, eds. *Muslim Travellers: Pilgrimage, Migration, and the Religious Imagination*. Berkeley: University of California Press, 1990.

Esin, Emel. *Mecca the Blessed, Medina the Radiant*. New York: Crown, 1963.

Ghafour, P. K. Abdul. "Foreign Pilgrims at Record High." *Arab News*, February 10, 2003. Available online at http://www.arabnews.com.

Ghafour, P. K. Abdul. "Pilgrims 'Must Imbibe the Spirit of Hajj.'" *Arab News,* February 9, 2003. Available online at http://www.arabnews.com.

Glassé, Cyril. *The Concise Encyclopedia of Islam*. San Francisco, CA: HarperSanFrancisco, 1991.

Grunenebaum, G. E., von. *Muhammadan Festivals*. Paperback ed. London, England: Curzon, 1988.

Is'harc, Istafiah. *Islam and Its Festivals*. London, England: Ta-Ha, 1997.

Kamal, Ahmad. *The Sacred Journey, Being Pilgrimage to Makkah*. New York: Van Rees Press, 1961.

Lunde, Paul. *Islam: Faith, Culture, History*. London, England: D. K. Publishing, 2002.

Nomachi, Ali Kazuyoshi, and Seyyed Hossein Nasr. *Mecca the Blessed, Medina the Radiant: The Holiest Cities of Islam*. New York: Aperture, 1997. (Photo essay)

Parker, Ann, and Avon Neal. *Hajj Paintings: Folk Art of the Great Pilgrimage*. Washington, D.C.: Smithsonian Institute Press, 1995.

Reese, Lyn. *Women in the Muslim World: Personalities and Perspectives from the Past*. Berkeley, CA: Women in World History Curriculum, 1998.

Reuters. "244 Die in Saudi Stampede During Muslim Pilgrimage." *New York Times*, February 2, 2004, A3.

Sakr, Ahmad H. *Feasts, Festivities, and Holidays*. Lombard, IL: Foundation for Islamic Knowledge, 1999.

Wahab, Siraj. "Satan Stoned in Symbolic Haj Ritual." *Arab News*, February 12, 2003. Available online at http://www.arabnews.com.

Wolfe, Michael. *The Hadj: An American's Pilgrimage to Mecca*. New York: Atlantic Monthly Press, 1993.

Wolfe, Michael, ed. *One Thousand Roads to Mecca*. New York: Grove, 1997.

During Hajj, millions of pilgrims visit the Kaba, Islam's holiest shrine, which is located in the center of the Grand Mosque in Mecca.

&c.

Britain's Channel 4 television station maintains a site on the Hajj which outlines the main events of the pilgrimage, discusses preparations, offers maps, gives prayers, and more: **http://www.channel4.com/life/microsites/H/hajj/index.html**

Those interested in the Saudi Arabian government's rules and regulations for Hajj pilgrims can find them on the web at: **http://saudiembassy.net/Travel/Hajj.asp**

The Saudi Embassy web site also carries press releases on events related to the Hajj: **http://saudiembassy.net**

Hidrellez

Turkish Muslims honor five religious holidays associated with events in the life of the prophet Muhammad by keeping their mosques lit all night. Taken together these special evenings are called the Kandil Geceleri. The word kandil means "candle," and the name of this observance is translated as Candle Feasts or Lamp Nights.

Ali, Ahmed, trans. *Al-Qur'an: A Contemporary Translation*. Rev. definitive ed. Princeton, NJ: Princeton University Press, 1988.

Glassé, Cyril. *The Concise Encyclopedia of Islam*. San Francisco, CA: Harper-SanFrancisco, 1991.

Halman, Hugh Talat. *Al-Khidr: The Green One*. Chicago, IL: Iqra, 2001.

Omar, Ifran. "Khidr in Muslim Tradition." *Muslim World* 83, no. 3-4 (July 1993): 279-93.

Owadally, Mohamad Yasin. *Khidr: The Mysterious Wandering Green Man*. Kuala Lumpur, Malaysia: A. S. Noordeen, 1997.

Walker, Warren S., and Ahmet E. Uysal. "An Ancient God in Modern Turkey: Some Aspects of the Cult of Hizir." *Journal of American Folklore* 86, no. 341 (September 1973): 286-89.

&c.

Turkey's Ministry of Culture and Tourism maintains a web page on "Hidrellez Traditions" at: **http://www.kultur.gov.tr/portal/kultur_en.asp?belgeno=5659**

Lamp Nights

Algar, Ayla. *Classical Turkish Cooking: Traditional Turkish Food for the American Kitchen*. New York: HarperCollins, 1991.

Schimmel, Annemarie. "Islamic Religious Year." In *The Encyclopedia of Religion*, edited by Mircea Eliade. Vol. 7. New York: Macmillan, 1987.

Laylat al-Bara'ah

Chowdury, Abdul Muqit. "The Call of Shab-e-Barat." *The New Nation Online Edition*, October 10, 2003. Available online at: http://nation.ittefaq.com/artman/publish/printer_5417.shtml.

Gibb, H. A. R., and J. H. Kramers. *Shorter Encylopedia of Islam*. Leiden, The Netherlands: E. J. Brill, 1965.

Glassé, Cyril. *The Concise Encyclopedia of Islam*. San Francisco, CA: HarperSanFrancisco, 1991.

Grunenbaum, G. E. von. *Muhammaden Festivals*. London, England: Curzon, 1988.

Padwick, Constance. *Muslim Devotions: A Study of Prayer-Manuals in Common Use*. Reprint, Oxford, England: Oneworld, 1997.

Renard, John. *Seven Doors to Islam: Spirituality and the Religious Life of Muslims*. Berkeley: University of California Press, 1996.

Rumi, Jalal al-Din. *Mystical Poems of Rumi: First Selection, Poems 1-200*. Translated by A. J. Arberry. Chicago, IL: University of Chicago Press, 1968.

Sakr, Amad H. *Feasts, Festivities, and Holidays*. Lombard, IL: Foundation for Islamic Knowledge, 1999.

Schimmel, Annemarie. "Islamic Religious Year." In *The Encyclopedia of Religion*, edited by Mircea Eliade. Vol. 7. New York: Macmillan, 1987.

Devout Muslims sometimes spend the last ten days of Ramadan in a spiritual retreat called i'tikaf.

Laylat al-Miraj

Al-Gailani, Noorah, and Chris Smith. *The Islamic Year: Surahs, Stories, and Celebrations*. Stroud, England: Hawthorn, 2002.

Ali, Ahmed, trans. *Al-Qur'an: A Contemporary Translation*. Rev. definitive ed. Princeton, NJ: Princeton University Press, 1988.

Chittick, William. "Miraj." In *The Oxford Encyclopedia of the Modern Islamic World*, edited by John L. Esposito. Vol. 3. Oxford, England: Oxford University Press, 1995.

Glassé, Cyril. *The Concise Encyclopedia of Islam*. San Francisco, CA: HarperSanFrancisco, 1991.

Rippin, Andrew, and Jan Knappert, eds. *Textual Sources for the Study of Islam*. Chicago, IL: University of Chicago Press, 1986.

Sakr, Ahmad H. *Feasts, Festivities, and Holidays*. Lombard, IL: Foundation for Islamic Knowledge, 1999.

Laylat al-Qadr

Al Hariri-Wendel, Tanja. *Symbols of Islam*. New York: Sterling, 2002.

Glassé, Cyril. *The Concise Encyclopedia of Islam*. San Francisco, CA: HarperSanFrancisco, 1991.

Is'harc, Istafiah. *Islam and Its Festivals*. London, England: Ta-Ha, 1997.

Kassamali, H., and T. Kassamali. *A Manual of Ramadhan Devotions*. Rev. ed. Richmond, Canada: Tayyiba, 2002.

Sakr, Ahmad H. *Feasts, Festivities, and Holidays*. Lombard, IL: Foundation for Islamic Knowledge, 1999.

Schimmel, Annemarie. "Islamic Religious Year." In *The Encyclopedia of Religion*, edited by Mircea Eliade. Vol. 7. New York: Macmillan, 1987.

◈

For more on Ramadan in Iran see the following site, compiled by writer and researcher Massoume Price: **http://www.cultureofiran.com/ramadan.php**

Mulid al-Nabi

An Egyptian girl holds a candy doll, made from hot, molten sugar in the shape of a female figure that she received in celebration of Mulid al-Nabi.

Abbas, Jailan. *Festivals of Egypt*. Cairo, Egypt: Hoopoe Books, 1995.

Ahsan, M. M. *Muslim Festivals*. Vero Beach, FL: Rourke Enterprises, 1987.

Al-Gailani, Noorah, and Chris Smith. *The Islamic Year: Surahs, Stories, and Celebrations*. Stroud, England: Hawthorn, 2002.

Gearhart, Rebecca. "Four Days for the Prophet: Kenya's Maulidi Festival Celebrates the Birth of Muhammad." *The World and I* 13, no. 9 (September 1998): 218-24.

Gibb, H. A. R., and J. H. Kramers. *Shorter Encylopedia of Islam*. Leiden, The Netherlands: E. J. Brill, 1965.

Glassé, Cyril. *The Concise Encyclopedia of Islam*. San Francisco, CA: HarperSanFrancisco, 1991.

Is'harc, Istafiah. *Islam and Its Festivals*. London, England: Ta-Ha, 1997.

Jayyusi, Salma Khadra. *Modern Arabic Poetry: An Anthology*. New York: Columbia University Press, 1987.

Renard, John. *Seven Doors to Islam: Spirituality and the Religious Life of Muslims*. Berkeley: University of California Press, 1996.

Sakr, Ahmad H. *Feasts, Festivities, and Holidays*. Lombard, IL: Foundation for Islamic Knowledge, 1999.

Schimmel, Annemarie. "Islamic Religious Year." In *The Encyclopedia of Religion*, edited by Mircea Eliade. Vol. 7. New York: Macmillan, 1987.

◈

An essay touching on the controversy over whether and how to celebrate Mulid al-Nabi, written by Dr. Sulayman Nyang, can be found on the web site of the Islamic Supreme Council of America at:
http://www.islamicsupremecouncil.org/bin/site/ftp/Mawlid-Nyang.pdf

Ramadan and Eid al-Fitr

Abbas, Jailan. *Festivals of Egypt*. Cairo, Egypt: Hoopoe Books, 1995.

Ahmad, Anis. "Ramadan." In *The Oxford Encyclopedia of the Modern Islamic World*, edited by John L. Esposito. Vol. 3. Oxford, England: Oxford University Press, 1995.

Ahmad, Nashiah, and Ihsan Bagby. "Schools Adapting to Muslim Holy Month." *Education Week* 22, no. 13 (November 27, 2002): 1-2.

Ahmed, Akbar S. *Islam Today: A Short Introduction to the Muslim World*. London, England: I. B. Tauris, 1999.

Ahsan, M. M. *Muslim Festivals*. Vero Beach, FL: Rourke Enterprises, 1987.

Al-Gailani, Noorah, and Chris Smith. *The Islamic Year: Surahs, Stories, and Celebrations*. Stroud, England: Hawthorn, 2002.

Algar, Ayla. *Classical Turkish Cooking: Traditional Turkish Food for the American Table*. New York: HarperCollins, 1991.

Al Hariri-Wendel, Tanja. *Symbols of Islam*. New York: Sterling, 2002.

Alhinai, Abdulrahman Bin Ali. *Ceremonies and Celebrations of Oman*. Reading, England: Garnet Publishing, 1999.

Ali, Ahmed, trans. *Al-Qur'an: A Contemporary Translation*. Rev. definitive ed. Princeton, NJ: Princeton University Press, 1988.

Ambrust, Walter. "The Riddle of Ramadan: Media, Consumer Culture, and the 'Christmasization' of a Muslim Holiday." In *Everyday Life in the Muslim Middle East*, edited by Donna Lee Bowen and Evelyn A. Early. 2nd ed. Bloomington: Indiana University Press, 2002.

Bakhtiar, Laleh. *Ramadan: Motivating Believers to Action*. Chicago, IL: Kazi Publications, 1995.

Bentley, John. "Muslims Begin Fasting, Celebrations for Holy Month of Ramadan." *Associated Press*, December 6, 2000. Available online at: http://www.canoe.ca/LifewiseHeartSoulwise00/1206_muslim_ap.html.

Berg, Elizabeth. *Egypt*. Milwaukee, WI: Gareth Stevens, 1997.

D'Agostino, Joseph A. "New York Schools Flip-Flop on Ramadan." *Human Events* 57, no. 44 (November 26, 2001): 4.

Early, Evelyn A. "Syrian Television Drama: Permitted Political Discourse." In *Everyday Life in the Muslim Middle East*, edited by Donna Lee Bowen and Evelyn A. Early. 2nd ed. Bloomington: Indiana University Press, 2002.

Esposito, John L., ed. *The Oxford Encyclopedia of the Modern Islamic World*. 4 vols. Oxford, England: Oxford University Press, 1995.

"Fasting and Feasting." *The Economist* 350, no. 8108 (January 1, 1999): 44.

Sunset—here seen against the Cairo Citadel—marks the end of the fasting hours of the month of Ramadan.

Gaouette, Nicole. "Let's Meet for Tea, at 3 O'Clock—in the Morning." *Christian Science Monitor* 94, no. 16 (December 14, 2001): 6.

Gatehouse, Jonathon. "The Holiest Month." *Maclean's* 114, no. 51 (December 17, 2001): 18-22.

Ghazi, Suhaib Hamid. *Ramadan*. New York: Holiday House, 1996.

Glassé, Cyril. *The Concise Encyclopedia of Islam*. San Francisco, CA: HarperSanFrancisco, 1991.

Griffin, Robert, and Ann H. Shurgin. *Junior Worldmark Encyclopedia of World Holidays*. Vol. 4. Detroit, MI: U.X.L., 2000.

Grunenbaum, G. E. von. *Muhammadan Festivals*. Reprint, London, England: Curzon, 1992.

Hajar, Rachel. "Recurring Happiness: Qatar Celebrates Eid al-Fitr." *The World and I* 14, no. 1 (January 1999): 202.

Hassan, Fayza. "Soup in a Tureen." *Al-Ahram Weekly Online* (Cairo, Egypt) no. 562 (November 29-December 5, 2001). Available online at: http://weekly.ahram.org.eg/2001/562/li1.htm.

Hassan, Javid. "Everything Connected with Ramadan Has Undergone a Change." *Arab News*, October 28, 2003. Available online at: http://www.arabnews.com.

Hoyt-Goldsmith, Diane. *Celebrating Ramadan*. New York: Holiday House, 2001.

Is'harc, Istafiah. *Islam and Its Festivals*. London, England: Ta-Ha, 1997.

Kassamali, H., and T. Kassamali. *A Manual of Ramadhan Devotions*. Rev. ed. Richmond, Canada: Tayyiba, 2002.

Kerven, Rosalind. *Id-ul-Fitr*. Austin, TX: Raintree Steck-Vaughn, 1997.

Layton, Leslie. *Singapore* (*Cultures of the World*). 2nd ed. Tarrytown, NY: Marshall Cavendish, 2002.

Lynfield, Ben. "Observing Ramadan in Jerusalem." *Christian Science Monitor*, December 4, 2000. Available online at: http://search.csmonitor.com/durable/2000/12/04/p6s1.htm.

Marchant, Kerena. *Id-Ul-Fitr*. Brookfield, CT: Millbrook Press, 1996.

Martin, Richard C. "Id al-Fitr." In *The Oxford Encyclopedia of the Modern Islamic World*, edited by John L. Esposito. Vol. 2. Oxford, England: Oxford University Press, 1995.

McCarthy, Kevin M. *Saudi Arabia: A Desert Kingdom*. Parsippany, NJ: Dillon Press, 1997.

Mirpuri, Gouri, and Robert Cooper. *Indonesia* (*Cultures of the World*). 2nd ed. Tarrytown, NY: Marshall Cavendish, 2002.

Moore, Daniel. *The Ramadan Sonnets*. San Francisco, CA: City Lights Books, 1996.

Before attending their annual Ramadan iftar, these Muslims perform tarawih, supplementary prayers for Ramadan.

Newby, Gordon D. *A Concise Encyclopedia of Islam*. Oxford, England: Oneworld, 2002.

Nigeria (Fiesta!). Danbury, CT: Grolier Educational, 1997.

Osama, Mohamed. "Eid: Celebration for the Young and Old." *Tour Egypt Monthly* 2, no. 1 (January 1, 2001). Available online at: http://www.touregypt.net/magazine/mag01012001/magf2.htm.

O'Shea, Maria. *Saudi Arabia (Festivals of the World)*. Milwaukee, WI: Gareth Stevens, 1999.

O'Shea, Maria. *Turkey (Festivals of the World)*. Milwaukee, WI: Gareth Stevens, 1999.

Radwan, Amany. "Ramadan Diary: One: The First Fast." *Time Europe*, December 7, 2000. Available online at: http://www.time.com/time/europe/webonly/mideast/2000/12/ramadan1.html.

Radwan, Amany. "Ramadan Diary: Two: Food for Thought." *Time Europe*, December 12, 2000. Available online at: http://www.time.com/time/europe/webonly/mideast/2000/12/ramadan2.html.

Radwan, Amany. "Ramadan Diary: Three: Festival of Light." *Time Europe*, December 15, 2000. Available online at: http://www.time.com/time/europe/webonly/mideast/2000/12/ramadan3.html.

Radwan, Amany. "Ramadan Diary: Four: Iftar." *Time Europe*, December 15, 2000. Available online at: http://www.time.com/time/europe/webonly/mideast/2000/12/ramadan4.html.

Radwan, Amany. "Ramadan Diary: Five: Out with a Boom." *Time Europe*, December 15, 2000. Available online at: http://www.time.com/time/europe/webonly/mideast/2000/12/ramadan5.html.

Radwan, Amany. "Ramadan Diary: Six: Remote Control." *Time Europe*, December 15, 2000. Available online at: http://www.time.com/time/europe/webonly/mideast/2000/12/ramadan6.html.

Radwan, Amany. "Ramadan Diary: Seven: Country Life." *Time Europe*, December 19, 2000. Available online at: http://www.time.com/time/europe/webonly/mideast/2000/12/ramadan7.html.

Radwan, Amany. "Ramadan Diary: Eight: The Final Feast." *Time Europe*, January 1, 2001. Available online at: http://www.time.com/time/europe/webonly/mideast/2001/01/ramadan8.html.

Rajendra, Vijeya, and Gisela Kaplan. *Iran (Cultures of the World)*. New York: Marshall Cavendish, 1993.

Ramdoyal, Ramesh. *Festivals of Mauritius*. Stanley, Rose-Hill, Mauritius: Edition de l'Océan Indien, 1990.

Roden, Claudia. *The New Book of Middle Eastern Food*. New York: Alfred A. Knopf, 2000.

A Ramadan lantern shop becomes a magical place after dark.

The minaret of the hospital, madrasa, and mausoleum of Sultan al-Mansur Qala'un, built in the 13th century, still bears the protruding wooden rods at its peak from which Ramadan lanterns were once hung.

Rodenbeck, Christine. *Egypt: A Portrait of the Country Though Its Festivals and Traditions*. Danbury, CT: Grolier, 1999.

Rodseth, Lars, Sally Howell, and Andrew Shryock. *Arab World Mosaic: A Curriculum Supplement for Elementary Teachers*. Dearborn, MI: ACCESS Cultural Arts Program, 1994.

Rumi, Jalal al-Din. *Mystical Poems of Rumi: First Selection, Poems 1-200*. Translated by A. J. Arberry. Chicago, IL: University of Chicago Press, 1968.

Sakr, Ahmad H. *Feasts, Festivities, and Holidays*. Lombard, IL: Foundation for Islamic Knowledge, 1999.

Schimmel, Annemarie. "Islamic Religious Year." In *The Encyclopedia of Religion*, edited by Mircea Eliade. Vol. 7. New York: Macmillan, 1987.

Schubel, Vernon James. "Islamic Calendar." In *The Oxford Encyclopedia of the Modern Islamic World*, edited by John L. Esposito. Vol. 2. Oxford, England: Oxford University Press, 1995.

Sheehan, Sam. *Pakistan (Cultures of the World)*. New York: Marshall Cavendish, 1994.

South, Coleman. *Syria (Cultures of the World)*. New York: Marshall Cavendish, 1995.

Tapper, Nancy. "*Ziyaret*: Gender, Movement, and Exchange in a Turkish Community." In *Muslim Travellers: Pilgrimage, Migration, and the Religious Imagination*, edited by Dale F. Eickelman and James Piscatori. Berkeley: University of California Press, 1990.

Turkey (Fiesta!). Danbury, CT: Grolier Educational, 1997.

Walker, Richard Kennedy. *Lebanon: A Portrait of the Country Through Its Festivals and Traditions*. Danbury, CT: Grolier, 1999.

Weiss-Armush, Anne Marie. *The Arabian Delights Cookbook*. Los Angeles, CA: Lowell House, 1993.

Muslims in two Yorkshire cities take to the airwaves during the holy month of Ramadan, binding together their minority communities with readings from the Quran, religious discussions, quizzes, and call-ins. Suhail Anjum Ali, age 12, broadcasts an Islamic quiz in Bradford, England.

☙❧

Safi, Omid. "The Essence of Ramadan," December 3, 2002, an editorial published through the Progressive Media Project and available on the web at:
http://www.progressive.org/Media%20Project%202/mpod302.html

Bledsoe, Helen Wiemen. "The Festival of Ramadan." *Calliope*. January-February 1997. This article, which is written for children ages nine through fourteen, is available on the web at:
http://www.cobblestonepub.com/pages/FACALLRamadan.html

"Ramadan in Egypt," by Sameh Arab, posted on *Tour Egypt Monthly*, a webzine sponsored by Tour Egypt, a company promoting tourism in Egypt:
http://www.touregypt.net/magazine/mag11012000/magf3.htm

A Palestinian Recipe for Qatayef is available in *This Week in Palestine*, issue 20, December 1999, posted online by the Jerusalem Media and Communication Centre, East Jerusalem, Palestine: **http://www.jmcc.org/ptw/99/Dec/recipe.htm**

"Breaking the Ramadan Fast with Soup," an article and recipes by Pat Soley, posted at Soupsong.com: **http://www.soupsong.com/z71100.html**

"Ramadan and Lebaran in Indonesia," an article posted on Expat Web Site Association in Jakarta, Indonesia, at: **http://www.expat.or.id/info/lebaran.html**

Marlowe, John. "Islam's First U.S. Postage Stamp for Muslim Eid Holiday," an article originally published in *Saudi Aramco World*, and posted to the web by the U.S. State Department: **http://usinfo.org/usia/usinfo.state.gov/usa/islam/a112101.htm**

The Kuwait Information Office offers information on Ramadan and Eid al-Fitr celebrations at: **http://www.kuwait-info.com/sidepages/festivals_ram.asp** **http://www.kuwait-info.com/sidepages/festivals_eid.asp**

For more on Muslim holidays in Senegal see the following page, sponsored by Lewis and Clark University: **http://www.lclark.edu/~nicole/SENEGAL/HOLIDAYS.HTM**

The Republic of Turkey's Ministry of Culture and Tourism posts a page on religious holidays in Turkey at: **http://www.kultur.gov.tr/portal/kultur_en.asp?belgeno=5657**

The government of Yemen offers information on Ramadan observances in that country at: **http://www.yemeninfo.gov.ye/ENGLISH/panorama/Celebrations.htm**

See also, "Ramadan in Yemeni Cities," an article from *The Yemen Times*, volume 10, issue 50, December 11 through December 17, 2000. Available on the web at: **http://www.yementimes.com/00/iss50/culture.htm**

See Kathleen Seidel's web cookbook, *Serving the Guest: A Sufi Cookbook*, for recipes from Muslim lands, especially those associated with religious figures and observances: **http://www.superluminal.com/cookbook**

For more on Ramadan in Iran see the following site, posted to the web by writer and researcher Massoume Price: **http://www.cultureofiran.com/ramadan.php**

At early morning prayers on the Eid al-Fitr, the celebration that concludes the holy month of Ramadan, friends greet each other with a handshake outside the Al-Kulafah' al-Rashidin Mosque in central Asmara located in Eritrea, Africa.

Saints and Their Festivals

Atia, Tarek. *Mulid! Carnivals of Faith*. Cairo, Egypt: American University in Cairo Press, 1999.

Barks, Coleman, ed. and trans. Introduction to *The Soul of Rumi: A New Collection of Ecstatic Poems*. San Francisco, CA: HarperSanFrancisco, 2001.

Barks, Coleman, and John Moyne, eds. and trans. *This Longing: Poetry, Teaching Stories, and Letters of Rumi*. Putney, VT: Threshold Books, 1988.

Biegman, Nicholaas, H. *Egypt: Moulids, Saints, Sufis.* The Hague, The Netherlands: SDU Publishers and Kegan Paul International, 1990.

Clarke, Lynda. "Sainthood." In *The Oxford Encyclopedia of the Modern Islamic World,* edited by John L. Esposito. Vol. 3. Oxford, England: Oxford University Press, 1995.

Denny, Frederick Mathewson. *An Introduction to Islam.* 2nd ed. New York: Macmillan, 1994.

Eickelman, Dale. "Popular Religion in the Middle East and North Africa." In *The Oxford Encyclopedia of the Modern Islamic World,* edited by John L. Esposito. Vol. 3. Oxford, England: Oxford University Press, 1995.

Eickelman, Dale. "Shrines." In *The Oxford Encyclopedia of the Modern Islamic World,* edited by John L. Esposito. Vol. 4. Oxford, England: Oxford University Press, 1995.

El Guindi, Fadwa. "Mawlid." In *The Oxford Encyclopedia of the Modern Islamic World,* edited by John L. Esposito. Vol. 3. Oxford, England: Oxford University Press, 1995.

Esposito, John L., ed. *The Oxford Encyclopedia of the Modern Islamic World.* 4 vols. Oxford, England: Oxford University Press, 1995.

Friedlander, Shems. *Rumi and the Whirling Dervishes.* New York: Parabola Books, 2003.

Glassé, Cyril. *The Concise Encyclopedia of Islam.* San Francisco, CA: HarperSanFrancisco, 1991.

Henderson, Helene, and Sue Ellen Thompson, eds. *Holidays, Festivals, and Celebrations of the World Dictionary.* 2nd ed. Detroit, MI: Omnigraphics, 1997.

Huda, Qamar-ul. "Celebrating Death and Engaging in Texts at Data Ganj Baksh's Shrine." *Muslim World* 90, no. 3-4 (fall 2000): 337-55.

Lewis, Franklin D. *Rumi, Past and Present, East and West: The Life, Teachings, and Poetry of Jalal al-Din Rumi.* Oxford, England: Oneworld, 2000.

Ohtsuka, Kazuo. "Sufi Shrine Culture." In *The Oxford Encyclopedia of the Modern Islamic World,* edited by John L. Esposito. Vol. 4. Oxford, England: Oxford University Press, 1995.

Renard, John. *Seven Doors to Islam: Spirituality and the Religious Life of Muslims.* Berkeley: University of California Press, 1996

Robinson, David. "Muridiyah." In *The Oxford Encyclopedia of the Modern Islamic World,* edited by John L. Esposito. Vol. 3. Oxford, England: Oxford University Press, 1995.

Schreibman, Jane. "At the Shrine of the Pir: India's Healing Saints." *The World and I* 5, no. 8 (August 1990): 642.

Entrance to the "Golden Mosque," center of one of the two districts identified as "preservation areas" in Baghdad.

Schubel, Vernon James. "Devotional Life and Practice." In *The Muslim Almanac: A Reference Work on the History, Faith, Culture and Peoples of Islam*, edited by Azim A. Nanji. Detroit, MI: Gale, 1996.

Schubel, Vernon James. "Islamic Calendar." In *The Oxford Encyclopedia of the Modern Islamic World*, edited by John L. Esposito. Vol. 2. Oxford, England: Oxford University Press, 1995.

Simpson, Chris. "The Annual Trek to Touba." *B.B.C. News*, May 14, 2001. Available online at: http://news.bbc.co.uk/1/hi/world/africa/1330324.stm.

Subhan, John A. *Sufism: Its Saints and Shrines*. New Delhi, India: Cosmo Publications, 1999.

Van Doorn, Nelly, and Kees de Jong. "The Pilgrimage to Tembayat: Tradition and Revival in Indonesian Islam." *Muslim World* 91, no. 3-4 (fall 2001): 325-53.

Waschsmann, Shelley. "Sailing into Egypt's Past." *Archeology* 6, no. 4 (July/August 2002): 36-40.

Wines, Leslie. *Rumi: A Spiritual Biography*. New York: Crossroads, 2000.

Zak, Susannah. "Whirling Before Allah: Mevlevis Dance to an Old World Song." *The World and I* 9, no. 5 (May 1994): 250.

Feet are washed before entering Fantasia tent.

☙❧

For more on the city of Touba see "Sacred Sites," a web site put together by writer, researcher, and photographer Martin Gray at: **http://www.sacredsites.com/africa/senegal.html**

UCLA's Fowler Museum of Cultural History web exhibit, "Passport to Paradise: Sufi Arts of Senegal and Beyond," offers photos and information on the life of Shaykh Amadou Bamba and the folk art created by members of the Mouride Brotherhood: **http://www.fmch.ucla.edu/paradise/main001.htm**

For information about Rumi, his mausoleum, and the Mevlevi Order, see the following site, posted by the family of Dr. Celaleddin B. Celebi, an expert on the Mevlevi Order and a descendant of Rumi. Includes links to sites featuring Rumi's poetry: **http://www.mevlana.net**

For more on Konya's Mevlana festival see the following site, posted by the Republic of Turkey's Ministry of Foreign Affairs: **http://www.mfa.gov.tr/grupc/ca/caa/uu/orta%20anadolu/mevlana.htm**

Turkey's Ministry of Culture and Tourism offers information on Rumi's life at: **http://www.kultur.gov.tr/portal/ARKEOLOJI_en.asp?belgeno=788**

For more information on Rumi's life, his recent popularity in the United States, and the Mevlevi Order see the following page, posted by the Islamic Supreme Council of America: **http://www.islamicsupremecouncil.org/bin/site/wrappers/default.asp?pane_2=content-spirituality-mevlevi**

Turkey's Ministry of Culture and Tourism provides a detailed description of the Mevlana Museum (Dervish Lodge) at:
http://www.kultur.gov.tr/portal/ARKEOLOJI_en.asp?belgeno=709

Travel writer Kamin Mohammadi's description of the Whirling Dervish festival can be found at: **http://www.travelintelligence.net/wsd/articles/art_2418.html**

For more on the Chapel Hill, North Carolina, Rumi festival see:
http://www.rumifest.com

White Nights

Grunenbaum, G. E. von. *Muhammaden Festivals*. London, England: Curzon, 1988.

Kassamali, H., and T. Kassamali. *A'Maal of Rajab and Shaban*. Richmond, Canada: Tayyiba Publishers and Distributors, 1996.

Schimmel, Annemarie. "Islamic Religious Year." In *The Encyclopedia of Religion*, edited by Mircea Eliade. Vol. 7. New York: Macmillan, 1987.

Last page of a Quran from the Sultan Barquq Mosque in Cairo, in Prisse's L'Art Arabe.

Photo Credits

Foreword—Ali A. Khalifa/*Saudi Aramco World*/PADIA: p.16.

Preface—S.M. Amin/*Saudi Aramco World*/PADIA: p.20; IslamiClip® Calligraphic Designs #1/ Sakkal Design p.23.

Opposite page: A Muslim from Ladakh, India, takes a moment for prayer.

SECTION ONE

Overview—Nik Wheeler/*Saudi Aramco World*/PADIA: p.30.

Chapter 1—Katrina Thomas/*Saudi Aramco World*/PADIA: p.32; IslamiClip® Calligraphic Designs #1/Sakkal Design pp.33, 34; Marie Docher/PhotoAlto p.35; Kevin Bubriski/*Saudi Aramco World*/PADIA: p.36; S.M. Amin/*Saudi Aramco World*/PADIA: p.38; Courtesy Jimmy Carter Library/PBS p.40; Brynn Bruijn/*Saudi Aramco World*/PADIA: p.41; Tor Eigeland/*Saudi Aramco World*/PADIA: pp.42, 44, 45; Dick Doughty/*Saudi Aramco World*/ PADIA: p.43.

Chapter 2—Great Silk Road/Corel Draw pp.49, 51.

Chapter 3—Miscellaneous Historical Photos Collection/*Saudi Aramco World*/PADIA: p.52; Tor Eigeland/*Saudi Aramco World*/PADIA: p.53; Robert Y. Richie/*Saudi Aramco World*/PADIA: p.54.

Chapter 4—S.M. Amin/*Saudi Aramco World*/PADIA: pp.56, 62; Norman MacDonald/ *Saudi Aramco World*/PADIA: p.58; Abdullah Y. Al-Dobais/*Saudi Aramco World*/PADIA: p.61; The New York Public Library, Astor, Lenox, and Tilden Foundations Spencer Collection — Turkish Manuscript, "Siyari-i-nabi" by Mustafa ibn Yusuf (al-Zarir) Istanbul, 1594-5/PBS p.64.

Chapter 5—David W. Tschanz/*Saudi Aramco World*/PADIA: p.66; John Feeney/*Saudi Aramco World*/PADIA: p.68; Tor Eigeland/*Saudi Aramco World*/PADIA: pp.69, 70; Illustrated by Michael Grimsdale/*Saudi Aramco World*/PADIA: p.72; Dorothy Miller/*Saudi Aramco World*/PADIA: p.75; Torben Larsen/*Saudi Aramco World*/PADIA: p.76; Ilene Perlman/*Saudi Aramco World*/ PADIA: p.77 (top); Dick Doughty/*Saudi Aramco World*/ PADIA: p.77 (bottom).

Chapter 6—Hussain A. Al-Ramadan/*Saudi Aramco World*/PADIA: pp.80, 83; Tor Eigeland/ *Saudi Aramco World*/PADIA: pp.81, 88, 90; Denise Applewhite/*Saudi Aramco World*/PADIA: p.82; IslamiClip®Calligraphic Designs #1/Sakkal Design p.84; Courtesy of Asia House Gallery/ *Saudi Aramco World*/PADIA: p.85; Sacred Places/Corel Draw p.87; Turkey/Corel Draw p.89 (top); World Landmarks/Corel Draw p.89 (bottom); Ilene Perlman/*Saudi Aramco World*/ PADIA: p.91.

Chapter 7—William Tracy/*Saudi Aramco World*/PADIA: p.92; Copyright © Bettmann/CORBIS p.94; Courtesy Jimmy Carter Library/PBS p.95; AFP/Getty Images p.96; Robert Azzi/*Saudi Aramco World*/PADIA: p.97; Amy Murphy p.98; John Filo/CBS. © 2003 CBS Worldwide Inc. All rights reserved. p.101; Dick Doughty/*Saudi Aramco World*/ PADIA: pp.102, 106; Brynn Bruijn/*Saudi Aramco World*/ PADIA: p.105.

Chapter 8—Harold Sequeira/*Saudi Aramco World*/PADIA: p.110; Gordon Parks/© W.D.M. Ministry Publications/PBS p.117.

Chapter 9—© Reza/PBS pp.118, 120 (top); S.M. Amin/*Saudi Aramco World*/PADIA: p.120 (bottom); Katrina Thomas/*Saudi Aramco World*/PADIA: p.121; Abdullah Y. Al-Dobais/*Saudi Aramco World*/PADIA: p.122; S.M. Amin/*Saudi Aramco World*/PADIA: p.123; William Tracy/*Saudi Aramco World*/PADIA: pp.124, 125; Great Silk Road/Corel Draw pp.126, 127 (top); Sacred Places/Corel Draw p.127 (bottom).

Additional Resources—Nik Wheeler/*Saudi Aramco World*/PADIA: pp.128, 129, 134; Near East Collections/Library of Congress: pp.130, 131; Dick Doughty/*Saudi Aramco World*/PADIA: p.132; Kathleen Burke/*Saudi Aramco World*/PADIA: p.133; Bill Tracy/*Saudi Aramco World*/ PADIA: p.135.

SECTION TWO

Overview — Nik Wheeler/*Saudi Aramco World*/PADIA: p.138.

Chapter 10 — Tor Eigeland/*Saudi Aramco World*/PADIA: p.142; John Feeney/*Saudi Aramco World*/PADIA: p.143; S.M. Amin/*Saudi Aramco World*/PADIA: p.144; Nik Wheeler/*Saudi Aramco World*/PADIA: pp.147, 149; Katrina Thomas/*Saudi Aramco World*/PADIA: p.150.

Chapter 11 — Brynn Bruijn/*Saudi Aramco World*/PADIA: p.152; Ilene Perlman/*Saudi Aramco World*/PADIA: p.153.

Chapter 12 — S.M. Amin/*Saudi Aramco World*/PADIA: p.154; Tor Eigeland/*Saudi Aramco World*/PADIA: p.155; IslamiClip®Calligraphic Designs #1/Sakkal Design pp.158, 159

Chapter 13 — Nik Wheeler/*Saudi Aramco World*/PADIA: p.161, 164; Tor Eigeland/*Saudi Aramco World*/PADIA: pp.162, 163; Stepheh Graham/*Saudi Aramco World*/PADIA: pp.165, 168; Katrina Thomas/*Saudi Aramco World*/PADIA: p.167.

Chapter 14 — Katrina Thomas/*Saudi Aramco World*/PADIA: p.170; Kevin Bubriski/*Saudi Aramco World*/PADIA: p.172; Tor Eigeland/*Saudi Aramco World*/PADIA: p.173; Eric Hasse/*Saudi Aramco World*/PADIA: p.174.

Chapter 15 — Dick Doughty/*Saudi Aramco World*/PADIA: p.178.

Chapter 16 — Tor Eigeland/*Saudi Aramco World*/PADIA: pp.182, 183, 184.

Chapter 17 — Tor Eigeland/*Saudi Aramco World*/PADIA: pp.186, 188; IslamiClip®Calligraphic Designs #1/Sakkal Design p.189.

Chapter 18 — Nik Wheeler/*Saudi Aramco World*/PADIA: pp.190, 191, 192 (top row, middle; bottom row, left); Harold Sequira/*Saudi Aramco World*/PADIA: p.192 (top row, left); Lorraine Chittock/*Saudi Aramco World*/PADIA: p.192 (top row, right); S.M. Amin/*Saudi Aramco World*/PADIA: p.192 (bottom row, middle and right); Bill Lyons/*Saudi Aramco World*/PADIA: p.193; S.M. Amin, Sa'id Ghamidi/*Saudi Aramco World*/PADIA: p.194; Cheryl Hatch/*Saudi Aramco World*/PADIA: p.195; Tor Eigeland/*Saudi Aramco World*/PADIA: p.196.

Chapter 19 — Nik Wheeler/*Saudi Aramco World*/PADIA: p.197.

Chapter 20 — Bill Strubbe/*Saudi Aramco World*/PADIA: p.199; Khalil Abou El-Nasr/*Saudi Aramco World*/PADIA: p.200

Chapter 21 — Khalil Abou El-Nasr/*Saudi Aramco World*/PADIA: p.204; Brynn Bruijn/*Saudi Aramco World*/PADIA: p.205.

Chapter 22 — Nik Wheeler/*Saudi Aramco World*/PADIA: p.206.

Chapter 23 — Katrina Thomas/*Saudi Aramco World*/PADIA: p.210; Ilene Perlman/*Saudi Aramco World*/PADIA: pp.214, 216; Cheryl Hatch/*Saudi Aramco World*/PADIA: pp.218, 219; Brynn Bruijn/*Saudi Aramco World*/PADIA: p.221; Kevin Bubriski/*Saudi Aramco World*/PADIA: p.223; Near East Collections/Library of Congress p.224.

Chapter 24 — Nik Wheeler/*Saudi Aramco World*/PADIA: p.226; © Reza/PBS p.228; S.M. Amin/*Saudi Aramco World*/PADIA: p.229.

Chapter 26 — Turkey/Corel Draw pp.234; Penny Williams/Paintings courtesy of Azem Palace Museum, John Fistere and W. Smalzer/*Saudi Aramco World*/PADIA: p.237.

Additional Resources — Brynn Bruijn/*Saudi Aramco World*/PADIA: pp.240, 241; Nik Wheeler/*Saudi Aramco World*/PADIA: p.242; S.M. Amin/*Saudi Aramco World*/PADIA: p.243; Ihsan Sheet/*Saudi Aramco World*/PADIA: p.244; Dick Doughty/*Saudi Aramco World*/PADIA: p.245.

SECTION THREE

Overview — Larry Luxner/*Saudi Aramco World*/PADIA: p.248.

Chapter 27 — S.M. Amin/*Saudi Aramco World*/PADIA: pp.252, 253; Tor Eigeland/*Saudi Aramco World*/PADIA: p.257.

Chapter 29 — Great Silk Road/Corel Draw pp.261, 264, 265, 266, 267; AFP/Getty Images p.271

Chapter 30 — Near East Collections/Library of Congress p.276; Katrina Thomas/*Saudi Aramco World*/PADIA: p.279.

Chapter 31 — William Tracy/*Saudi Aramco World*/PADIA: pp.282, 284 (left); J. W. "Soak" Hoover/*Saudi Aramco World*/PADIA: p.284 (right); © Art Resource, NY p.287.

Chapter 32 — Great Silk Road/Corel Draw pp.290, 291; Robert Azzi/*Saudi Aramco World*/PADIA: p.292.

Chapter 33 — Sa'id al-Ghamidi/*Saudi Aramco World*/PADIA: pp.296, 314; Lorraine Chittock/*Saudi Aramco World*/PADIA: pp.301, 307, 313; Brynn Bruijn/*Saudi Aramco World*/PADIA: pp.304, 309.

Chapter 34 — John Feeney/*Saudi Aramco World*/PADIA: pp.316, 317; 334, 335; Brynn Bruijn/ *Saudi Aramco World*/PADIA: pp.319, 323; M. S. Al-Shabeeb/*Saudi Aramco World*/ PADIA: p.321; Lorraine Chittock/*Saudi Aramco World*/PADIA: p.324; S.M. Amin/*Saudi Aramco World*/PADIA: p.327; Burnett H. Moody/*Saudi Aramco World*/PADIA: p.328; Sa'id al-Ghamidi/ *Saudi Aramco World*/PADIA: p.331; Khalil Abou El-Nasr and Waseem Tchorbachi/*Saudi Aramco World*/PADIA: p.333; Kathleen Burke/*Saudi Aramco World*/PADIA: p.337; Bob Wilkins/*Saudi Aramco World*/PADIA: p.338.

Chapter 35 — Katrina Thomas/*Saudi Aramco World*/PADIA: p.340.

Chapter 36 — S.M. Amin/*Saudi Aramco World*/PADIA: pp.344, 350, 353, 354 (bottom), 356 (top), 357, 359 (left and bottom right), 360; © Reza/PBS pp.347, 354 (top), 356 (top), 362; Frank and Frances Carpenter Collection/Library of Congress p.349; Samia El-Moslimany p.359 (top right), 361.

Chapter 37 — Tor Eigeland/*Saudi Aramco World*/PADIA: p.364; Dick Doughty/*Saudi Aramco World*/PADIA: p.366.

Chapter 38 — Tor Eigeland/*Saudi Aramco World*/PADIA: p.372; Brynn Bruijn/*Saudi Aramco World*/PADIA: p.374.

Chapter 42 — Great Silk Road/Corel Draw p.382, 387; Sacred Places/Corel Draw p.385.

Chapter 43 — Arthur Clark/*Saudi Aramco World*/PADIA: p.390; Nik Wheeler/*Saudi Aramco World*/PADIA: p.391; Morocco/Corel Draw p.396; Photograph courtesy of www.sacredsites .com pp.397, 398; Turkey/Corel Draw pp.402, 404; Sacred Places/Corel Draw pp.403, 406.

Additional Resources — S.M. Amin/*Saudi Aramco World*/PADIA: pp.408, 409; Great Silk Road/ Corel Draw p.410; Ian Yeomans/*Saudi Aramco World*/PADIA: p.411; Ilene Perlman/*Saudi Aramco World*/PADIA: p.412; Peter Harrigan/*Saudi Aramco World*/PADIA: p.413; Larry Luxner/*Saudi Aramco World*/PADIA: p.414; Near East Collections/Library of Congress p.415; Sa'id al-Ghamidi/*Saudi Aramco World*/PADIA: p.416; Brynn Bruijn/*Saudi Aramco World*/ PADIA: p.417; John Feeney/*Saudi Aramco World*/PADIA: p.418; Sacred Places/Corel Draw p.419; Great Silk Road/Corel Draw p.420.

Glossary — John Feeney/*Saudi Aramco World*/PADIA: pp.422, 423, 425 (top), 434; IslamiClip® Calligraphic Designs #1/Sakkal Design p.424; Brynn Bruijn/*Saudi Aramco World*/ PADIA: pp.425 (bottom), 432 (bottom), 436 (bottom), 439 (bottom), 440; Katrina Thomas/*Saudi Aramco World*/PADIA: pp.426 (top), 431 (bottom), 436 (top); Turkey/Corel Draw p.426 (bottom); Near East Collections/Library of Congress p.427; © Reza/PBS pp.428 (top), 431 (top), 439 (top); Khalil Abou El-Nasr/*Saudi Aramco World*/PADIA: pp.428 (bottom), 439 (bottom); S.M. Amin/*Saudi Aramco World*/PADIA: pp.429, 433 (bottom); Nik Wheeler/*Saudi Aramco World*/ PADIA: p.430; Cheryl Hatch/*Saudi Aramco World*/PADIA: p.432 (top); Abdullah Y. Al-Dobais/ *Saudi Aramco World*/PADIA: p.433 (top); Dick Doughty/*Saudi Aramco World*/ PADIA: p.435; Lorraine Chittock/*Saudi Aramco World*/PADIA: p.437; Michael Spenser/*Saudi Aramco World*/ PADIA: p.438.

Topical Bibliography — Katrina Thomas/*Saudi Aramco World*/PADIA: pp.442, 443, 464, 465; S.M. Amin/*Saudi Aramco World*/PADIA: pp.444, 450, 451, 462; Bill Lyons/*Saudi Aramco World*/PADIA: pp.445, 458; Near East Collections/Library of Congress p.446; Photodisc p.447; Tor Eigeland/*Saudi Aramco World*/PADIA: p.448; Brynn Bruijn/*Saudi Aramco World*/PADIA: p.449; Nik Wheeler/*Saudi Aramco World*/PADIA: pp.452, 454; Robert Azzi/*Saudi Aramco World*/PADIA: p.453; Khalil Abou El-Nasr/*Saudi Aramco World*/PADIA: p.455; Calligraphy by Aftab Ahmad/*Saudi Aramco World*/PADIA: p.456; Michael Winn/*Saudi Aramco World*/PADIA: p.457; Great Silk Road/Corel Draw p.459; U.S. Post Office p.460; Gian Luigi Scarfiotti/*Saudi Aramco World*/PADIA: p.461; Dick Doughty/*Saudi Aramco World*/PADIA: p.463; John Feeney/ *Saudi Aramco World*/PADIA: pp.466, 468, 473; Lorraine Chittock/*Saudi Aramco World*/PADIA: pp.467, 470; Michael Friend/*Saudi Aramco World*/PADIA: p.469; Jill Brown/*Saudi Aramco World*/PADIA: p.471; Morocco/Corel Draw p.472.

Photo Credits & Index — Brynn Bruijn/*Saudi Aramco World*/PADIA: pp.474, 478.

Index

The index for *Understanding Islam and Muslim Traditions* includes personal names, place names, and subject terms that appear in the book. Photo captions have also been included in the index, with these page references marked in italic type. To facilitate use of the glossary, the index also features references for its definitions of terms. For these entries, the page reference for each glossary term is marked after the heading "defined."

Page references to photo and illustration captions appear in italic type.

483

Page references to glossary definitions appear with the term "defined."

Page references to glossary definitions appear with the term "defined."

Khidr, 229, 375-77
  defined, 431
  folklore associated with, 377
Khomeini, Ayatollah Ruhollah, 97-98, 225, 263
khutba, 166, 374
  defined, 431
Khwarizmi, Muhammad ibn Musa al-, 81
kiswa, 355
  defined, 431
Konya, Turkey, 403
Koran. *See* Quran
Korite, 332
kunya, 212
  defined, 431
kursi, defined, 431
Kuwait, observance of Ramadan in, 321

L

la ilaha ill-Allah, defined, 432
Lamp Nights, 280, 379-80
  See also Laylat al-Bara'ah; Laylat al-Miraj;
    Laylat al-Qadr; Mulid al-Nabi
  defined, 432
lanterns, Ramadan, *316, 316-17, 317*
laqab, 212
  defined, 432
Laylat al-Bara'ah, 291-95
  as observed in India, Bangladesh, and
    Pakistan, 293
  defined, 432
laylat al-hinna, defined, 432
Laylat al-Miraj, 50, 283-89
  celebrations of, 288
  defined, 432
Laylat al-Qadr, 298, 320, 339-43
  as observed by Shia Muslims in Iran, 343
  defined, 432
  Muslim folklore surrounding, 342
  prayers during, 342
Lebanon, observance of Ramadan in, 321
loqaimat, 329
Lusignan, Guy De, *72*

M

madh, 178-79
  defined, 432
maghrib, defined, 432
Mahal, Mumtaz, 87
Mahdi, 292
  defined, 432
mahr, 218
  defined, 432
mahram, defined, 432
majalis, 268, 372
  defined, 432
Majdhoub, Muhammad al-Mahdi al-, 280, 281
Makkah Mosque, Hyderabad, India, *161*
Maliki, 48-49
  defined, 432
Mamluk sultans, 278
Mansur, al-, 79
marabout, 385
  defined, 432
Mary, 286
ma sha Allah, 189
  defined, 433
Mashad, Iran, 127
mashakik, 325
mashallah. *See* ma sha Allah
masjid, defined, 433
Masjid Raya, Sumantra, Indonesia, *31*
Masnavi, 402, 403
Masud, Fariduddin. *See* Baba Farid Shakar Ganj
matam, 265
  defined, 433
mathematics and physics, Muslim
    contributions to, 81
Maulid, al-, 281
Maulidi, 280
Mauritania, 62
Mauritius, observance of Ramadan in, 322
mawlay, defined, 433
mawlid. *See* mulid
mawlud, 276
  defined, 433

    Page references to glossary definitions appear with the term "defined."

Page references to photo and illustration captions appear in italic type.

489

Page references to glossary definitions appear with the term "defined."

Page references to glossary definitions appear with the term "defined."

Page references to glossary definitions appear with the term "defined."